Project-Based Learning in Integrated STEM Education

Project-Based Learning in Integrated STEM Education

Guest Editors

Mi Yeon Lee
Jean S. Lee

MDPI

Basel • Beijing • Wuhan • Barcelona • Belgrade • Novi Sad • Cluj • Manchester

Guest Editors

Mi Yeon Lee
Mary Lou Fulton College for Teaching and Learning Innovation
Arizona State University
Tempe, AZ
USA

Jean S. Lee
Department of Education Studies
University of California San Diego
San Diego, CA
USA

Editorial Office
MDPI AG
Grosspeteranlage 5
4052 Basel, Switzerland

This is a reprint of the Special Issue, published open access by the journal *Education Sciences* (ISSN 2227-7102), freely accessible at: https://www.mdpi.com/journal/education/special_issues/Q0F47U3T57.

For citation purposes, cite each article independently as indicated on the article page online and as indicated below:

Lastname, A.A.; Lastname, B.B. Article Title. *Journal Name* **Year**, *Volume Number*, Page Range.

ISBN 978-3-7258-4673-3 (Hbk)
ISBN 978-3-7258-4674-0 (PDF)
https://doi.org/10.3390/books978-3-7258-4674-0

Contents

About the Editors

Mi Yeon Lee

Mi Yeon Lee is an Associate Professor of Mathematics Education in the Division of Teacher Preparation at the Mary Lou Fulton College for Teaching and Learning Innovation, Arizona State University. She teaches undergraduate mathematics content and methods courses for pre-service teachers. Her scholarship, teaching, and service bridge mathematics education and teacher preparation, with a focus on professional noticing, technology integration, and project-based learning. Dr. Lee is PBL-certified and has served as a Managing Editor for the *Mathematical Education* journal and as an Academic Editor for *Education Sciences*. She has also contributed as a Guest Editor for several Special Issues.

Jean S. Lee

Jean S. Lee is the Director of Teacher Education at the University of California, San Diego. She has been involved in leading various professional development projects, working with teachers at the state, national, and international levels. Dr. Lee's research interests include project-based learning and the preparation of teachers for high-need, urban school settings. She is also PBL-certified and supports K-16 educators in using PBL approaches.

Preface

This volume brings together a collection of scholarly works centered on *Project-Based Learning (PBL)* as a transformative approach to teaching and learning, particularly within the context of STEM education in K–16 settings. Rooted in real-world problem-solving and collaborative inquiry, PBL offers a powerful framework for helping students develop not only disciplinary knowledge, but also critical thinking, creativity, and a deeper understanding of how knowledge is constructed and applied.

The *scope* of this work is intentionally broad, encompassing both theoretical and practical perspectives on the implementation of PBL. It includes empirical research, conceptual analyses, and descriptions of innovative practices that reflect the evolving role of PBL in contemporary classrooms. The articles explore PBL's potential to foster interdisciplinary STEM learning, civic engagement, equity and identity development, and pedagogical innovation.

The *aim and purpose* of this volume are to advance the understanding of PBL's role in education and to provide educators, researchers, and policymakers with insights into its possibilities and challenges. By highlighting diverse approaches and outcomes, this work seeks to contribute to the growing conversation about how we can meaningfully engage students in complex learning experiences that prepare them for the demands of an interconnected and rapidly changing world.

The *motivation* behind assembling this collection arises from a shared recognition among educators and scholars that effective STEM education must go beyond memorization and procedural fluency. PBL offers a pathway toward more authentic and equitable learning experiences—ones that empower students to take ownership of their learning while engaging with content that matters.

This volume is addressed to a broad audience, including teacher educators, K–16 instructors, curriculum designers, education researchers, and graduate students who are interested in research-based strategies that connect theory with practice. Whether you are exploring PBL for the first time or refining your existing approach, we hope the contributions in this collection will inform and inspire your work in advancing student learning and educational equity through project-based teaching.

Mi Yeon Lee and Jean S. Lee
Guest Editors

education sciences

MDPI

Editorial

Project-Based Learning as a Catalyst for Integrated STEM Education

Mi Yeon Lee [1,*] and Jean S. Lee [2]

1 Mary Lou Fulton College for Teaching and Learning Innovation, Arizona State University, Tempe, AZ 85281, USA
2 Department of Education Studies, University of California San Diego, La Jolla, CA 92093, USA; jeanlee@ucsd.edu
* Correspondence: mlee115@asu.edu

1. Introduction

The call for enhancing Science, Technology, Engineering, and Mathematics (STEM) education to prepare students for tackling complex global challenges has become increasingly urgent (Becker & Park, 2011; Contribution 1; English, 2016; Contribution 7; Sokolova et al., 2025). Addressing these issues require not only deep disciplinary knowledge but also the ability to integrate multiple perspectives across fields and apply this level of understanding in real-world contexts creatively (Contribution 1; Kokotsaki et al., 2016; Kwon & Lee, 2025; Contribution 7). Moreover, traditional teacher-centered approaches are being challenged by the recognition that students must be active participants in their own learning (Dole et al., 2016; Contribution 2; Contribution 5; Strobel & van Barneveld, 2009). Project-Based Learning has emerged as a promising pedagogical approach positioned to meet this need by engaging students in authentic, real-world problems and meaningful projects over extended periods (Diana & Sukma, 2021; Contribution 5; Krajcik & Blumenfeld, 2006; M. Y. Lee & Robles, 2019; Markham et al., 2003; PBL Works, 2019; Contribution 8; Contribution 10).

2. Project-Based Learning

A Project-Based Learning (PBL) curriculum engages learners in meaningful problems that are important to them while advancing their creativity and problem-solving abilities (Kokotsaki et al., 2016). The PBL model is based on the assumption that most academic content is learned best in the context of projects (Blumenfeld et al., 1991).

PBL is an inquiry-based instructional approach that reflects a learner-centered environment and concentrates on learners' application of disciplinary concepts, tools, experiences, and technologies to research the answers to questions and solve real-world problems (Condliffe et al., 2017; Larmer et al., 2015). PBL can aid in enhancing both the range of learners' interests and their conceptual understanding of content. Teachers support ways for learners to construct their own understanding and orchestrate conversations in which learners explore complex connections and relationships among ideas.

General core principles and practices of PBL include the following (J. S. Lee & Galindo, 2021):

- Promoting a professional culture of trust, respect, and responsibility among the learners and the teacher
- Focusing on 21st-century skills and content standards
- Improving character education traits such as leadership, civic responsibility, and compassion
- Scaffolding activities that include student-centered instruction to increase relevance and rigor

- Connecting learning to other subject areas
- Infusing technology as a tool for communicating, collaborating, and learning
- Partnering with community institutions so that learners can build relationships with other local stakeholders

In this commentary, we explore how PBL serves as a critical approach for integrated STEM education. We synthesize insights from ten research papers in this Special Issue, focusing on its role in (1) fostering interdisciplinary learning; (2) supporting civic engagement; (3) promoting equity, identity, and inclusion; and (4) examining innovative pedagogical approaches. A discussion on future directions follows.

3. Interdisciplinary STEM Learning

Integrated STEM education emphasizes combining discrete subject areas in relevant contexts to deepen students' understanding and awareness of connections across disciplines (Hall & Miro, 2016; Contribution 7). PBL provides a robust framework for this integration by engaging students in authentic problems that inherently require drawing upon knowledge and skills from multiple STEM fields (M. Y. Lee & Robles, 2019; Contribution 8; Contribution 10).

Several examples in this Special Issue illustrate how PBL facilitates this interdisciplinary STEM approach. The Challenges in the STEM Learning Framework integrates features of PBL, Design-Based Learning, and Entrepreneurial-Based Learning to center mathematics learning within innovative pitch competitions (Contribution 1). This approach explicitly aims to foreground the mathematics within interdisciplinary STEM activities by making visible and central the contribution of mathematics to addressing challenges involved with entrepreneurial solutions (Contribution 1; Contribution 7). Another innovative combination involves integrating PBL with flipped classrooms, which has demonstrated significant improvement in students' computational thinking skills in mathematics, specifically decomposition, pattern recognition, and abstraction (Contribution 4).

Interdisciplinary PBL provides rich opportunities for students to integrate knowledge, collaborate across fields, and engage with real-world issues. In higher education, multidisciplinary Capstone Senior Design Projects in fields such as Electrical Engineering, Mechanical Engineering, and Computer Science require collaborative efforts across these domains (Contribution 6). Similarly, the STEM Oriented Alliance for Research project engages university students across Electrical Engineering, Communications, and Marketing majors to foster collaborative abilities crucial for navigating diverse professional fields (Contribution 9). In one study (Contribution 3), the authors described an undergraduate engineering course that successfully integrated engineering with social issues by using homelessness as the context for an engineering design project, connecting technical learning with public welfare and ethics. The authors of another study (Contribution 2) reported a case study involving university exchange students in education tasked with developing interdisciplinary STEM lessons combining mathematics and environmental science, leveraging place-based education to ground learning in local contexts. At the K-12 level, gardening-based learning exemplifies integrated PBL, naturally drawing connections across environmental studies, mathematics, science, and language arts (Contribution 8).

Despite these successes, challenges persist in ensuring rigorous and deep integration of disciplinary content within PBL frameworks. Teachers often struggle to design projects that effectively drive the learning of core disciplinary standards, particularly for mathematics (Contribution 7; Contribution 10), while balancing them with PBL elements (Contribution 10). In one of the included studies, pre-service teachers, for instance, varied in their ability to integrate mathematics as a core, not auxiliary, part of STEM PBL units (Contribution 7).

4. Civic Engagement

A hallmark of effective PBL in integrated STEM is its emphasis on authenticity, often achieved by grounding projects in real-world problems or contexts that allow for civic engagement and impact (Contribution 5; Contribution 7; Contribution 8). This approach prepares students to be active and responsible citizens capable of addressing societal challenges.

One powerful example is the engineering design project referenced above in which university students engaged with issues faced by people experiencing homelessness (Contribution 3). The aim of this project was to shift students' views on homelessness by linking engineering skills to ethical and societal considerations. The researchers (Contribution 3) noted that a major goal of the project was to combat a "culture of disengagement" by relating learning directly to sociotechnical applications. Similarly, a group of researchers (Contribution 2) studied university exchange students focusing on localized environmental problems in their STEM lessons. The Design & Pitch framework also situates its challenges within real-world contexts that affect various stakeholders, addressing pressing issues such as pollution, food waste, and economic viability, empowering students with the autonomy to identify personally meaningful pursuits (Contribution 1). The Community Garden Project (Contribution 10) is a discipline-rich PBL, tasking students to serve as activists and urban farmers to address food insecurity in their community by designing a school garden and proposing its implementation to the administration.

Beyond disciplinary content, PBL in integrated STEM environments is a vital vehicle for developing essential 21st-century skills critical for civic participation and professional life (Bell, 2010; Rehman et al., 2023). Collaboration, critical thinking, problem-solving, and communication are inherently fostered through the PBL process (Contribution 7). The authors of a comparative analysis of multidisciplinary Capstone Senior Design Projects found that both industry-sponsored and faculty-sponsored projects aided in the development of professional skills; industry-sponsored projects led to higher performance in overall project execution and professional skills development such as punctuality and listening, while faculty-sponsored projects were particularly effective in nurturing teamwork and communication abilities (Contribution 6). The aim of the STEM Oriented Alliance for Research project (Contribution 9) was to develop collaborative abilities such as positive interdependence, accountability, proactive interaction, group processing, and social skills, directing students' learning orientations towards future professional work. These examples demonstrate how PBL provides a structured environment for students to develop the essential 21st-century skills in interdisciplinary workforces and active civic engagement (Contribution 6; Contribution 9).

Furthermore, projects grounded in social issues cultivate social awareness, empathy, and a sense of responsibility. The homelessness project led to statistically significant shifts in students' perceptions. Their views moved away from biases about personal choices or moral deficiencies, and toward more compassionate, empathetic perspectives. The project reinforced the idea that engineers have a duty to care for those experiencing homelessness. It also showed that PBL can counter a technocratic view of engineering by emphasizing its sociotechnical nature and the importance of compassion and empathy (Contribution 3).

5. Equity, Identity, and Inclusion

Culturally responsive approaches are central to achieving equity and inclusion. PBL holds significant potential for addressing long-standing issues of underrepresentation in multiple STEM fields, particularly for groups such as women and Hispanic communities (Contribution 1; Contribution 8). By connecting learning to students' lives, cultures, and communities, PBL can foster STEM identity development and narrow achievement gaps for underrepresented students (Cross et al., 2012; Contribution 8; Contribution 10).

A group of researchers (Contribution 8) provide a compelling example of this point in the Family Project-Based Learning, a garden-based STEM program for Latina girls and their parents centered around planning, growing, and harvesting food. The authors describe this program as actively leveraging community cultural wealth, including aspirational, linguistic, familial, social, navigational, and resistance capital, to support STEM identity development through authentic, hands-on activities. The provision of English/Spanish bilingual instruction was critical, validating and building upon families' linguistic capital. This approach directly addresses the lack of access and role models that contribute to the underrepresentation of Latinas in STEM, promoting the idea that diverse perspectives and talents are essential for innovation (Contribution 8).

Another group of researchers (Contribution 1) report on how the framework also contributes to inclusion by featuring diverse STEM professionals as "challenge champions" who introduce projects, showcasing a range of careers and backgrounds. These role models aid students in seeing their own identities reflected in STEM and entrepreneurship, empowering them to draw on their unique experiences and STEM knowledge to invent solutions. Similarly, the homelessness project in engineering education (Contribution 3) advocates for a more inclusive, justice-oriented education that addresses systemic inequities and encourages students to reflect on privilege and disadvantage, further supporting an equity-focused approach (Contribution 3).

Furthermore, integrating social justice and global awareness into PBL STEM units aids in preparing pre-service teachers to address issues such as environmental, racial, gender, disability, and economic inequities with their future students (Contribution 7). PBL, in this context, becomes a tool for future educators to make a tangible difference in the lives of their students, though challenges in integrating potentially controversial topics may emerge (Contribution 7). The collaborative nature of PBL supports inclusion, as seen in a case study wherein culturally diverse exchange students used technology to enhance communication and understanding while developing curricula together (Contribution 2). The STEM Oriented Alliance for Research project showed that despite initial challenges, interdisciplinary teamwork across various majors fosters understanding, mutual appreciation, and a growth mindset (Contribution 9).

6. Pedagogical Innovations and Frameworks

PBL is defined by core elements such as a challenging problem, sustained inquiry, authenticity, student voice and choice, reflection, and a public product, shifting the focus from teacher-directed instruction to students' active construction of knowledge (Contribution 5; Contribution 7; Contribution 8; Contribution 10). The papers included in this Special Issue highlight various innovative adaptations and frameworks aimed at enhancing the effectiveness of PBL in integrated STEM contexts.

One such innovation is the framework involving Launch, Design, and Pitch phases (Contribution 1), which synthesizes PBL, Design-Based Learning, and Entrepreneurial-Based Learning into an integrated model for mathematics education, drawing on key features from each, such as sustained inquiry from PBL, iterative design from Design-Based Learning, and persuasive pitching from Entrepreneurial-Based Learning. This approach emphasizes authenticity and entrepreneurial viability through technical briefs and public critiques like expert check-ins and the final pitch (Contribution 1). Another integrated model combines PBL with flipped classrooms, wherein students engage in independent learning outside of class using resources such as videos and then apply and discuss their understanding in interactive face-to-face sessions, significantly improving their computational thinking skills (Contribution 4).

Innovative adaptations of interdisciplinary STEM PBL expand its potential by integrating new pedagogical approaches, fostering student agency, family engagement, and professional collaboration. Students acted as "lesson architects" to develop an interdisciplinary STEM curriculum through a unique adaptation integrating PBL with place-based education, lesson study, and the "students as partners" pedagogy (Contribution 2). This approach positions students as decision-makers and co-creators, embedding iterative processes through lesson study (Contribution 2). The Family Project-Based Learning in a gardening context (Contribution 8) offers a model specifically designed for engaging families from underrepresented communities, in which they practice emphasizing discussion before action and exploration before explanation within a hands-on project. The STEM Oriented Alliance for Research project (Contribution 9) represents an industry-modeled interdisciplinary PBL approach for university students, structured with multiple checkpoints and feedback loops to emulate professional settings and foster collaborative abilities.

However, challenges to implementing these innovations persist. Teachers not only struggle to design projects that effectively integrate and drive the learning of core disciplinary standards but also find it difficult to balance the elements of PBL with specific content and practice pathways (Contribution 10). In particular, pre-service teachers are likely to have difficulty consistently integrating key PBL elements such as sustained inquiry, student voice and choice, reflection, and public product or ensuring that mathematics is genuinely integral to the project (Contribution 7). Challenges also include teachers' need for strong facilitation skills and adequate resources (Contribution 4), in addition to mentorship and varying expectations in industry-sponsored projects (Contribution 6). Furthermore, current assessment instruments may be constrained by limitations in accurately capturing the nuanced shifts in students' perceptions that occur in PBL environments (Contribution 3).

To address these challenges, frameworks and conceptual tools are currently being developed. To support teachers in managing the complex goals of STEM PBL design, a group of researchers (Contribution 10) propose the Project Planning Pyramid. This conceptual tool aids teachers in designing 'discipline-rich' STEM projects by explicitly integrating key elements. It combines the PBL framework with a Content Storyline—a coherent sequence of content ideas—and a Practice Pathway, which provides sequenced opportunities to build disciplinary practices. Embedding formative assessment processes within projects, as in the STEM Oriented Alliance for Research project, provides opportunities for iterative application of criteria, feedback, and self-reflection, aiding students in understanding expectations and improving their work (Contribution 9). Comparing different student-centered methods, such as PBL and Problem-Based Learning, highlights the unique characteristics of PBL. These include its broader scope, emphasis on sustained inquiry, and the creation of tangible products. PBL often encompasses other methods within its wider project framework (Contribution 5).

7. Future Directions

Building upon these four sections, the trajectory for future exploration of PBL in integrated STEM education must focus on methodological rigor and nuanced assessment. There is an urgent need for researchers to conduct larger-scale, longitudinal studies across diverse contexts to capture the multifaceted learning and perception shifts fostered by interdisciplinary PBL. Such studies are crucial for understanding the sustained development and transferability of skills, such as computational thinking, to real-world and professional settings (Contribution 4; Contribution 8). Utilizing robust mixed-methods approaches is important, allowing researchers to integrate quantitative data for generalizability and qualitative insights for a more nuanced understanding, as demonstrated or recommended in several studies (Contribution 3; Contribution 4; Contribution 8). This scope includes employing strategies like theoretical sampling and thematic analysis in qualitative phases (Contribution 2; Contribution 4; Contribution 8). In this regard, further work is needed to refine assessment instruments that are sensitive to the unique learning outcomes and attitude shifts in integrated STEM PBL, which potentially includes adapting or revalidating existing instruments for specific contexts (Contribution 3). Exploring innovative data collection and analysis methods, such as visual analysis or detailed case studies, will aid in capturing the nuances of student engagement and learning processes.

The authors of future studies should also include in-depth investigation of the long-term impacts of integrated PBL on student outcomes, including how participation influences mindsets, collaborative abilities, and career trajectories in multiple STEM fields. Clarifying PBL's long-term impacts requires understanding how integrated models and PBL elements support learning and identity formation, such as exploring the effectiveness of combining PBL with flipped classrooms for specific skill enhancement (Contribution 4), integrating Design-Based Learning and Entrepreneurial-Based Learning to authentically center disciplines such as mathematics (Contribution 1), or leveraging place-based education and "students as partners" pedagogies for engagement with complex issues (Contribution 2). Further study of various models, such as faculty-sponsored versus industry-sponsored projects, can highlight their unique benefits and challenges in developing practical skills and teamwork (Contribution 6).

Lastly, supporting educators in effectively designing and implementing discipline-rich PBL in integrated STEM remains paramount to improve the long-term impacts of PBL. Thus, further research is needed to understand how various conceptual frameworks or models support teachers' pedagogical design capacity for creating projects that meaningfully integrate content, disciplinary practices, and PBL elements. In addition, providing sustained professional learning experiences built on such frameworks or models is crucial for aiding teachers in balancing the demands of integrated STEM PBL. Most urgent is the targeted mathematics support that is often marginalized in integrated contexts (English, 2016). By pursuing these interconnected avenues, the field can continue to harness PBL's transformative power to prepare students for a complex and interdisciplinary future.

Author Contributions: Conceptualization, M.Y.L. and J.S.L.; writing—original draft preparation, M.Y.L.; writing—review and editing, J.S.L. All authors have read and agreed to the published version of the manuscript.

Conflicts of Interest: The authors declare no conflicts of interest.

List of Contributions

1. Belcher, M., Confrey, J., Krupa, E. E., & Borden, M. L. (2025). The design & pitch challenges in STEM: A theoretical framework for centering mathematics learning in entrepreneurial pitch competitions. *Education Sciences*, *15*(6), 651. https://doi.org/10.3390/educsci15060651.
2. Bolick, M. A., Thomassen, M., Apland, J., Spencer, O., Nicole, F., Tran, S. K. N., Voigt, M., & Lazar, K. B. (2024). Project-based learning in interdisciplinary spaces: A case study in Norway and the United States. *Education Sciences*, *14*(8), 866. https://doi.org/10.3390/educsci14080866.
3. Chen, D. A., Chapman, M. A., & Mejia, J. A. (2025). Shifting students' perceptions about homelessness: Quantitative assessment of a project-based approach. *Education Sciences*, *15*(5), 608. https://doi.org/10.3390/educsci15050608.
4. Fitrah, M., Sofroniou, A., Setiawan, C., Widihastuti, W., Yarmanetti, N., Jaya, M. P. S., Panuntun, J. G., Arfaton, A., Beteno, S., & Susianti, I. (2025). The impact of integrated project-based learning and flipped classroom on students' computational thinking skills: Embedded mixed methods. *Education Sciences*, *15*(4), 448. https://doi.org/10.3390/educsci15040448.
5. Goodwin, J. R. (2024). What's the difference? A comparison of student-centered teaching methods. *Education Sciences*, *14*(7), 736. https://doi.org/10.3390/educsci14070736.

6. Morsy, M. M., Uddin, M. N., & Znidi, F. (2024). Multidisciplinary capstone senior design projects: A comparative analysis of industry–sponsored and faculty–sponsored projects using comprehensive performance metrics. *Education Sciences*, *14*(3), 314. https://doi.org/10.3390/educsci14030314.
7. Pitot, L. N., McHugh, M. L., & Kosiak, J. (2024). Establishing a PBL STEM framework for pre-service teachers. *Education Sciences*, *14*(6), 571. https://doi.org/10.3390/educsci14060571.
8. Rillero, P., Jiménez-Silva, M., Short-Meyerson, K., & Rillero, K. M. (2025). From seeds to harvest in seven weeks: Project-based learning with Latina girls and their parents. *Education Sciences*, *15*(2), 246. https://doi.org/10.3390/educsci15020246.
9. Seo, S., Van Orman, D. S. J., Beattie, M., Paxson, L. C., & Murray, J. (2024). Transforming learning orientations through STEM interdisciplinary project-based learning. *Education Sciences*, *14*(11), 1154. https://doi.org/10.3390/educsci14111154.
10. Sircar, M., Orr, S., Madis, C., & DiMaria, S. (2024). Conceptualizing an initial framework to support discipline-rich project-based learning in STEM. *Education Sciences*, *14*(7), 793. https://doi.org/10.3390/educsci14070793.

References

Becker, K., & Park, K. (2011). Effects of integrative approaches among science, technology, engineering, and mathematics (STEM) subjects on students' learning: A preliminary meta-analysis. *Journal of STEM Education: Innovations & Research*, *12*(5/6), 23–37.

Bell, S. (2010). Project-based learning for the 21st century: Skills for the future. *The Clearing House: A Journal of Educational Strategies, Issues and Ideas*, *83*(2), 39–43. [CrossRef]

Blumenfeld, P. C., Soloway, E., Marx, R. W., Krajcik, J. S., Guzdial, M., & Palincsar, A. (1991). Motivating project-based learning: Sustaining the doing, supporting the learning. *Educational Psychologist*, *26*(3–4), 369–398. [CrossRef]

Condliffe, B., Quint, J., Visher, M., Bangser, M., Drohojowska, S., Saco, L., & Nelson, E. (2017). *Project-based learning: A literature review* (Working paper). MDRC. Available online: https://www.mdrc.org/publication/project-based-learning (accessed on 14 June 2025).

Cross, D., Hudson, R., Adefope, O., Lee, M. Y., Rapacki, L., & Perez, A. (2012). Success made probable: Creating equitable mathematical experiences through project-based learning. *Journal of Urban Mathematics Education*, *5*(2), 55–86. [CrossRef]

Diana, N., & Sukma, Y. (2021). The effectiveness of implementing project-based learning (PjBL) model in STEM education: A literature review. In *Journal of physics: Conference series* (Vol. 1882, No. 1, p. 012146). IOP Publishing.

Dole, S., Bloom, L., & Kowalske, K. (2016). Transforming pedagogy: Changing perspectives from teacher-centered to learner-centered. *Interdisciplinary Journal of Problem-Based Learning*, *10*(1), 10. [CrossRef]

English, L. D. (2016). Advancing mathematics education research within a STEM environment. In K. Maker, S. Dole, J. Visnovska, M. Goos, A. Bennison, & K. Fry (Eds.), *Research in mathematics education in Australasia 2012–2015* (pp. 353–371). Springer.

Hall, A., & Miro, D. (2016). A study of student engagement in project-based learning across multiple approaches to STEM education programs. *School Science and Mathematics*, *116*(6), 310–319. [CrossRef]

Kokotsaki, D., Menzies, V., & Wiggins, A. (2016). Project-based learning: A review of the literature. *Improving Schools*, *19*(3), 267–277. [CrossRef]

Krajcik, J. S., & Blumenfeld, P. C. (2006). Project-based learning. In R. K. Sawyer (Ed.), *The Cambridge handbook of the learning sciences* (pp. 317–334). Cambridge University Press.

Kwon, H., & Lee, Y. (2025). A meta-analysis of STEM project-based learning on creativity. *STEM Education*, *5*(2), 275–290. [CrossRef]

Larmer, J., Mergendoller, J., & Boss, S. (2015). *Setting the standard for project-based learning*. ASCD.

Lee, J. S., & Galindo, E. (Eds.). (2021). *Project-based learning in elementary classrooms: Making mathematics come alive*. National Council of Teachers of Mathematics.

Lee, M. Y., & Robles, R. (2019). Using project-based learning method as a way to engage students in STEM Education. *Research in Mathematical Education*, *22*(2), 83–97.

Markham, T., Larmer, J., & Ravitz, J. (2003). *Project based learning handbook: A guide to standards-focused project based learning* (2nd ed.). Buck Institute for Education.

PBL Works. (2019). *What is PBL? Buck Institute for Education*. Available online: http://my.pblworks.org (accessed on 11 June 2025).

Rehman, N., Zhang, W., Mahmood, A., Fareed, M. Z., & Batool, S. (2023). Fostering twenty-first century skills among primary school students through math project-based learning. *Humanities and Social Sciences Communications*, *10*(1), 424. [CrossRef]

Sokolova, E. V., Blaginin, V. A., & Shatrova, A. Y. (2025). Evolution and current trends in STEM education: A retrospective and bibliometric analysis. *Journal of Hypermedia & Technology-Enhanced Learning*, *3*(1), 90–107.

Strobel, J., & van Barneveld, A. (2009). When is PBL more effective? A meta-synthesis of meta-analyses comparing PBL to conventional classrooms. *Interdisciplinary Journal of Problem-Based Learning*, *3*(1), 44–58. [CrossRef]

education sciences

MDPI

Article

The Design & Pitch Challenges in STEM: A Theoretical Framework for Centering Mathematics Learning in Entrepreneurial Pitch Competitions

Michael Belcher *, Jere Confrey, Erin E. Krupa and Margaret L. Borden

College of Education, North Carolina State University, Raleigh, NC 27695, USA; jere_confrey@ncsu.edu (J.C.); eekrupa@ncsu.edu (E.E.K.); margaretleakborden@gmail.com (M.L.B.)
* Correspondence: mjbelche@ncsu.edu

Abstract: Solving many of the pressing issues facing the world today will require a deep and integrated understanding of science, technology, engineering, and mathematics (STEM). To prepare today's K-12 students to tackle these challenges, STEM education must create opportunities to learn disciplinary content while inventing actionable solutions to messy, interdisciplinary problems. Learning frameworks, such as Project-Based Learning (PBL), Design-Based Learning (DBL), and Entrepreneurial-Based Learning (EBL), could support this reconceptualization of STEM education. New approaches are needed that leverage and integrate what works from these frameworks to better prepare students for success post-schooling. This means leveraging frameworks that emphasize practices and ways of thinking that support students to build and justify solutions that create value for users, while also creating a need for disciplinary content knowledge. This is especially necessary for mathematics, a discipline that is often treated insufficiently in interdisciplinary STEM activities. This paper introduces the Design & Pitch (D&P) Challenges in STEM Learning Framework, a novel learning framework that leverages features of PBL, DBL, and EBL, situating math learning within entrepreneurial pitch competitions. It describes the D&P Learning Framework and explores how each contributing learning framework combines to enhance students' work, focusing their mathematical reasoning, while also empowering them to invent relevant solutions to authentic problems.

Keywords: project-based learning; design-based learning; entrepreneurial-based learning; mathematics; STEM

1. Introduction

Today's K-12 students will be confronted with unprecedented environmental, economic, and social challenges. Solving many of these significant and pressing issues will likely require a deep and integrated understanding of science, technology, engineering, and mathematics (STEM) combined with an entrepreneurial mindset that prioritizes innovation, actionability, empathy, and value creation (Organisation for Economic Co-operation & Development [OECD], 2018). To prepare students to take on these challenges, STEM education must create opportunities for students to engage with authentic interdisciplinary problems, while also learning specific disciplinary content (Organisation for Economic Co-operation & Development [OECD], 2018; Pearson, 2017). Novel curricular approaches are needed that allow students the autonomy to identify meaningful problems and pursue innovative solution paths, establish connections between in-school learning and their out-of-school experiences, and learn and apply targeted STEM content.

Curriculum theorists have developed learning frameworks that could support this reconceptualization of STEM education. These include, among others, Project-Based Learning (PBL) and Design-Based Learning (DBL), two learning frameworks that situate STEM learning within authentic contexts and challenges. More recently, researchers have begun exploring how Entrepreneurial-Based Learning (EBL; Pérez Yuste et al., 2014), a framework that uses authentic entrepreneurial processes to teach disciplinary content (Lackéus, 2015), can motivate learning and increase interest and engagement in STEM (Deveci & Seikkula-Leino, 2023; Newton et al., 2018; Yu et al., 2025). In isolation, each of these frameworks has shown promise for supporting interest, engagement, and learning in STEM (Cruz et al., 2022; Doppelt et al., 2008; Newton et al., 2018; Penner et al., 1998; Stevens, 2000; Wendell & Rogers, 2013). Synthesizing these frameworks within a single cohesive learning framework could enhance their potential for reconceptualizing STEM education, allowing researchers to leverage specific features from each.

The purpose of this paper is to introduce the Design & Pitch (D&P) Challenges in STEM Learning Framework (Confrey et al., 2019) that situates the learning and application of grade-level-specific mathematics content within week-long entrepreneurial pitch competitions. The framework was designed to allow for a variety of use cases, including as the primary activity that drives the learning of new mathematics content and skills or as a summative application of previously learned mathematics content. During the experience, teams of students invent their own entrepreneurial solutions to math-focused design challenges, define business plans, and deliver five-minute pitches to a panel of judges. We explain how the D&P Learning Framework combines elements of Project-Based Learning (PBL), Design-Based Learning (DBL), and Entrepreneurial-Based Learning (EBL) to enhance students' mathematical reasoning, while also empowering them to invent solutions to authentic problems that are both personally and socially relevant. We also provide details on the D&P Learning Framework and describe the nine curricular activities (challenges) we created to align to the framework. We conclude with a vision for how and why this novel curricular form can transform the teaching and learning of mathematics.

2. The Design & Pitch Challenges in STEM

The D&P Learning Framework uses authentic entrepreneurial processes to motivate the learning or application of curricular STEM content (Moberg, 2014), especially mathematics. More specifically, the D&P Learning Framework engages teams of students to collaboratively invent, prototype, and pitch innovative and actionable solutions to the real-world math-focused entrepreneurial design challenge detailed in a D&P curricular activity. The pitch, the culminating event for a challenge, is a short (maximum of five minutes) persuasive presentation in which teams attempt to convince a panel of external judges that their products or services are entrepreneurially viable. The following sections describe the novel integrated D&P Learning Framework and highlight how each component leverages specific features of Project-Based Learning (PBL), Design-Based Learning (DBL), and Entrepreneurial-Based Learning (EBL), the three learning frameworks that informed its design. This paper defines the Design & Pitch Challenges in STEM as a learning framework that drove the development of coherent curricular activities: tasks that can be used in classrooms to teach standards-aligned disciplinary content (Jukic Matić, 2019). To help illustrate the components of the D&P Learning Framework, we include descriptions of one challenge, Pollution Solution. Several student solutions, and their potential for supporting mathematical reasoning, are discussed to show how features of PBL, DBL, and EBL are leveraged to support interest, engagement, and targeted mathematical reasoning.

2.1. A Brief Overview of PBL, DBL, and EBL

The D&P Learning Framework integrates compatible features of Project-Based Learning (PBL), Design-Based Learning (DBL), and Entrepreneurial-Based Learning (EBL). The purpose of this integration was to build a novel learning framework that focuses and scaffolds students' innovative thinking and mathematical reasoning.

Project-Based Learning (PBL) uses authentic driving questions and relevant contexts to motivate the learning of curricular content (Barron et al., 1998; Capraro & Slough, 2013). Through sustained collaborative inquiry (Capraro & Slough, 2013; Schneider et al., 2002), students build artifacts and deliver culminating presentations that address an authentic driving question (Blumenfeld et al., 2006; J. S. Krajcik & Blumenfeld, 2006; Thomas, 2000). As students work, they continually reflect and iterate on their ideas, identifying gaps in their skills and working towards the disciplinary content goals of the project (Barron et al., 1998; J. Krajcik et al., 2007).

Design-Based Learning (DBL) engages students in design thinking as they iteratively build, test, and refine user-focused solutions to specific design challenges that, like PBL, are intended to create a need for the learning of disciplinary skills and content (English et al., 2020). As students progress through a challenge, they expose their prototypes to critique, which helps them to identify gaps in their understanding (relative to the content, context, and original designs) that need filling (Kolodner, 2002; Penner et al., 1998). DBL involves iteratively gathering and analyzing information (Fortus et al., 2004), generating possible solutions (Apedoe & Schunn, 2013), building, testing, presenting, and refining prototype solutions (Doppelt et al., 2008; Kolodner, 2002; Penner et al., 1998; Razzouk & Shute, 2012), and reflecting on their process (Fortus et al., 2004; Kolodner, 2002). At the end of a DBL challenge, students produce a final design artifact that meets the needs of intended users.

Lastly, Entrepreneurial-Based Learning (EBL) supports students to learn to think and act like an entrepreneur (Lackéus, 2015; Pérez Yuste et al., 2014). It can involve teaching students about entrepreneurial concepts or supporting them to learn entrepreneurial skills through engaging in authentic entrepreneurial processes (Lackéus, 2015; Moberg, 2014; Passaro et al., 2017). These include (a) "... defining situations, imagining scenarios and deciding what is to be done while minimizing risks" (Filion, 1994, p. 70); (b) collaborating, arguing, and debating ideas and processes with peers (Passaro et al., 2017); (c) reflecting on their knowledge and skills relative to a specific entrepreneurial opportunity; and (d) considering ways of providing value to customers (Lackéus, 2015). Although researchers and private companies have begun exploring ways of using entrepreneurship to motivate the learning of STEM content (Deveci & Seikkula-Leino, 2023; Yu et al., 2025) or to leverage DBL in entrepreneurial settings (Laptev & Shaytan, 2022), EBL does not require an explicit connection to the learning of such content.

While PBL, DBL, and EBL are similar in many ways, they also have distinct elements that serve to enhance learning environments. The D&P Learning Framework was designed to take these unique elements and build upon the overlapping foundation of the three frameworks to create a novel approach to mathematics learning. The following sections describe how the D&P Learning Framework leverages and integrates select features of PBL, DBL, and EBL to promote interest, engagement, and targeted mathematics learning.

2.2. Introducing the Competition

Each competition, prior to engaging with a specific challenge, begins with introducing entrepreneurship and elements of pitch competitions. The overarching pitch competition is designed to engage students in authentic entrepreneurial processes (e.g., idea generation, opportunity and resource analysis, building business models, iterating, problem solving, building diverse teams, and pitching) and supports the development of entrepreneurial characteristics, such as resourcefulness, adaptability, and courage.

During the introduction of the competition, teachers facilitate a whole-class discussion in which students share their knowledge of entrepreneurship and pitch competitions and review the rules and specifications for the upcoming pitch competition. As part of this discussion, students explore the D&P Entrepreneurial Characteristics and Processes (see Figure 1), which focus their attention on several key characteristics (e.g., problem solving, resourcefulness, empathy) and processes (e.g., prototyping, iterating, market research) that promote an empathetic and action-oriented conception of entrepreneurship.

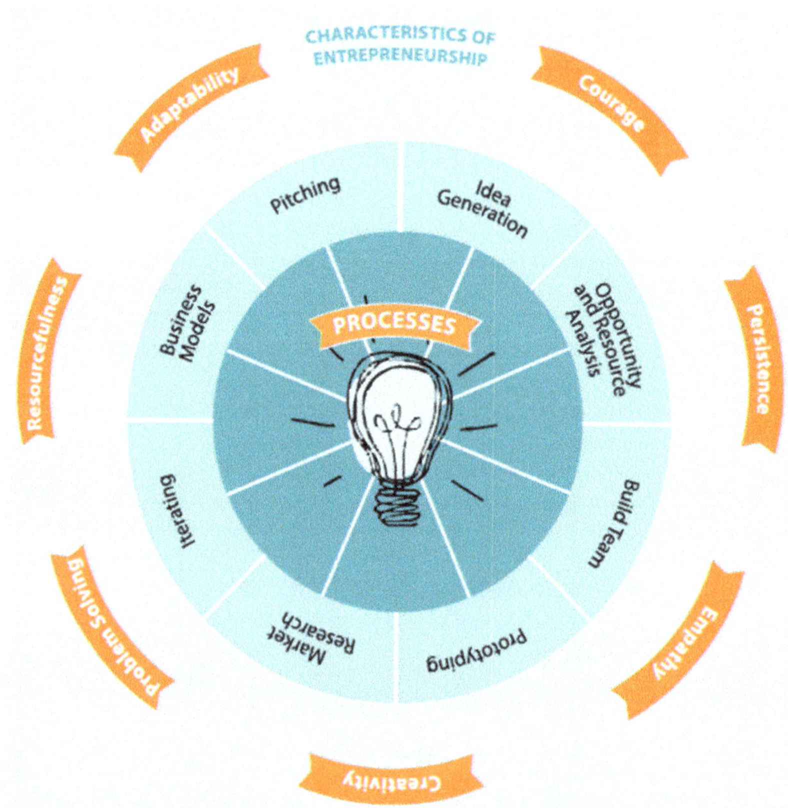

Figure 1. This is a figure of the D&P Entrepreneurial Characteristics and Processes developed by Confrey et al. (2019) in partnership with JASON Learning and informed by the work of Cristal Glanchai (2019).

The competition launch also includes watching a role model video in which a STEM or entrepreneurial professional discusses their experiences in entrepreneurship. The competition launch serves to orient students to the general goals of the activity (i.e., developing a solution to a challenging problem and pitching it to potential investors) and to get students excited about participating in a competition. It also helps focus students' attention on solving real problems in ways that are actionable and financially viable, as opposed to prioritizing profit for profit's sake.

Lastly, and most importantly for engagement and mathematics learning, the competition launch establishes a tangible and immediate purpose for students' work (Blumenfeld et al., 2006; Condliffe et al., 2016; J. S. Krajcik & Blumenfeld, 2006). Students will work in teams to design a physical solution or artifact that addresses a given design challenge (Fortus et al., 2004; Wendell & Rogers, 2013), provide evidence of its potential entrepreneurial viability (Lackéus, 2015), and deliver a culminating presentation, in the form of a pitch, to investors (J. S. Krajcik & Blumenfeld, 2006; Passaro et al., 2017; Thomas, 2000).

2.3. *The D&P Learning Framework*

Creativity and innovation are defining characteristics of entrepreneurship (Bilen et al., 2005; Lackéus, 2015; Laptev & Shaytan, 2022). Although these characteristics can excite and inspire students, they also present an obstacle often confronted by mathematics educators: authentic entrepreneurial problems require innovative and unanticipated solutions, both in terms of the context of the solution and the mathematics used to design it. The D&P Learning Framework (see Figure 2) aims to overcome this obstacle by focusing students' entrepreneurial innovations through design challenges and criteria written to elicit specific mathematics content.

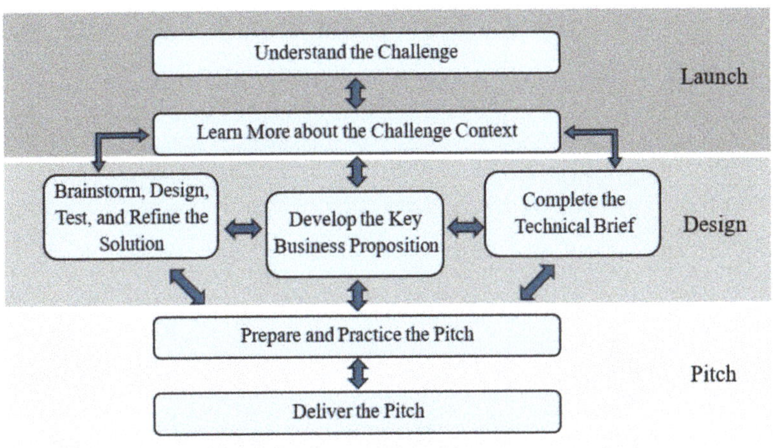

Figure 2. This figure shows the iterative design process that defines the D&P Learning Framework.

The D&P Learning Framework describes an iterative process through which students make sense of the challenge and context (Launch); brainstorm, prototype, refine, and describe entrepreneurial solutions to those challenges (Design); and pitch their solutions to a panel of external judges (Pitch). An in-depth exploration of how students' mathematical reasoning relative to a specific mathematics topic has been reported on in other publications (see e.g., Belcher et al., 2021, 2024). This paper willdescribe the phases of the process, using the Pollution Solution challenge to highlight how each phase draws on features of PBL, DBL, and EBL.

Following the description of the D&P Learning Framework, an overview of the complete set of aligned middle grades challenges will be provided. It is important to note that, although the framework and this paper are organized around the student process, teachers play an essential role in facilitating a challenge. Teachers are encouraged to frequently check in with teams, probe student thinking, reinforce challenge criteria, and provide targeted math support, in the form of individualized support or small group workshops, when needed. Key teacher moves will be discussed as they arise within the D&P Learning Framework sections.

2.3.1. Launch

After introducing the competition and orienting students to the characteristics and processes of entrepreneurship, teachers launch the specific math-focused entrepreneurial design challenge with students. The D&P Learning Framework engages students in addressing authentic driving questions through designing entrepreneurial solutions to math-focused design challenges. For example, in Pollution Solution (see Figure 3), students are tasked with addressing the broad driving question of how to decrease plastic pollution through the challenge of designing a non-plastic container for a liquid product.

Your challenge is to **propose a business around producing and selling a liquid consumer product that is packaged in a dissolvable or edible non-plastic container**. Your business should include:

1. A description of the liquid consumer product your business will sell and its purpose.
2. A 3D sketch and justification of the most appropriate shape and size for your product, given its purpose.
3. A detailed plan, with a 3D sketch and justification, for how you will package and ship your product.

Figure 3. This figure shows the challenge statement for Pollution Solution.

The challenge focuses students' project work and innovation, which places boundaries on the mathematics students are likely to use, while also allowing them the autonomy to identify both the liquid product and the material they use to package it. The challenge launch supports students to understand the challenge, learn more about the broader context in which the challenge is situated, reflect on their experiences with the context and challenge, and begin to empathize with their intended users and define what they need in a solution.

Understand the Challenge

Drawing from PBL and DBL, the D&P Learning Framework follows the introduction of the competition with a challenge launch in which students work collaboratively to understand the challenge and learn more about the challenge context. Students often have experiences with the challenge, context, or existing products that relate to the challenge and context. The challenge launch leverages these experiences to generate excitement through a brief whole-class discussion in which students reflect on and share their experiences with the challenge context. This discussion encourages students to connect their out-of-school experiences with the design challenge and positions them as both designers and clients/consumers of the product or service. Additionally, this initial launch centers the authenticity of the challenge and allows it to drive students' mathematical decision-making as they build their solutions. For example, in the Pollution Solution challenge, students reflect on their usage of single-use plastics, reasons that make single-use plastic ubiquitous, the environmental impact of single-use plastics, and existing solutions with which they are familiar. Through these reflections and conversations, students are primed to connect with and understand the scope of the problem, begin to consider and internalize the needs of their target consumers, and define the criteria that would make their proposed solution viable.

Following the whole-class discussion, students are shown a challenge champion video and the challenge statement. Each challenge in the D&P Learning Framework includes a challenge champion video. In the challenge champion video, a STEM or entrepreneurial professional whose work is related to the challenge context introduces the challenge and describes the general criteria for a solution. In the Pollution Solution challenge, the challenge of designing a liquid product contained in a plastic alternative is introduced by Clifford Okoth Owino. The chief executive officer (CEO) of Chemolex, Okoth Owino, invented a way to turn a harmful invasive plant into an alternative to plastic. In doing so, he found a way to help his community by removing (and repurposing) an invasive plant, while also inventing an eco-friendly replacement for single-use plastics.

Students then read the challenge statement, which adds detail to the challenge champion video and includes: (a) a summary of the challenge, (b) a detailed description of the context in which the design challenge is situated, (c) a statement of the specific design challenge, and (d) a description of the criteria against which final designs will be evaluated. In the Pollution Solution challenge, the criteria specify that student solutions must include: a description of the liquid consumer product their business will sell and its purpose; a three dimensional (3-D) sketch and justification of the most appropriate shape and size for their product given its purpose; and a detailed plan, with a 3-D sketch and justification, for how the product will be packaged and shipped that includes the size, shape, surface area, and volume of the product container.

The challenge launch is intended to engage students in entrepreneurial processes, highlight entrepreneurial characteristics (e.g., empathy, creativity, idea generation, opportunity, and resource analysis), and establish a concrete foundation that will drive students' mathematics learning. The launch of the design challenge may also "trigger" certain student ideas or actions (Fortus et al., 2004), giving them an entry into the challenge. Although these activities are started in the challenge launch, it is an iterative process, with students developing a deeper understanding of both the challenge and the context as they build, test, and refine their solutions.

In both PBL and DBL, the launch is essential to students' understanding of the project or challenge. In PBL, it provides students the opportunity to collectively focus the task and identify the content and skills needed to complete it (Barron et al., 1998; J. S. Krajcik & Blumenfeld, 2006; J. Krajcik et al., 2007), thereby creating a need for new learning. In DBL, it engages students (individually, in groups, or as a class) in a process of "problem scoping" or "problem formulating" in which they begin "clarifying and restating the goal of the problem, identifying constraints to be met in problem solution, exploring feasibility issues, drawing on related context to add meaning, experimenting with materials, and establishing collaborative group work" (English & King, 2015, p. 4). This problem-scoping stage focuses students' attention on the specific criteria that will determine the success of a design (Kolodner, 2002; Fortus et al., 2004; Penner et al., 1998; English & King, 2015). It helps orient the class, supports students to attend to the relationship between the problem and any proposed solutions (Penner et al., 1998), and can initiate student action through their familiarity with the context (Fortus et al., 2004).

Learn More about the Challenge Context

Once students have a fundamental understanding of the challenge, they begin learning more about the challenge context as they collaboratively research the overarching driving question and the ways entrepreneurs and scientists are currently addressing it. This initial step of research engages students in entrepreneurial processes such as empathy and opportunity and resource analysis, and encourages them to think big, attending to the viability and authenticity of a solution.

The research phase includes two additional resources designed to support students to learn more about the challenge context. The first is the Helpful Resources document, a set of internet hyperlinks to news stories about the context or to websites of companies doing work relating to the challenge context. Understanding the needs of users, often through market research, is essential to entrepreneurship. The Helpful Resources document is an effort to translate this entrepreneurial experience to the classroom. Through the set of links, the resource provides students with additional information about the context, users, and existing entrepreneurial solutions to help them gain insight into how others have solved the problem and what users may want in a solution. These links were curated and designed to jumpstart student thinking and highlight the authenticity of their work. In Pollution Solution, the set of resources explores the extent and environmental implications of the single-use plastics problem and lists innovative alternatives that are either currently in use or being developed. The research phase and the Helpful Resources not only provide deeper insight into the importance and urgency of the broader context of the driving question, but also help students connect, on a personal level, with the challenge.

The second resource is a background video in which the challenge champion gives students more information about their careers and provides tips for students to consider when building their solutions. Integrating the Helpful Resources and Background Video within the research process is intended to further support students to attend to constraints authentic to the challenge context and the needs of their intended users. Additionally, it positions them as both the designer and user of the solution, which gives them a frame of reference for evaluating the completeness and success of their solutions. For Pollution Solution, the challenge champion discusses in greater depth the origin of his innovative bioplastic, how it connects to his life experiences as the son of a fisher, and how his company considered the unique needs and desires of his community: the people he most wanted to help with his solution. Okoth Owino's decision to use an invasive plant as the primary material for his bioplastic emerged from his experiences witnessing the damage the plant was doing to his father's livelihood. Okoth Owino was uniquely positioned, through the combination of his life experiences and STEM training, to capitalize on this entrepreneurial opportunity. In this way, the background video not only gives students insight into the importance of understanding one's community and empathizing with the needs of their users, but also empowers them to draw on their experiences and STEM knowledge in inventing entrepreneurial solutions. This was evident in a solution from one team of middle school students. Like Okoth Owino, they identified a locally invasive plant with which they were familiar (bamboo) and designed a cylindrical water bottle made from sections of that plant. In this way, the background video may have jump-started students' idea generation, leading them to a solution that was authentic, personally relevant, and that would provide the focus of their engagement with the intended mathematics content.

2.3.2. Design

Following the challenge launch, students start working through three parallel and iterative components of the D&P Learning Framework: (a) brainstorm, design, test, and refine solutions; (b) develop the Key Business Proposition; and (c) build the Technical Brief. The work of designing a prototype solution, defining its entrepreneurial viability through a business proposition, and documenting its mathematical foundation happens within this Design phase. Although these three phases are depicted in the D&P Learning Framework as distinct, they are nevertheless highly interactive and iterative, with each phase informing the other two and students frequently cycling between the three.

Brainstorm, Design, Test, and Refine Solutions

The brainstorming phase of the solution design process establishes an essential foundation that will drive students' mathematical and entrepreneurial reasoning throughout the competition. It is during this phase that students collaboratively draw on their personal out-of-school experiences, interests, and expertise to identify entrepreneurial opportunities and begin defining solutions that capitalize on those opportunities. This accomplishes several beneficial outcomes for students' mathematics learning. First, it engages students more broadly in authentic mathematics problem solving. Rather than providing students with a pre-selected or pre-configured "real-world" problem, students are empowered to identify, within the challenge context, their own problem to solve and define the relevant parameters. Second, it connects students' in-school learning to their out-of-school experiences, demonstrating the utility of mathematics learning beyond the classroom. Finally, it positions students as experts, relative to their chosen solution path, empowering them to self-evaluate the correctness or completeness of their solutions and the underlying mathematics. Take for example, the team of students who addressed the Pollution Solution challenge by inventing a water bottle made from a cylindrical bamboo stalk. Although one could argue this solution does not meet the challenge requirement that the container be made from "dissolvable or edible non-plastic material," the bamboo water bottle would nevertheless allow students to address the math-focused criteria and, thus, engage with the intended mathematics content. To be able to determine the amount of water their bottle could hold, students would need to make assumptions about how to model a bamboo stalk (bamboo stalks are not uniformly cylindrical and have thick outer walls), define the dimensions of a section of the stalk, and consider the relationship between those dimensions and the amount of water the stalk could hold. Other solutions included beeswax cubes that would hold honey and spherical edible pods containing water. Each of these liquid products introduces unique and authentic constraints for students to consider in quantifying the volume and surface area of the containers.

Once students have arrived at a general idea for a solution, they begin designing, testing, and refining it, often using D&P-identified technological tools. In each challenge, the D&P Learning Framework includes technological tools, specifically identified to support students in prototyping their solutions and engaging with the targeted mathematics content. In Pollution Solution, students use the free online 3-D design software TinkerCAD (Autodesk, 2025) to create 3-D models of their containers. TinkerCAD allows students to design and manipulate 3-D figures, supporting the development of students' spatial reasoning and highlighting the relationship between the dimensions/shape of a figure and its apparent capacity.

The process of brainstorming, designing, testing, and refining their prototypes to meet the design criteria is intended to help students identify gaps in their math content knowledge or skills and work to fill those gaps by seeking out additional resources (Capraro & Slough, 2013; Kolodner, 2002; J. Krajcik et al., 2007; Penner et al., 1998), including teacher support and a math resource tailored to each challenge. It also leverages students' design preferences and real-world experiences as consumers to motivate and inform valuable mathematical considerations. For example, in the Pollution Solution challenge, students need to coordinate between the design of their liquid container, its volume and surface area, and the needs of users. This coordination requires students to draw on their experiences as users of the product, their aesthetic preferences for the appearance and form of the container, the financial incentive of minimizing the container's surface area, and the industry expectations for the container's volume. For example, users' expectations for the volume of a water bottle are likely different from their expectations for the volume of a honey cube or an edible water pod, and students must consider those expectations in designing their containers.

The theory informing the brainstorm, design, test, and refine component of the D&P Learning Framework leverages features of EBL, PBL, and DBL. In PBL, students work collaboratively in "communities of learners... including peers, teachers, and members of the community" (Schneider et al., 2002, p. 3) to address the driving question through the creation of a tangible artifact, which can include physical products, sketches, plans, or even posters (Blumenfeld et al., 2006; Capraro & Slough, 2013; Condliffe et al., 2016; Cruz et al., 2022; Fisher et al., 2020; Thomas, 2000). The creation of the final product provides a concrete outcome for students' schoolwork (Blumenfeld et al., 2006), which can create an immediate purpose for learning that motivates student engagement (Ainley et al., 2005; T. J. Moore et al., 2020). DBL uses design thinking to provide a structure for students' collaborative work (Dym et al., 2005; Kolodner, 2002) and includes opportunities to more explicitly connect that work to specific mathematics learning goals (Apedoe & Schunn, 2013; Mehalik et al., 2008; Penner et al., 1998). After launching the design challenge and establishing initial conditions and criteria against which designs will be evaluated, students engage in an iterative process of gathering and analyzing information (Fortus et al., 2004), generating possible solutions (Apedoe & Schunn, 2013), building, testing, presenting, and refining prototypes (Doppelt et al., 2008; Kolodner, 2002; Penner et al., 1998; Razzouk & Shute, 2012), and reflecting on their process (Fortus et al., 2004; Kolodner, 2002).

Develop the Key Business Proposition

For an entrepreneurial solution to succeed, it must create value for consumers or customers (Jones et al., 2020; Lackéus, 2015). That is, it must solve a problem, fixing something a user dislikes or enhancing something they like about their situation. If an entrepreneur cannot communicate a convincing value proposition to investors, consumers, and customers, the product or service is unlikely to succeed. As students brainstorm, design, test, and refine their solutions, they are also supported to define their solutions' value propositions using the Key Business Proposition (KBP). The KBP includes three parts. The first part of the KBP is shown in Figure 4.

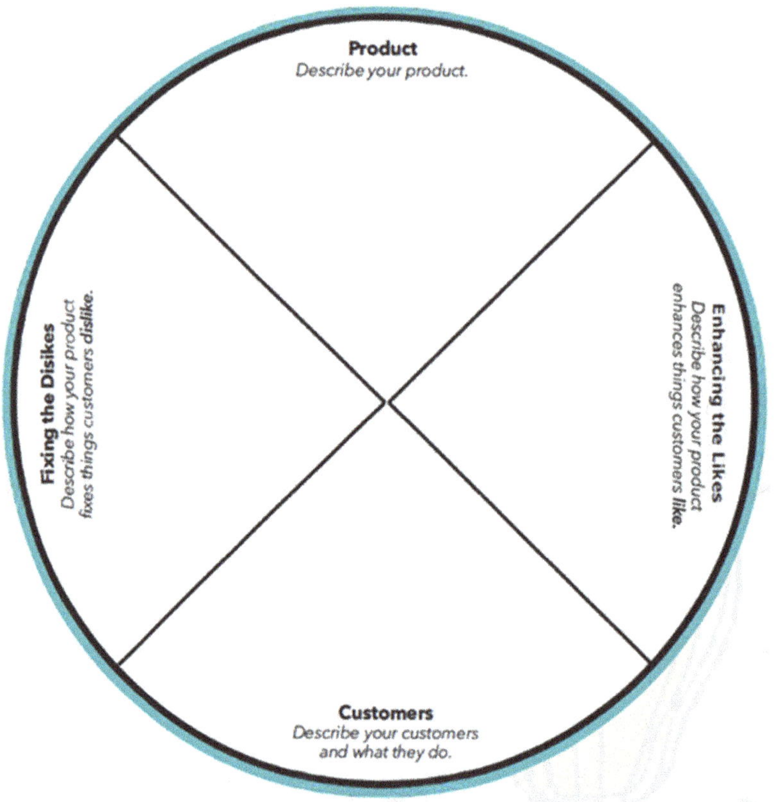

Figure 4. This figure represents the first part of the Key Business Proposition.

It provides a structure for students to describe the features of their product, identify their target customers, and define how their product will fix something customers dislike about their situation or enhance something they like about their situation. For example, in Pollution Solution, students need to coordinate between enhancing features that consumers like about bottles (e.g., ease of use, lightweight and durable materials, portability, aesthetics) and fixing features they dislike about plastic bottles (e.g., plastic pollution, release of harmful chemicals over time, use of a non-renewable resource). These considerations inform students' design decisions, which then often introduce mathematical constraints on their solutions, such as guaranteeing that the resulting container is lightweight, made from eco-friendly materials, and holds an amount of liquid that fits users' expectations. This requires students to coordinate between the volume and surface area of the container as they make adjustments to meet users' expectations. For example, students would need to consider the relationship between the dimensions of a section of bamboo stalk and the amount of water it can contain. Similarly, meeting user expectations for the amount of honey in an edible honey cube or water in an edible water pod requires students to coordinate between the dimensions of the container and its volume.

The second part of the KBP prompts students to identify a type of business model they will use to make their solutions financially viable. The D&P Learning Framework includes a Business Model Types resource that describes several common business model types. It is intended to introduce students to different types of business models while also focusing their attention on the actionability of their solutions. The final part of the KBP is an Elevator Pitch template (see Figure 5).

Hi, our names are ____________ (group member's name), ____________ (group member's name), **and** ____________ (group member's name).

Our company, ____________ (company name), **invented** ____________ (product name).

It helps ____________ (customers), **who** ____________ (customer's situation or job).

Unlike ____________ (competitor), **which** ____________ (competitor weakness 1), **and** ____________ (competitor weakness 2)

our product ____________ (improves, makes easier, lessens, etc.) **the** ____________ (a customer dislike), **by**

____________ (how the product lessens a customer dislike). **It also**

____________ (increases, enhances, etc.) **the** ____________ (a customer like), **by**

____________ (how the product enhances a customer like).

Figure 5. This figure shows the Elevator Pitch Template included in the Key Business Proposition.

The Elevator Pitch template provides students with a structured way to begin planning how to effectively and concisely communicate the features of their solution, describe its value proposition, and position it in the market relative to competitors. Focusing students' attention on their consumers and competitors, the elevator pitch not only creates opportunities for students to continue practicing communicating and defending their reasoning, but it also introduces additional considerations that can lead students to self-evaluate and iterate on their designs. As students reflect on how their solutions compare to their competitors, they often discover ways in which those solutions fall short of their competitors and are, thus, in need of improvement.

PBL and DBL both emphasize authenticity, through engaging in career-connected processes (Grossman et al., 2019; J. S. Krajcik & Blumenfeld, 2006; Thomas, 2000), addressing real-world driving questions (Capraro & Slough, 2013; Grossman et al., 2019; Schneider et al., 2002), and designing tangible artifacts or prototypes (Blumenfeld et al., 2006; Capraro & Slough, 2013; Condliffe et al., 2016; Cruz et al., 2022; Fortus et al., 2004; Mehalik et al., 2008; Wendell & Rogers, 2013). The KBP draws on EBL to enhance the authenticity of projects and design challenges, by focusing students' attention on the entrepreneurial viability of their solutions. That is, to be authentically actionable, students' solutions must create value for a specific group of customers or consumers (Borasi & Finnigan, 2010; Jones et al., 2020; Lackéus, 2015). In both DBL and EBL, students play a central role in defining the criteria for a successful solution and making necessary adjustments to those criteria based on value judgments (Apedoe & Schunn, 2013; Dym et al., 2005; Kolodner, 2002). Where EBL differs from DBL is in its emphasis on not just the needs of the customer, but on identifying and communicating the value proposition of a design (Lackéus, 2015). Through the KBP, the D&P Learning Framework provides students with a way of defining the criteria for a complete solution that takes into consideration the needs of the target user/consumer and the actionability of the solution.

The KBP supports learning and promotes entrepreneurial characteristics and processes in several ways. First, it encourages empathy, as students consider the needs of customers. Second, it promotes problem solving, as students consider how to adapt or better position their ideas to create value for customers. Third, it supports learning by leveraging the evaluation and critique component of DBL. In DBL, it is important for students to consider alternative designs, to make value judgments relative to the criteria for success, and to select the optimal or preferred design for the final product (Dym et al., 2005). Finally, the KBP utilizes an elevator pitch framework (see Figure 4) to help students begin considering how to concisely describe their business and product, while positioning it in the market relative to competitors.

Build the Technical Brief

The third component of the Design phase of the D&P Learning framework is completing the Technical Brief. In completing the Technical Brief, students describe the specifics of their solutions, including mathematical and scientific justifications, and discuss the process through which they developed their solutions. The goal of the Technical Brief is to encourage students to demonstrate how they know a solution will work and that it meets the specific challenge criteria, using the targeted mathematics content. It includes two parts. In the first part of the Technical Brief, students reflect on their process of designing, testing, and refining their solution, including describing the research they conducted and the solutions they considered but chose not to pursue. In the second part of the Technical Brief, students describe the specifics of their solution and how it addresses the challenge criteria, which involves explicitly showing their mathematical reasoning.

In the Pollution Solution challenge, the Technical Brief makes explicit the requirement for students to create 3-D models and calculate the volume and surface area of their liquid container. Students are also prompted to describe how they arrived at their final designs and justify the entrepreneurial and scientific viability of their designs. These requirements connect students' entrepreneurial designs to the intended mathematical content relating to the measurement of 3-D figures. The D&P Learning Framework also includes a Technical Brief Rubric aligned to the Technical Brief that makes students aware of the expectations of what to include in the Technical Brief and guides teachers in their assessment of students' understanding of the intended mathematics content.

In both PBL and DBL, reflecting on the process of developing the final artifact is essential for connecting the design or project tasks with the underlying STEM content and skills (Kolodner, 2002; J. Krajcik et al., 2007; Penner et al., 1998). In PBL, this reflection may occur through scaffolded lessons implemented during the unit (J. Krajcik et al., 2007) or through project journals in which students document their process and the problems they choose to solve (Stevens, 2000). In DBL, reflection might involve whole-class presentations (Fortus et al., 2004; Penner et al., 1998), gallery walks, design journals, guided inquiry lessons during the design process (Kolodner, 2002), or through testing and reflecting on the success of prototypes (Doppelt et al., 2008; Kolodner, 2002; Penner et al., 1998; Razzouk & Shute, 2012). The Technical Brief provides a structure for supporting this reflection, while also encouraging students to show how their solution meets the specific design criteria, using the intended mathematics content.

Exposing Ideas to Critique

As students design their solutions, define value propositions through the KBP, and describe the entrepreneurial and mathematical specifications of their solutions through the Technical Brief, the D&P Learning Framework incorporates frequent opportunities for students to practice sharing their thinking, expose their ideas to critique, and receive feedback from teachers and external audiences. Throughout the competition, teachers are encouraged to conduct informal check-ins, asking students to explain their solutions, describe how those solutions address specific challenge criteria, identify their target customers, and justify how their solutions create value for those customers. These informal check-ins leverage the authenticity and entrepreneurial viability of student solutions to prompt students to reflect on the targeted mathematics. For example, in the Pollution Solution challenge, teachers frequently ask questions like, "What type of liquid product will your container hold? How much liquid will it hold? How did you decide on that amount? Who are your target customers? And what aspects of your product will make customers want to use it?" These questions prompt students to reflect on the relationship between the design of their container, its volume and surface area, and the expectations and needs of the customers. In this way, the authenticity of the situation leads students to evaluate the accuracy of their prototypes and calculations and iterate as needed.

The D&P Learning Framework includes a more formal opportunity for students to expose their solutions to critique through the Expert Check-In, in which students describe their solutions to a member of the community who has not engaged with the students about their solutions previously. During the Expert Check-In, the expert, like the teacher, is encouraged to follow student thinking, asking questions about the real-world and entrepreneurial viability of solutions to drive back at the math-focused challenge criteria. The Expert Check-In provides students with another opportunity to test the viability of their solutions, this time with a new audience, and to practice explaining and defending their design decisions. Together, the teacher, through their frequent informal check-ins, and the experts, through their more formal check-ins halfway through the competition, press students to explain and defend features of their solution and value proposition. These check-ins (a) provide students with helpful guidance for improving their solutions; (b) create opportunities for students to practice explaining and defending their solutions; (c) help students identify gaps in their solutions that to fill require engagement with the intended mathematics content; and (d) build students' investment and confidence in their solutions.

Peer feedback is central to PBL, driving students to iterate and improve on their tangible artifacts and final presentations, while also creating opportunities to identify gaps in their discipline-specific knowledge or skills (Condliffe et al., 2016; J. S. Krajcik & Blumenfeld, 2006; Schneider et al., 2002; Thomas, 2000). The D&P Learning Framework draws on the feedback structures characteristic of DBL and EBL to focus and enhance this component of PBL. In DBL, students are given frequent opportunities to expose their prototypes to critique, often through testing their designs under real-world circumstances. This could include things like testing a parachute design by dropping it from some height

(Kolodner, 2002) or testing a physical model of an elbow to evaluate whether it behaves as expected (Penner et al., 1998). The purpose of exposing the prototype to critique is to allow real-world constraints to determine the success or failure of a design. When a design fails (or does not behave as expected), students must reflect on their prototypes, identify and work to fill gaps in their understanding that led to the design failure, and refine their designs using the newly learned knowledge or skills (Skinner & Harlow, 2022). Entrepreneurs similarly build, test, and refine prototypes of their products. They also frequently seek out feedback from peers, experts, and their intended users and utilize that feedback to improve their designs.

2.3.3. Pitch

The final component of the D&P Learning Framework is pitching and includes both a practice pitch with an external judge and the final pitch competition with a panel of judges. The final pitch in the D&P Learning Framework is restricted to five minutes, without time for questions, which requires students to clearly, concisely, and thoroughly communicate the features of their solution and convince the judges of its viability. This final pitch situates and reframes the presentation components of both PBL and DBL within an authentic, exciting, and high-pressure entrepreneurial experience of the start-up competition (Bilen et al., 2005; R. A. Moore et al., 2017; Passaro et al., 2017).

Prepare and Practice the Pitch

To help students learn to build a pitch deck and plan their entrepreneurial pitch, the D&P Learning Framework provides a set of pitch resources. These resources include a How to Build a Pitch document, which outlines the key components of an effective pitch, a set of sample pitches from real companies, which helps students understand what a pitch looks like and important elements to include, and a pitch judging rubric that will be used by the judges to evaluate each of the solutions and choose a winning team.

One to two days before the final pitch competition, students are given an opportunity to complete a practice pitch to an external practice judge. External practice judges can be anyone who is not the students' teacher because the teacher already has a deep understanding of each solution. Not only is the practice pitch an opportunity for students to have a trial run at their pitch, but this provides time for the students to receive critical feedback so they can develop their ideas and how they communicate those ideas more completely before the final pitch. The practice pitch is intended to give students one more opportunity to expose their ideas to critique and make necessary improvements before the final pitch, while also continuing to build their confidence in their solutions and their excitement to share those solutions with the judges and their peers.

The importance of preparing and practicing the pitch goes beyond improving the solution and final pitch. The act of communicating one's thinking thoroughly, convincingly, and concisely to an unfamiliar audience is a challenging and intimidating prospect that requires considerable courage. It increases student accountability and inspires action. Typically, halfway through the competition, students start to feel the pressure of the practice pitch, and their intensity and collaboration inevitably increase. They start to assign roles for the pitch, identify the key elements they need to communicate in their pitch, and plan how to do so effectively through visuals, text in their pitch decks, and a verbal script. After delivering their practice pitches, they come to understand the daunting nature of the task, often realizing just how short five minutes feels when they are excited to share their ideas with the judges, and how much practice they need to be able to comfortably explain and pitch their innovations. This often leads teams to repeatedly and iteratively plan, discuss, write, practice, and reflect on what and how they are communicating to the judges, including both the purely entrepreneurial aspects of their solutions and the underlying mathematics.

Deliver the Pitch

Each D&P challenge culminates with a five-minute pitch to a panel of judges. Depending on the setting and the resources available, the panel of judges could be members of the community, local entrepreneurs, or school stakeholders. The only requirement for judges is that they are not familiar with students' entrepreneurial solutions prior to the final pitch. By the time students make it through the week of designing their solutions, defining their business value propositions, defending their thinking to teachers and outside experts, and preparing and practicing their pitches, students are often nervous and excited to show off what they have accomplished. On the day of the final pitch competition, students continue running through their pitches (often pacing back and forth with notecards) and tinkering with their slide decks (typically a Google Slides or PowerPoint presentation), which provides additional opportunities for students to practice communicating and reflecting on their solutions and the underlying mathematics. The autonomy afforded by the entrepreneurial pitch format adds to the appeal and excitement of a final presentation. While daunting and requiring courage, it allows students the opportunity to share something unique and personally relevant with outside experts. Students get excited to share what they have learned with adults who want to listen to what they have been working on. Upon completing their final pitches, students often report feeling proud of their work and identify ways they could have improved.

Preparing for and delivering the final pitch has roots in all three instructional frameworks that informed the design of the D&P Learning Framework. In PBL, projects culminate with a final presentation in which students share their work with an external audience. The final presentation provides added accountability to students' work and an opportunity to reflect on the connections between the project work and the targeted disciplinary content (Condliffe et al., 2016; Grossman et al., 2019; J. S. Krajcik & Blumenfeld, 2006; J. Krajcik et al., 2007; Thomas, 2000). Similarly, in DBL, the expectation that students continually expose their ideas to critique is intended to allow students to evaluate their prototypes and connect the features of their designs to the intended STEM content (Kolodner, 2002; Penner et al., 1998). EBL adds a unique twist to these public presentations, making them persuasive and investor-focused. In EBL, the final presentation of a solution, product, or service often takes the form of a persuasive pitch to investors (Bilen et al., 2005; Passaro et al., 2017). Like PBL and DBL, the pitch, delivered to an external audience, requires students to develop and deliver a clear, concise, and convincing explanation of their solutions.

2.3.4. Summary

The D&P Learning Framework leverages and enhances compatible features of PBL, DBL, and EBL to create an integrated learning framework that can support targeted mathematics learning. Table 1 shows how PBL, DBL, and EBL informed the D&P Learning Framework. It should be noted that PBL, DBL, and EBL all share similar features, and most of the D&P Learning Framework components were informed by more than one framework. For example, PBL and DBL both include opportunities for students to expose their ideas to critique through a final presentation or testing of a prototype. The D&P Learning Framework leverages the entrepreneurial pitch competition (an authentic entrepreneurial process) to heighten the excitement, accountability, and autonomy of this public presentation. Likewise, while PBL emphasizes autonomy and EBL emphasizes innovation and uniqueness in the development of artifacts and products, DBL's emphasis on design challenges and user-focused design criteria was leveraged to focus students' innovations and provide predictability in the math that will emerge as students build those innovations. Lastly, while both DBL and EBL are intended to motivate the learning of disciplinary STEM content, PBL provides a structure, through workshops and content rubrics, for supporting students to draw connections between their project work and the intended STEM learning goals.

Table 1. The D&P Learning Framework Components Summary.

D&P Components	PBL	DBL	EBL
		Launch	
Understand the Challenge	Identify content and skills needed to address the driving question.	Focus the problem and understand the design challenge.	
Learn More about the Challenge Context	Consider authentic constraints.	Define the authentic constraints and user-focused criteria.	Consider entrepreneurial opportunities and available resources.
		Design	
Brainstorm, Design, Test, and Refine Solutions	Collaboratively build an artifact that addresses the driving question.	Iteratively design a prototype that meets user criteria.	Design a viable product or service.
Develop the Key Business Proposition		Evaluate design against user-focused criteria.	Define how the product/service creates values for users (clients).
Complete the Technical Brief	Connect project work to intended disciplinary content.	Reflect on the process using a design journal.	Define product specifications for the users (clients).
		Pitch	
Prepare and Practice the Pitch	Give, receive, and incorporate feedback.	Test and expose prototypes to critique.	Practice pitch with external experts.
Deliver the Pitch	Deliver culminating presentation.		Deliver a persuasive pitch to external judges.

2.4. The D&P Learning Framework Challenges

The D&P Learning Framework includes nine entrepreneurial design challenges targeting middle school mathematics content. The challenges were designed to target a variety of mathematical topics and real-world contexts. The challenge champions were selected to expose students to a diverse range of STEM professionals in hopes that students would be able to see their own identities reflected in the world of STEM and entrepreneurship. Table 2 presents the complete set of middle grades challenges, describing each challenge, its challenge champion, and intended mathematics content.

Table 2. D&P Learning Framework Challenges.

Challenge Title	Description	Champion	
 Building Algorithms	Students build algorithms that use people's opinions to rate or rank something they care about. Math Focus: Expressions and Equations		Cathy Yee CEO, Founder, Incluvie
 Erase Food Waste	Students design food-related businesses that use sliding price scales to reduce food waste. Math Focus: Percents, Data Analysis		Oscar Ekponimo Founder, CEO Chowberry

Table 2. *Cont.*

Challenge Title	Description	Champion
 Fix It: Design for Community Impact	Students design physical products that will help solve a problem facing their communities. Math Focus: 3-D Figures, Surface Area, Volume	 Gitanjali Rao Inventor, STEM Promoter
 Flashy Fashion	Students design wearable technology products that use LED lighting systems. Math Focus: Transformations, Coordinate Plane	 Kelsy Dominick Designer, CEO DiDomenico Design
 Keep It Real	Students design apps that use data representations to help people put down their phones and connect, face-to-face. Math Focus: Data Analysis and Representation	 Dr. Cardell PatilloExecutive Director, Head StartProgram
 Operation Lifeline	Students design medical packs that can be used to deliver refrigerated medications in times of natural disasters. Math Focus: 3-D Figures; Surface Area, Volume	 Kris Ludwig Scientist, US Geological Survey
 Pollution Solution	Students design containers, made from dissolvable or edible materials, to package and sell liquid products. Math Focus: 3-D Figures, Surface Area, Volume	 Clifford Okoth Owino Founder, CEO Chemolex
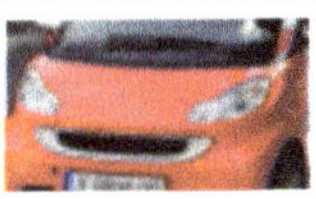 Power Me Up	Students design companies that make it easier for people to charge their electric vehicles. Math Focus: Ratios, Data Analysis, Equations	 Kristin Vicari Senior Chemical Engineer, Tesla
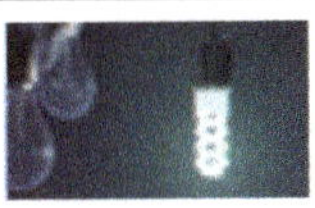 Prototype to Profit	Students build business plans and pitches to make existing product ideas economically viable. Math Focus: Building Linear Functions, Solving Linear Equations	 Tyler Maloney Materials Science Engineer, Entrepreneur

2.4.1. Contexts

The D&P challenges are situated within real-world contexts selected to be accessible to students and open enough to allow them to pursue innovative and authentic solutions using the intended mathematics content. As described in Table 1, the set of D&P challenges targets a variety of contexts that address current and pressing issues. These include environmental contexts, such as pollution, food waste, and emissions from gas-powered vehicles (Pollution Solution, Erase Food Waste, and Power Me Up); economic contexts focused on how to make innovative solutions financially viable (Prototype to Profit); social contexts, such as finding solutions to problems facing one's community and delivering medical supplies following a natural disaster (Fix It: Design for Community Impact and Operation Lifeline); and technological contexts, such as understanding bias in rating algorithms, reducing smartphone dependence, and designing tech-infused fashion (Building Algorithms, Keep It Real, and Flashy Fashion).

Each challenge is situated within an authentic driving question relating to a broad context, such as the new application of a technology, or a multi-dimensional, thorny, and global problem, such as plastic pollution or climate change. Addressing these questions requires one to identify manageable and solvable local opportunities. In the D&P Learning Framework challenges, students are given the autonomy to identify those necessary and personally meaningful local opportunities and capitalize on them in ways that meet the criteria of the challenge and the needs of the people most in need of a solution. In this way, the contexts are engaging and accessible, allowing students to meaningfully draw on their personal interests and experiences in building their entrepreneurial and mathematical solutions. For example, the Flashy Fashion challenge is situated within the broad context of infusing LED technology in fashion. Students have the autonomy to identify opportunities that can be addressed using this technology. In one particularly powerful example, students drew on their experiences wearing masks during the COVID-19 pandemic, specifically the challenge of reading someone's emotions when a mask prevents one from reading facial expressions. To solve this problem, the students designed programmable facemasks that would allow the wearer to show a facial expression using LED lights. They identified and addressed a personally meaningful problem within the broader context of technology-infused fashion.

2.4.2. Champions

Each challenge includes a challenge champion who launches the challenge and gives background information about the context. The champions represent a diverse collection of STEM and entrepreneurial professionals, whose work is closely connected to their challenge and context (see Table 2 above). They provide students with authentic examples of how pursuing solutions to personally meaningful and relevant problems can lead to STEM-focused careers. For example, in the Erase Food Waste challenge, students use sliding price scales to tackle food waste. The champion for this challenge is Oscar Ekponimo. Ekponimo is the CEO of Chowberry, an app that reduces food waste by connecting food-insecure customers with grocery stores looking to sell soon-to-expire foods at a discount. Ekponimo's work inventing the app and convincing grocery stores to offer discounts provides students with a real-world example of the work they are doing in the challenge.

The challenge champions also provide students with a powerful entrepreneurial lens for thinking about career paths. Often, students express interest in working in well-known careers without a complete understanding of the nature of those careers (Mann et al., 2020). Through the stories of the challenge champions, students are exposed to examples of people who built careers around solving problems that they found meaningful. For example, in the Building Algorithms challenge, students are introduced to Cathy Yee, the founder and CEO of Incluvie, a company that rates movies based on their treatment of diversity. Yee found a personally meaningful problem (the movie industry's inaccurate and harmful representation of groups who have been marginalized) and built a career around solving it.

2.4.3. Mathematics Content

Just as the challenge contexts and champions were intentionally designed to represent a diverse range of options, the challenges were also designed to target a diverse range of mathematics content (see Table 2). Middle grades mathematics standards changed significantly with the release of the Common Core State Standards for Mathematics (Confrey & Krupa, 2012). As such we intentionally wrote challenges to align with the six mathematical domains of the Common Core: Ratio and Proportional Reasoning, the Number System, Expressions and Equations, Functions, Geometry, and Statistics and Probability. While each challenge focuses on one mathematical topic, many of the challenges have the potential for students to engage with multiple mathematical concepts as they build their solutions. For example, in Power Me Up, students are tasked with designing a business that expands the electric vehicle charging infrastructure. The challenge primarily targets ratio and proportional reasoning as students compare the refueling costs of electric vehicles and gas-powered vehicles to determine pricing. Students must also create a prototype plan for where they will build their initial set of charging stations, requiring them to analyze data to determine the locations of existing charging stations and identify gaps. The intended mathematics is woven into the challenge criteria such that building the solution creates a need for students to engage with and develop a deeper understanding of the intended mathematics.

2.4.4. Technology Tools

The D&P Learning Framework includes technological tools with each challenge to support students' prototyping efforts. These freely available online tools were selected based on their utility for building the desired prototype and their ability to support and enhance the intended mathematical reasoning. For three of the challenges (Fix It: Design for Community Impact, Operation Lifeline, and Pollution Solution), the technology tool is TinkerCAD (Autodesk, 2025). TinkerCAD is a 3-D modeling tool that can be used to create 3-D designs by combining and manipulating (e.g., moving, rotating, resizing) figures. It helps students visualize 3-D figures from multiple perspectives, while also attending to the relationships between the features of their designs and the volume and surface area of those designs.

For three other challenges, the technological tool is a spreadsheet. Like with TinkerCAD, the spreadsheet tool (Excel and Google Sheets are both supported) provides students with a way to build a functioning prototype of their solutions, which include rating/ranking algorithms (Building Algorithms), sliding price scales (Erase Food Waste), or a component of financial business plans (Prototype to Profit). The spreadsheet is also a powerful tool for helping students develop a nuanced understanding of variables, algebraic expressions, and functions (Belcher et al., 2024; Filloy et al., 2007; Rojano, 1996; Tabach et al., 2008).

Two challenges (Flashy Fashion and Power Me Up) use GeoGebra (2025) to help engage students with geometric transformations and properties of circles. GeoGebra is an online, dynamic geometry tool that allows students to construct and transform figures. Students use the tool to create transforming fashion (Flashy Fashion) or plan the locations of their charging stations (Power Me Up). The tool allows students to offload the work of manually constructing and transforming geometric figures, which allows them to attend to the properties of those constructions and transformations.

Finally, Keep It Real includes the data representation tool, Datawrapper (Datawrapper GmbH, 2025), which students can use to input data and explore and manipulate different visual representations of that data. Like TinkerCAD and GeoGebra, Datawrapper allows students to offload the task of manually building data representations and instead focus their attention on how changing a representation can alter the story it communicates to an audience. Across the nine challenges, the technological tools not only enhance the authenticity of students' mathematics learning but also enable students to engage deeply with the intended mathematics content.

3. Discussion

This paper presented the components of the D&P Learning Framework, highlighting how it integrates and, through that integration, enhances features of PBL, DBL, and EBL to create distinct opportunities for mathematics learning and engagement. The framework was created to support the learning and application of specific and standards-aligned mathematics content. The design of the D&P Learning Framework drew on a constructivist perspective of learning, in which students, in response to a perceived problematic (Confrey, 1991), iteratively build, test, and refine models of a given situation. Throughout this iterative process, students continuously reflect on the viability of their models (von Glasersfeld, 1982) and the problematic they are working to address (Confrey & Maloney, 2007; Dewey, 1938/1981). As they progress through this cycle, students develop a deeper understanding of both the problematic they are working to address and the mathematics underlying their solutions (Confrey & Maloney, 2007). By combining features of PBL, DBL, and EBL, the D&P Learning Framework supports and enhances this iterative cycle for students in several important ways that are instructive for STEM education.

First, the D&P Learning Framework demonstrates that an interdisciplinary STEM challenge situated within an entrepreneurial pitch competition can engage students in rich, curricular-aligned mathematics content. One critique often leveled at these types of context-situated STEM challenges is that they sacrifice conceptual rigor for contextual authenticity (Brantlinger, 2022). Students, in their efforts to invent solutions authentic to the real-world context, will either not attend to the targeted mathematics content at all or will engage with the math only superficially. This is especially true for integrated STEM activities, which often lessen the cognitive demand of mathematics (Forde et al., 2023). Although this is a potential limitation, the D&P Learning Framework was designed to address this limitation through its inclusion of design criteria aligned to specific middle grades mathematics content standards. Each challenge was written to include specific design criteria that draw on targeted curricular mathematics content from the six domains of middle grades mathematics: ratios and proportional relationships, the number system, expressions and equations, functions, geometry, and statistics and probability (National Governors Association Center for Best Practices, Council of Chief & State School Officers [CCSSO], 2010). These criteria increase the likelihood that students will engage with the intended mathematics while allowing them to pursue innovative and personally relevant entrepreneurial solutions. However, more work is needed to understand how to better support teachers and students to maintain focus on the intended mathematics content and ensure that students' use and understanding of it deepens throughout the course of a challenge. This work could improve the scalability of the D&P Learning Framework by helping teachers see its value for supporting mathematics learning and feel comfortable implementing a challenge with their students.

Second, by prioritizing the authenticity and entrepreneurial viability of solutions during brainstorming and prototyping, the framework broadens and deepens students' participation in authentic mathematical reasoning, beyond what is typical of middle grades instruction. Each challenge is situated within a broad context and authentic driving question, and students must work collaboratively to identify and address personally relevant entrepreneurial opportunities within that context. Students must draw on their out-of-school interests, knowledge, and experiences to find the entrepreneurial opportunity for which they possess the unique resources to address. This positions students as the experts and equips them with real-world insights that help sustain their engagement, take pride in their accomplishments during a challenge, and deepen their mathematical reasoning. By encouraging students to draw on their deep knowledge of the context and the opportunity they identify, the D&P Learning Framework engages them in essential mathematical activities. This can include defining constructs, creating or selecting appropriate representations, finding measurements of irregular figures, or defining and operationalizing hard-to-measure variables. DBL and EBL's emphasis on users and customers, respectively, establishes a purpose that drives these considerations and provides a lens for self-evaluating their progress.

By positioning them as both designers and users, the D&P Learning Framework empowers students to take responsibility for making mathematical decisions, determining whether those decisions meet the requirements of the challenge, context, and users, deciding when iteration is needed, and defending and justifying their decisions to both external audiences and their teammates.

Third, team diversity and collaboration are essential characteristics of successful entrepreneurship that create opportunities for all students to contribute meaningfully during a competition. Combined with the fast-paced experience of participating in a week-long pitch competition, the D&P Learning Framework requires all students on a team to work collaboratively to design, justify, and pitch an innovative solution to the math-focused challenge. In this way, the D&P Learning Framework leverages entrepreneurship to provide a method for encouraging and supporting meaningful collaboration in a mathematics classroom.

Finally, the expectation that students frequently expose their ideas to critique through teacher check-ins, expert check-ins, the practice pitch, and the culminating pitch creates opportunities for them to reflect on the relationship between the real-world viability of their solution and its underlying mathematics. Communicating ideas is a malleable skill that is foundational to mathematics learning (Gutiérrez, 1999; Herbel-Eisenmann et al., 2013; Moschkovich, 2002). As students practice explaining and justifying their solutions, they become better at doing so, developing a deeper understanding of the solution and the mathematical considerations that informed its design (Warshauer, 2015). Additionally, as their understanding of their solution improves, students become more invested in the solution and more willing to engage with their teachers and the external experts as peers. This investment makes the final pitch, an entrepreneurial twist on the culminating presentation, an appealing opportunity for students to share their unique creations with an external audience. It also provides an immediate and high-stakes purpose that helps students sustain their engagement as they use every opportunity leading up to the competition to continue to practice explaining, justifying, and refining their reasoning.

4. Conclusions

If we recognize the importance of preparing students to tackle thorny, multidisciplinary problems, educators need to develop a variety of curricular innovations to support them in gaining the skills necessary to do so. For too long, we have neglected such preparation, and made questionable claims that such competency will naturally and developmentally be gained by using "structure of the discipline" (Bruner, 1960, p. 20) approaches. As expectations for a broader accumulation of skills and knowledge increase, and students and teachers experience the fatigue of the curricular gallop, the protective reaction is to restrict entry to new approaches and to try, like the sorcerer's apprentice, to do more and more with less and less satisfaction and effectiveness. Ironically, substantial content is repeated each year from the previous year due to the ineffectiveness of the current approaches, thus exacerbating the problem and increasing the self-imposed vicious cycle.

Today's culture is fast-paced, interactive, and constantly changing. Students are accustomed to highly engaging activities and learning informally, through dialogic exchange, how to master and use new features of technology. Their tolerance for dull and repetitious practice is low, and yet, when invited to participate in activities with rapid feedback and motivating contexts, they jump at the opportunity. Mathematics teachers must be supported to break out of the tyranny of content coverage in order to excite students and capitalize on this new reality.

In science education, many schools and districts have embraced learning frameworks intended to motivate the learning of disciplinary content through engaging real-world contexts, including project-based learning (PBL), design-based learning (DBL), and entrepreneurial-based learning (EBL). Mathematics education has been slow and reluctant to adopt many of these situation-based approaches, and by doing so, has convinced too many students of its irrelevance to their future aspirations. This has led too many teachers to underestimate students' capabilities. To get students to persist in studying mathematics and pursuing careers requiring depth and conceptual knowledge, teachers need to believe in students' ability to reason and problem solve.

In this paper, we introduced an innovative approach (the D&P Learning Framework) that leverages and synthesizes key features of PBL, DBL, and EBL for use in mathematics classrooms, offering novelty through their integration within a single cohesive framework. We also described the nine challenges developed as part of the D&P Learning Framework to show the depth and breadth of the mathematical content that can be included in such an approach. We are not suggesting that the entire mathematics curriculum be taught in this manner, but we do argue for the value of multiple occasions to experience this approach to learn or apply select mathematics concepts. The D&P Learning Framework situates mathematics learning within compelling projects, design challenges, and contexts that are socially and personally relevant to students and call for meaningful social actions. We have observed teachers adapt the framework for a variety of use cases, including as a summative application at the end of an instructional unit, as the primary activity to support the learning of new content, or the launch of community and norm building at the very beginning of the school year. The breadth and openness of the challenges and contexts leave space for taking a variety of approaches, which interjects a key element of design into the solutions. The entrepreneurial framing of the activities grounds students' solutions, positioning them to take on the perspective of a client or consumer and demonstrate economic viability through the development of business proposals.

To support teachers, many of whom are unlikely to have participated in an entrepreneurial pitch competition, this paper provides a description of the processes and practices involved in entrepreneurial design activities and the D&P Learning Framework. The D&P Learning Framework was described as involving three major components (launching the challenge, designing a possible solution, and pitching that solution to a panel of judges). The approach was illustrated with one example, Pollution Solution, and included an overview of the eight other challenges developed as part of the D&P Learning Framework. The complete set of nine challenges encompasses a diverse array of contexts, careers, and professionals (challenge champions). The challenge champions who introduce each challenge, discussing how they built careers around solving similar challenges, show students that their unique experiences have value in the mathematics classroom and that STEM careers are attainable and can be built around inventing solutions to meaningful and thorny problems.

The second part of the framework describes the process of designing a solution and framing it in the context of a business. It involves periods of brainstorming, mutual critique, search for further knowledge of the topic, and the preparation of a Technical Brief to explain the related mathematics. Students must also consider how to make the solution actionable by defining a viable business plan. This requires them to consider what they are proposing, how to accomplish it, and how to market it to potential customers. Relating their proposed solutions to people around them can be an eye-opening experience that not only drives iteration and innovation but also creates opportunities for students to assume new perspectives that they may have previously taken for granted.

Finally, the students prepare and deliver their pitches in five minutes. They must learn to be collaborative in this effort, clearly outline their ideas with figures and graphs, and figure out how to get the attention of the judges to make their ideas pop. It is remarkable how well one has to understand the mathematics of a solution when under time pressure and the scrutiny of judges and peers. Watching students get excited about their ideas, learn to speak mathematics fluently with each other, access resources to learn more, build their case, and then act as an audience to their classmates is an opportunity that can add to the ways to revitalize mathematics instruction.

Author Contributions: Conceptualization, J.C., M.B. and E.E.K.; resources, J.C., M.B. and E.E.K.; writing—original draft preparation, M.B., J.C., E.E.K. and M.L.B.; writing—review and editing, M.B., J.C., E.E.K. and M.L.B.; supervision, J.C. and E.E.K.; project administration, J.C. and E.E.K.; funding acquisition, J.C. All authors have read and agreed to the published version of the manuscript.

Funding: This material is based upon work supported by the National Science Foundation under Grant No. 1759167. Any opinions, findings, and conclusions or recommendations expressed in this material are those of the author(s) and do not necessarily reflect the views of the National Science Foundation.

Institutional Review Board Statement: The study was conducted in accordance with the Declaration of Helsinki, and approved by the North Carolina State University Institutional Review Board (protocol code: #12603; date of approval: 12 December 2017).

Informed Consent Statement: Informed consent was obtained from all subjects involved in the study.

Data Availability Statement: Data are unavailable due to privacy restrictions.

Conflicts of Interest: The authors declare no conflicts of interest. The funders had no role in the design of the study; in the collection, analyses, or interpretation of data; in the writing of the manuscript; or in the decision to publish the results.

Abbreviations

The following abbreviations are used in this manuscript:

STEM	Science, Technology, Engineering, and Mathematics
PBL	Project-Based Learning
DBL	Design-Based Learning
EBL	Entrepreneurial-Based Learning

References

Ainley, J., Bills, L., & Wilson, K. (2005). Designing spreadsheet-based tasks for purposeful algebra. *International Journal of Computers for Mathematical Learning, 10*(3), 191–215. [CrossRef]

Apedoe, X. S., & Schunn, C. D. (2013). Strategies for success: Uncovering what makes students successful in design and learning. *Instructional Science, 41*(4), 773–791. [CrossRef]

Autodesk. (2025). *TinkerCAD* [Computer software]. Available online: https://tinkercad.com (accessed on 18 February 2025).

Barron, B. J., Schwartz, D. L., Vye, N. J., Moore, A., Petrosino, A., Zech, L., & Bransford, J. D. (1998). Doing with understanding: Lessons from research on problem-and project-based learning. *Journal of the Learning Sciences, 7*(3–4), 271–311.

Belcher, M., Confrey, J., & Krupa, E. (2024). Algorithms, spreadsheets and functions: Exploring middle graders' functional reasoning during a STEM entrepreneurial pitch competition. *International Journal of Mathematical Education in Science and Technology*. [CrossRef]

Belcher, M., Mannix, J. P., & Krupa, E. E. (2021, October 14–17). *Exploring students' statistical thinking during an entrepreneurial design challenge*. The 43rd Annual Conference of the North American Chapter of the International Group for the Psychology of Mathematics Education (PME-NA), Philadelphia, PA, USA.

Bilen, S., Kisenwether, E., Rzasa, S., & Wise, J. (2005). Developing and assessing students' entrepreneurial skills and mind-set. *Journal of Engineering Education, 94*(2), 233–243. [CrossRef]

Blumenfeld, P. C., Kempler, T. M., & Krajcik, J. S. (2006). Motivation and cognitive engagement in learning environments. In K. R. Sawyer (Ed.), *The Cambridge handbook of the learning sciences* (pp. 475–488). Cambridge University Press.

Borasi, R., & Finnigan, K. (2010). Entrepreneurial attitudes and behaviors that can help prepare successful change-agents in education. *The New Educator, 6*(1), 1–29. [CrossRef]

Brantlinger, A. (2022). Critical and vocational mathematics: Authentic problems for students from historically marginalized groups. *Journal for Research in Mathematics Education*, *53*(2), 154–172. [CrossRef]

Bruner, J. S. (1960). *The process of education*. Harvard University Press.

Capraro, R. M., & Slough, S. W. (2013). Why PBL? Why STEM? Why now? An introduction to STEM project-based learning: An integrated science, technology, engineering, and mathematics (STEM) approach. In *STEM project-based learning* (pp. 1–5). Brill.

Condliffe, B., Visher, M. G., Bangser, M. R., Drohojowska, S., & Saco, L. (2016). *Project-based learning: A literature review*. MDRC.

Confrey, J. (1991). Learning to listen: A student's understanding of powers of ten. In E. von Glasersfeld (Ed.), *Radical constructivism in mathematics education* (pp. 111–138). Springer Netherlands.

Confrey, J., Krupa, E., & Belcher, M. (2019). *Design & pitch challenges in STEM*. Available online: https://sites.ced.ncsu.edu/design-and-pitch/ (accessed on 18 February 2025).

Confrey, J., & Krupa, E. E. (2012). The arrival of the Common Core State Mathematics Standards: How did we get here and what needs to happen next? In C. R. Hirsch, G. Lappan, & B. J. Reys (Eds.), *Curriculum issues in an era of common core state standards for mathematics*. National Council of Teachers of Mathematics.

Confrey, J., & Maloney, A. (2007). A theory of mathematical modelling in technological settings. In W. Blum, P. L. Galbraith, H. W. Henn, & M. Niss (Eds.), *Modelling and applications in mathematics education: The 14th ICMI study* (pp. 57–68). Springer Science + Business Media.

Cristal Glanchai, L. (2019). *The case for youth entrepreneurship education*. Venture Lab. Available online: https://venturelab.org/wp-content/uploads/2019/12/State-of-Youth-Entrepreneurship_2019.pdf (accessed on 18 February 2025).

Cruz, S., Viseu, F., & Lencastre, J. A. (2022). Project-based learning methodology as a promoter of learning math concepts: A scoping review. *Frontiers in Education*, *7*, 1–11. [CrossRef]

Datawrapper GmbH. (2025). *Datawrapper* [Computer software]. Available online: https://www.datawrapper.de/ (accessed on 18 February 2025).

Deveci, İ., & Seikkula-Leino, J. (2023). The link between entrepreneurship and STEM education. In *Enhancing entrepreneurial mindsets through STEM education* (pp. 3–23). Springer International Publishing.

Dewey, J. (1981). Logic: The theory of inquiry. In J. J. McDermott (Ed.), *The philosophy of John Dewey* (Vol. 1–2, pp. 442–453). The University of Chicago Press. (Original work published 1938).

Doppelt, Y., Mehalik, M. M., Schunn, C. D., Silk, E., & Krysinski, D. (2008). Engagement and achievements: A case study of design-based learning in a science context. *Journal of Technology Education*, *19*(2), 22–39.

Dym, C. L., Agogino, A. M., Eris, O., Frey, D. D., & Leifer, L. J. (2005). Engineering design thinking, teaching, and learning. *Journal of Engineering Education*, *94*(1), 103–120. [CrossRef]

English, L. D., Adams, R., & King, D. (2020). Design learning in STEM education. In *Handbook of research on STEM education* (pp. 76–86). Routledge.

English, L. D., & King, D. T. (2015). STEM learning through engineering design: Fourth-grade students' investigations in aerospace. *International Journal of STEM Education*, *2*(1), 14. [CrossRef]

Filion, L. J. (1994). Ten steps to entrepreneurial teaching. *Journal of Small Business & Entrepreneurship*, *11*(3), 68–78.

Filloy, E., Rojano, T., & Puig, L. (2007). *Educational algebra: A theoretical and empirical approach* (Vol. 43). Springer Science & Business Media.

Fisher, D., Kusumah, Y. S., & Dahlan, J. A. (2020). Project-based learning in mathematics: A literatur review. *Journal of Physics: Conference Series*, *1657*, 012032. [CrossRef]

Forde, E. N., Robinson, L., Ellis, J. A., & Dare, E. A. (2023). Investigating the presence of mathematics and the levels of cognitively demanding mathematical tasks in integrated STEM units. *Disciplinary and Interdisciplinary Science Education Research*, *5*(1), 3. [CrossRef]

Fortus, D., Dershimer, R. C., Krajcik, J., Marx, R. W., & Mamlok-Naaman, R. (2004). Design-based science and student learning. *Journal of Research in Science Teaching*, *41*(10), 1081–1110. [CrossRef]

GeoGebra. (2025). *GeoGebra* [Computer software]. Available online: https://geogebra.org (accessed on 18 February 2025).

Grossman, P., Dean, C. G. P., Kavanagh, S. S., & Herrmann, Z. (2019). Preparing teachers for project-based teaching. *Phi Delta Kappan*, *100*(7), 43–48. [CrossRef]

Gutiérrez, R. (1999). Advancing urban Latina/o youth in mathematics: Lessons from an effective high school mathematics department. *The Urban Review*, *31*(3), 263–281. [CrossRef]

Herbel-Eisenmann, B. A., Steele, M. D., & Cirillo, M. (2013). (Developing) teacher discourse moves: A framework for professional development. *Mathematics Teacher Educator*, *1*(2), 181–196. [CrossRef]

Jones, C., Penaluna, K., & Penaluna, A. (2020). Value creation in entrepreneurial education: Towards a unified approach. *Education + Training*, *63*, 101–103. [CrossRef]

Jukic Matić, L. (2019). The pedagogical design capacity of a lower secondary mathematics teacher and her interaction with curriculum resources. *REDIMAT—Journal of Research in Mathematics Education*, *8*(1), 53–75. [CrossRef]

Kolodner, J. L. (2002). Facilitating the learning of design practices: Lessons learned from an inquiry into science education. *Journal of Industrial Teacher Education, 39*(3), 9–40.

Krajcik, J., McNeill, K. L., & Reiser, B. J. (2007). Learning-goals-driven design model: Developing curriculum materials that align with national standards and incorporate project-based pedagogy. *Science Education, 92*(1), 1–32. [CrossRef]

Krajcik, J. S., & Blumenfeld, P. C. (2006). Project-based learning. In K. R. Sawyer (Ed.), *The Cambridge handbook of the learning sciences* (pp. 317–333). Cambridge University Press.

Lackéus, M. (2015). *Entrepreneurship in education—What, why, when, how. Entrepreneurship 360. Background paper*. OECD.

Laptev, G., & Shaytan, D. (2022). Co-design-based learning for entrepreneurs in the digital age. *Measuring Business Excellence, 26*(1), 93–105. [CrossRef]

Mann, A., Denis, V., Schleicher, A., Ekhtiari, H., Forsyth, T., Liu, E., & Chambers, N. (2020). *Dream jobs: Teenagers' career aspirations and the future of work*. Available online: https://www.mmllen.com.au/wp-content/uploads/2021/10/dream-jobs-teenagers-report.pdf (accessed on 18 February 2025).

Mehalik, M. M., Doppelt, Y., & Schuun, C. D. (2008). Middle-school science through design-based learning versus scripted inquiry: Better overall science concept learning and equity gap reduction. *Journal of Engineering Education, 97*(1), 71–85. [CrossRef]

Moberg, K. (2014). Two approaches to entrepreneurship education: The different effects of education for and through entrepreneurship at the lower secondary level. *The International Journal of Management Education, 12*(3), 512–528. [CrossRef]

Moore, R. A., Newton, S. H., & Baskett, A. D. (2017). The InVenture challenge: Inspiring STEM learning through Invention and Entrepreneurship. *International Journal of Engineering Education, 33*(1), 361–370.

Moore, T. J., Johnston, A. C., & Glancy, A. W. (2020). STEM integration: A synthesis of conceptual frameworks and definitions. In *Handbook of research on STEM education* (pp. 3–16). Routledge.

Moschkovich, J. (2002). A situated and sociocultural perspective on bilingual mathematics learners. *Mathematical Thinking and Learning, 4*(2–3), 189–212. [CrossRef]

National Governors Association Center for Best Practices, Council of Chief and State School Officers [CCSSO]. (2010). *Common core state standards for math*. National Governors Association Center for Best Practices, Council of Chief State School Officers.

Newton, S. H., Alemdar, M., Moore, R. A., & Cappelli, C. J. (2018, June 24–27). *An investigation of students' experiences in a K-12 invention program (evaluation)*. The 2018 ASEE Annual Conference & Exposition, Salt Lake City, UT, USA.

Organisation for Economic Co-operation and Development (OECD). (2018). *The future of education and skills: Education 2030*. OECD.

Passaro, R., Quinto, I., & Thomas, A. (2017). Start-up competitions as learning environment to foster the entrepreneurial process. *International Journal of Entrepreneurial Behavior & Research, 23*(3), 426–445.

Pearson, G. (2017). National academies piece on integrated STEM. *The Journal of Educational Research, 110*(3), 224–226. [CrossRef]

Penner, D. E., Lehrer, R., & Schauble, L. (1998). From physical models to biomechanics: A design-based modeling approach. *Journal of the Learning Sciences, 7*(3–4), 429–449. [CrossRef]

Pérez Yuste, A., Herradón Díez, R., Blanco Cotano, J., Sánchez Fernández, J. A., & de Diego Martínez, R. (2014, July 9–10). *An entrepreneurship-based learning (EBL) experience in information and communication technologies (ICTs)*. The 2nd International Conference of E-Learning and E-Educational Technology (ICELEET 2014), Zurich, Switzerland.

Razzouk, R., & Shute, V. (2012). What is design thinking and why is it important? *Review of Educational Research, 82*(3), 330–348. [CrossRef]

Rojano, T. (1996). Developing algebraic aspects of problem solving within a spreadsheet environment. In *Approaches to algebra* (pp. 137–145). Springer. [CrossRef]

Schneider, R. M., Krajcik, J., Marx, R. W., & Soloway, E. (2002). Performance of students in project-based science classrooms on a national measure of science achievement. *Journal of Research in Science Teaching, 39*(5), 410–422. [CrossRef]

Skinner, R. K., & Harlow, D. B. (2022). Recognition of design failure by fourth-grade students during an engineering design challenge. *Journal of Pre-College Engineering Education Research (J-PEER), 12*(2), 10. [CrossRef]

Stevens, R. (2000). Who counts what as math? Emergent and assigned mathematics problems in a project-based classroom. In J. Boaler (Ed.), *Multiple perspectives on mathematics teaching and learning* (pp. 105–144). Ablex Publishing.

Tabach, M., Hershkowitz, R., & Arcavi, A. (2008). Learning beginning algebra with spreadsheets in a computer intensive environment. *The Journal of Mathematical Behavior, 27*(1), 48–63. [CrossRef]

Thomas, J. W. (2000). *A review of research on project-based learning*. Available online: https://tecfa.unige.ch/proj/eteach-net/Thomas_researchreview_PBL.pdf (accessed on 18 February 2025).

von Glasersfeld, E. (1982). An interpretation of Piaget's constructivism. *Revue Internationale de Philosophie, 36*(4), 612–635.

Warshauer, H. K. (2015). Strategies to support productive struggle. *Mathematics Teaching in the Middle School, 20*(7), 390–393. [CrossRef]

Wendell, K., & Rogers, C. (2013). Engineering design-based science, science content performance, and science attitudes in elementary school. *Journal of Engineering Education*, *102*(4), 513–540. [CrossRef]

Yu, W., Zheng, Z., & He, J. (2025). Integrating entrepreneurial education into STEM education: A systematic review. *Research in Science Education*, *55*(1), 159–185. [CrossRef]

education sciences

MDPI

Article

Project-Based Learning in Interdisciplinary Spaces: A Case Study in Norway and the United States

Margaret Ann Bolick [1,*], Malena Thomassen [2], Jennifer Apland [3], Olivia Spencer [4], Fantasi Nicole [1], Sonja Kim Ngan Tran [2], Matthew Voigt [1] and Kelly Best Lazar [1]

1 Department of Engineering and Science Education, Clemson University, Clemson, SC 29634, USA; fcurry@clemson.edu (F.N.); mkvoigt@gmail.com (M.V.); klazar@clemson.edu (K.B.L.)
2 Department of Engineering Sciences, University of Agder, 4630 Kristiansand, Norway; malenat@student.uia.no (M.T.); sonja.tran@live.no (S.K.N.T.)
3 Department of Plant Biology, Michigan State University, East Lansing, MI 48824, USA; aplandje@msu.edu
4 Department of Civil Engineering, Clemson University, Clemson, SC 29634, USA; ocspenc@clemson.edu
* Correspondence: bolick4@clemson.edu

Abstract: The research described in this case study features a cohort of five exchange students from post-secondary institutions in Norway and the United States who collaboratively engaged in a project-based learning experience infused with aspects of place-based education, lesson study, and the pedagogical technique "students as partners". The students were tasked with crafting an interdisciplinary lesson combining mathematics and environmental science to address a localized problem in the Southeastern United States. This study reflects on how the students participated in project-based learning as well as the instructional practices that supported student engagement. Students identified an increase in understanding of interdisciplinary and multicultural Science, Technology, Engineering, and Mathematics (STEM) education, a broader understanding of instructional practices, and exposure to educational research. Data were collected throughout the study using a variety of techniques, including discussion posts, collaborative documents, and reflections to gauge student experience and project progress. The results provide evidence to support the use of project-based learning in postsecondary STEM classrooms and emphasize the benefits of engaging students in curriculum development.

Keywords: project-based learning; lesson study; students as partners; curriculum development; interdisciplinary STEM; cultural exchange; higher education

1. Introduction

The traditional model of education, with the instructor as the sole source of knowledge, has been challenged by calls for more student-centered, real-world learning experiences [1,2]. Project-based learning, combined with place-based education, offers a promising approach to meet this need by empowering students to actively engage in the creation of meaningful, contextually relevant curricula [3–8]. This case study examines a unique project-based learning course in which post-secondary STEM exchange students from Norway and the United States collaborated to develop and implement an interdisciplinary lesson integrating mathematics and environmental science. The course, designed for both undergraduate and graduate students, fostered an environment of co-creation, where students became "lesson architects", driving the curriculum development process [9]. This approach not only equipped students with practical skills but also deepened their understanding of interdisciplinary STEM education, cultural exchange, and instructional practices [8–10]. This study explores how the integration of project-based learning, place-based education, lesson study, and the "students as partners" pedagogy created a transformative learning experience [2,7,9].

By examining the students' engagement as decision-makers, the instructional supports and barriers encountered, and the impact on their conceptual understanding of interdisciplinary STEM education, this research provides valuable insights into fostering inclusive, student-led project-based learning environments in higher education STEM classrooms. The findings shed light on the potential of project-based learning to empower students, enhance their understanding of STEM concepts, and promote their development as future educators and researchers. As such, this study seeks to answer the following research questions focusing on the engagement, implementation, and conceptual impact of the lesson architects' experience:

1. Student Engagement: How did exchange students actively participate as partners in the project-based learning process to create an interdisciplinary STEM lesson integrating mathematics and environmental science concepts?
2. Implementation: What were the key instructional barriers and supports encountered when implementing a project-based interdisciplinary STEM lesson where students were involved as co-creators?
3. Conceptual Impact: How did participation in the project-based lesson development process influence exchange students' understanding of interdisciplinary STEM education and its practical applications?

2. Conceptual Framing and Background

This study uses the tenets of project-based learning to engage a group of undergraduate and graduate students in a student-led lesson study. This study melds the world of project-based learning with lesson study [3–6,11,12] and serves as a novel adaptation of the two concepts where students and instructors act as partners in curriculum development [9]. We frame the entire study as a project-based learning experience that leverages and infuses (1) place-based education, (2) lesson study, and (3) students as partners in curriculum development (see Figure 1).

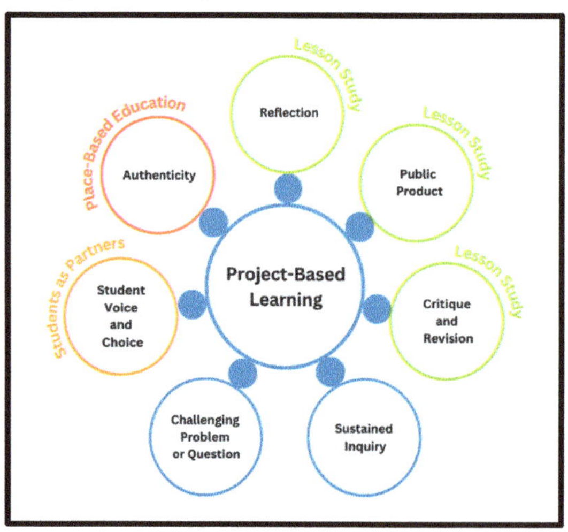

Figure 1. Adapted conceptual framework from the Buck Institute for Education's [3] design elements infused with aspects of place-based education, lesson study, and students as partners in curriculum development.

2.1. Project-Based Learning: Design Elements

Project-based learning has been implemented in a variety of forms and contains a multitude of different design principles, yet there is no consensus on a standard set of principles that make project-based learning successful [6]. We aligned our study with the framework of "gold standard" design elements from Ref. [3] adapted from Ref. [13]'s depiction of exemplary design practices to create a project-based learning classroom. These design elements include (1) a challenging problem or question, (2) sustained inquiry, (3) authenticity, (4) student voice and choice, (5) reflection, (6) critique and revision, and (7) public product [3]. Each design principle contributes to implementing a thoughtfully crafted project that students can engage in for an extended period. A common thread in project-based learning includes providing students with a challenging, complex problem or question that is open-ended and serves as a starting point for student thinking [3,5,14]. While project-based tasks need to maintain student inquiry for an extended period of time, they also require an iterative process of investigative inquiry to solve a challenging problem or answer a challenging question [3]. By incorporating these seven design elements, instructors develop strong project-based learning environments that engage students in a larger scale, self-sustained task that can promote creativity and independence [15].

2.2. *Connection to Place-Based Education*

Study [14] suggests that in addition to being complex, the problem or question students are provided should also be realistic or, as Ref. [3] claims, authentic. Article [13] defines authenticity as (1) featuring real-world context, including (2) the ability to make a real impact and (3) the potential to connect to students' lives. Thus, a requirement for the students was to design a lesson that included a place-based aspect. Place-based education is influenced by Freire's beliefs in developing critical consciousness and Dewey's emphasis on learner-centered, socially collaborative approaches to foster real-world learning experiences [2,16,17]. Through place-based learning, students are taught the curriculum through the lens of their local community and are encouraged to develop their own solutions to identified problems. Emphasizing the importance of physical space and surrounding environment in education allows for a better understanding of culture, social atmospheres, and community engagement and resilience [7]. With an overlap of living and learning concepts, students are often able to see beyond the content of a classroom and can apply the curriculum to a larger picture, fostering the students' ability to expand their realm of knowledge on an independent level [7].

2.3. *Infusion of Lesson Study*

The students addressed an educational problem by creating a lesson study, an iterative Japanese teaching technique where a group of educators plan a lesson on a specific instructor-generated vision of a pedagogical practice [11]. By engaging in a lesson study, the students were naturally able to incorporate reflection, critiques, and revisions into their projects. A key feature of lesson study includes recording the implementation via observational protocols as a way to gather data for reflection during the debrief of the observed lesson [11]. The research in [12] references similar features of a successful lesson study while describing an iterative process of revising and re-teaching the lesson. The re-taught lesson would also be observed and debriefed on, which leads to the last step of sharing results with communities of educators, a public product [9]. The cyclical nature of a lesson study produced numerous opportunities to reflect, critique, and revise the lesson throughout the process, all key elements of project-based learning.

2.4. *Engaging Students as Partners in Curriculum Development*

The intent of incorporating student voice and choice into project-based learning is to hear differing perspectives from students and embrace students incorporating outside knowledge into their solutions [3]. Encouraging students to make decisions for themselves and be "producers of knowledge" pushes students to think critically about a problem and develop a solution on their own [14]. Due to prevailing beliefs of instructor-led curricula, students are rarely engaged in a course where they guide the decision-making process and learning outcomes of the course. However, student–instructor co-creation of the curriculum is increasing in popularity due to its active nature and collaboration between students and instructors [9]. By positioning students as experts in curriculum creation, student–

instructor co-creation has the potential to produce a transformative experience for students and instructors, as well as empower students to elevate their unique knowledge, skills, and perspectives [18].

2.5. Project-Based Learning: Teaching Practices

Project-based learning teaching practices were developed to support the project-based learning design elements [4,19]. The intent of having specific teaching practices is to provide educators with the tools to adjust from traditional teaching methods to project-based learning teaching methods, which focus on supporting students' curiosity [4]. The teaching practices identified in [19] include (1) design and plan, (2) align to standards, (3) build the culture, (4) manage activities, (5) scaffold student learning, (6) assess student learning, and (7) engage and coach [4]. The research in [20] found similar practices identified by instructors actively practicing project-based learning.

A successful project-based learning course is supported by both the design elements and teaching practices defined by the authors of [3,4]. In conjunction with these practices, educators must develop a project that is aligned with standards, includes a challenging prompt, has a clear timeline for completion, and incorporates formative and summative assessments [4,20]. Educators need to ensure students are organized and on schedule by actively managing their activities or providing concrete project management tools students are responsible for to scaffold student learning [4,20]. Similar to scaffolding student learning, instructors need to engage and coach students to identify when they need assistance or praise to support student growth [4]. Yet, without the collective commitment of the course, the designing, planning, managing, and scaffolding, the course will not be successful. Students need to be exposed to a classroom culture that fosters independence, self-management, and individual exploration with clear expectations of student work [4,20]. Each teaching practice contributes to ensuring students are receiving a rich learning experience that addresses more than the aligned standards.

3. Methods

3.1. Data Context

The data analyzed for this study originates from a larger project focused on cultural exchange between two universities (note these university names are used in place of the true names of the universities to protect the identities of the participants): one in Norway and the other in the United States. The larger exchange program was funded by an Anonymized Funding Source and had a lifespan of three academic years. The exchange program started in the Fall of 2023 with three Norwegian students spending the Fall Semester at Isunigu University, Southeastern United States (the Cherokee town of Isunigu was flooded in the 20th century by the creation of Lake Hartwell in South Carolina, resulting in the loss of artifacts and the history of the place, Isunigu), and continued into the Spring of 2024 with two American students spending the Spring Semester at the University of Egðir, Norway (an Old Norse word from the Viking Age that describes the people of the Southern region of Norway). As a focus of the exchange, the students engaged in this project-based interdisciplinary STEM course. Due to the participants' success and autonomy in developing the lesson, the term *lesson architects* was used to distinguish them from the students in the class where the lesson was implemented. The term lesson architects aimed to capture the co-construction of knowledge that was instrumental in the finished lesson.

3.2. Course Description

The course encouraged the lesson architects to think in terms of interdisciplinary STEM disciplines while attending to place-based problems within the localized context of Isunigu University. The unique nature of the course included students as co-creators to explore a variety of STEM topics, with the learning objectives centered around interdisciplinary STEM education. The course aimed for students to meet the following learning objectives through the creation of an interdisciplinary STEM lesson and engagement in a lesson study: (1) demonstrate critical thinking through the design and analysis of an integrated STEM education place-based lesson study to address a global challenge; (2) evaluate how varying perspectives influence the outreach and communication with communities impacted by a global challenge; (3) identify the contextual factors (regional, national, global, and ethnic) that impact how an integrated STEM education place-based research project can be implemented in a localized context; (4) define and provide examples of integrated STEM research, education, and outreach. The lesson architects were tasked with developing an interdisciplinary STEM lesson that included mathematics and environmental science, focused on a challenge within the localized context of the Southeastern United States, and had the potential to be scaled to a globalized context. Students were required to implement the lesson in either a classroom or an alternative setting.

The course leaned on the disciplinary and cultural backgrounds of the lesson architects and instructors to construct the interdisciplinary place-based STEM lesson to implement in a water sustainability course. Additional time was dedicated to learning about STEM education research methods and creating data collection tools that assess the success of the lesson. By the end of the semester, the lesson architects created and implemented an interactive environmental science and mathematics lesson set in the localized context of the Savannah River Watershed, South Carolina, United States, and within the international context of Norway.

3.3. Participants

Five students from two universities, Isunigu University and the University of Egðir, participated in this course as part of a larger STEM education cultural exchange program. Students were recruited from the two universities through platforms promoting cultural exchange programs at Isunigu University, tutoring programs at the University of Egðir, and snowball sampling. In order for the lesson architects to partake in the abroad program and the course, they were required to be in a STEM field and have an interest in STEM education. The student participants, who represented a diverse group of STEM disciplines, collaboratively constructed new knowledge utilizing various cultural and educational experiences to develop a place-based and interdisciplinary lesson on harmful algal blooms in the Southeastern United States and the coast of Norway. As a way to capture the backgrounds of participants, Table 1 includes a brief biography of the lesson architects and course instructors.

Table 1. The lesson architects (students) and instructors in this project-based learning course.

Pseudonym	Position	Brief Biography
Florence	Undergraduate Lesson Architect (United States)	She is a Bachelor of Science student in Civil Engineering at Isunigu University.
Maria	Undergraduate Lesson Architect (Norway)	She is a Bachelor of Science student in Civil Engineering at the University of Egðir.
Red	Graduate Lesson Architect (Norway)	She is a Master of Science student in Civil Engineering and Industrial Economy and Technology Management at the University of Egðir.
Salix	Graduate Lesson Architect (United States)	She is a recent graduate with a Master of Science in Biological Sciences from Isunigu University. Her research focus is plant ecology.
Sophia	Graduate Lesson Architect (Norway)	She is a Master of Science student in Industrial Economy and Technology Management with a Bachelor of Science degree in Electronics and Electrical Engineering from the University of Egðir.
Gigi	Graduate Student Teacher of Record; Lead Researcher (United States)	She is a current PhD student in Engineering and Science Education at Isunigu University with previous secondary mathematics and science teaching experience, as well as experience in Biomedical Engineering.

Table 1. *Cont.*

Pseudonym	Position	Brief Biography
Saoirse	Faculty Co-Instructor (United States)	She is an assistant professor at Isunigu University with a joint appointment in the Department of Engineering and Science Education and the Department of Environmental Engineering and Earth Sciences.
Maximilian (Max)	Faculty Co-Instructor (United States)	He is an assistant professor at Isunigu University in the Department of Engineering and Science Education.

3.4. Study Design

The researchers of this study held multiple responsibilities within the course. The lead researcher was tasked with the development of the course structure, leading classes, analyzing data, and crafting the narrative of the article. Additional researchers acted as faculty co-instructors during the course or lesson architects during the course. All researchers collectively contributed to the interpretation of themes and "thick descriptions" [21] (p. 29) encountered in this study.

To capture the unique nature of the project-based learning course, we situate our collective experiences as a case study [21] with an ethnographic lens. Our deep involvement in planning, implementing, and engaging in the course allowed us to approach this qualitative case study with an increased depth of understanding. We used Merriam's [21] definition of a case study, which characterizes a case study as particularistic, descriptive, and heuristic, meaning a case study should provide thick descriptions and provide the audience with an in-depth understanding of the specific phenomenon [22]. Due to the duality of researchers as instructors and lesson architects within the course, we were able to draw on our experiences to provide a more narrative-focused analysis and additional context to our data. The immersive nature of this case study assisted in developing a collaborative partnership [21,23] between the researchers and participants since the roles were fluid throughout the course. Engaging in the cultural exchange, as well as a project-based learning course that empowered the lesson architects to develop a lesson of their choosing and the educational research, not only broke the all too common "sage on the stage" narrative of undergraduate education but reversed the narrative of what it means to be a student.

3.5. Data Collection

Throughout the semester, the lesson architects engaged in various assignments that contributed to data sources for this study and included collaborative documents, discussion posts, and end-of-semester reflections. The collaborative documents contain any lesson architect-generated material, including the class agenda, the three final lesson plan documents, and the two observation protocols. The class agenda was particularly rich with qualitative data as it included a timeline of how the course was structured, evidence of the multitude of activities the lesson architects engaged in, and lesson architect-generated ideas. In addition to collaborative documents, the lesson architects were asked to reflect and respond to five discussion posts to generate ideas about localized problems, reflect on the course overall, and provide constructive feedback for how the implementation of their lesson could be improved. Lastly, the lesson architects individually wrote one-page reflections on the course and the lesson they implemented. The end-of-semester reflections provided additional context for lesson architect growth and insight into their experiences in a project-based learning course. Each type of data was utilized to capture the full picture of the course, including how lesson architects engaged in curriculum development, the pedagogical approaches used, and the impact this course had on lesson architects' knowledge of interdisciplinary place-based STEM education.

3.6. Data Analysis

Due to the research team's positioning within the course, we were already familiarized with the raw data; however, we read through the data multiple times to re-orient ourselves. The data were coded abductively using a combination of deductive and inductive coding. Using the Seven Essential Project Design Elements and Seven Project Based Teaching Practices from [3,4], the data were coded deductively using the qualitative coding software MAXQDA v. 22.2.1, with each coding pass focused on a single standard. The data were then coded inductively to determine the lesson architects' shifts in conceptual understanding. The codes were collapsed into themes using thematic analysis [24] to gain a better understanding of the answers to our research questions. Once the initial analysis was completed, the lesson architects engaged in member checking to provide feedback on the analysis and ensure the validity of the study.

3.7. Validity and Reliability

Merriam's [21] definition of a case study includes six strategies for internal validity, including triangulation, member checking, long-term observation, peer examination, participatory research, and disclosure of researcher bias [22]. Due to the ethnographic lens of this case study, member checking, peer examination, and participatory research were woven into the data collection, analysis, and reporting processes. Triangulation and disclosure of researcher bias took place throughout the data analysis phase, and long-term observation was inherent in our semester-long case study. Similarly, Marriam's standards for reliability include stating the investigators' positionalities, triangulation, and well-kept records of qualitative data and analysis [21,22]. All three of these standards took place during the data analysis or reporting phase. Lastly, a main technique to ensure external validity is reporting thick descriptions of the case/results to which the results section adheres [21,22]. Due to the qualitative nature of the case study, this study is unable to be generalizable; however, this study is transferable.

4. Results

Three major themes emerged from the data that encapsulated each research question. The first theme discusses how the lesson architects engaged as the primary decision-makers while engaging in project-based learning. The second theme addresses the instructional supports and barriers that assisted or hindered the lesson architects' progress in the development of the lesson study. The third theme amplifies the areas of self-growth the lesson architects identified.

4.1. Students as Decision Makers and Lesson Architects

Students were the lead decision makers throughout the entire course, earning the title of lesson architect because of their commitment to designing and building the lesson from minimal instruction. The course provided the lesson architects with scaffolded activities to guide the process of building a lesson, prompting them to think about aspects they may not have been familiar with that are important in creating a lesson (e.g., learning objectives, scaffolding, and assessment).

Throughout the semester, the lesson architects engaged in active decision-making while collaborating on the end-of-semester product: the place-based, interdisciplinary STEM lesson. Their voices were heard throughout the choices they were making. The lesson architects had to decide on everything, including the lesson's focus on mathematics and environmental sciences and how the lesson was implemented. As a scaffold, the lesson architects were prompted to brainstorm local-to-them challenges in Southern and Western Norway and the Southeastern United States using Jamboard. The challenges identified included limited public transportation, high electricity costs, and flooding across the Southeastern United States and Southern Norway. Florence, originally from the Southeastern United States, demonstrated her extensive expertise in the Southeastern United States by focusing on the Savannah River Watershed, a body of water that runs along the border of South Carolina and Georgia. Florence's Jamboard can be seen in Figure 2. Her Jamboard evoked conversation from the other lesson architects on the similarity of flooding between the two locations, which ultimately resulted in the lesson architects narrowing in on water-based challenges.

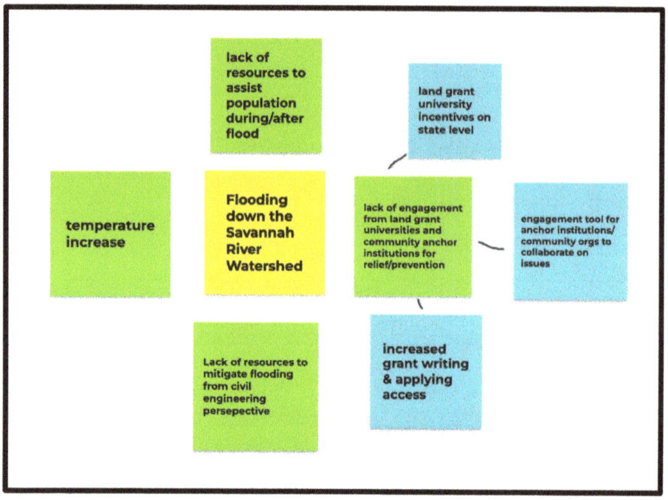

Figure 2. Florence's Jamboard from brainstorming challenges on the Savannah River Watershed.

Once the lesson architects agreed to focus on the flooding of the Savannah River Watershed, Gigi (the graduate teacher of record) tasked the lesson architects with exploring resources that could provide a deeper understanding of problems the Savannah River Watershed faces and assess the stakeholders who are affected by these problems. Overall, the lesson architects narrowed down their search to pollutants within the watershed and the effects on minoritized communities. Florence elaborated in a discussion post on flooding in the Savannah River Watershed by identifying possible causes:

> *"One problem that affects the Savannah River Watershed and the surrounding communities is heavy pollution into the basin. . .Communities are affected by this problem because it damages the aesthetic of the environment, but also because pollution can cause blockages that can contribute to things like flooding."* Florence

Maria unearthed new knowledge about a racially minoritized community in Savannah, Georgia, which was "experiencing the brunt of climate change, pollution, and environmental racism" because of pollution from a nearby "nuclear weapons production site". Red identified chemical pollution's effect on the environment, citing, "the habitats get less suitable for native species that are depending on this habitat to survive". With new knowledge of the local watershed, primary sources of pollution, and the communities most affected, the lesson architects advanced to selecting a lesson topic.

Together, the class brainstormed overarching questions, including "How badly is the water contaminated?", "What are the factors contributing to water contamination?", "What are effective mitigation strategies?" and "How can we use technology to understand the distribution of contamination?". The lesson architects brainstorming about the Savannah River Watershed became focused on testing the water quality for varying forms of contaminants. After assessing the feasibility of having future students conduct water testing within the limited time frame, they reassessed the type of pollution students could investigate. Saoirse, one of the two faculty co-instructors who specialized in geology, suggested that the lesson architects consider an alternative type of pollution: algal blooms. The lesson architects, having little prior knowledge of algal blooms, were interested in learning more and decided to investigate further. Ultimately, deciding on algal blooms as the environmental science topic would be the foundation for the lesson.

After deciding on the lesson topic of algal blooms in the Savannah River Watershed, the lesson architects individually wrote learning objectives on mathematics, environmental science, and environmental justice. Yet, when the lesson architects began to create activities that resulted in each learning objective, they found that the activities they were creating were not interdisciplinary. The monodisciplinary activities did not meet the criteria of the final lesson, prompting the lesson architects to adjust the learning objectives. However, Salix and Sophia, together, came up with the mathematics activity of students graphing and running a t-test or other statistical tests. The rest of the team supported this activity idea and suggested that graphing and running statistical tests should be the primary activity with different datasets. With the primary activity chosen, the lesson architects finalized the learning objectives, which can be seen in Table 2.

Table 2. The learning objectives developed by the lesson architects for their lesson study project.

Learning Objective	Description
Learning Objective 1	Students will plot various types of algal bloom data and conduct multiple statistical tests on data derived from different locations, including the Savannah River Watershed and Norwegian Coastline.
Learning Objective 2	Students will be able to interpret the results of the graphs and statistical tests by making connections within and across data sets to draw conclusions about how algal blooms grow and the impact algal blooms have on the environment.

The lesson architects searched for different datasets that could demonstrate a holistic understanding of algal blooms in the Savannah River Watershed and on the coast of Norway. The data from the Savannah River Watershed demonstrated the effects of land runoff on harmful algal bloom growth, connecting the type of land use to the increase in runoff. The data from Trøndelag, Norway, connected the longitudinal fish population data to the amount of cytotoxins over time. However, the lesson architects also wanted students to have an active learning experience, so Gigi suggested having students collect water samples and grow algae themselves. The third data set was created using student-collected water samples from the on-campus pond and varying the levels of phosphates and nitrates to promote algae growth.

Once the vision was firmly established, the lesson architects collaboratively created the prompts and slides for the implementation (see Supplementary Materials). The lesson architects wanted to set the stage for the lesson and started with an introduction to who they were and why they were teaching this lesson. They then contextualized algal blooms and their effects on individuals through a launch activity where the students observed a video posted on social media, read comments on the video, and discussed what was happening and its impact. Prior to implementation, the lesson architects completed each task to assess the clarity and feasibility of the tasks with the future students in mind. They adjusted their drafts to provide greater clarity on where the data came from, how to access the data, how to plot graphs using Google Sheets, what statistical tests were, and how to interpret graphs and test results. In their slides, the lesson architects also provided context on the format of the lesson, explicitly describing how the jigsaw activity would work.

In addition to constructing the lesson, Maria, Red, and Sophia developed qualitative and quantitative observation protocols to collect field note data on how the lesson was received by the students as part of the lesson study. These protocols streamlined the observations by allowing observers to document the data the lesson architects found most interesting, which would help inform the evolution of the lesson when the lesson is revised and re-implemented in a Norwegian classroom. During the lesson, unbiased observers were brought in to record their observations of the lesson, utilizing the observation protocols.

Additionally, Maria, Red, and Sophia created a focus group protocol and conducted a focus group with students from the class who engaged with the lesson to gain more insight into how the lesson was received.

Not only did the lesson architects orchestrate data collection on student engagement with the lesson, but they also reflected on their individual observations of student perception of the lesson. Each lesson architect shared their insight on the implementation and provided constructive criticism for improvements. The criticisms included adding different pedagogical techniques such as "think-pair-share or turn-and-talk to engage multiple voices" or addressing the different groups' needs. The lesson architects found that some groups "needed prompting to collaborate" and found that "Group 3's [task] was less straightforward" whereas "Group 1's was more straightforward". The lesson architects also discussed how the overall layout of the classroom limited peer-to-peer collaboration, citing that "a different physical layout of the classroom would have allowed for more conversation". The suggestions the lesson architects produced will serve as a guiding force for the ongoing revisions during the Spring 2024 semester.

With the help of scaffolding, the lesson architects were positioned as the primary decision-makers throughout the course. They engaged in thought-provoking activities to connect different aspects of curriculum development to ideas they already generated. By learning about lesson development as they approached different decision points in the process, they were able to make informed and decisive decisions about the lesson, as well as learn about the nuanced details of student learning.

4.2. *Effective Instructional Supports and Barriers*

The following section presents multiple supports that proved effective in engaging students in project-based learning as well as effectively eliminating the barriers the lesson architects faced during the semester.

4.2.1. Create a Welcoming and Collaborative Culture

The course intentionally started by creating a collaborative set of norms that every student contributed to and agreed upon. Instead of vocalizing their expectations out loud, the lesson architects engaged in an anonymous brainstorming session via Jamboard. Figure 3 shows the Jamboard the lesson architects populated.

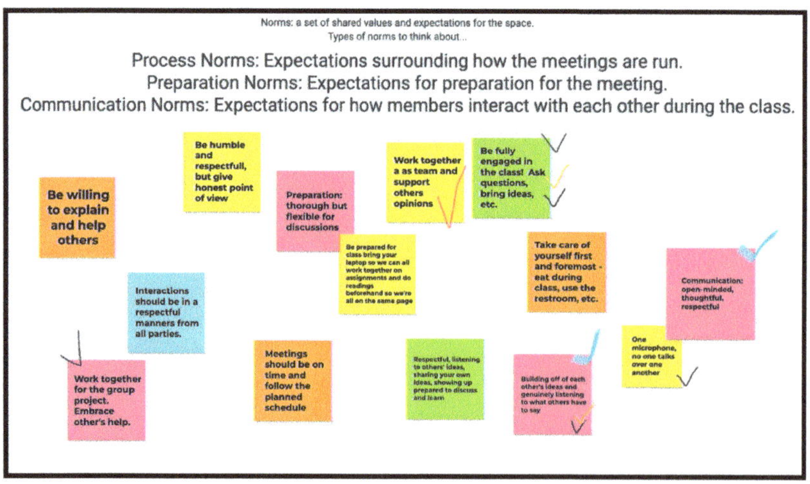

Figure 3. The Jamboard the lesson architects brainstormed expectations for each other and the instructors. Checkmarks indicate norms that were agreed upon by lesson architects and implemented into the top of the agenda.

After filling out the Jamboard, the lesson architects had the opportunity to speak to any norm on the document. Once the norms were finalized (see Figure 4), they remained at the top of the running agenda throughout the semester to remind the lesson architects of our agreed-upon expectations.

Communal Norms

Team Work/Engagement:
- Work together as a team and support others opinions
- Be willing to explain, help others, and embrace other's help
- Be fully engaged in the class! Ask questions, bring ideas, etc.
- Building off of each other's ideas and genuinely listening to what others have to say

Preparation:
- Be prepared for class bring your laptop so we can all work together on assignments and do readings beforehand so we're all on the same page
- Preparation is thorough but flexible for discussions
- Show up prepared to discuss and learn

Communication:
- Be humble and respectful, but give honest point of view
- Share your own ideas
- Open-minded, thoughtful, respectful
- One microphone, no one talks over one another

Structure:
- Meetings should be on time and follow the planned schedule
- Take care of yourself first and foremost, eat during class, use the restroom, etc.

Figure 4. The finalized communal norms that were placed at the top of the running agenda for the course.

In their final reflections from the course, Sophia and Red both discussed the comfort they felt within the course. Red referred to the course as "a safe and low-key environment". Sophia emphasized that "the dynamics within the class have been nothing but amazing" and cited that "the creation of a safe and inclusive environment for open discussions and the sharing of thoughts has been an important aspect of [her] learning experience". Throughout the semester, the lesson architects engaged in many collaborative activities to provide structured avenues for students to form connections. The groups would fluctuate between being from the same institution (the University of Egðir and Isunigu University) and being mixed as the students became more comfortable. It is important to note that the Norwegian students spoke English in mixed groups but were encouraged to speak in Norwegian when together as a way to recognize their ability to linguistically code-switch, honor their native language, and ensure they felt comfortable engaging with their peers. Red disclosed that initially, "it was a bit hard to adapt to the language and ways things are done [at Isunigu University]," and Sophia expressed that initially, "I felt the challenge of formulating my thoughts in English in a precise manner". Yet, Sophia continued by saying, "this safe environment has encouraged me to keep trying to formulate my thoughts and engage in discussion without any reservation about my proficiency in English".

4.2.2. Scaffold Activities Responsive to the Lesson Architect's Needs

Multiple scaffolded activities took place throughout the semester to assist in broadening the lesson architects' knowledge of interdisciplinary STEM, place-based education, and lesson design. Two scaffolded activities involved the lesson architects reading articles on interdisciplinary STEM education and place-based education outside of class. During class, the lesson architects derived definitions from the articles and their own experiences to accurately define interdisciplinary STEM education and place-based education. When defining interdisciplinary STEM education, the lesson architects were tasked with combining two random STEM disciplines into an interdisciplinary lesson. Figure 5 shows one group of lesson architects' work combining physics/technology, and Figure 6 shows the other group of lesson architects' work combining precalculus/geology into two interdisciplinary lessons.

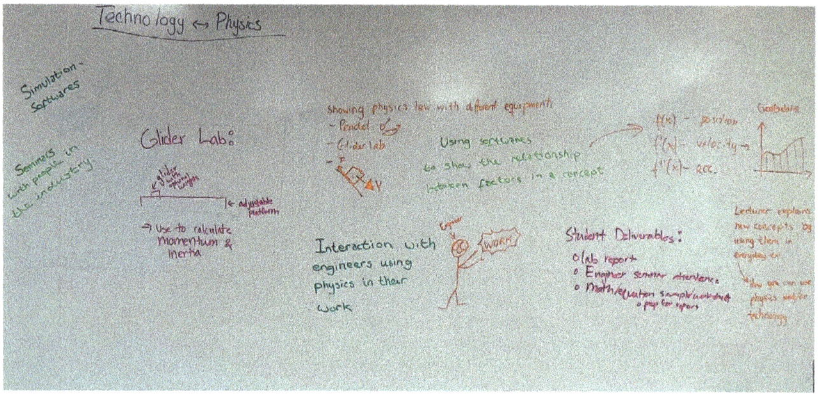

Figure 5. One group of lesson architects practiced combining physics and technology into an interdisciplinary lesson.

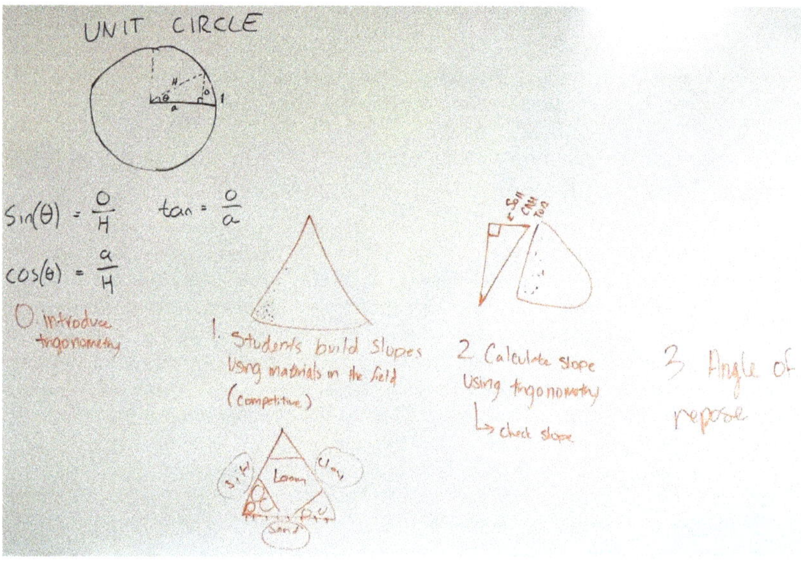

Figure 6. The other group of lesson architects practiced combining precalculus and geology into an interdisciplinary lesson.

An additional scaffolded activity the lesson architects engaged in was qualitative and quantitative observational data collection. They watched an open-access physics lesson while taking observational notes and evaluating what they thought was important data to collect as a way to consider what data the lesson architects were interested in collecting during their lesson implementation. The lesson architects used this experience to decide on the types of data they wanted to collect during the lesson study, including qualitative observational data answering, "how do students interact with each other during the task?" and "how do students interact with the task?" and quantitative observational data counting the number of times "students ask clarifying questions related to the task or activity" or "students ask questions related to the topic to further their understanding".

4.2.3. Additional Structure to Assist the Lesson Architects in Decision Making

Although the scaffolding supported the lesson architects' decision-making throughout the lesson development, the lesson architects still struggled to coalesce on a finalized topic for their lesson. The structure provided at the beginning of the course was responsive to where the lesson architects were in the design process, but as they built out the activities, the scaffolding was removed to allow them the space to work collaboratively on what they deemed important. In the middle of the semester, the decision-making process stalled. The lesson architects crafted four distinct learning objectives (two for mathematics, one for environmental science, and one for geography), yet the categorized learning objectives made it difficult for the lesson architects to envision an interdisciplinary lesson, and they found themselves at a standstill. At this point, Gigi realized she was not managing the activities as closely as necessary for the lesson architect's success. As a response, she took a more active role in managing the process by leading the collaborative effort of reimagining the learning objectives into two interdisciplinary objectives (see Table 2) and creating a document of necessary lesson components and tasks that needed to be accomplished. By delegating what tasks remained, the lesson architects were given momentum to continue finishing the lesson, and as Salix stated, "our final project was truly a team effort".

4.3. Multifaceted Understanding of Interdisciplinary STEM Education

The following theme highlights the lesson architects' reflections on their experiences and areas of growth the lesson architects identified. As Florence eloquently stated, "I believe I have learned more practical knowledge in this class than I do in most of my content-based classes". The sentiment from Florence's end-of-semester reflection was echoed in the other lesson architect's reflections. Salix similarly expressed that she "learned a lot about the need for implementing interdisciplinary STEM education at all levels, and the high need for an interdisciplinary understanding of STEM in the workforce". Together, the lesson architects identified five nuanced areas of growth in their conceptual understanding of interdisciplinary STEM education: environmental science, multiculturalism, learning theories, research, and instructional practices.

4.3.1. Expanding Knowledge of Environmental Science

One lesson architect, Red, was adamant that she expanded her knowledge of environmental science and scientific methods by engaging in this project-based interdisciplinary STEM lesson. Through the course, she "learned a lot [about] algae bloom and how one can create a lesson of STEM, collecting water samples and measur[ing] pH, turbidity, and color". Prior to this course, the lesson architects had limited to no exposure to algal blooms and their effects on the environment and local ecosystems. The lesson architects engaged deeply in researching algal blooms, discovering how algal blooms appear, how algal blooms affect the surrounding environment, including various stakeholders, and how to measure the growth of algal blooms.

4.3.2. Multiculturalism within Interdisciplinary STEM Education

As a way to define place-based education and explore local and global problems, the lesson architects read multiple articles on interdisciplinary STEM education within the context of other countries in addition to the United States. Red recognized these articles as "interesting" and "really liked the international perspective of STEM". The articles led to discussions that enabled students to gain insight into other cultures, education systems, and other countries' views of STEM. Additionally, the conversations branched into the lesson architect's own experiences in the United States and Norway, which allowed them to compare the educational structures between Norway and the United States. Florence identified growth "in [her] ability to recognize multicultural differences in education" and how her new understanding of multiculturalism expanded how she perceives her future as she hopes "to work around the world, in a variety of different cultures, backgrounds, community structures, and levels of resilience".

4.3.3. Understanding of Learning Theories

The learning architects' conceptualization of learning and learners' experiences expanded throughout the course. The lesson architects completed scaffolded activities to encourage them to consider components of a lesson that they were unfamiliar with, including learning objectives and scaffolding for diverse groups of students. The majority of the lesson architects did not have prior experience with the research in [25] or the learning objectives, so they initially reflected on their own learning to inform the lesson development. In particular, Maria was fascinated with "how students learn and motivate themselves within STEM courses", while Sophia found the research in [25] to be an interesting insight into how her previous education considered various levels of learning. The lesson architects similarly engaged in discussion about various forms of instruction for different levels of students and different types of students. Florence found addressing "approaches to differences in student learning and developing adequate instructions for diverse groups of students" to be insightful in recognizing each student as an individual learner. Sophia acknowledged "that designing a lesson that engages the students to work with their peers in [addition] to being memorable/interesting will foster a good learning environment for the students".

4.3.4. Engagement in Educational Research

Prior to this course, the lesson architects had experience as students, tutors, mentors, and teaching assistants; however, they had limited experience engaging in educational research. An integral aspect of a lesson study is collecting data throughout the implementation, and by engaging in a lesson study, the lesson architects naturally participated in educational research. The lesson architects were responsible for determining what data would provide valuable feedback for the team to revise the lesson. The three Norwegian lesson architects were responsible for creating data collection instruments. Through this task, Maria, Red, and Sophia learned about qualitative and quantitative observational protocols, Likert-scale surveys, and focus group protocols. They developed two observation protocols (one qualitative and one quantitative), an exit ticket questionnaire, and a focus group interview protocol. The experience of engaging in educational research left an impression on all three lesson architects as each identified educational research in their end-of-semester reflections. For example, Red emphasized how this project-based lesson development broadened her mindset on what data is and taught her "how to collect different [types of] data". Maria similarly cited how she grasped "various methods for collecting data and the diverse data that can be obtained by choosing different methods (both qualitative and quantitative)". Engaging in project-based lesson development influenced how the lesson architects saw data and the tools used to collect them.

Similarly to Maria's and Red's accounts of expanding their educational research abilities and definitions, Sophia's end-of-semester reflection described how the entire project-based lesson development course influenced how she saw education research:

> *"The exposure to various theories through reading research papers has been crucial in broadening my understanding for conducting research. Delving into these papers has not only enhanced my theoretical knowledge but has also offered practical insights into the methodologies employed in research. It's even more fascinating to witness how these theories come to life through the implementation of the algal bloom lesson."* Sophia

Sophia discussed how the scaffolds throughout the course provided insights into how to use various theories and methodologies when conducting educational research. The experience provided Sophia and the rest of the lesson architects with the practical knowledge of how to turn educational theories into educational practices, something they had previously not been able to witness in their STEM courses.

4.3.5. Broadening the Understanding of Instructional Practices

The majority of the lesson architect's reflections emphasized how they would have revised the lesson and instructional practices to support the students' learning. Red called out that the lesson implementation "could have been more effective" and expressed the need for the more targeted practice of implementing a lesson "as it could have enhanced the overall flow of the lesson". The four other lesson architects had similar critiques and specific suggestions for improvement, which demonstrated their expanding knowledge of instructional practices.

Collectively, the lesson architects noticed that "some of the student[s] struggled identifying the objective of the task and that they were to combine their knowledge to reach a collective conclusion"; thus, "some students did not respond to the objectives. . .failing to draw the conclusions we intended". Through an instructional lens, Red suggested that "we should have encouraged the students to evaluate each case and then foster the connection between the three 'big groups'". Maria proposed to have "the specific objectives presented on a slide. . . [to] help students understand what they need to answer". As students were divided into groups, initial student engagement was low, which could have been due to the lack of clarity on the objectives of the task. Florence similarly noted that student engagement initially started low but "progressed over time throughout the lesson" and established that in the future, she would mitigate the lack of engagement by "prepar[ing] more questions to ask [students] to enhance understanding throughout the lesson". Red, Maria, and Florence recognized the students' confusion around the task, which hindered the students' ability to work with each other. Yet, all three provided instructional-based solutions that they could implement to improve the students' experiences with the lesson.

The lesson architects identified specific content components that students were fixated on, specifically conducting and interpreting a *t*-test. Red observed that the "*t*-test might have been too ambitious to make students do", while Maria concluded that "it might be wise to introduce the *t*-test to the students earlier". In a similar vein, Sophia recommended providing students with a preparatory homework assignment, including a short video on how to interpret a *t*-test. "This way, the educators can ensure the students [have an] understanding of [the *t*-test] before the lesson is implemented". Red also proposed to assign preparatory homework that includes some pre-selected statistical tests where "they had to read about [statistical tests] and identify which one to use where". The lesson architects developed plans to restructure how students were introduced to the *t*-test as a response to observations that were made during implementation.

Not only did the lesson architects' knowledge of instructional techniques grow through a critical analysis of the implementation, but the lesson architects' pedagogical knowledge increased throughout the whole process. In reflecting on instructional practices beneficial to student learning, the lesson architects thought having the students jigsaw into multidisciplinary groups was beneficial in engaging all students and having students gain different perspectives. Although the "classroom layout also didn't quite work" because "at times, it was difficult to move around" due to the immobile nature of the seating, the lesson architects appreciated trying an unfamiliar instructional technique. Florence even found that "having three different groups [was] a great technique in teaching a wide variety of content at once as the students are then able to teach each other".

5. Discussion

The success of the lesson architect's engagement and growth is tied to three primary lessons learned: (1) facilitation of effective communication, (2) centering of the lesson architects, and (3) inclusion of authentic engagement with interdisciplinary STEM education. In this discussion, we describe key takeaways from lessons learned and future directions of project-based learning with students as partners.

5.1. Facilitate Effective Communication

A key component of the course that supported the lesson architects was facilitating open and effective communication throughout the course. Students rarely engage in project-based learning in higher education STEM disciplines [26], which is why course design [4] should emphasize the importance of fostering an environment that is inclusive to students from different backgrounds and conducive to project-based learning. By having the lesson architects create their own classroom norms, they were able to express their expectations of their peers and their instructors. These expectations could differ between the cultures of the United States and Norway or even regionally across the United States. However, having the lesson architects relay their unspoken expectations to their peers allowed everyone to have a shared understanding of the expectations within the course. The anonymity allowed the lesson architects to be honest with their expectations without having the initial discomfort of speaking to a group of people they just met.

By modeling effective communication and establishing classroom norms, the lesson architects were able to address possible cultural differences between Norway and the United States. Cultural differences, together with speaking in a foreign language (in this case, in English for the Norwegian lesson architects), can easily result in the native speakers taking the lead in conversations, potentially leaving the Norwegian lesson architects to simply agree with what is being said due to possible language barriers. Using Jamboard and discussion posts, the Norwegian lesson architects could more easily express their thoughts individually without being influenced by the other students. Another positive effect of using these tools was increasing the number of visible opinions, as well as encouraging all parties to share their thoughts on an issue. Given that the Norwegian lesson architects have different cultural perspectives and localized issues, the ability to express differing opinions highlighted multiple facets of society. During the development of the lesson plan, the lesson architects provided a different perspective on a local issue, in this case, algal blooms, and attempted to draw connections between their previous experiences in Norway and the United States. In this way, facilitating an environment with open communication allowed new connections to be made and seen across cultures and STEM disciplines, which was pivotal to the success of developing an interdisciplinary STEM lesson.

5.2. Lesson Architect-Centered: Focus on the Interests, Experiences, and Knowledge of the Lesson Architects

The class was designed to have structure for the lesson architects but was also responsive to their needs throughout the lesson design process. The open-endedness of the course allowed students to call on their previous knowledge and interests. For example, Florence employed previous knowledge from growing up in the Southeastern United States as well as experiences testing the Savannah River Watershed to suggest the location for the lesson. Florence's valuable insight into problems affecting the Savannah River Watershed was the foundation of the place-based aspect of the lesson and made it easier to determine a focus area every lesson architect could work on, namely water pollution. Equally as passionate about the topic of water pollution, the Norwegian lesson architects brainstormed water-based challenges in localized regions of Norway, resulting in the parallel challenge of harmful algal blooms. Finding a joint environmental problem between the Southeastern United States and Norway increased the authenticity of the lesson, providing strong reasoning for why algal blooms are important in real life, a key pillar in place-based learning [2].

Similar to Florence's place-based expertise, Salix expressed continued interest in using statistics in the lesson, given her strong background in the subject. Salix quickly became the statistics expert and provided suggestions for how to intertwine statistics with the environmental science topic of algal blooms. The use of statistics expanded to include technology skills and data interpretation, with Sophia and Salix suggesting that students make two graphs and run two statistical tests to prove or disprove an algal bloom incidence. The use of statistics prompted the lesson architects to think about potential datasets that could be incorporated into the lesson. The group landed on incorporating fish mortality data from Norway, algal bloom toxin data from water testing sites along the Savannah River Watershed, and student-collected algal growth data from localized water sources, including the pond on Isunigu University's campus.

5.3. Include Authentic Engagement with Interdisciplinary STEM Education

Structuring the course to promote an authentic and engaging project-based learning experience was critical in the lesson architects' personal and academic development. After engaging in this course, the lesson architects grew their understanding of what defines education, what tools educators employ to develop a successful lesson, and how to conduct education research. The lesson architects expanded their own knowledge base of environmental science as they quickly had to become experts in the causes of algal blooms as well as affected ecosystems. Through this expansion of knowledge, the lesson architects grew to recognize how local problems can have a global impact or how local problems can exist on a global scale.

Not only did the lesson architects expand their personal knowledge of environmental science, but they witnessed first-hand that educators can initially be novices on a topic and expand their knowledge enough to create a well-thought-out lesson. Their view of an educator expanded to include a wider variety of instructional practices as well as recognition that exceptional educators tend to have an understanding of how a multitude of students learn and construct learning objectives catered to the depth in which students are to learn a topic. Broadening the view of educators included recognizing that educators engage in education research even through techniques as accessible as lesson study. Lesson architects were also introduced to the importance of including more underutilized methods in STEM education, including place-based and interdisciplinary methodology. As we foster passion and skills in future educators, it is valuable to include these methods in order to create ripples of passion in STEM and continued community engagement.

5.4. Future Directions for Project-Based Learning with Students as Partners

This case study provides a dive into student perspectives of a novel undergraduate course framework, where students played the leading role in curriculum development. Developing a classroom where students and instructors share responsibility for course development creates a community where students are encouraged to challenge themselves (see discussion in Section 5.2 for the lesson architect-centered focus), and participation in a safe learning community simulates the group dynamic that students may experience in the workforce or "the real world" [9,10,27]. In our study, these elements were strengthened by instructor scaffolding and effective communication facilitated through the use of Google apps (Jamboard, Docs, and Sheets) and a learning management system (Canvas; see discussion in Section 5.1 on facilitating effective communication). The use of technology in this case study facilitated an open discussion space for the lesson architects to brainstorm ideas and provide feedback during the process of lesson development. Across other studies, the use of technology has facilitated learning and peer-to-peer collaboration [28,29]. As technology continues to advance through increasingly collaborative and interactive platforms and through the use of artificial intelligence, the way students learn and complete projects will continue to evolve. Increasing student autonomy and investment in their coursework may lead to authentic work and participation by students in the classroom and allow them to engage with STEM topics in realistic ways.

6. Conclusions

The semester proved to be a challenging and rewarding experience for the five lesson architects and instructors from Norway and the United States. Aligning the course instruction with project-based learning standards and teaching methods [3,4] assisted the lesson architects in developing a successful place-based, interdisciplinary lesson on algal bloom growth in Norway and the United States. Ultimately, the project-based standards were key frameworks that influenced the structure of the course and contributed to student growth.

The structure of the course was unique for a higher education institution, yet the authentic, open-ended task of creating an interdisciplinary lesson provided the lesson architects with a variety of directions to take the lesson while also allowing them to recall previous knowledge they had. By engaging in a place-based, project-based learning course focused on creating an interdisciplinary STEM lesson study, the lesson architects gained a greater understanding of the inner workings of interdisciplinary STEM education, inclusion of multiculturalism within STEM education, ways in which students learn, and instructional practices that enhance student learning and engagement. The lesson architects ultimately participated and highly benefited from the concepts of place-based and interdisciplinary methodology, allowing them to further develop their global perspectives and lesson development skills.

Although the course featured in this case study took place in the Fall of 2023, the exchange program continued into the Spring of 2024, and the second iteration of the course took place at the University of Egðir. During the Spring of 2024, the lesson architects and Gigi traveled (or returned) to Norway to revise and re-implement the algal bloom lesson in Norwegian higher education classrooms. In the Fall of 2024, the exchange program will continue at Isunigu University with a new group of instructors, exchange students, and students. From this experience and our subsequent research on the project-based learning course, we encourage other educators to use project-based learning to foster an inclusive environment with appropriate scaffolding to construct a transformative experience for all students.

Supplementary Materials: The following supporting information can be downloaded at https://www.mdpi.com/article/10.3390/educsci14080866/s1, File S1: Group 1: Reflection Pond Algal Blooms; File S2: Group 2: Impact of Algal Blooms in Trøndelag, Norway; File S3: Group 3: Land Use and Algal Blooms in the Savannah River Watershed.

Author Contributions: Conceptualization, M.A.B., K.B.L. and M.V.; Methodology, M.A.B., M.V. and F.N.; Formal Analysis, M.A.B.; Writing—Original Draft Preparation, M.A.B., M.T., J.A. and O.S.; Writing—Review & Editing, J.A., K.B.L., M.V., F.N., S.K.N.T. and O.S.; Supervision, M.A.B., M.V. and K.B.L.; Project Administration, M.A.B., M.V. and K.B.L.; Funding Acquisition, M.V. and K.B.L. All authors have read and agreed to the published version of the manuscript.

Funding: Norwegian Directorate for Higher Education and Skills, project number: UTF-2021/10111. Supplemental funding was provided by Clemson University Creative Inquiry Program.

Institutional Review Board Statement: The study was conducted in accordance with the Declaration of Helsinki, and approved by the Institutional Review Board of Clemson University (protocol code IRB 2023-0649 and date of approval is 4 December 2023).

Informed Consent Statement: Informed consent was obtained from all subjects involved in the study.

Data Availability Statement: The data presented in this article are not readily available because the data contains sensitive information and may be re-identifiable given the rich nature of the data. The raw data from this study may be made available upon request after providing a written rationale and intended use of the data. Requests to access the datasets should be directed to mkvoigt@gmail.com.

Acknowledgments: We would like to acknowledge Anna Haakonsen, Thomas Gjesteland, and Halvard Øysæd for their contributions to the collection of data and support throughout the course. We would also like to acknowledge Sarah Otterbeck for her feedback throughout the writing process of this article.

Conflicts of Interest: The authors declare no conflict of interest.

References

1. King, A. From Sage on the Stage to Guide on the Side. *Coll. Teach.* **1993**, *41*, 30–35. [CrossRef]
2. Gruenewald, D.A. The Best of Both Worlds: A Critical Pedagogy of Place. *Educ. Res.* **2003**, *32*, 3–12. [CrossRef]

3. Buck Institute for Education. Gold Standard PBL: The Essential Project Design Elements. 2022. Available online: https://my.pblworks.org/resource/document/gold_standard_pbl_essential_project_design_elements (accessed on 27 February 2024).
4. Buck Institute for Education. Gold Standard PBL: Project Based Teaching Practices. 2019. Available online: https://my.pblworks.org/resource/document/gold_standard_pbl_project_based_teaching_practices1 (accessed on 27 February 2024).
5. Krajcik, J.S.; Shin, N. Project-based learning. In *The Cambridge Handbook of the Learning Sciences*, 2nd ed.; Sawyer, R.K., Ed.; Cambridge University Press: Cambridge, UK, 2014; pp. 275–297.
6. Condliffe, B. *Project-Based Learning: A Literature Review*; Working Paper; MDRC: New York, NY, USA, 2017.
7. Yemini, M.; Engel, L.; Ben Simon, A. Place-based education–A systematic review of literature. *Educ. Rev.* **2023**, 1–21. [CrossRef]
8. Van den Beemt, A.; MacLeod, M.; Van der Veen, J.; Van de Ven, A.; Van Baalen, S.; Klaassen, R.; Boon, M. Interdisciplinary engineering education: A review of vision, teaching, and support. *J. Eng. Educ.* **2020**, *109*, 508–555. [CrossRef]
9. Lubicz-Nawrocka, T. From partnership to self-authorship: The benefits of co-creation of the curriculum. *Int. J. Stud. Partn.* **2018**, *2*, 47–63.
10. Ngereja, B.; Hussein, B.; Andersen, B. Does Project-Based Learning (PBL) Promote Student Learning? A Performance Evaluation. *Educ. Sci.* **2020**, *10*, 330. [CrossRef]
11. Lewis, C.C.; Tsuchida, I. A Lesson Is Like a Swiftly Flowing River: How Research Lessons Improve Japanese Education. *Improv. Sch.* **1999**, *2*, 48–56. [CrossRef]
12. Stigler, J.W.; Hiebert, J. *The Teaching Gap: Best Ideas from the World's Teachers for Improving in the Classroom*; The Free Press: New York, NY, USA, 1999; pp. 103–128.
13. Larmer, J.; Mergendoller, J.R. *Gold Standard PBL: Essential Project Design Elements*; Buck Institute for Education: Novato, CA, USA, 2015; pp. 1–4.
14. Darling-Hammond, L.; Barron, B.; Pearson, P.D.; Schoenfeld, A.H.; Stage, E.K.; Zimmerman, T.D.; Cervetti, G.N.; Tilson, J.L. *Powerful Learning: What We Know about Teaching for Understanding*; Jossey-Bass: Hoboken, NJ, USA, 2008.
15. Yu, H. Enhancing creative cognition through project-based learning: An in-depth scholarly exploration. *Heliyon* **2024**, *10*, e27706. [CrossRef] [PubMed]
16. Freire, P. *Pedagogy of the Oppressed*, 30th Anniversary ed.; Continuum: New York, NY, USA, 2005; pp. 43–70.
17. Williams, M.K. John Dewey in the 21st century. *J. Inq. Action Educ.* **2017**, *9*, 7.
18. Lubicz-Nawrocka, T.; Bovill, C. Do students experience transformation through co-creating curriculum in higher education? *Teach. High. Educ.* **2023**, *28*, 1744–1760. [CrossRef]
19. Larmer, J.; Mergendoller, J.; Boss, S. *Setting the Standard for Project Based Learning*; ASCD: Alexandria, VA, USA, 2015; pp. 1–54.
20. Mergendoller, J.R.; Thomas, J.W. Managing project based learning: Principles from the field. In Proceedings of the 2000 Annual Meeting of the American Educational Research Association, New Orleans, LA, USA, 24–28 April 2000.
21. Merriam, S.B. *Qualitative Research and Case Study Applications in Education*, 2nd ed.; Jossey-Bass Publishers: San Francisco, CA, USA, 2009; pp. 39–55.
22. Yazan, B. Three Approaches to Case Study Methods in Education: Yin, Merriam, and Stake. *Qual. Rep.* **2015**, *20*, 134–152. [CrossRef]
23. Brown, P.A. A review of the literature on case study research. *Can. J. New Sch. Educ./Rev. Can. Jeunes Cherch. Cherch. Educ.* **2008**, *1*, 1–13.
24. Braun, V.; Clarke, V. Thematic analysis. In *APA Handbook of Research Methods in Psychology: Research Designs: Quantitative, Qualitative, Neuropsycholog-Ical, and Biological*; Cooper, H., Camic, P.M., Long, D.L., Panter, A.T., Rindskopf, D., Sher, K.J., Eds.; American Psychological Association: Washington, DC, USA, 2012; Volume 2, pp. 57–71.
25. Bloom, B.S. *Taxonomy of Educational Objectives, Handbook: The Cognitive Domain*; David McKay Company, Inc.: New York, NY, USA, 1956.
26. Chang, Y.; Choi, J.; Şen-Akbulut, M. Undergraduate Students' Engagement in Project-Based Learning with an Authentic Context. *Educ. Sci.* **2024**, *14*, 168. [CrossRef]
27. Kaya, T.; Bowlyn, K.N. Building an Innovative Engineering Curriculum from the Ground Up: Lessons and Success Stories Paper. In Proceedings of the 2024 ASEE North East Section, Fairfield, CT, USA, 19–20 April 2024.
28. Tsui, E.; Dragicevic, N.; Fan, I.; Cheng, M. Co-creating curriculum with students, teachers, and practitioners in a technology-enhanced environment. *Educ. Tech. Res. Dev.* **2024**, *72*, 869–893. [CrossRef]
29. Abuhassna, H.; Al-Rahmi, W.M.; Yahya, N.; Zakaria, M.A.Z.M.; Kosnin, A.B.M.; Darwish, M. Development of a new model on utilizing online learning platforms to improve students' academic achievements and satisfaction. *Int. J. Educ. Technol. High. Educ.* **2020**, *17*, 38. [CrossRef]

education sciences

MDPI

Article

Shifting Students' Perceptions About Homelessness: Quantitative Assessment of a Project-Based Approach

Diana A. Chen [1,*], Mark A. Chapman [1] and Joel Alejandro Mejia [2]

1 Department of Integrated Engineering, University of San Diego, San Diego, CA 92110, USA; markchapman@sandiego.edu
2 Department of Engineering and Computing Education, University of Cincinnati, Cincinnati, OH 45220, USA; mejiaja@ucmail.uc.edu
* Correspondence: dianachen@sandiego.edu; Tel.: +1-619-260-4622

Abstract: Although engineering institutional bodies uphold public welfare and the impact of engineering on people and society, engineering curricula rarely scaffold students to connect their technical learning with sociotechnical perspectives. This paper describes a project-based learning approach where engineering students engaged with issues faced by people experiencing homelessness to better understand the sociotechnical nature of effective, user-centered, engineering design. We conducted a quantitative assessment to determine how well and in what ways the project-based learning curriculum shifted students' perceptions about homelessness. We collected pre-/post-survey data from students on 21 statements about their perceptions and attitudes about homelessness prior to and after an engineering project with a focus on homelessness in San Diego, CA, USA. The study aimed to measure the effectiveness of the course/project on shifting students' perceptions from myths about homelessness towards reality, which supported the course objectives regarding diversity, inclusion, and social justice. We found that, from data from 166 students over 8 semesters, students' perceptions had statistically significant ($p < 0.05$) shifts in five survey statements, which regarded beliefs about the personal choices or perceived moral decisions of those experiencing homelessness, and that students were able to more strongly identify with an engineer's duty to care for those experiencing homelessness.

Keywords: sociotechnical; project-based learning; homelessness; engineering design; perceptions; attitudes; quantitative assessment; empathy; critical consciousness

1. Introduction

Two institutional bodies that drive engineering morals, values, and change include engineering accreditation, such as the Accreditation Board for Engineering and Technology (ABET), and engineering professional societies, such as the American Society of Mechanical Engineers among many others. Annually, ABET releases a set of student outcomes (SOs) that it uses to assess engineering students and the programs from which they graduate (Criteria for Accrediting Engineering Programs, 2025–2026). In its latest iteration (established 2019), three SOs in particular have led to some consternation across engineering faculty. These SOs state that upon graduation students should have the following:

- SO2: an ability to apply engineering design to produce solutions that meet specified needs with consideration of public health, safety, and welfare, as well as global, cultural, social, environmental, and economic factors.

- SO4: an ability to recognize ethical and professional responsibilities in engineering situations and make informed judgments, which must consider the impact of engineering solutions in global, economic, environmental, and societal contexts.
- SO5: an ability to function effectively on a team whose members . . . create a collaborative and inclusive environment. . ..

On the other hand, engineering professional societies each have their own Codes of Ethics, which are used to guide engineers' behavior as they produce work that is used by people and affects society. Across several of the largest disciplines' societies, the American Society of Mechanical Engineers (ASME.org, n.d.; Criteria for Accrediting Engineering Programs, 2025–2026), the Biomedical Engineering Society (2024 BMES Annual Meeting Policies & Code of Conduct—Biomedical Engineering Society, n.d.), the American Society of Civil Engineers (Code of Ethics, n.d.-a), the Institute of Electrical and Electronics Engineers (IEEE Code of Ethics, n.d.), and the National Society of Professional Engineers (Code of Ethics, n.d.-b), the first tenet of each Code of Ethics is for a professional engineer to use their knowledge and skills for the enhancement of human welfare, and/or to hold paramount the safety, health, and welfare of the public.

The ABET outcomes described above emphasize the complexity of real-world engineering and the impact it has on people more explicitly and in a more integrated way than previous iterations have. Similarly, the Codes of Ethics all emphasize human welfare/welfare of the public. It is evident that both institutional bodies prioritize engineering's impact on people; however, the way engineering is taught rarely discusses the impact of engineering technologies on society (Mejia et al., 2018). One study found that, despite many students entering engineering with a commitment to public welfare, engineering's "culture of disengagement" leads students to be disenfranchised when they graduate (Cech, 2014). One reason for this decline in student concern for public welfare may be the lack of exposure and practice students receive around how human life and decision-making are involved in engineering (Mejia et al., 2021). Another reason is the framing of engineering as apolitical and decontextualized. Several scholars have studied the role of objectivity in engineering culture that has led to engineering's problem with decontextualization (Chen & Wodin-Schwartz, 2019; Downey, 2015; Lucena & Leydens, 2015; Moseley, 2017). Others have also found that a sociotechnical lens can help students tie their technical skills to real-world problems. For example, Chen et al. (2023) found that framing engineering content as sociotechnical increased student engagement and helped students to think more deeply about their own goals as future engineers. By directly relating engineering to its sociotechnical and public welfare applications, we hope to combat the culture of disengagement in our own curricula.

Project-based learning (PBL) courses are especially well suited for the integration of sociotechnical context. We consider 'sociotechnical' to indicate the complex ways in which the social and technical aspects of these issues are interconnected. Successful PBL courses often base a project on a meaningful problem and operationalize the project with an open-ended, engaging question (de Graaff & Kolmos, 2007). In addition, sustained inquiry, where students find and use resources of their own over time; authenticity of a real-world context, process, and impact that connects to students' own concerns, interests, and identities; and student voice and choice in how they use their time and the products they create are key elements to creating an engaging project (Buck Institute for Education, 2015). Engineering design projects, particularly those that take user contexts into account, lend themselves especially well to PBL when students are asked to consider sociotechnical aspects that influence their technical design solutions. This study uses PBL to integrate local issues faced by people experiencing homelessness into an engineering design course to garner student engagement. Homelessness is an escalating global issue that has worsened over the last few years due to economic instability, housing shortages, and other systemic factors. Homelessness has become a growing crisis in recent years, particularly in the United States and in cities like San Diego, CA, where rising housing costs and insufficient shelter capacity have contributed to an increasing unhoused population. As the crisis grows, it is increasingly becoming an engineering challenge that requires innovative solutions in areas such as sustainable housing, infrastructure design, and resource accessibility. Given this perspective, our research explores how project-based learning can equip future engineers with the skills and social awareness needed to tackle complex societal issues like homelessness.

Existing literature has explored homelessness from social, economic, and public health perspectives. However, there is a gap in research that explicitly connects engineering education—particularly project-based learning—with addressing homelessness as both a technical and social challenge. Our study fills this gap by examining how project-based learning can cultivate engineers who are not only technically proficient but also socially responsible and equipped to develop empathy toward these issues. Recent comments from technocrats claiming that empathy has been the demise of the Western civilization demonstrate the idea that technical and social work must be taught separately. This rhetoric can be dangerous for engineering education because it reinforces an outdated, technocratic view of engineering that prioritizes efficiency, logic, and innovation at the expense of human-centered considerations. This perspective risks devaluing the ethical and social dimensions of engineering, which are essential for addressing complex global challenges such as homelessness.

It is important to note that the existing engineering education framework in the U.S. continues to largely prioritize Western, White, and male epistemologies (Leydens & Lucena, 2018; Momo et al., 2020; Riley, 2008). These dominant perspectives shape the way engineering students engage with community-based projects, often privileging top-down, technocratic solutions rather than collaborative, culturally responsive approaches. By interrogating these underlying tendencies to see empathy as an interfering force to conducting transformative engineering work, our research seeks to challenge traditional engineering education paradigms and reimagine project-based learning as a tool for ethical, community-centered reflection. Through a localized case study on homelessness, we aim to demonstrate how engineering students make sense of social issues. This work contributes to a growing body of scholarship advocating for a more inclusive, justice-oriented engineering education that critically examines its own epistemological foundations and redefines its role in addressing systemic inequities.

1.1. Course Context and Institutional Resources

The study described in this paper is based within an undergraduate engineering course, User-Centered Design, that is required of students in all engineering majors at the University of San Diego (USD). The course is typically taken in a student's second or third semester in the engineering curriculum. As a result of the campus environment, the User-Centered Design course evolved over time to be unique in its objective to cover topics including justice, power, intersectionality, and privilege and oppression (Mejia et al., 2018).

The unique nature of this User-Centered Design course grew out of an opportunity in the School of Engineering to align engineering requirements with the institution's mission and initiatives. The University of San Diego is a primarily undergraduate, liberal arts, contemporary Catholic institution that embraces the Catholic moral and social tradition in its mission and values, which emphasizes the importance of sustainability and social justice. USD is also designated as an Ashoka U "Changemaker Campus", a recognition of our university's commitment to finding sustainable solutions to the world's most pressing problems. Furthermore, the university's last strategic plan, "Because the World Needs Changemakers", aligned university-wide curricula with the values of the institution. In keeping with the mission, all undergraduate students are required to complete two courses with the diversity, inclusion, and social justice (DISJ) Core flag, which seeks to help students develop critical self-reflection and the ability to analyze the complexities of social constructions in everyday life.

In Spring 2017, the engineering faculty body voted to designate the User-Centered Design course as a lower level DISJ course. While the impetus for the change was to ensure that students were seeing the relevance of DISJ topics within an engineering context, the benefit was two-fold, as it also led to one fewer additional (i.e., external to engineering) graduation requirement for the already lengthy engineering curricula. The integration of the DISJ topics with engineering design proved to be challenging, and the progression of the course is detailed elsewhere for the reader (Chen et al., 2019, 2020; Lord et al., 2018; Mejia et al., 2018). In Fall 2019, after reviewing the efficacy of the course, the primary instructors decided to shift the final design project (which was previously situated around building solar water heaters with a context divorced from the local area) towards homelessness (Chen et al., 2020; Mejia et al., 2021). Not only does San Diego rank as the sixth highest for rates of individuals experiencing homelessness in the United States (Johnson et al., 2025), providing a pressing context for a locally visible issue, but the context allowed for topics around social justice to be better tied to course content. In addition, USD's Changemaker Hub—which is described as both a place and a process that highlights the interconnections of people, activities, and organizations that constitute changemaking—launched an Urgent Challenges Collective initiative in 2019 to study and address homelessness and food insecurity in our local community. The timing of the homelessness initiative aligned well with the redevelopment of the course to provide activities, events, and resources on campus to help students engage with and learn about the issues faced by individuals experiencing homelessness.

Based on the required learning objectives for the DISJ designation, the full list of course objectives are presented below. By the end of the course, students will have achieved the following:

1. Have reflected on and be able to communicate about their own identity and personal experiences (i.e., privilege and disadvantage) in relation to others.
2. Have demonstrated empathy for users by describing how users' experiences may be influenced by societal norms around the intersectionality of issues such as race, ethnicity, gender, age, physical ability, immigration status, literacy, and language.
3. Be familiar with qualitative research methodologies (e.g., interviews, observation, and immersion) to engage users and identify user issues related to intersectionality.
4. Be able to demonstrate empathy and other mindsets that support a user-centered approach to engineering design.
5. Be able to analyze and design consumer products by applying principles of design.
6. Be able to translate customer needs to product specifications.
7. Be able to develop a plan to complete a design task.
8. Be able to use prototyping techniques and iteration to develop design ideas.
9. Be able to elicit feedback from users to improve designs.
10. Be able to describe and practice attributes of effective teams and team members.
11. Be able to collaborate with people, especially users, throughout a design process to develop user-oriented concepts, products, or services.
12. Be able to communicate design solutions to various stakeholders.

1.2. Collaboration with Think Dignity

As a part of the course redesign, the primary instructors cultivated a relationship with a local non-profit organization, Think Dignity, which is a legal advocacy group that strives to provide services and programs that focus on advancing the basic dignity for those living on the streets (Think Dignity, n.d.). One of the goals of the partnership was to provide a more realistic situation for students to engage with the DISJ content, local to San Diego. As a part of the collaboration, a staff member from Think Dignity was invited every semester to give a guest lecture to the engineering students. The talk included statistics about homelessness both nationally and locally for the county and presented different myths regarding homelessness that were often surprising to students. For example, four myths and their realities are provided below (Watanabe, 2019):

1. Myth: A large majority of homeless individuals have issues with substance abuse that prevents them from maintaining stability in their lives. (Reality: Only 3% of homeless individuals have these issues).
2. Myth: A large majority of homeless individuals have a severe mental illness. (Reality: Only 4% of homeless individuals have these issues).
3. Myth: A large majority of homeless individuals abuse free services or welfare. (Reality: Less than 20% of homeless individuals know about/are qualified for free services or welfare).
4. Myth: Homeless people are criminals. (Reality: Homeless people are more likely to be victims of crime).

The presentation also often included topics such as compounding legal ramifications that individuals experiencing homelessness often faced and were left to navigate on their own, as well as presenting resources that these individuals could engage with, which often inspired students' project topics.

This paper describes a four-year study that investigates, "How well and in what ways did the project-based learning curriculum contribute to a shift in students' perceptions about homelessness?" While this paper focuses on quantitative data, the reader is directed to Chen et al. (2020) for a discussion of the qualitative data collected that describes how the project-based approach affected students' learning outcomes around the idea that engineering alone cannot solve complex socio-political problems. Together, our overall goal was to use the context of homelessness embedded into PBL to help students to meet course objectives around developing empathy and learning about social justice topics within an engineering context. Our hope with this project-based approach and community collaboration was that we could dispel myths that students might hold about homelessness in order to encourage more students to become more compassionate engineers. The context of homelessness helped to better integrate the diversity, inclusion, and social justice course elements with the engineering design concepts (whereas previous iterations of the course had modules on topics such as race and privilege separated from the engineering design project), serving as a conduit for achieving the course objectives and reinforcing the idea that engineering is a sociotechnical endeavor.

2. Methods

At the start of each semester, as a part of the first homework assignment, students in the class were provided with a pre-survey to gather data on their preconceptions about homelessness prior to the information discussed throughout the course. The survey included 21 statements about homelessness and individuals experiencing homelessness, where students were asked to indicate the option that most closely represented their views using a Likert scale with five options, ranging from strongly disagree to strongly agree. The prompt reassured students that there were no right or wrong answers, and that they did not need to spend long on each statement, as often their first response would be the most accurate representation of their perceptions. At the conclusion of the survey, students were asked to type the last four digits of their cell phone number so that future responses (identical post-survey) could be linked anonymously.

The 21 statements about homelessness were adapted from the Health Professional Attitudes Towards the Homeless Inventory (HPATHI)[1], developed by Buck et al. for use in the medical community (2005). The HPATHI targets three subscales: (1) Personal Advocacy, which reflects a personal commitment to work with people experiencing homelessness, (2) Social Advocacy, which reflects society's responsibility to care for the homeless population, and (3) Cynicism, which reflects a negative attitude and sense of futility in working with the homeless (Crow, 2013). The HPATHI is a validated instrument that measures medical providers' attitudes toward the homeless in the hopes that results can point towards the design and implementation of educational activities that foster more compassionate homeless health care (Buck et al., 2005).

Medicine, in particular, is a profession that attempts to develop an ethic of service to the underserved in its students; however, studies have indicated that progression through the medical curriculum is linked with a rise in cynicism, a decrease in empathy, and a decreased interest in caring for the poor (Fine et al., 2013). The undergraduate engineering curriculum presents a similar conundrum: while engineering, broadly, upholds and values the welfare of the public and the impact of engineering and technology on people and society, the traditional engineering curriculum does not tend to scaffold students in learning and applying these values. In fact, Cech (2014) found that the culture of engineering education causes students to become more disengaged with the public good over time.

While the original HPATHI instrument presents 19 statements, the survey we used for this project presented students with 21 statements that were reworded for an engineering context. Of the original HPATHI statements, we kept and/or adapted 9 and added 12 more. Table 1 shows the 21 statements used in our engineering study. In particular, our survey targeted four subscales (themes):

- T1: Beliefs about homelessness being a real (as opposed to trivial or imaginary) issue.
- T2: Beliefs about individuals experiencing homelessness, reflecting a bias against personal choices or moral deficiencies.
- T3: Relevance of homelessness for engineers/engineering.
- T4: Government responsibility towards addressing homelessness.

Gjersing et al. (2010) make the case that previously validated instruments are not necessarily valid in another time, culture, or context. Given that the original HPATHI instrument was written specifically for medical professionals, it was not only appropriate but necessary for us to adapt the statements to our own discipline. By adapting the instrument, the study preserves the integrity of the original subscales—Personal Advocacy, Social Advocacy, and Cynicism—while making them more suitable for the target engineering population. This adaptation seeks to retain the validated structure and intent of the HPATHI while adjusting the language and context of the statements to align with an engineering context. Since the HPATHI has already demonstrated reliability in measuring attitudes toward homelessness, modifying it for a different but related audience allows for meaningful comparisons while maintaining the rigor of the original instrument. However, we did conduct a reliability check and determined that the Cronbach's alpha = 0.553, indicating some internal consistency. While this indicates medium internal consistency, the instrument was retained due to its conceptual relevance and prior validation in other domains. The medium reliability may be attributed to contextual differences between disciplines, potentially affecting how participants interpreted certain items. This limitation is acknowledged, and future work should consider refining or revalidating the instrument for use with engineering populations. Furthermore, the adaptation supports the goal of assessing attitudes to inform educational interventions, ensuring that findings can still contribute to strategies for fostering empathy and advocacy in homelessness-related work.

Table 1. Statements used in pre-/post-survey with themes labeled.

#	Statement Text	Theme			
		T1	T2	T3	T4
Q1	Homeless people do not choose to be homeless.		X		
Q2	Nearly all homeless people are drug addicts.		X		
Q3	You only need to learn about homelessness if you want to be a social worker.			X	
Q4	Homeless people are victims.		X		
Q5	Homeless people are rude.		X		
Q6	Engineers have a duty to care for the homeless.			X	
Q7	Homeless people are aggressive.		X		
Q8	Homelessness is a major problem in our society.	X			
Q9	Homelessness is a self-inflicted state.		X		
Q10	Homelessness is not a health issue.	X			
Q11	The government should not waste its resources on the homeless.				X
Q12	I entered engineering because I want to help those in need.			X	
Q13	People make themselves homeless to get government benefits.		X		
Q14	No one in this country has to 'sleep rough'.	X			
Q15	The government should spend more money on providing housing.				X
Q16	Alcoholism is a personal weakness.		X		
Q17	I entered engineering because I was good at math and/or science.			X	
Q18	Homelessness is not a significant problem in San Diego.	X			
Q19	Engineers should address technical and social problems.			X	
Q20	The government should spend more money on the care of the homeless.				X
Q21	Homelessness can be solved using technology.			X	

While the pre-/post-survey was identical for all instructors that participated, every instructor inevitably has their own teaching style and may have delivered course content differently. Over the course of 9 semesters, 7 instructors (named A–F below) had their students participate in the study. Course enrollments are typically limited to 24 students total per section. Table 2 shows the total student enrollment in each section with the participating instructors, alongside the resulting survey success rate. Data collection was concluded after the Fall 2023 semester due to the course developers no longer being consistently assigned to teach the course.

A total of 318 students were enrolled in the version of the course that explored homelessness (there were some instructors in the school who offered different versions of the course). However, the instructors opted not to collect data in Fall 2021, resulting in only 276 students who were instructed to complete the pre-/post-survey. Of the 276 students, only 166 adequately completed the pre-/post-surveys, resulting in a total completion rate of 60%. The survey was conducted in Qualtrics, which enabled us to match the unique ID numbers of each entry (students' self-reported last four digits of their cell phone number). To condition the data down to the final N = 166, incomplete responses were removed, and only unique pairs were used (i.e., one unique ID appeared only twice in one semester—once for pre and once for post). In cases where students mistakenly completed a pre- or post-survey multiple times, the later entry was used. In later semesters, several instructors moved towards making the post-survey an extra credit opportunity to reduce excess assignments at the end of the semester during final exams. However, it does not appear that this shift in requirements played a significant role (either positively or negatively) in the success rate of the post-survey.

Table 2. Student participation rate by semester.

Semester	Total Enrollment by Instructor	Total Student Participation (S)	Usable Responses (N)	Success Rate
Fall 2019	Instructor A—24 Instructor B—24 Instructor C—11	59	38	64%
Spring 2020 *	Instructor B—14 Instructor C—17 Instructor D—7 Instructor D—21	59	38	64%
Fall 2020 **	Instructor B—9	9	6	67%
Spring 2021 **	Instructor B—24 Instructor C—21	45	18	40%
Fall 2021 ***	Instructor A—20 Instructor B—22	0	0	0%
Spring 2022	Instructor A—22 Instructor A—20	42	24	57%
Fall 2022	Instructor E—10	10	7	70%
Spring 2023	Instructor B—11 Instructor F—17	28	18	64%
Fall 2023	Instructor A—24	24	17	71%
	Total	S = 276	N = 166	60%

* Spring 2020 Switched to Emergency Remote Teaching halfway through the semester. ** Fall 2020 and Spring 2021 Entirely online due to global pandemic. *** Fall 2021 Did not collect data.

There are also changes between each semester that are important to note, which may have affected students' learning outcomes and shifts in their perceptions of homelessness. First, the scope of the project changed slightly from semester to semester, as described in Table 3.

Additionally, the participation of our invited speaker from Think Dignity varied from semester to semester. We believe this guest talk played a major role in shifting students' perceptions about homelessness, so the format and requirement of attending the talk may have influenced the results of our study. For the most part, the guest talk was held over Zoom during "dead hours", which spans 12:15–2:20 p.m. on Tuesdays and Thursdays during which no classes are scheduled (intending to give students time for extracurricular activities such as meetings through student organizations). The primary reason for this was that there were multiple sections of students, and scheduling the talk during these hours reduced the coordination and time commitment from the guest speaker. However, using this time block also meant that not all students could or did attend the talk, due to other engagements. In every semester, the talk was recorded and all students were required to submit a written reflection about the talk, but those that did not attend were not able to ask questions and engage in exploring potential project topics more deeply with the speaker. Table 4 shows the semesters in which the guest speaker presented in-person on campus versus online via Zoom, and if the presentation was during class time when all students were present or during dead hours, so that multiple sections could attend at the same time.

Table 3. Description of final project prompt by semester.

Semester	Final Project Description
Fall 2019	This project will be aiming to assist Think Dignity with their Fresh Start Showers Program. Design a solar water heater that interfaces with Think Dignity's mobile shower unit.
Spring 2020 *	Design a prototype or process aimed at an unmet need associated with COVID-19 and homelessness.
Fall 2020 **	
Spring 2021 **	
Fall 2021 ***	Investigate the issues facing our unhoused neighbors and create a design that addresses an unmet need in their community. (open-ended)
Spring 2022	Investigate the issues facing our unhoused neighbors and create a design that addresses an unmet need in their community. Choose one aspect of hygiene to tackle: bathing, laundry, toilet access, feminine care, other. Note: all of these depend on access to fresh clean water. What is an engineering solution you could create to help with this?
Fall 2022	Investigate the issues facing our unhoused neighbors and create a design that addresses an unmet need in their community. (open-ended)
Spring 2023	Investigate the issues facing our unhoused neighbors and create a design that addresses an unmet need in their community. Choose one aspect of hygiene to tackle: bathing, laundry, toilet access, feminine care, other. Note: all of these depend on access to fresh clean water. What is an engineering solution you could create to help with this?
Fall 2023	Investigate the issues facing our unhoused neighbors and create a design that addresses an unmet need in their community. San Diego instated an "Unsafe Camping Ban", which prohibits outdoor sleeping in any open areas or near schools and transit hubs. In conjunction, two new "Safe Sleeping Sites" have been opened as temporary "housing" for those experiencing homelessness. What is an engineering solution you could create to help with these two new initiatives?

* Spring 2020 Switched to Emergency Remote Teaching halfway through the semester. ** Fall 2020 and Spring 2021 Entirely online due to global pandemic. *** Fall 2021 Did not collect data.

Table 4. Variations in Guest Speaker Presentation.

Semester	In-Person vs. Online Talk	Dead Hours vs. In-Class
Fall 2019	In-Person	Dead Hours
Spring 2020 *	Online	Dead Hours
Fall 2020 **	Online	In-Class
Spring 2021 **	Online	Dead Hours
Fall 2021 ***	Online	Dead Hours
Spring 2022	Online	Dead Hours
Fall 2022	In-Person	In-Class
Spring 2023	In-Person	Dead Hours
Fall 2023	In-Person	In-Class

* Spring 2020 Switched to Emergency Remote Teaching halfway through the semester. ** Fall 2020 and Spring 2021 Entirely online due to global pandemic. *** Fall 2021 Did not collect data.

Notably, in Fall 2020, Fall 2022, and Fall 2023, there was only one section of this version of the course offered; in these cases, the guest speaker was invited to give her talk within the boundaries of the class meeting time. (In Fall 2020, this meant still on Zoom due to completely remote teaching due to the global pandemic, but in Fall 2022 and Fall 2023, the guest speaker was invited to attend class in person).

3. Results

We performed statistical analysis on the students' responses on the pre-/post-survey by adapting the Likert scale to be a numerical scale, with 1 corresponding with 'strongly disagree' and 5 with 'strongly agree'. To determine whether or not we could reasonably group all survey data collected across eight different semesters (data was not collected in Fall 2021), we conducted a one-way ANOVA based on semester. The Tukey post hoc analysis found no significant differences in 33 out of 42 prompts (the 21 statements were each presented twice, once for pre and once for post) between semesters. Of the nine comparisons that did show significance (Q8 pre and post, Q11 pre, Q15 post, Q17 pre, Q19 post, Q20 post, and Q21 post), only minor differences were found between a few semesters, and no systematic patterns were revealed across the prompts (i.e., certain semesters were not driving the identified differences). Accordingly, due to the limited inter-semester differences, all pre- and post-data across semesters for each prompt are pooled and analyzed for aggregate differences.

Table 5 shows the group descriptive statistics for each prompt for the data pooled across semesters. Figure 1 shows a diverging stacked bar chart to visualize the main patterns and statistical differences in the data. Notably, a paired *t*-test revealed significant shifts in student perspectives in Statements 1, 2, 6, 9, and 16 (Table 5, Figure 1), with effect sizes (i.e., Cohen's d) of −0.22, 0.40, −0.17, 0.29, and 0.16, respectively.

Table 5. Descriptive group statistics for each prompt across 8 semesters, with paired *t*-test sample statistics. 1 = strongly disagree and 5 = strongly agree. Statistical significance was set to $p \leq 0.05$.

Statement Text		Mean	Std. Deviation	Std. Error Mean	*p* Value
Q1: Homeless people do not choose to be homeless.	Pre	3.63	0.987	0.077	0.006
	Post	3.86	0.974	0.076	
Q2: Nearly all homeless people are drug addicts.	Pre	2.36	0.915	0.071	0.000
	Post	2.01	0.809	0.063	
Q3: You only need to learn about homelessness if you want to be a social worker.	Pre	1.80	0.840	0.065	0.896
	Post	1.79	0.907	0.070	
Q4: Homeless people are victims.	Pre	3.28	0.837	0.065	0.073
	Post	3.41	0.860	0.067	
Q5: Homeless people are rude.	Pre	2.40	0.794	0.062	0.455
	Post	2.36	0.747	0.058	
Q6: Engineers have a duty to care for the homeless.	Pre	3.40	0.927	0.072	0.031
	Post	3.55	0.931	0.072	
Q7: Homeless people are aggressive.	Pre	2.46	0.799	0.062	0.367
	Post	2.40	0.755	0.059	
Q8: Homelessness is a major problem in our society.	Pre	4.52	0.620	0.048	0.231
	Post	4.45	0.743	0.058	
Q9: Homelessness is a self-inflicted state.	Pre	2.64	0.908	0.070	0.000
	Post	2.43	0.812	0.063	
Q10: Homelessness is not a health issue.	Pre	2.16	0.978	0.076	0.820
	Post	2.17	0.947	0.073	
Q11: The government should not waste its resources on the homeless.	Pre	1.81	0.808	0.063	0.100
	Post	1.72	0.769	0.060	
Q12: I entered engineering because I want to help those in need.	Pre	3.73	1.068	0.083	0.419
	Post	3.79	1.072	0.083	
Q13: People make themselves homeless to get government benefits.	Pre	1.88	0.785	0.061	0.239
	Post	1.81	0.814	0.063	
Q14: No one in this country has to 'sleep rough'.	Pre	2.73	1.257	0.098	0.312
	Post	2.66	1.352	0.105	
Q15: The government should spend more money on providing housing.	Pre	3.60	0.978	0.076	0.399
	Post	3.65	0.953	0.074	
Q16: Alcoholism is a personal weakness.	Pre	2.89	1.246	0.097	0.037
	Post	2.71	1.096	0.085	
Q17: I entered engineering because I was good at math and/or science.	Pre	3.78	0.987	0.077	0.465
	Post	3.82	1.023	0.079	

Table 5. *Cont.*

Statement Text		Mean	Std. Deviation	Std. Error Mean	*p* Value
Q18: Homelessness is not a significant problem in San Diego.	Pre	1.68	0.860	0.067	0.373
	Post	1.61	0.807	0.063	
Q19: Engineers should address technical not social problems.	Pre	2.16	0.867	0.067	0.683
	Post	2.19	0.850	0.066	
Q20: The government should spend more money on the care of the homeless.	Pre	3.69	0.887	0.069	0.579
	Post	3.72	0.919	0.071	
Q21: Homelessness can be solved using technology.	Pre	3.38	0.798	0.062	0.191
	Post	3.29	0.902	0.070	

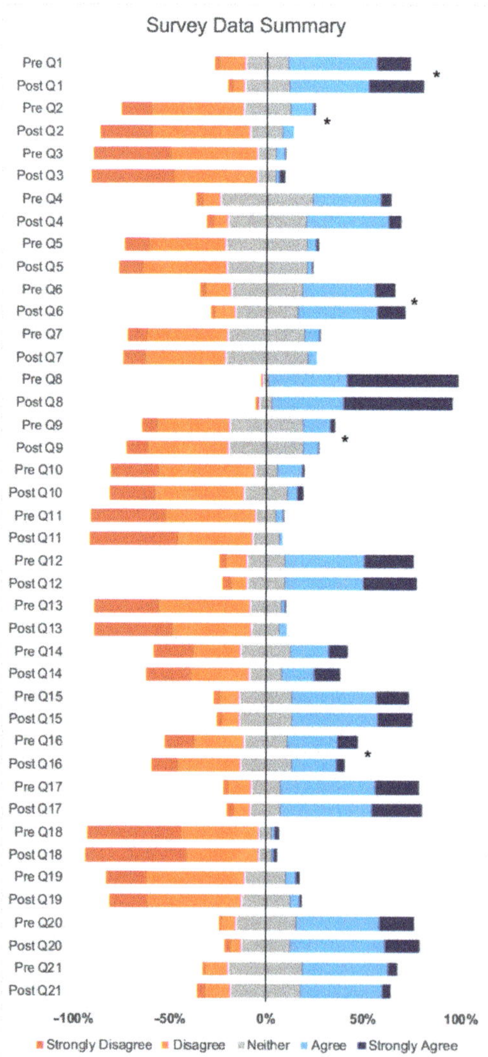

Figure 1. Aggregated Likert scale data collected over 8 semesters. A paired *t*-test comparing pre- and post-survey data found significant shifts in the responses to Statements 1, 2, 6, 9, and 16. Significance is indicated by an asterisk ($p \leq 0.05$).

4. Discussion

Our goal with this study was to evaluate how the PBL course elements contributed to shifts in students' perceptions about homelessness in order to analyze the impact of the course in meeting its objectives related to diversity, inclusion, and social justice. Of the statements provided in the pre-/post-survey, the results of the paired *t*-test revealed statistically significant shifts in student responses from before and after the course interventions in the following five (of twenty-one) statements, suggesting that the intervention had a measurable impact on certain attitudes or beliefs.

- Q1: Homeless people do not choose to be homeless.
- Q2: Nearly all homeless people are drug addicts.
- Q6: Engineers have a duty to care for the homeless.
- Q9: Homelessness is a self-inflicted state.
- Q16: Alcoholism is a personal weakness.

Notably, Statement 2 showed a moderate positive effect size (Cohen's d = 0.40), indicating a meaningful shift in student responses. Statement 9 also showed a small-to-moderate effect (d = 0.29), while the remaining significant statements reflected smaller shifts. The negative effect sizes for Statements 1 and 6 (d = −0.22 and −0.17, respectively) may point to nuanced changes in student interpretation or unexpected reactions that warrant further exploration. Overall, these findings suggest that while the instrument had limitations in internal consistency, it was still sensitive enough to detect changes in specific areas of student thinking. This supports the potential value of the intervention, though further refinement of the instrument for use in engineering contexts is recommended to strengthen future interpretations.

Interestingly, Q1, Q6, Q9, and Q16 were all related to Theme 2: Beliefs about individuals experiencing homelessness. These questions captured preconceived notions and stereotypes, such as the idea that homelessness is primarily the result of poor life choices or a lack of moral responsibility. In all four cases, students' post-survey responses shifted to a more sympathetic perspective following the class project. We believe these shifts in the perceptions of homelessness were tied to the project activities, such as the guest talk that debunked the myths regarding homelessness and the additional research students were asked to conduct. The requirement for students to conduct in-depth research about the specific need they identified ensured that their designs were user-centered, encouraging them to consider the lived experiences of individuals facing homelessness. These activities compelled students to move beyond surface-level assumptions and engage critically with the intersectionality of privilege, disadvantage, and social inequities. All of these shifts towards a more sympathetic perspective were positively correlated with our course learning objectives (e.g., demonstrating empathy, identifying user issues related to intersectionality, reflecting on how their own personal experiences may be different than others with different privileges and disadvantages).

The last statement in which we observed a shift in student perceptions was Q6: Engineers have a duty to care for the homeless, which was related to Theme 3: Relevance of homelessness for engineers/engineering. This outcome aligned with the overarching goal of the class to help students see that engineering as a whole is a sociotechnical endeavor. By framing engineering as a discipline with responsibilities that extend beyond technical problem-solving, the course encouraged students to see themselves as agents of positive societal change. Furthermore, although this course does not present ABET outcomes or professional societies' codes of ethics to the students, this shift in perception also aligned with these institutional bodies' goals for students to have "an ability to apply engineering design to produce solutions that meet specified needs with consideration of public health, safety, and welfare", to have "an ability to recognize ethical and professional responsibilities in engineering situations and make informed judgments, which must consider the impact of engineering solutions in ... societal contexts", and to "use their knowledge and skill for the enhancement of human welfare." This shift toward a more socially conscious view of engineering highlights what the course sought to do in terms of fostering a sense of purpose and responsibility among students. The results suggest that students are beginning to see themselves not only as problem-solvers but also as contributors to addressing pressing societal challenges, such as homelessness. This evolution in their perspectives underscores the importance of incorporating sociotechnical considerations into engineering education to prepare students for the complex challenges they will encounter in their professional lives.

Other prompts in Theme 3 related to the relevance of homelessness to engineering (Q3, Q12, Q17, Q19, and Q21) did not reveal significant shifts in student perceptions. The low pre-survey mean for Q3 (1.8), and above-neutral means for Q6 (3.4) and Q12 (3.73) indicated that students entered the course with attitudes already aligned with our desired student outcomes—possibly due to the student population that self-selected into our university, based on the values of the institution. If anything, the lack of shift in these prompts can be perceived as a positive outcome, suggesting that this course did not contribute to the "culture of disengagement" described by Cech (2014). We are hopeful that our unique take on user-centered design helped students to see why it is important for them to continue caring about social issues as engineers.

Two prompts in which we may have expected significant shifts but did not were Q19 and Q21. For a course that emphasizes the role of engineering as a sociotechnical endeavor, it was surprising that we observed a significant shift in Q6, which specifically tied engineering to "a duty to care for the homeless", but not significant shifts in engineering's relation to broader sociotechnical issues (outside of homelessness). This observation suggests an opportunity for the course to expand its focus and more effectively showcase the breadth of sociotechnical issues that engineers can address through their work. Additionally, the course could place greater emphasis on the importance of interdisciplinary collaboration, particularly with social scientists, to achieve truly user-centered design. Highlighting the value of diverse expertise and perspectives can help students appreciate that engineering solutions are most effective when informed by a deep understanding of social contexts and human experiences. This approach not only enriches the learning experience but also fosters empathy, empowering students to become more thoughtful and inclusive engineers.

Notably, we did not observe significant shifts in either Theme 1: Beliefs about homelessness being a real issue, or Theme 4: Government responsibility towards addressing homelessness. However, these themes were not explicitly addressed through course content, so the lack of shift is not surprising. Nonetheless, it is important to acknowledge that some of the observed shifts in student responses may not be solely attributable to the intervention itself. For instance, students may have had prior exposure to similar content through coursework, lived experiences, or extracurricular experiences, which could have influenced their perspectives independently of the study. Additionally, variations in student motivation or engagement levels—either at the time of the intervention or during the assessment—may have affected how thoughtfully or critically they responded to the instrument. These factors could contribute to both positive and negative shifts in responses, and highlight the importance of accounting for contextual variables when interpreting changes in attitudes or perceptions. Future studies should consider collecting additional background data, increasing the reliability of the instrument, or implementing control conditions to better isolate the effects of the intervention.

5. Conclusions

This paper describes a study conducted in an engineering design course that implemented a project-based learning approach to help students meet course objectives around developing empathy and learning about social justice topics in a way that demonstrates that engineering is a sociotechnical endeavor. To integrate social issues with engineering, the instructors chose to use the context of homelessness to achieve said objectives. The intervention involved a collaboration with a local non-profit organization and a final course project that asked students to identify a need related to homelessness and design a solution to alleviate hardships. This study investigated, "How well and in what ways did the project-based learning curriculum contribute to a shift in students' perceptions about homelessness?" The study explored the applicability of an established instrument—originally developed in the medical sciences—for assessing changes in student perspectives regarding homelessness within an engineering education context. The results revealed significant shifts in student responses on select items, indicating that the intervention may have positively influenced certain dimensions of student thinking—primarily shifting biases away from believing individuals experiencing homelessness suffer due to their own personal choices or moral deficiencies and towards more sympathetic and compassionate beliefs following the course intervention. However, the internal consistency of the instrument in this context was relatively low (Cronbach's alpha = 0.553), suggesting that while some items may resonate with engineering students, others may not fully align with their disciplinary context or experience. This finding underscores the need for future research where cultural or disciplinary norms differ.

The positive results of the study suggest that students began to see themselves as agents of positive change in addressing homelessness. The shift in student perspectives regarding homelessness highlights the importance of integrating sociotechnical considerations into engineering curricula through project-based learning, rather than leaving social issues (and the impact engineering and technology has on these issues) to the humanities. The shifts towards more compassionate perspectives on the human experience aligned with the course's objectives.

However, the study is not without limitations. First, student perceptions prior to the course may have aligned with our study's end goals, based on students' self-selection into our university which upholds values regarding compassion and social issues in the mission statement. Students may also have had previous courses that exposed them to similar content. Second, we did not observe significant shifts in student perceptions of engineers' duty to broader sociotechnical issues outside of homelessness, pointing to an area for improvement for the course. While the project may center on homelessness, future iterations of the course should highlight homelessness as just one example of a social issue that engineering solutions intersect with. Moreover, there are several issues that future studies could consider addressing. First, adapting and revalidating the instrument for use in engineering contexts could enhance measurement accuracy. Second, implementing a mixed-methods approach—including interviews or open-ended surveys—may help uncover how students interpret key items and provide richer insight into the observed changes. Finally, future studies should consider larger, more diverse samples and the inclusion of control groups to better isolate intervention effects.

Overall, while preliminary, the findings suggest promise in adapting reflective or attitudinal assessments across disciplines while emphasizing the impact of critical reflection among engineering students. We encourage engineering educators to continue our work in combatting a technocratic view of engineering that prioritizes efficiency, logic, and innovation at the expense of human well-being. By emphasizing the compassion and empathy needed both for good engineering designs and for addressing social issues, engineering educators can use project-based learning as one approach for highlighting the sociotechnical nature of engineering work. This study's insights contribute to the broader conversation about the development of critical consciousness among future engineers, and the importance of measuring shifts in attitudes toward complex problems in society. We hope our work has impacts beyond just the students in the study and contributes to on-going scholarly efforts that seek to transform engineering education into a more inclusive, justice-oriented field and redefines its role in addressing systemic inequities.

Author Contributions: Conceptualization, D.A.C., M.A.C. and J.A.M.; methodology, D.A.C., M.A.C. and J.A.M.; software, M.A.C.; formal analysis, D.A.C. and M.A.C.; resources, D.A.C. and M.A.C.; data curation, D.A.C.; writing—original draft preparation, D.A.C. and M.A.C.; writing—review and editing, D.A.C. and M.A.C.; project administration, D.A.C. All authors have read and agreed to the published version of the manuscript.

Funding: This research received no external funding.

Institutional Review Board Statement: The study was conducted in accordance with the Declaration of Helsinki, and approved by the Institutional Review Board of University of San Diego (IRB-2020-49, 29 June 2020; IRB-2022-239, 4 December 2023; IRB-2024-63, 30 October 2023).

Informed Consent Statement: Informed consent was obtained from all subjects involved in the study.

Data Availability Statement: The original contributions presented in this study are included in the article. Further inquiries can be directed to the corresponding author.

Conflicts of Interest: The authors declare no conflict of interest.

Notes

1 While terminology has been shifting towards the use of "unhoused" as a way to focus on a person's lack of shelter, in this paper we use the term "people experiencing homelessness" to highlight the distressing experiences caused by the lack of housing, which can be both temporary or long-term. In places where the term "the homeless" is used, we are referring directly to the survey we adopted, which uses this terminology, to retain the instrument's validity.

References

2024 BMES Annual Meeting Policies & Code of Conduct—Biomedical Engineering Society. (n.d.). Available online: https://assets.noviams.com/novi-file-uploads/bmes/PDFs_and_Documents/Governance/BMES_Code_of_Ethics_2021_-_Revised_October_2021.pdf (accessed on 9 May 2025).

ASME.org. (n.d.). *Society policy: Ethics*. Available online: https://www.asme.org/getmedia/3e165b2b-f7e7-4106-a772-5f0586d2268e/p-15-7-ethics.pdf (accessed on 8 January 2025).

Buck, D. S., Monteiro, F. M., Kneuper, S., Rochon, D., Clark, D. L., Melillo, A., & Volk, R. J. (2005). Design and validation of the health professionals' attitudes toward the Homeless Inventory (HPATHI). *BMC Medical Education, 5*(1), 2. [CrossRef] [PubMed]

Buck Institute for Education. (2015). *Essential project design elements checklist*. Available online: https://cpb-us-w2.wpmucdn.com/wp.wpi.edu/dist/e/220/files/2017/06/Essential-Project-Design-Elements-Checklist.pdf (accessed on 2 July 2020).

Cech, E. A. (2014). Culture of disengagement in engineering education? *Science, Technology & Human Values, 39*(1), 42–72.

Chen, D. A., Chapman, M. A., & Mejia, J. A. (2020). Balancing complex social and technical aspects of design: Exposing engineering students to homelessness issues. *Sustainability: Science Practice and Policy, 12*(15), 5917. [CrossRef]

Chen, D. A., Forbes, M. H., Hoople, G., Lord, S., & Mejia, J. (2023). The "who" in engineering: Sociotechnical engineering as memorable and relevant. *International Journal of Engineering Pedagogy, 13*(5), 72–90. [CrossRef]

Chen, D. A., Mejia, J. A., & Breslin, S. (2019). Navigating equity work in engineering: Contradicting messages encountered by minority faculty. *Digital Creativity, 30*(4), 329–344. [CrossRef]

Chen, D. A., & Wodin-Schwartz, S. (2019, June 16–19). *Contextualizing statics: Our process and examples*. 2019 ASEE Annual Conference & Exposition, Tampa, FL, USA. Available online: https://peer.asee.org/contextualizing-statics-our-process-and-examples (accessed on 8 January 2025).

Code of Ethics. (n.d.-a). Available online: https://www.asce.org/career-growth/ethics/code-of-ethics (accessed on 8 January 2025).

Code of Ethics. (n.d.-b). Available online: https://www.nspe.org/resources/ethics/code-ethics (accessed on 8 January 2025).

Criteria for Accrediting Engineering Programs. (2025–2026). *ABET*. Available online: https://www.abet.org/accreditation/accreditation-criteria/criteria-for-accrediting-engineering-programs-2025-2026/ (accessed on 9 May 2025).
Crow, S. M. (2013). Critical synthesis package: Health professional's attitude towards the homeless inventory (HPATHI). *MedEdPORTAL: The Journal of Teaching and Learning Resources*, *9*(1), 9589. [CrossRef]
de Graaff, E., & Kolmos, A. (2007). *Management of change: Implementation of problem-based and project-based learning in engineering*. Sense.
Downey, G. L. (2015). PDS: Engineering as problem definition and solution. In S. Christensen, C. Didier, A. Jamison, M. Meganck, C. Mitcham, & B. Newberry (Eds.), *International perspectives on engineering education* (Vol. 20, pp. 435–455). Springer.
Fine, A. G., Zhang, T., & Hwang, S. W. (2013). Attitudes towards homeless people among emergency department teachers and learners: A cross-sectional study of medical students and emergency physicians. *BMC Medical Education*, *13*(1), 112. [CrossRef] [PubMed]
Gjersing, L., Caplehorn, J. R. M., & Clausen, T. (2010). Cross-cultural adaptation of research instruments: Language, setting, time and statistical considerations. *BMC Medical Research Methodology*, *10*(1), 13. [CrossRef] [PubMed]
IEEE Code of Ethics. (n.d.). Available online: https://www.ieee.org/about/corporate/governance/p7-8.html (accessed on 8 January 2025).
Johnson, S. R., Haines, J., & Jeffrey-Wilensky, J. (2025). *The 25 major U.S. cities with the largest homeless populations*. U.S. News & World Report. Available online: https://www.usnews.com/news/best-states/slideshows/cities-with-the-largest-homeless-populations-in-the-u-s (accessed on 8 January 2025).
Leydens, J. A., & Lucena, J. C. (2018). *Engineering justice: Transforming engineering education and practice*. John Wiley & Sons.
Lord, S. M., Mejia, J. A., Hoople, G., Chen, D., Dalrymple, O., Reddy, E., Przestrzelski, B., & Choi-Fitzpatrick, A. (2018, November 12–16). *Creative curricula for changemaking engineers*. 2018 World Engineering Education Forum—Global Engineering Deans Council (WEEF-GEDC) (pp. 1–5), Albuquerque, NM, USA.
Lucena, J. C., & Leydens, J. A. (2015, June 14–17). *From sacred cow to dairy cow: Challenges and opportunities in integrating of social justice in engineering science courses*. 2015 ASEE Annual Conference & Exposition, Seattle, WA, USA. Available online: https://peer.asee.org/24143 (accessed on 27 September 2022).
Mejia, J. A., Chen, D. A., Chapman, M. A., & Fledderman, B. (2021, July 26). *"Drugs, Alcohol, Joblessness, and Lifestyle": Engineering students' perceptions of homelessness and implications for social justice education*. 2021 ASEE Virtual Annual Conference Content Access, Virtual Conference. Available online: https://peer.asee.org/36531 (accessed on 21 October 2022).
Mejia, J. A., Chen, D. A., Dalrymple, O., & Lord, S. M. (2018, June 24–27). *Revealing the invisible: Conversations about–Isms and power relations in engineering courses* [2018 ASEE Annual Conference Proceedings]. 2018 ASEE Annual Conference, Salt Lake City, UT, USA. Available online: https://peer.asee.org/revealing-the-invisible-conversations-about-isms-and-power-relations-in-engineering-courses (accessed on 22 July 2021).
Momo, B., Hoople, G. D., Chen, D. A., Mejia, J. A., & Lord, S. M. (2020). Broadening the engineering canon: How culturally responsive pedagogies can help educate the engineers of the future. *Murmurations*, *2*, 6–21. [CrossRef]
Moseley, S. (2017, June 24). *One paragraph and a few simple questions—Giving statics problems human context*. 2017 ASEE Annual Conference & Exposition, Columbus, OH, USA. Available online: https://peer.asee.org/28719 (accessed on 27 September 2022).
Riley, D. (2008). Engineering and social justice. *Synthesis Lectures on Engineers, Technology, and Society*, *3*(1), 1–152.
Think Dignity. (n.d.). *Who we are*. Available online: https://thinkdignity.org/about/ (accessed on 9 May 2025).
Watanabe, M. (2019). *"Don't look away": Addressing homelessness in San Diego county* [Invited Talk]. University of San Diego.

education sciences

MDPI

Article

The Impact of Integrated Project-Based Learning and Flipped Classroom on Students' Computational Thinking Skills: Embedded Mixed Methods

Muh Fitrah [1,2], Anastasia Sofroniou [3,*], Caly Setiawan [1], Widihastuti Widihastuti [1], Novi Yarmanetti [4], Melinda Puspita Sari Jaya [1], Jontas Gayuh Panuntun [5], Arfaton Arfaton [6], Septrisno Beteno [4] and Ika Susianti [4]

1 Graduate School, Universitas Negeri Yogyakarta, Yogyakarta 55281, Indonesia; muhfitrah.2023@student.uny.ac.id (M.F.); csetiawan@uny.ac.id (C.S.)
2 Department of Civil Engineering, Universitas Muhammadiyah Bima, Bima 84111, Indonesia
3 School of Computing and Engineering, University of West London, London W5 5RF, UK
4 Department of Primary Education, Faculty of Education and Psychology, Universitas Negeri Yogyakarta, Yogyakarta 55281, Indonesia; septrisno0299fipp.2023@student.uny.ac.id (S.B.)
5 Educational Management, Universitas Negeri Yogyakarta, Yogyakarta 55281, Indonesia
6 Faculty of Social Sciences, Law, and Political Science, Universitas Negeri Yogyakarta, Yogyakarta 55281, Indonesia; arfaton.2023@student.uny.ac.id
* Correspondence: anastasia.sofroniou@uwl.ac.uk

Abstract: Computational thinking skills among high school students have become a global concern, especially in the context of the ever-evolving digital education era. However, the attention given by teachers to this skill during mathematics instruction has not been a priority. This study aims to evaluate and explore the impact of project-based learning (PBL) integrated with flipped classroom on high school students' computational thinking skills in mathematics. The research design employed a mixed-method approach with a quasi-experimental, nonequivalent pre-test post-test control group design. The experimental group (46 students) and control group (45 students) were selected through simple random sampling from 12th-grade science students. Data were collected through tests, questionnaires, and in-depth interviews, using instruments such as computational thinking skills assessment questions, questionnaires, and interview protocols. Quantitative data analysis was performed using SPSS Version 26 for *t*-tests and ANOVA, while qualitative analysis was conducted using ATLAS.ti with an abductive-inductive and thematic approach. The findings indicate that PBL integrated with flipped classrooms significantly improved students' decomposition, pattern recognition, and abstraction skills. The implementation of PBL, integrated with a flipped classroom, created an interactive learning environment, fostering active engagement and enhancing students' understanding and skills in solving mathematical concepts. Although there was an improvement in algorithmic thinking skills, some students still faced difficulties in developing systematic solutions. The results of this study suggest that further research could explore other methodologies, such as grounded theory and case studies integrated with e-learning, and emphasize visual analysis methods, such as using photo elicitation to explore thinking skills.

Keywords: project-based learning; flipped classroom; computational thinking skills; mathematics learning; learning technology

1. Introduction

The 21st century education demands learners to develop higher-order thinking skills essential for adapting to an increasingly complex and dynamic world. Transformations in education now require more innovative pedagogical approaches that not only facilitate knowledge transfer but also promote the development of thinking skills such as computational thinking. Amid the evolving teaching practices, the project-based learning (PBL) model has emerged as an effective approach that can be further optimized when integrated with the flipped classroom concept. This combination encourages not only active and collaborative learning but also provides students with opportunities to cultivate 21st-century skills (Dong et al., 2024).

Previous studies have provided empirical evidence on the effectiveness of PBL and flipped classrooms in education. For instance, research by Li and Tu (2024) demonstrated that integrated PBL significantly enhances students' creative thinking skills, engagement, and collaboration (AlAli, 2024; Maros et al., 2021; Rehman et al., 2024). In mathematics education, PBL creates a more positive learning environment and improves student outcomes (Holmes & Hwang, 2016; Rehman et al., 2024). This effectiveness stems from maximizing students' roles, such as collaborating, coordinating, communicating, leading, practicing, and exerting effort in integrated design project activities (Çakiroğlu & Erdemir, 2018).

Through direct and in-depth investigations and authentic interviews conducted over a semester (six months) with teachers in schools, we observed that traditional teacher-centered methods frequently fail to equip students with the skills required by advancements in science and technology, such as computational thinking skills. Traditional teaching often focuses excessively on rote memorization and rigid, procedural problem-solving approaches, which do not encourage students to develop critical and innovative thinking. Furthermore, the utilization of technology as a learning tool is underwhelming, and many teachers we observed lacked proficiency in using technology. Consequently, the presence of technology in schools often serves as a facade rather than a reality in mathematics education. This complexity underscores the need for more in-depth research. Findings from Charbonneau-Gowdy et al. (2023) revealed that, in the past two years (2021–2022), computational thinking skills, active learning, and the use of technology are closely interconnected. The meta-analysis by Alonso-García et al. (2024) indicates that the development of educational practices emphasizing technology is predominantly observed in Asia, yet it does not specifically include Indonesia. This finding highlights the importance of further research on computational thinking skills in Indonesia, particularly by integrating technology-based learning models. Such research has the potential to significantly contribute to a more critical transformation of education in addressing complex problem-solving challenges (Alonso-García et al., 2024).

Despite these field observations, we also reviewed challenges identified by previous researchers underpinning PBL studies. For instance, Rijken and Fraser (2023) highlighted a decline in student engagement in mathematics learning during the transition from primary to secondary school, often due to less favorable classroom environments and curriculum changes. This decline in engagement adversely affects students' performance in mathematics exams (Craig & Marshall, 2019). Moreover, students tend to be passive, struggle with independent learning, and perceive mathematics as difficult, boring, or uninteresting (Remijan, 2017).

In light of these issues, the integration of PBL with flipped classrooms emerges as one of the most promising approaches in the era of technology. This integration enables students to engage in independent learning outside the classroom and subsequently apply and discuss their understanding in more dynamic and interactive face-to-face sessions. This aligns with the ideas presented by Charbonneau-Gowdy et al. (2023), who emphasized flipped classrooms as an innovative teaching method involving new explorations. Furthermore, Egara and Mosimege's (2023) research illustrated that this approach improves students' achievement, interest, and attitudes in mathematics learning (Tekin &

Sarıkaya, 2020), fostering interactive and active environments for both individual and group learning. Additionally, Gondal et al. (2024) reported significant improvements in students' average scores and high satisfaction levels with flipped classrooms (Deng et al., 2023; Egara & Mosimege, 2023). Specifically, flipped classroom designs with instructional videos effectively enhance knowledge retention (Shen, 2024).

Flipped learning, when combined with active methodologies such as project-based learning, significantly improves students' critical thinking, creativity, and collaboration skills, particularly in secondary education (Bolivar et al., 2023; Hossein-Mohand et al., 2021; Mohamed et al., 2019). According to the framework designed by Cubric and Tripathi (2009), the collaboration of these two methods fosters personalized and collaborative online learning spaces. Research by Zarouk et al. (2020) supported this, showing that PBL implementation within flipped classrooms enhances students' motivation, strategic planning, and self-monitoring skills, especially when students actively engage with peers (Dinh & Phuong, 2025; Liu et al., 2024; Pokhrel et al., 2024). However, a critical gap remains in both the literature and our investigations: the combination of PBL and flipped classrooms in developing computational thinking skills has not been extensively explored. Computational thinking involves a set of skills, including problem decomposition, pattern recognition, abstraction, and algorithm design, which are foundational for effective problem-solving across disciplines. Through project-based learning, students have opportunities to tackle complex problems, decompose them into manageable components, design efficient solutions, and test hypotheses.

This study aims to explore the impact of PBL integrated with flipped classroom on the development of computational thinking skills among senior high school students studying geometric transformations in Grade 12. We believe that this study will provide significant contributions to the mathematics education literature by offering empirical evidence that strengthens the argument that this approach not only enhances computational thinking skills but also prepares students for future challenges aligned with technological advancements in the workplace. By integrating PBL and flipped classrooms, we aim to reinforce and recommend the implementation of a learning model that promotes active and independent learning, fosters computational thinking abilities, and enhances students' skill sets. This research is crucial not only in the local context but also has global implications for developing education that is more responsive to contemporary needs.

Based on the theoretical issues and direct observations, this research seeks to answer the following questions: Is there a difference in computational thinking skills between students taught using PBL integrated with a flipped classroom and those taught using PBL alone? How does the integrated PBL and flipped classroom process influence students' computational thinking skills? From these research questions, the hypotheses are as follows:

H_1: *There is a difference in decomposition skills between students taught using PBL integrated with flipped classroom and those taught using PBL.*

H_2: *There is a difference in pattern recognition skills between students taught using PBL integrated with flipped classroom and those taught using PBL.*

H_3: *There is a difference in abstraction skills between students taught using PBL integrated with flipped classroom and those taught using PBL.*

H_4: *There is a difference in algorithmic thinking skills between students taught using PBL integrated with flipped classroom and those taught using PBL.*

2. Literature Review

2.1. Project-Based Learning in Mathematics Instruction

Project-Based Learning (PBL), as a student-centered approach, plays a significant role in enhancing 21st-century skills such as computational thinking and problem-solving within mathematics education. PBL emphasizes that meaningful learning occurs when students actively construct their knowledge through experience and interaction. Students are encouraged to connect abstract concepts with real-world situations through challenging and relevant projects (Nayak et al., 2024; Singha & Singha, 2024). PBL promotes the completion of projects that require data analysis, solution creation, and presentations, fostering active engagement and providing a learning experience that significantly differs from conventional teaching methods (Holmes & Hwang, 2016).

Since its introduction, the concept of PBL has evolved alongside the integration of technology in education. Meyer et al. (1997) emphasized that PBL engages students in solving real-world problems that require them to apply mathematical knowledge in meaningful contexts. Kim and Lee (2002) highlighted that technology not only serves as a tool but also as a pivotal element that deepens the reflection process in PBL, enhancing students' learning experiences. Moreover, Gibson et al. (2002) argued that technology, particularly ICT, plays a crucial role in supporting the learning process in PBL, allowing students to utilize software and the internet for research and collaboration. However, the implementation of PBL in mathematics instruction faces significant challenges. Rijken and Fraser (2023) highlight the necessity for strong facilitation skills from teachers to accommodate long-term projects. Furthermore, constraints such as limited resources and lack of teacher training are significant concerns (My Nguyen et al., 2024). Nevertheless, PBL integrates collaboration and knowledge sharing through online learning communities, creating an enriched learning ecosystem (Kramer et al., 2007). Moss (2000) further emphasized that technology-supported PBL creates a dynamic and interactive learning environment, which not only enhances academic content skills but also prepares students to face real-world challenges by using digital tools effectively.

The concept of PBL has been widely applied across countries, with an emphasis on using technology to support more authentic and relevant learning. Erstad (2002) noted that in Norway, PBL combined with technology enables students to develop collaborative skills, critical thinking, and the ability to integrate knowledge from various sources. Blumenfeld et al. (1991) and Krajcik et al. (1994) also argued that PBL is not just about completing projects but also about supporting the learning process through active engagement and providing the necessary support to ensure its successful implementation in classrooms. Specifically, the use of digital technology in PBL further expands access and facilitates inclusive learning. Ndiung and Menggo (2024) underline PBL's potential in creating contextual and relevant learning environments, though it requires further enhancement.

2.2. Flipped Classroom with Active Learning

The flipped classroom is an instructional method that transforms traditional teaching models by providing foundational content for students to study independently outside of class, using digital technologies such as videos or reading materials, before engaging in integrated activities like discussions and problem-solving in class. This model allows class time to be used more efficiently for deepening complex concepts and fostering collaborative learning, particularly in mathematics instruction (Isabel Santos & Serpa, 2020). Bergmann and Sams (2012) highlighted that flipped learning enhances student engagement by shifting direct instruction outside of class, allowing more opportunities for active learning and deeper interaction. Tucker (2012) further described this model as an approach where instructional content is accessed beforehand through digital resources, enabling students to maximize in-class time for collaboration and problem-solving. Research shows that this approach significantly increases student engagement, as students not only memorize formulas but also develop critical thinking skills and the ability to apply concepts in real-world contexts (Fernández-Martín et al., 2020).

The flipped classroom approach can also be adapted to support various active methodologies that integrate technology. Students learn material independently through videos, followed by critical exploration and interactive activities in class, which deepens conceptual understanding (Fredriksen et al., 2024). This approach does not always have to be complicated, as shown by Patterson et al. (2018), who found that minimal preparation, such as reading materials before class, is still effective. Kong (2014) emphasized that flipped learning fosters information literacy and critical thinking by integrating domain knowledge learning in digital classrooms, supporting students in active and inquiry-based learning. See and Conry (2014) also demonstrated how flipped classrooms enhance student engagement by utilizing digital content for pre-class preparation, freeing up class time for case studies and collaborative projects. Furthermore, integrating the flipped classroom with technology and scaffolding yields significant results. For example, the use of learning management systems facilitates independent learning and provides relevant formative feedback (Awi et al., 2024).

A flipped classroom model supported by social learning communities fosters deeper interaction, where collaboration and instant feedback accelerate the learning process (Wang, 2024). A meta-analysis by Gong et al. (2023) also demonstrates that this approach is significantly more effective than traditional methods in improving student academic performance, with activities that link home and classroom learning, such as quizzes and group discussions, reinforcing student learning outcomes. Clark (2015) further confirmed that the flipped classroom model positively impacts student engagement and academic performance, particularly in mathematics instruction. These findings reinforce that flipped classrooms not only support academic achievement but also enhance student autonomy and engagement in the learning process.

2.3. Computational Thinking Skills and Their Impact on Mathematics Instruction

Computational thinking skills are a set of cognitive abilities that are crucial in modern mathematics instruction, including problem decomposition, pattern recognition, abstraction, and algorithm design. Sung et al. (2017) explain that integrating these skills into mathematics instruction aims to break down complex problems into simpler components and design systematic algorithmic solutions. This approach, which also includes the use of embodied cognition methods, connects physical activity with abstract concepts, strengthening students' mathematical understanding and programming skills (Sung & Black, 2020). In practice, these skills equip students with explicit processes for thinking and acting like computer scientists, which are relevant for solving 21st-century problems. Weintrop et al. (2015) emphasize that these skills encompass data processing, modeling, and simulation, which train students to analyze information, make data-integrated decisions, and understand phenomena through simulation.

Meanwhile, the use of visual programming tools such as Scratch introduces students to algorithmic principles in an accessible and engaging way, encouraging collaborative and exploratory problem-solving in mathematics (Rodríguez-Martínez et al., 2019). Integrated technology approaches, such as computer-based math games, have also been shown to enhance students' computational thinking skills. Soboleva et al. (2021) explain that these games not only motivate students but also promote systematic and algorithmic thinking, which is essential in mathematics (del Olmo-Muñoz et al., 2023). Moreover, Durak and Saritepeci (2018) found that students' academic success in mathematics significantly influences their computational thinking skills, highlighting the importance of a cognitive approach to learning. Ersozlu et al. (2023) add that authentic and relevant learning experiences strengthen the application of these skills.

3. Methods

3.1. Research Design

This study employs a mixed-method embedded design (Creswell, 2014), with a quasi-experimental approach and qualitative descriptive methods. The aim is to explore the comprehensive implementation of PBL integrated with the flipped classroom approach by teachers in mathematics instruction. The rationale for choosing this research design is that the combination of quantitative and qualitative data provides a more critical emphasis compared to a single approach. Moreover, identifying the influence and testing are complex tasks. Quantitative data will serve as the basis for generalizing findings, while qualitative data will support these generalizations. Using the mixed-method embedded design, we analyze quantitative data first and support these findings with qualitative research results.

The quasi-experimental approach uses a nonequivalent pre-test post-test control group design. In this design, both the experimental and control groups are given a pre-test to measure their initial conditions before the treatment, followed by a post-test to measure the outcomes after the treatment. The experimental group receives instruction using the PBL model integrated with the flipped classroom, while the control group follows PBL.

3.2. Population and Sample

3.2.1. Quantitative

The population for this study consists of 171 twelfth-grade students in the Science Program at a senior high school, from six classes. The selection of this school was based on its accessibility and the limited technological resources supporting learning, such as a school internet quota of only 30 Mbps per school. Additionally, the learning environment was predominantly conventional, and the teacher's creativity in integrating other learning models was weak pedagogically. The sample for this study is 91 students (45 in the control group and 46 in the experimental group), selected using simple random sampling to give every class in the population an equal chance of being chosen. This technique was chosen to avoid selection bias and improve the external validity of the study.

3.2.2. Qualitative

For the qualitative phase, the researcher used theoretical sampling. Theoretical sampling involves selecting participants who can provide relevant information to develop or test the emerging theory. The sample was chosen based on student activity during the teaching and learning process and their final grades. A total of 6 female and 4 male students were selected based on their achievement of the minimum standard score ($\geq$75) and engagement. The qualitative sample is anonymized to protect student identities. See Table 1.

Table 1. Qualitative sample.

Initial	Gender	Age	Activity Level	Score
Creswel	Male	18 Years	Active	80.00
Albert	Male	18 Years	Active	80.00
Donald	Male	17 Years	Active	80.00
Joseph	Male	18 Years	Active	85.00
Charmaz	Female	18 Years	Active	85.00

Table 1. *Cont.*

Initial	Gender	Age	Activity Level	Score
Collins	Female	17 Years	Less Active	80.00
Cohen	Female	16 Years	Less Active	75.00
Donna	Female	18 Years	Less Active	80.00
Patricia	Female	16 Years	Active	85.00
Katy	Female	17 Years	Active	85.00

3.3. Techniques and Instruments for Data Collection

The data in this study were collected using three main instruments: tests (pre-test and post-test), questionnaires, and interviews. The pre-test and post-test were used to measure computational thinking skills in transformation geometry, focusing on four main dimensions: decomposition, pattern recognition, abstraction, and algorithmic thinking. The pre-test was administered before the intervention to assess students' initial understanding of the material to be taught, while the post-test was given after the intervention to evaluate improvements in students' thinking skills. The pre-test was conducted in the first session, and the PBL intervention integrated with the flipped classroom was carried out from the second session to the eighth session (seven weeks). The post-test was then administered in the eighth session, i.e., the eighth week. Therefore, the time span between the pre-test and post-test was eight weeks.

The test consisted of 15 questions in multiple-choice, short-answer, and problem-solving formats. These questions were designed with varying levels of difficulty to explicitly measure the four dimensions of computational thinking skills. Decomposition was assessed through students' ability to break down complex problems into smaller parts. Pattern recognition examined the process of students recognizing patterns or similarities in mathematical problems. Abstraction measured students' ability to filter out irrelevant information and focus on the details necessary for problem-solving. Meanwhile, algorithmic thinking assessed students' ability to design systematic solutions and logical steps to solve problems.

The development of test items was based on the Basic Competencies and Competency Achievement Indicators established in the Regulation of the Minister of Education and Culture of the Republic of Indonesia Number 37 of 2018 concerning Core Competencies and Basic Competencies of Subjects in the 2013 Curriculum for Primary and Secondary Education levels. Table 2 presents the test blueprint, which outlines the relationship between basic competencies, competency achievement indicators, test indicators, the level of computational thinking being measured, and the number of questions included in the test.

An example of a test question used to measure students' CT skills is provided below. This question represents various CT levels, including decomposition, pattern recognition, abstraction, and algorithmic thinking, as reflected in problem-solving processes, transformation pattern identification, filtering relevant information, and systematically structuring a solution.

Table 2. Computational thinking test.

Basic Competency	Competency Achievement Indicator	Test Indicator	CT Level	Number of Questions
Analyzing and comparing transformations and compositions of transformations using matrices	Identifying transformation matrices (reflection) at point $O(0,0)$	Given point $A(x,y)$, students determine the reflection transformation matrix at point O(0,0) and the shadow coordinates.	Decomposition	2 (1 multiple choice, 1 Essay)
	Identifying transformation matrices (reflection) on the x-axis	Given point $A(x,y)$, students determine the reflection matrix on the x-axis and explain the changes in coordinates.	Pattern Recognition	2 (1 multiple choice, 1 Essay)
	Identifying transformation matrices (reflection) on the y-axis	Given point $A(x,y)$, students determine the reflection matrix on the y-axis and identify the pattern differences compared to the reflection on the x-axis.	Pattern Recognition	3 (2 multiple choice, 1 Essay)
	Determining the shadow of a transformation composition (reflection) using matrices	Given a point and two consecutive reflection transformations, students determine the final shadow using the composition transformation matrix.	Abstraction	4 (2 multiple choice, 1 Short Answer, 1 Essay)
Solving problems related to geometric transformation matrices (translation, reflection, dilation, and rotation)	Solving problems involving transformation (reflection)	Students are given a real-world problem requiring the application of the reflection concept in problem-solving.	Algorithmic Thinking	4 (2 multiple choice, 1 Short Answer, 1 Essay)

Example Question:

A rectangular billiard table has four corner points: $A(5,6), B(-5,6),\ C(-5,0)$ and $D(5,0)$. A ball is located at point $E(-3,3)$ and is hit towards another ball positioned at point $F(3,3)$. However, before reaching the ball at point F, the ball must first bounce off side CD of the billiard table. Determine the coordinates of the reflection point of the ball on side CD before reaching point F.

Solution:

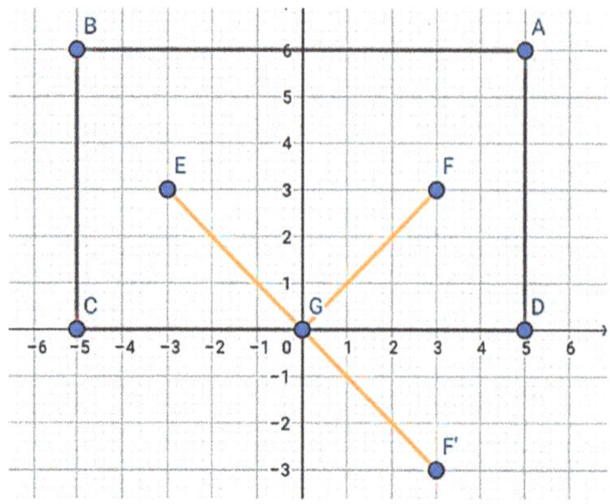

The billiard table is a rectangle ABCD, with the ball at $E(-3,3)$ and aimed at hitting ball $F(3,3)$ after bouncing on side CD. To determine the target point on CD, we first find the reflection of point $F(3,3)$ with respect to $CD(x - axis)$, which is $F'(3,-3)$. Next, we determine the intersection of the line connecting $E(-3,3)$ and $F'(3,-3)$ with the line $CD(y = 0)$. The equation of line EF' is $y = -x$. Substituting $y = 0$ gives $x = 0$, so the intersection point is $(0,0)$. Therefore, the target point where the ball will bounce off side CD before reaching $F(3,3)$ is $(0,0)$.

Student test scoring was aligned with the characteristics of each question type to ensure an effective measurement of computational thinking skills. The assessment included multiple-choice, short-answer, and essay questions, each with specific scoring criteria (see Table 3). The final scores were computed and normalized to a 0–100 scale.

Table 3. Scoring criteria for computational thinking assessment.

Question Type	CT Dimension Assessed	Scoring Criteria	Max Score
Multiple-Choice	All CT dimensions	1 = Correct. 0 = Incorrect.	1
Short-Answer	Abstraction, Algorithmic Thinking	3 = Correct and structured problem-solving steps. 2 = Minor inaccuracies in problem-solving steps. 1 = Most steps are incorrect. 0 = No problem-solving steps written.	3
Essay	All CT dimensions	90–100 = Deep analysis, logical solution, systematic approach. 70–89 = Mostly logical, minor errors in reasoning or structure. 50–69 = Partial understanding, significant logical or procedural errors. <50 = Lacks conceptual understanding, unsystematic response.	100

Additionally, the questionnaire was used to measure students' responses to the PBL method integrated with the flipped classroom and the development of their computational thinking skills. The questionnaire consisted of 15 statements developed based on computational thinking theory and previous research on assessing computational thinking in mathematics education and technology. The statements in the questionnaire were arranged in a Likert scale with five response levels, ranging from strongly disagree to strongly agree, to capture a deeper variation in students' understanding and experiences. Each item in the questionnaire directly represented one of the four dimensions of computational thinking being measured. The questionnaire was administered in Google Forms format and completed by students under the supervision of the teacher.

Furthermore, interviews were conducted to gain deeper insights into students' experiences during the learning process and the challenges they faced in computational learning. The interviews were conducted after the lessons, considering students' activities and the learning outcomes obtained. The interview process lasted between 45 and 82 min with a semi-structured approach. The duration was determined based on the accumulated time students spent responding to questions guided by their answers in the essay and short-answer sections. The interviews extended up to 82 min as, at this point, responses met the criteria, and response saturation was reached. The interview protocol consisted of three main themes: challenges in computational thinking, students' involvement in problem-solving strategies, and their reflections on the teaching methods used.

To ensure scoring reliability, both the researcher and the mathematics teacher independently evaluated student responses. Any discrepancies, particularly in essay and short-answer questions, were resolved through discussion and consensus.

The total score from essay questions was normalized to a 0–100 scale. Based on the final accumulated test scores, students were selected for qualitative interviews to ensure representation across different performance levels (see Table 1).

3.4. Validity and Reliability of the Instruments

To ensure the reliability and validity of the instruments, we conducted a comprehensive validity and reliability assessment prior to their use in data collection. The validity of the instruments was assessed through two main approaches: content validity and construct validity. Content validity was evaluated by analyzing the alignment of each test item, questionnaire statement, and interview protocol with the competencies outlined in the curriculum. Construct validity was established through an expert review process involving three experts in the fields of learning models, mathematics education, and educational technology, all of whom hold the academic rank of Senior Lecturer and have published scholarly works in the relevant fields. Additionally, the experts provided feedback on the clarity, difficulty level, and relevance of the items in relation to the four dimensions of CT. Based on evaluations by the three experts, the average Aiken's V value was 0.83, indicating a high level of validity. Reliability was tested using Cronbach's Alpha to ensure the internal consistency and dependability of the instruments. The results of the reliability test are presented in Table 4.

Table 4. Results of instrument validity and reliability tests.

Skill	Cronbach's Alpha
Decomposition	0.94
Pattern recognition	0.86
Abstraction	0.83
Algorithmic thinking	0.91

3.5. Data Analysis Techniques

Data analysis was carried out in several stages to ensure the validity and accuracy of the research results. First, a normality test using Kolmogorov–Smirnov was conducted to check if the data were normally distributed (see Table 5). For normally distributed data, parametric statistics such as *t*-tests and ANOVA were used. Second, a homogeneity test using Levene's test was conducted to ensure that the variance between groups was homogeneous, which is a prerequisite for further analysis.

Table 5. Results of normality tests.

Category	Control				Experiment			
	V1	V2	V3	V4	V1	V2	V3	V4
N	45				46			
Exact Sig. (2-tailed)	0.22	0.53	0.251	0.17	0.25	0.51	0.28	0.35

Based on the results of the normality test using the Exact Sig. (2-tailed) values, all variables in the control and experimental groups showed values greater than 0.05. Therefore, it can be concluded that the data are normally distributed. Thus, the assumption of normality is met, and we used parametric statistical approaches, such as *t*-tests and ANOVA, for further analysis to answer the research questions. All these analyses were conducted using SPSS version 26. In addition, qualitative data analysis in this study was conducted using ATLAS.ti version 24, employing thematic analysis with abductive (deductive) reasoning. The analysis using ATLAS.ti included 87 codes, 8 categories, and 2 themes with 210 quotations (see Figure 1).

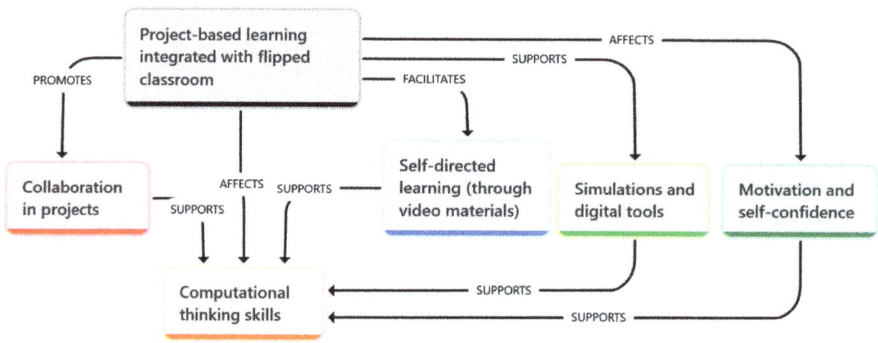

Figure 1. Contribution of integrated PBL and flipped classroom to students' computational thinking skills.

3.6. Hypothesis Testing

This study used two main statistical methods: *t*-test and ANOVA. The *t*-test was used to compare the means between the control and experimental groups. This test aimed to determine whether there was a significant difference in computational thinking skills between the two groups. If the *t*-test results showed a p-value < 0.05, the difference would be considered significant. ANOVA was used to examine the overall effect of the integrated PBL and flipped classroom method on students' computational thinking skills. With ANOVA, the researcher can determine whether the treatment had a significant overall effect. If the calculated F-value is greater than the F-table value, the null hypothesis (H0) is rejected, indicating that the integrated PBL and flipped classroom method has a significant effect. The *t*-test was used because this study compared two groups with one dependent variable, while ANOVA was necessary to test the effects of multiple factors simultaneously.

3.7. Ethics in Mixed Methods Research

Ethics in mixed methods research is crucial due to the complexity involved, which may present potential ethical issues (Stadnick et al., 2021). In this study, we are committed to adhering to ethical principles throughout each phase of the research, as outlined by Saheb and Saheb (2024), who emphasize the importance of respecting participants' rights and privacy while ensuring the reliability and validity of the data. Before the research commenced, we obtained informed consent from students, teachers, and the school principal through signed consent forms. These forms included detailed information about the purpose of the study, the methods used, potential risks, and participants' rights, including their right to withdraw at any time without any consequences. To ensure data confidentiality, participants' identities were protected using initials (see Table 1), and no personally identifiable information was recorded or disclosed. Additionally, regular discussions among researchers were conducted to ensure that data collection and analysis remained objective, minimizing potential biases that could influence the research outcomes. This approach aims to ensure transparency and uphold ethical standards in research.

4. Results

This study evaluates the impact of integrated PBL and flipped classroom on computational thinking skills (decomposition, pattern recognition, abstraction, algorithmic thinking) among high school students. Descriptive statistics obtained show a significant difference between the performance of the control and experimental classes in all four aspects of computational skills, as presented in Table 6.

Table 6. Descriptive statistics of computational thinking skills.

Skill	Class	N	Mean	Standard Deviation
Decomposition	Control	45	49.64	8.49
	Experiment	46	60.01	9.91
Pattern recognition	Control	45	36.22	6.17
	Experiment	46	40.74	6.52
Abstraction	Control	45	30.51	5.87
	Experiment	46	35.78	5.95
Algorithmic thinking	Control	45	34.30	6.44
	Experiment	46	38.78	5.66

This table shows that the average decomposition skill score for the control class is 49.64 with a standard deviation of 8.49, while the experimental class shows an improvement with an average score of 60.01 and a standard deviation of 9.91. Interview results support this finding, with many respondents explaining how the projects helped them break down complex problems into smaller, manageable parts. Albert mentioned, "The projects in class helped me see how the theory we learned applies to real-life situations". Patricia added, "in the transformation geometry project, I had to break a big problem into smaller, more manageable steps".

For pattern recognition skills, the control class recorded an average of 36.22 with a standard deviation of 6.17, while the experimental class had an average of 40.74 with a standard deviation of 6.52, indicating the effectiveness of this learning method in helping students better recognize patterns. Interview results support this finding, with Albert explaining, "I now understand how certain patterns in geometry transformations can be applied to other problems". Patricia added, "When I break down geometry problems, I can see patterns in the shape changes and how the steps relate to each other".

Next, the average score for abstraction skills in the control class is 30.51 with a standard deviation of 5.87, while the experimental class shows an improvement with an average of 35.78 and a standard deviation of 5.95. Interviews indicate that students were more capable of filtering out important information and focusing on the key aspects of the problems. Collins said, "With the flipped classroom method, I can learn to filter important information before the project starts, so I can focus on relevant parts". Patricia stated, "The group projects taught me to focus on the essential elements of the problem and ignore irrelevant details".

Finally, for algorithmic thinking skills, the control class had an average of 34.30 with a standard deviation of 6.44, while the experimental class showed a higher average of 38.78 with a standard deviation of 5.66. The flipped classroom process helped prepare students to think more systematically when solving problems. Albert revealed, "the flipped classroom helped me create systematic steps to solve math problems". Donna added, "When I had to create a simple algorithm for the project, I learned to organize the solution steps more neatly".

Integrated PBL and flipped classrooms proved to be effective in improving computational thinking skills (decomposition, pattern recognition, abstraction, algorithmic thinking) in students. PBL integrated with a flipped classroom helps develop computational thinking skills through structured, interactive, and PBL experiences. The combination of online videos, class discussions, and project activities enables students to directly practice concepts, effectively improving decomposition, pattern recognition, abstraction, and algorithmic thinking skills. To test the research hypothesis comprehensively, statistical analysis involved normality tests (Table 7), homogeneity tests, F-tests, and *t*-tests.

Table 7. Results of homogeneity test.

Skill	Levene Statistic	Significance
Decomposition	0.31	0.59
Pattern recognition	0.08	0.79
Abstraction	1.30	0.26
Algorithmic thinking	2.60	0.12

Levene's test showed that all variables had homogeneous variances ($p > 0.05$). The homogeneity of variance between the control and experimental groups ensures that the comparison of results can be made fairly, without distortion from differences in data distribution. This uniformity provides confidence in the results of the *t*-test and F-test, as shown in Table 8, which are used to measure the impact of the treatment, namely the integrated PBL and flipped classroom method, more accurately and convincingly.

Table 8. Results of F-test.

Model	Sum of Squares	Mean Square	F	Significance
Regression	2184.437	546.109	10.88	0.000
Residual	1053.425	50.163		
Total	3237.862			

The calculated F value of 10.88 with $p = 0.000$ indicates a highly significant difference between the control and experimental groups. This result shows that integrated PBL and flipped classrooms make a significant contribution to influencing students' computational thinking skills. Based on interviews with 10 students, integrated PBL and flipped classrooms facilitate self-directed learning, supported by video materials, which help students prepare better before collaborating on the transformation geometry project. A student expressed, "Patricia mentioned, 'I feel more prepared with the material before the class meeting because I already have an idea of what will be discussed. However, I sometimes need more explanation about some parts of the material I don't understand from the video.'" and "The videos provided are clear and to the point, but sometimes some materials are too long, requiring more time to understand them" (Creswell's expression).

The projects not only enhance computational thinking skills but also utilize simulations and digital tools to deepen the understanding of more complex concepts. Additionally, motivation and self-confidence play crucial roles in motivating students to feel more confident in solving complex problems, which impacts their computational thinking skills. One student shared, "I feel more confident, Sir. I can now more easily analyze and solve complex problems, especially in math and geometry, where I need to think critically and analytically" (Katy's expression). "Alhamdulillah (an expression of gratitude in Arabic), I am confident, Sir, because this method trains me to always think before acting. I've become more skilled at analyzing problems" (Albert's expression).

The figure illustrates how the integration of PBL with the flipped classroom contributes to the development of students' computational thinking skills. This approach not only fosters collaboration in projects but also facilitates self-directed learning through video materials, enabling students to grasp concepts before face-to-face sessions. Additionally, self-directed learning is reinforced by simulations and digital tools, which assist students in deepening their conceptual understanding and enhancing their problem-solving skills systematically. Beyond improving conceptual understanding, this approach also plays a crucial role in cultivating students' motivation and self-confidence. Active engagement in problem-based projects allows students to feel more prepared and confident in analyzing and solving complex challenges. Thus, the integration of PBL and the flipped classroom not only supports computational thinking skills but also fosters a more independent, interactive, and technology-driven learning environment.

Table 9 presents the results of the *t*-test for the regression model, which evaluates the contribution of each independent variable decomposition, pattern recognition, abstraction, and algorithmic thinking toward the dependent variable. The constant coefficient of 55.92 with a t-value of 5.50 and significance of 0.000 shows that when all independent variables are zero, the dependent variable still holds a significant value. This p-value < 0.05 confirms that the constant in the model has a relevant contribution.

Table 9. Results of *t*-test.

Model	Unstandardized Coefficients	Standardized Coefficients	t	Significance
(Constant)	55.92		5.50	0.000
Decomposition	1.92	1.67	5.58	0.000
Pattern recognition	−1.99	−1.16	−3.76	0.001
Abstraction	1.03	0.54	2.15	0.044
Algorithmic thinking	−1.45	−0.72	−3.59	0.002

The decomposition variable has an unstandardized coefficient of 1.92 and a standardized coefficient of 1.67, with a t-value of 5.58 and significance of 0.000, indicating that decomposition has a strong and significant positive effect on the dependent variable. Each unit increase in decomposition will increase the dependent variable by 1.92 units. In contrast, pattern recognition has an unstandardized coefficient of −1.99 and a standardized coefficient of −1.16, with a t-value of −3.76 and significance of 0.001. This result indicates that pattern recognition has a significant negative effect, reducing the dependent variable by 1.99 units for every one-unit increase in this variable.

Meanwhile, abstraction has an unstandardized coefficient of 1.03 and a standardized coefficient of 0.54, with a t-value of 2.15 and significance of 0.044, indicating a positive and significant contribution, although the level of significance is lower than the other variables. Each unit increase in abstraction will increase the dependent variable by 1.03 units. Finally, algorithmic thinking has an unstandardized coefficient of −1.45 and a standardized coefficient of −0.72, with a t-value of −3.59 and significance of 0.002, which indicates a significant negative effect on the dependent variable. Each unit increase in algorithmic thinking will decrease the dependent variable by 1.45 units.

5. Discussion

The results of this study indicate that the implementation of project-based learning (PBL) integrated with flipped classrooms significantly impacts the enhancement of students' computational thinking skills. This method has proven effective in facilitating active student engagement, enriching the learning process, and deepening the understanding of complex concepts. Specifically, this study tested four hypotheses related to computational thinking skills: decomposition, pattern recognition, abstraction, and algorithmic thinking. The findings confirmed that the experimental group outperformed the control group in all four dimensions, highlighting the efficacy of the integrated flipped PBL classroom approach in fostering computational thinking development.

The most striking improvement was observed in decomposition skills. The significantly higher average scores of students in the experimental group compared to the control group underscore the effectiveness of integrated PBL with flipped classroom in helping students break down complex problems into simpler components. Shin et al. (2021) support this finding, as PBL provides a complex structure for students to focus on key elements of a problem. This approach encourages students to analyze and understand each component in an organized manner, thereby improving their ability to solve computational problems more efficiently. Additionally, Buitrago-Florez et al. (2019) emphasized that the integrated project strategy strengthens students' analytical skills, facilitating in-depth understanding and application of concepts in various situations. These results suggest that integrating project-based approaches with flipped learning not only enhances computational thinking but also fosters critical problem-solving abilities applicable across different disciplines.

Pattern recognition skills also showed significant improvement. The integration of PBL and flipped classroom created a learning environment that nurtures students' ability to recognize patterns in data and identify relevant patterns. This aligns with the findings of Yasin and Nusantara (2023), who identified pattern recognition as a key aspect in the development of computational thinking. Abdullah et al. (2019) further emphasized that the use of integrated gaming technology accelerates the pattern recognition process, making students more responsive and accurate in identifying patterns. Chan et al. (2021) also support this finding, as computational thinking activities integrated with digital tools deepen students' understanding of patterns and mathematical relationships, enhancing the positive impact of integrated PBL and flipped classrooms (Saad & Zainudin, 2024; Xing & Zeng, 2024). In a broader context, these findings indicate that incorporating structured pattern recognition activities into computational learning can lead to better problem-solving capabilities in real-world applications, such as data analysis and artificial intelligence development.

In the area of abstraction, students taught with integrated PBL and flipped classrooms demonstrated a better ability to simplify information and focus on essential elements. This result is in line with the findings of Nurbekova et al. (2020), who emphasized that visualization technology helps students manage and simplify complex information by disregarding irrelevant details. The integrated project approach encourages students to effectively practice abstraction through active performing activities, which enhances their ability to devise efficient and relevant solutions. This finding is also supported by Indriati et al. (2024), who found that authentic tasks in PBL strengthen critical thinking skills, prompting students to separate essential information from secondary data (Zhang et al., 2024). Given that abstraction is a crucial skill in computational problem-solving, the observed improvements suggest that educators should integrate more visualization tools and real-world problem scenarios to strengthen students' ability to generalize and apply knowledge beyond the classroom.

However, algorithmic thinking, while showing improvement, still presents challenges. Some students struggled with constructing systematic algorithmic solutions, indicating the need for additional strategies. Ergin and Arıkan (2023) demonstrated that while PBL enhances algorithmic skills, students often require additional scaffolding before mastering text-based programming. This aligns with Voon et al. (2022), who stated that the use of constructivist argumentation can assist students in designing more effective algorithms through discussion and reflection. These findings imply that while PBL and flipped classroom methods are beneficial, additional instructional support such as guided practice in algorithm design and step-by-step debugging exercises is necessary to optimize students' algorithmic thinking skills.

This research underscores that integrated PBL with a flipped classroom is an effective approach in computational education, where students develop essential skills to tackle real-world challenges. Wang (2024) highlighted that computational thinking is key to innovation in various fields, and this study demonstrates that integrated PBL with a flipped classroom can successfully integrate these skills into the curriculum in a productive manner. A meta-analysis by Zhang et al. (2024) further reinforces this finding, stating that PBL significantly enhances students' creativity, collaboration, and critical thinking. Online PBL has been proven to increase students' metacognitive awareness (Kalemkuş & Bulut-Özek, 2022; Shekh-Abed, 2024; Tu et al., 2025). From a practical standpoint, these results suggest that implementing a structured and well-supported flipped PBL classroom model can be beneficial not only for computational education but also for broader STEM-based learning environments. Future research should explore the long-term impact of this approach on students' ability to transfer computational thinking skills to real-world technological and professional settings.

6. Conclusions

This study demonstrates that the implementation of project-based learning (PBL) integrated with a flipped classroom significantly enhances students' computational thinking skills. The findings confirm that students in the experimental group outperformed those in the control group across all four dimensions: decomposition, pattern recognition, abstraction, and algorithmic thinking. Specifically, students using this approach were able to break down complex problems into simpler parts (decomposition), recognize patterns more effectively (pattern recognition), and simplify information by focusing on key elements (abstraction). These improvements highlight the effectiveness of integrated PBL in fostering problem-solving skills and optimizing class time for deeper conceptual engagement.

While improvements were also observed in algorithmic thinking, challenges remain. Some students experienced difficulty in constructing systematic and efficient algorithmic solutions, indicating the need for additional scaffolding and structured guidance. This suggests that supplementary instructional strategies, such as guided coding exercises or adaptive learning tools, may be necessary to reinforce algorithmic reasoning.

The results of this study provide valuable insights for educators, curriculum developers, and policymakers. The integration of PBL with flipped classrooms can serve as an effective pedagogical model to promote computational thinking in mathematics and computer science education. Schools and institutions should consider adopting structured PBL frameworks with digital resources to maximize student engagement and learning outcomes. Additionally, teacher training programs should incorporate strategies for implementing flipped PBL effectively, particularly in subjects requiring higher-order cognitive skills.

This study has some limitations, namely that the sample was limited to a single school, which restricts the generalization of the results. Differences in cultural contexts, classroom environments, and technological accessibility may influence the effectiveness of this method. Additionally, the quasi-experimental design used has limitations in controlling external variables that may impact the results.

Future research should explore larger-scale studies across multiple schools to assess the scalability and adaptability of the integrated PBL approach. Longitudinal studies are also needed to examine the long-term effects of computational thinking development. Furthermore, qualitative research using grounded theory could provide deeper insights into students' conceptual understanding of transformational geometry. Additionally, integrating adaptive learning technologies could support students struggling with algorithmic thinking, making the learning process more personalized and effective. These findings underscore the transformative potential of PBL and flipped classrooms in preparing students for computational problem-solving in the digital era.

Author Contributions: Conceptualization, M.F. and A.S.; Methodology, M.F., C.S., W.W., N.Y., M.P.S.J. and S.B.; Software, M.F. and S.B.; Validation, A.S. and C.S.; Formal analysis, M.F., W.W. and I.S.; Investigation, N.Y., M.P.S.J., J.G.P., A.A. and I.S.; Resources, N.Y., M.P.S.J., J.G.P., A.A. and I.S.; Data curation, N.Y., J.G.P. and A.A.; Writing—original draft, M.F.; Writing—review & editing, M.F. and A.S.; Visualization, M.F. and S.B.; Supervision, A.S., C.S. and W.W.; Project administration, N.Y., M.P.S.J., J.G.P., A.A. and I.S. All authors have read and agreed to the published version of the manuscript.

Funding: This research was funded by BPPT Kemendikbudristek and LPDP (grant number 01627/BPPT/BPI.06/9/2023).

Institutional Review Board Statement: The study was conducted in accordance with the Declaration of Helsinki, and approved by the Dean of the Faculty of Social Sciences, Universitas Negeri Yogyakarta (protocol code B/1711/UN34.14/PT.01.04/2024; date of approval: 30 April 2024).

Informed Consent Statement: Informed consent was obtained from all subjects involved in the study.

Data Availability Statement: The research data can be accessed upon request and with approval from the research team. For inquiries regarding the data, please contact the principal investigator, Muh. Fitrah, via email at muhfitrah.2023@student.uny.ac.id or through LinkedIn at Muh. Fitrah.

Conflicts of Interest: The authors declare no conflict of interest.

References

Abdullah, A. H., Othman, M. A., Ismail, N., Rahman, S. N. S. A., Mokhtar, M., & Zaid, N. M. (2019, December 10–13). *Development of mobile application for the concept of pattern recognition in computational thinking for mathematics subject*. TALE 2019—2019 IEEE International Conference on Engineering, Technology and Education, Yogyakarta, Indonesia. [CrossRef]

AlAli, R. (2024). Enhancing 21st century skills through integrated STEM education using project-oriented problem-based learning. *Geo Journal of Tourism and Geosites, 53*(2), 421–430. [CrossRef]

Alonso-García, S., Fuentes, A.-V. R., Navas-Parejo, M. R., & Victoria-Maldonado, J.-J. (2024). Enhancing computational thinking in early childhood education with educational robotics: A meta-analysis. *Heliyon, 10*(13), e33249. [CrossRef] [PubMed]

Awi, A., Naufal, M. A., Sutamrin, S., & Huda, M. (2024). Enhancing geometry achievement in pre-service mathematics teachers: The Impact of a scaffolded flipped classroom using a learning management system. *Journal of Ecohumanism, 3*(6), 637–645. [CrossRef]

Bergmann, J., & Sams, A. (2012). Before you flip, consider this. *Phi Delta Kappan, 94*(2), 25. [CrossRef]

Blumenfeld, P. C., Soloway, E., Marx, R. W., Krajcik, J. S., Guzdial, M., & Palincsar, A. (1991). Motivating project-based learning: Sustaining the doing, supporting the learning. *Educational Psychologist, 26*(3–4), 369–398. [CrossRef]

Bolivar, R., Triviño Jaimes, N. R., & Gonzalez, E. A. (2023). Implementation and benefits of hybrid methodology: Flipped classroom and project-based learning in mechanical engineering courses. *International Journal of Mechanical Engineering Education, 53*(1), 102–124. [CrossRef]

Buitrago-Florez, F., Danies, G., Restrepo, S., & Hernandez, C. (2019). Boosting 21st century competences through computational thinking and student centered strategies. In R. M. Lima, V. Villas-Boas, L. Bettaieb, & K. Akrout (Eds.), *International symposium on project approaches in engineering education* (Vol. 9, pp. 48–55). University of Minho. Available online: https://www.scopus.com/inward/record.uri?eid=2-s2.0-85074940602&partnerID=40&md5=a4b4579100d67026f1f9a85e993fc03b (accessed on 14 September 2024).

Çakiroğlu, Ü., & Erdemir, T. (2018). Online project based learning via cloud computing: Exploring roles of instructor and students. *Interactive Learning Environments, 27*(4), 547–566. [CrossRef]

Chan, S.-W., Looi, C.-K., Ho, W. K., Huang, W., Seow, P., & Wu, L. (2021). Learning number patterns through computational thinking activities: A Rasch model analysis. *Heliyon, 7*(9), e07922. [CrossRef]

Charbonneau-Gowdy, P., Cubric, M., Pechenkina, K., Dyer, R., Pyper, A., Söbke, H., & Spangenberger, P. (2023). EJEL editorial 2023: Trends and research gaps in e-learning. *Electronic Journal of E-Learning, 21*(3), 248–257. Available online: http://www.ejel.org/ (accessed on 15 September 2024).

Clark, K. R. (2015). The effects of the flipped model of instruction on student engagement and performance in the secondary mathematics classroom. *Journal of Educators Online, 12*(1), 91–115. Available online: https://files.eric.ed.gov/fulltext/EJ1051042.pdf (accessed on 7 March 2025).

Craig, T. T., & Marshall, J. (2019). Effect of project-based learning on high school students' state-mandated, standardized math and science exam performance. *Journal of Research in Science Teaching, 56*(10), 1461–1488. [CrossRef]

Creswell, J. W. (2014). *Research design: Qualitative, quantitative, and mixed methods aapproaches*. Sage Publications, Inc.

Cubric, M., & Tripathi, V. (2009). A semantic web framework for generating collaborative e-learning environments. *International Journal of Emerging Technologies in Learning, 4*(3), 4–7. [CrossRef]

del Olmo-Muñoz, J., Bueno-Baquero, A., Cózar-Gutiérrez, R., & González-Calero, J. A. (2023). Exploring gamification approaches for enhancing computational thinking in young learners. *Education Sciences, 13*(5), 487. [CrossRef]

Deng, R., Feng, S., & Shen, S. (2023). Improving the effectiveness of video-based flipped classrooms with question-embedding. *Education and Information Technologies, 29*(10), 12677–12702. [CrossRef]

Dinh, C. T., & Phuong, H. (2025). Teaching self-regulated learning strategies on efl students in moocs: A case study in Vietnam. *Turkish Online Journal of Distance Education, 26*(1), 101–121. [CrossRef]

Dong, X., Zhang, X., & Li, X. (2024, July 29–August 1). *Project-based flipped classroom model focusing on outcome communication and evaluation*. 2024 International Symposium on Educational Technology (ISET) (pp. 305–309), Macau, Macao. [CrossRef]

Durak, H. Y., & Saritepeci, M. (2018). Analysis of the relation between computational thinking skills and various variables with the structural equation model. *Computers & Education, 116*, 191–202. [CrossRef]

Egara, F. O., & Mosimege, M. (2023). Effect of flipped classroom learning approach on mathematics achievement and interest among secondary school students. *Education and Information Technologies, 29*(7), 8131–8150. [CrossRef]

Ergin, H., & Arıkan, Y. D. (2023). The effect of project based learning approach on computational thinking skills and programming self-efficacy beliefs. *AJIT-e: Academic Journal of Information Technology, 14*(55), 320–334. [CrossRef]

Ersozlu, Z., Swartz, M., & Skourdoumbis, A. (2023). Developing computational thinking through mathematics: An evaluative scientific mapping. *Education Sciences, 13*(4), 422. [CrossRef]

Erstad, O. (2002). Norwegian students using digital artifacts in project-based learning. *Journal of Computer Assisted Learning, 18*(4), 427–437. [CrossRef]

Fernández-Martín, F.-D., Romero-Rodríguez, J.-M., Gómez-García, G., & Ramos Navas-Parejo, M. (2020). Impact of the flipped classroom method in the mathematical area: A systematic review. *Mathematics, 8*(12), 2162. [CrossRef]

Fredriksen, H., Rebenda, J., Rensaa, R. J., & Pettersen, P. (2024). Inquiry-based linear algebra teaching and learning in a flipped classroom framework: A case study. *PRIMUS*, 1–21. [CrossRef]

Gibson, I. S., O'Reilly, C., & Hughes, M. (2002). Integration of ICT within a project-based learning environment. *European Journal of Engineering Education, 27*(1), 21–30. [CrossRef]

Gondal, S. A., Khan, A. Q., Cheema, E. U., & Dehele, I. S. (2024). Impact of the flipped classroom on students' academic performance and satisfaction in Pharmacy education: A quasi-experimental study. *Cogent Education, 11*(1), 2378246. [CrossRef]

Gong, J., Cai, S., & Cheng, M. (2023). Exploring the effectiveness of flipped classroom on STEM student achievement: A meta-analysis. *Technology, Knowledge and Learning, 29*(2), 1129–1150. [CrossRef]

Holmes, V.-L., & Hwang, Y. (2016). Exploring the effects of project-based learning in secondary mathematics education. *The Journal of Educational Research, 109*(5), 449–463. [CrossRef]

Hossein-Mohand, H., Trujillo-Torres, J.-M., Gómez-García, M., Hossein-Mohand, H., & Campos-Soto, A. (2021). Analysis of the use and integration of the flipped learning model, project-based learning, and gamification methodologies by secondary school mathematics teachers. *Sustainability, 13*(5), 2606. [CrossRef]

Indriati, L., Mai, N., & Tan, H. Y.-J. (2024). Enhancing authentic assessment in large-class design education through authentic project-based learning. *International Journal of Learning, Teaching and Educational Research, 23*(9), 432–452. [CrossRef]

Isabel Santos, A., & Serpa, S. (2020). Flipped classroom for an active learning. *Journal of Education and E-Learning Research, 7*(2), 167–173. [CrossRef]

Kalemkuş, F., & Bulut-Özek, M. (2022). The effect of online project-based learning on metacognitive awareness of middle school students. *Interactive Learning Environments, 32*(4), 1533–1551. [CrossRef]

Kim, D., & Lee, S. (2002). Designing collaborative reflection supporting tools in e-project-based learning environments. *Journal of Interactive Learning Research, 13*(4), 375–392. Available online: https://www.learntechlib.org/primary/p/9530/ (accessed on 7 March 2025).

Kong, S. C. (2014). Developing information literacy and critical thinking skills through domain knowledge learning in digital classrooms: An experience of practicing flipped classroom strategy. *Computers & Education, 78*, 160–173. [CrossRef]

Krajcik, J. S., Blumenfeld, P. C., Marx, R. W., & Soloway, E. (1994). A collaborative model for helping middle grade science teachers learn project-based instruction. *The Elementary School Journal, 94*(5), 483–497. [CrossRef]

Kramer, B. S., Walker, A. E., & Brill, J. M. (2007). The underutilization of information and communication technology-assisted collaborative project-based learning among international educators: A Delphi study. *Educational Technology Research and Development, 55*(5), 527–543. [CrossRef]

Li, M.-M., & Tu, C.-C. (2024). Developing a project-based learning course model combined with the think–pair–share strategy to enhance creative thinking skills in education students. *Education Sciences, 14*(3), 233. [CrossRef]

Liu, L., Hew, K. F., & Du, J. (2024). Design principles for supporting self-regulated learning in flipped classrooms: A systematic review. *International Journal of Educational Research, 124*, 102319. [CrossRef]

Maros, M., Korenkova, M., Fila, M., Levicky, M., & Schoberova, M. (2021). Project-based learning and its effectiveness: Evidence from Slovakia. *Interactive Learning Environments, 31*(7), 4147–4155. [CrossRef]

Meyer, D. K., Turner, J. C., & Spencer, C. A. (1997). Challenge in a mathematics classroom: Students' motivation and strategies in project-based learning. *The Elementary School Journal, 97*(5), 501–521. [CrossRef]

Mohamed, H., Saidalvi, A., & Tashiron, N. A. (2019). Project based learning in flipped classroom based on student's cognitive style. *International Journal of Recent Technology and Engineering, 7*(6S3), 696–700.

Moss, D. M. (2000). Bringing together technology and students: Examining the use of technology in a project-based class. *Journal of Educational Computing Research, 22*(2), 155–169. [CrossRef]

My Nguyen, H. T., Chau Nguyen, G. T., Hong Thai, L. T., Truong, D. T., & Nguyen, B. N. (2024). Teaching Mathematics through project-based learning in K-12 Schools: A systematic review of current practices, barriers, and future developments. *TEM Journal, 13*, 2054–2065. [CrossRef]

Nayak, A., Satpathy, I., & Jain, V. (2024). The project-based learning approach (PBL): Enthralling students through Project-Based Learning approach (PBL) in Education 5.0. In *Preconceptions of Policies, Strategies, and Challenges in Education 5.0* (pp. 158–174). IGI Global. [CrossRef]

Ndiung, S., & Menggo, S. (2024). Project-based learning in fostering creative thinking and mathematical problem-solving skills: Evidence from primary education in Indonesia. *International Journal of Learning, Teaching and Educational Research, 23*(8), 289–308. [CrossRef]

Nurbekova, Z., Grinshkun, V., Aimicheva, G., Nurbekov, B., & Tuenbaeva, K. (2020). Project-based learning approach for teaching mobile application development using visualization technology. *International Journal of Emerging Technologies in Learning (IJET), 15*(08), 130. [CrossRef]

Patterson, B., McBride, C. R., & Gieger, J. L. (2018). Flipped active learning in your mathematics classroom without videos. *PRIMUS, 28*(8), 742–753. [CrossRef]

Pokhrel, M., Sharma, L., Sharma, T., Prasad, M., & Poudel, L. G. C. (2024). Enhancing mathematics learning through self-directed pedagogy: Strategies and evaluation techniques for effective student engagement. *Journal of Computational Analysis and Applications, 33*(8), 841–854. Available online: https://eudoxuspress.com/index.php/pub/article/view/1471 (accessed on 22 October 2024).

Rehman, N., Huang, X., Mahmood, A., AlGerafi, M. A. M., & Javed, S. (2024). Project-based learning as a catalyst for 21st-Century skills and student engagement in the math classroom. *Heliyon, 10*(23), e39988. [CrossRef]

Remijan, K. W. (2017). Project-based learning and design-focused projects to motivate secondary mathematics students. *Interdisciplinary Journal of Problem-Based Learning, 11*(1), 1–15. [CrossRef]

Rijken, P. E., & Fraser, B. J. (2023). Effectiveness of project-based mathematics in first-year high school in terms of learning environment and student outcomes. *Learning Environments Research, 27*(2), 241–263. [CrossRef]

Rodríguez-Martínez, J. A., González-Calero, J. A., & Sáez-López, J. M. (2019). Computational thinking and mathematics using Scratch: An experiment with sixth-grade students. *Interactive Learning Environments*, *28*(3), 316–327. [CrossRef]

Saad, A., & Zainudin, S. (2024). A review of teaching and learning approach in implementing Project-Based Learning (PBL) with Computational Thinking (CT). *Interactive Learning Environments*, *32*(10), 7622–7646. [CrossRef]

Saheb, T., & Saheb, T. (2024). Mapping ethical artificial intelligence policy landscape: A mixed method analysis. *Science and Engineering Ethics*, *30*(2), 9. [CrossRef]

See, S., & Conry, J. M. (2014). Flip My Class! A faculty development demonstration of a flipped-classroom. *Currents in Pharmacy Teaching and Learning*, *6*(4), 585–588. [CrossRef]

Shekh-Abed, A. (2024). Metacognitive self-knowledge and cognitive skills in project-based learning of high school electronics students. *European Journal of Engineering Education*, *50*(1), 214–229. [CrossRef]

Shen, Y. (2024). Examining the efficacies of instructor-designed instructional videos in flipped classrooms on student engagement and learning outcomes: An empirical study. *Journal of Computer Assisted Learning*, *40*(4), 1791–1805. [CrossRef]

Shin, N., Bowers, J., Krajcik, J., & Damelin, D. (2021). Promoting computational thinking through project-based learning. *Disciplinary and Interdisciplinary Science Education Research*, *3*(1), 7. [CrossRef] [PubMed]

Singha, R., & Singha, S. (2024). Application of experiential, inquiry-based, problem-based, and project-based learning in sustainable education. In *Teaching and learning for a sustainable future: Innovative strategies and best practices* (pp. 109–128). IGI Global. [CrossRef]

Soboleva, E. V., Kirillova, E. P., Lomakin, D. E., & Gribkov, D. N. (2021). Formation of computational thinking skills in the development of computer games for educational purposes. *Perspektivy Nauki i Obrazovania*, *49*(1), 464–477. [CrossRef]

Stadnick, N. A., Poth, C. N., Guetterman, T. C., & Gallo, J. J. (2021). Advancing discussion of ethics in mixed methods health services research. *BMC Health Services Research*, *21*(1), 577. [CrossRef]

Sung, W., Ahn, J., & Black, J. B. (2017). Introducing computational thinking to young learners: Practicing computational perspectives through embodiment in mathematics education. *Technology, Knowledge and Learning*, *22*(3), 443–463. [CrossRef]

Sung, W., & Black, J. B. (2020). Factors to consider when designing effective learning: Infusing computational thinking in mathematics to support thinking-doing. *Journal of Research on Technology in Education*, *53*(4), 404–426. [CrossRef]

Tekin, O., & Sarıkaya, E. E. (2020). Flipped classroom model in high school mathematics. *Bartın University Journal of Faculty of Education*, *9*(2), 301–314.

Tu, F., Wu, L., Kinshuk, Ding, J., & Chen, H. (2025). Exploring the influence of regulated learning processes on learners' prestige in project-based learning. *Education and Information Technologies*, *30*, 2299–2329. [CrossRef]

Tucker, B. (2012). The flipped classroom. *Education Next*, *12*(1), 82–83. Available online: https://www.educationnext.org/wp-content/uploads/2023/04/ednext_XII_1_what_next.pdf (accessed on 7 March 2025).

Voon, X. P., Wong, S. L., Wong, L.-H., Khambari, M. N. M., & Syed-Abdullah, S. I. S. (2022). Developing computational thinking competencies through constructivist argumentation learning: A problem-solving perspective. *International Journal of Information and Education Technology*, *12*(6), 529–539. [CrossRef]

Wang, J. (2024). Research on the flipped classroom + learning community approach and its effectiveness evaluation—Taking college german teaching as a case study. *Sustainability*, *16*(17), 7719. [CrossRef]

Weintrop, D., Beheshti, E., Horn, M., Orton, K., Jona, K., Trouille, L., & Wilensky, U. (2015). Defining computational thinking for mathematics and science classrooms. *Journal of Science Education and Technology*, *25*(1), 127–147. [CrossRef]

Xing, D., & Zeng, Y. (2024). Exploring the effects of secondary school student's information and communication technology literacy on computational thinking skills in the smart classroom environment. *Education and Information Technologies*. [CrossRef]

Yasin, M., & Nusantara, T. (2023). Characteristics of pattern recognition to solve mathematics problems in computational thinking. In *AIP conference proceedings* (vol. 2569, p. 40009). AIP Publishing. [CrossRef]

Zarouk, M. Y., Olivera, E., Peres, P., & Khaldi, M. (2020). The impact of flipped project-based learning on self-regulation in higher education. *International Journal of Emerging Technologies in Learning (IJET)*, *15*(17), 127. [CrossRef]

Zhang, W., Guan, Y., & Hu, Z. (2024). The efficacy of project-based learning in enhancing computational thinking among students: A meta-analysis of 31 experiments and quasi-experiments. *Education and Information Technologies*, *29*(11), 14513–14545. [CrossRef]

education sciences

MDPI

Review

What's the Difference? A Comparison of Student-Centered Teaching Methods

Joshua R. Goodwin

Department of Curriculum and Instruction, College of Education, Purdue University, West Lafayette, IN 47907, USA; goodwin3@purdue.edu

Abstract: Many approaches to teaching and learning are classified as student-centered. The current literature evaluates these methods in-depth either individually or by comparing two or three at a time. This article provides a comparison of multiple student-centered teaching methods, with examples, employed in contemporary education. The aim is to assess the key characteristics associated with different approaches by investigating five popular student-centered teaching methodologies: activity-based learning, inquiry-based learning, cooperative learning, problem-based learning, and project-based learning. The results enable educators to make informed decisions about instructional strategies and provide a stepping stone for further research.

Keywords: student-centered teaching; pedagogy; problem-based learning; project-based learning; cooperative learning; situated learning; inquiry-based learning

1. Introduction

There has been a significant shift in educational paradigms in recent decades, with a growing emphasis on student-centered teaching methods (SCTs). Traditional teacher-centric approaches, where the instructor plays a central role in knowledge dissemination, have been challenged by the recognition that students are active participants in their own learning process [1–3]. SCTs prioritize student engagement, autonomy, and critical thinking, fostering a deeper understanding of concepts and enhancing the overall learning outcomes. Most teaching strategies can be placed into one of two categories: teacher-centered [2,4] or student-centered [1,3,5]. Though many definitions exist for both, for the purposes of this paper, I will rely on the following definitions to distinguish the two strategies: student-centered learning is "an instructional approach in which students influence the content, activities, materials, and pace of learning" [5] (pp. 338–339); teacher-centered learning is "an instructional approach in which the teacher controls the content, the activities, the materials, and the pace of learning" [5] (p. 349). Teacher-centered learning is often also referred to as a "traditional learning model" and is characterized by generally seeing students as passive learners rather than active learners in terms of engagement and motivation [5].

When investigating these two strategies in more detail, an array of styles and strategies that teachers and researchers use are found to have been developed with a focus on different aspects of a specific style. There are many names given to various SCT instructional methods. Some are quite similar to other SCTs but with different names, such as personalized learning and individualized learning. Some methods are technically different but can be difficult to differentiate between because they share similar definitions or assumed preconceived understanding. For example, when researching project-based learning and problem-based learning, one may find that both have a general definition of a student-centered approach to classroom instruction that involves students working collaboratively on solutions to authentic problems [6–9]. The difference between the two actually lies in the nuance and implementation, not only their definitions, which will be discussed below.

Based on this, we can see why it would be difficult for someone exploring the use of SCTs to understand the differences among them. It becomes even more difficult to decide which of these methods to use for your classroom. This is where further clarification on the differences between many of these methods is needed. The purpose of this article is to provide a brief comparison of five different SCTs employed in education: activity-based learning, inquiry-based learning, cooperative learning, problem-based learning, and project-based learning. By examining the definitions and key characteristics of each approach, I provide educators with an introduction to these SCTs to gain valuable insights into their suitability for different learning contexts and classroom use.

2. Background on Student-Centered Teaching

The theoretical roots of SCTs can be traced back to early American educational theory from John Dewey in the early 1900s. Dewey was a major proponent of experiential learning. His writings highlighted the importance of experience, engagement, social interaction, and authentic situational learning contexts for students. Building on Dewey's work, theorists like Vygotsky and Piaget worked towards explaining how children learn through experience and internalizing knowledge. Vygotsky [10] shared his belief of social interaction as a key component of learning and built upon Dewey's work from a psychological perspective. Piaget [11] built upon Dewey's work from a cognitive development perspective, providing a theoretical foundation for how learning takes place throughout childhood. These three seminal theorists' writings are essential to the foundation for constructivism, which is the epistemological foundation of many popular student-centered methods.

Constructivist work has been expanded upon since that time, notably by Bruner with the expansion of scaffolding in discovery learning [12,13], Lave and Wenger with the introduction of situated learning [14] and communities of practice [15], and others (e.g., [16–18]). These works further add to the understanding of how people learn and students develop knowledge. Collectively, their works led to methods of instruction in which the teacher and student dynamic is more fluid, and the students' learning is conceptualized as building new knowledge upon prior knowledge. They advocated for a view of teachers as being facilitators of students' knowledge construction more so than being distributors of knowledge [19].

On the one hand, advancements in understanding how children learn have influenced methods of instruction. Several strands of constructivism have been developed as a result of further research into how students learn. These strands have been taken up in classrooms and used to develop new methods of teaching. Such theories and methods include Vygotskian [10] social constructivism as seen in problem-based learning [8] and collaborative learning [20] with the characteristic of requiring group work and student interaction, Bruner's [12,13] guided discovery as seen in inquiry-based learning [21] with the characteristics of exploration and retesting hypotheses, and Papert and Harel's [22] constructionism as seen in project-based learning [7] with its characteristic of producing a tangible product. Studies have shown that, by having the student be the focus of the lessons rather than the teacher, children gain an increase in motivation, a deeper understanding of the content, a greater connection of the material to authentic situations, and improved test scores [6,7,23].

On the other hand, learning theories such as behaviorism and cognitivism do not provide a model of learning consistent with SCTs. Ertmer and Newby [24] alluded to this in their discussion on these learning theories alongside constructivism. According to them, the goal of behaviorism is to "focus on the importance of consequences" (p. 55), and correct responses are positively reinforced to ensure repetition in the future. From an instructional viewpoint, the student is responding to environmental stimuli rather than assuming an "active role in discovering the environment" (p. 55). The cognitivist perspective of learning focuses more on the organization of mental structures and how new information is stored and retrieved in a student's memory. They explain that cognitivist instructional methods "emphasize the role that environmental conditions play in facilitating learning [using methods such as] explanations, demonstrations, illustrative examples and matched non-examples" (p. 58). In this theory, the student plays a more active role in the learning process but only in the "mental activities of the learner that lead up to a response" (p. 59, italics in original), much like in that of behaviorism. Constructivism, according to these authors, views learning not as a transfer from the world into students' minds but, rather, "they build personal interpretations of the world based on individual experiences and interactions" (p. 63). Here, we see that students are creating and building an understanding within themselves as a result of interacting with the world around them. Ertmer and Newby [24] explained with these three theories, from an instructional perspective, that,

> As one moves along the behaviorist–cognitivist–constructivist continuum, the focus of instruction shifts from teaching to learning, from the passive transfer of facts and routines to the active application of ideas to problems. Both cognitivist and constructivist view the learner as being actively involved in the learning process, yet the constructivists look as the learner as more than just and active processor of information; the learner elaborates upon and interprets the given information (p. 66).

Understanding now how the various strands of constructivism provide the theoretical underpinning of SCTs, also referred to as student-centered learning, we can move toward a definition of what SCTs are and why we should work toward a better understanding of them. SCTs are instructional methods that shift the focus of the learning process from the teacher to the students [5]. For SCTs, the instruction, planning, decision-making, content, activities, pace of learning, etc. are all influenced more by concerns about student learning than concerns about the teacher's specific mode of knowledge transmission. When teachers adopt a student-centered approach, course material, activities, resources, and speed of instruction are more tailored to students' strengths, background knowledge, and social context, and in some cases, students can have more direct control over them as well. Students also have more opportunities to learn on their own and from one another while the instructor helps them develop the skills they need to do so [5]. Using SCTs, teachers take on the role of a facilitator of students' knowledge construction instead of a knowledge disseminator.

The definition of SCT has shifted and changed over time as researchers and teachers have taken ownership of its meaning, leading to a somewhat convoluted understanding of the term. O'Neill and McMahon [3] illustrated how the term SCT has become a complex term with varying definitions and conceptualizations. In their literature review, they described several different interpretations of the term and offered a consensus stating:

> In summary, it appears from the literature that some view student-centered learning as the concept of the student's choice in their education; others see it as the being about the student doing more than the lecturer (active versus passive learning); while others have a much broader definition which includes both of these concepts but, in addition, describes the shift in the power relationship between the student and the teacher (p. 32).

A common misconception is that there is no room for teacher-led instruction and didactic approaches within SCT. However, teacher-led and/or didactic approaches could occur within a SCT-based lesson when a teacher provides prerequisite knowledge or a foundational vocabulary before the student exploration of a new project-focused inquiry. For example, in a math lesson on graphing, the students may need to understand what a coordinate system is and what ordered pairs are by name before exploring how they work on the rate of change, velocity, and position of vehicles on a nearby road, leading to a larger investigation into their uses. By our definitions, this example has some teacher-led portions; however, they are not the primary means of learning but rather a means to begin the students' learning process and, thus, are still student-centered.

In the last century, SCTs have taken on many different forms and have been called by many different names. Larmer [9], for example, established a working list of over 100 SCT methods that included names like land-based learning, passion learning, and even zombie-based learning. Below, I share a comparative analysis and provide educators with insights into some of the most popular approaches available. This comparison can serve as a launching point for further research and investigations and an introductory reference piece for those interested in SCT.

3. Comparing Five SCT Instructional Methods

For this comparison, I evaluated online teaching resources to identify what appeared to be the most commonly discussed or used SCT methods. The sources (e.g., [25–30]) used to locate common methods were based on my experience as a teacher and coaching other teachers in developing instructional materials. The five methods identified were (a) activity-based learning, (b) collaborative learning, (c) inquiry-based learning, (d) problem-based learning, and (e) project-based learning. I then reviewed the relevant literature for each to establish a definition and list out the key characteristics of the method. These methods selected for comparison lay the groundwork for what SCTs are and what they can become. The aim of this article is to provide an overview of what they are and how they can be implemented more so than to delve into the history or theory behind these methods. This serves as a valuable resource for teachers seeking to implement SCT instructional strategies that align with their specific educational context and goals.

For each SCT, I provide a definition, key characteristics of the method as found in the literature, an example, and its relevance to teaching, meaning how the example is representative of the chosen method. The key characteristics are in no particular order of importance, and the examples provided are based on the associated definitions. Because of open sourcing, mislabeling of ideas, and perhaps a lack of universally accepted definitions, projects, materials, and information specific to each method can be difficult to find. For some of the examples provided, educators may interpret them differently from the way they have been labeled. Such divergence is welcome, as the purpose of this article is not to correct or challenge others' perspectives. Not every definition is understood in the exact same way by all scholars, as demonstrated previously by O'Neill and McMahon [3]. The premise of this article is not rigidity but in advocating for the principles of SCTs. Each method and example listed below has flexibility, allowing for manipulation, alteration, and use in various contexts.

3.1. *Activity-Based Learning*

3.1.1. Definition

Activity-based learning is an educational approach consisting of tasks, situations, and other short interactive exercises developed to guide children in learning. These tasks may be completed individually or in small groups and should include some instructor-led sections and allow students to respond and process new information. Prior knowledge is acquired, understood, and applied to new information and skills as the lessons continue [31,32].

3.1.2. Key Characteristics

The main characteristics of activity-based learning, in no particular order, are that it (a) uses activities to construct new knowledge, (b) employs a high level of student investment, (c) requires student exploration, (d) may be performed individually or as a group, and (e) involves activities that are either teacher-focused (more structured) or student-focused (less structured) [31,32]. The main component of this method is the use of activities as described above. Many SCTs incorporate activities to enhance or guide student learning, but in this method, the activities are the crux of the learning. The activities need to be shorter in length and scale than all-encompassing projects or week-long problems. They should be designed to encourage full student engagement, leading to a desire to explore further. Teacher-led sections help fill in the gaps during the activities or facilitate reflection afterward.

3.1.3. Example

One example of an activity-based learning task is Pizza Fractions (adapted from [25]) for recommended grades 2–5. In this activity, students create a pizza using classroom materials such as colored pencils, cardboard, construction paper, and manipulatives. Students create the toppings separately and then use them to decorate a certain fraction of the pizza. For example, if the teacher asks for one-fourth, the student will cover one-quarter of the pizza in mushrooms or pepperonis. This can be extrapolated to the students developing their own fractions, multiple fractions simultaneously, and fraction addition and subtraction. Teachers can visit http://mathseeds.com (accessed on 11 May 2024) for more examples of activity-based learning and other lessons.

3.1.4. Relevance to Teaching

Pizza Fractions is an example of activity-based learning, as it fits the key characteristics, definition, and is not better represented by another SCT. This example uses a short activity in which students are engaged with the material because of its familiarity and hands-on approach. It provides students with a visual and manipulative representation of fractions, which can be difficult for children to grasp. It provides teachers with an avenue for inserting students' voice and choice, as well as entry points for teacher-led sections where new information can be developed, challenged, and applied [25,31,32].

3.2. Collaborative Learning

3.2.1. Definition

In the original collaborative learning model developed by Reid et al. [33], there are "five phases for designing instruction for collaborative learning: engagement, exploration, transformation, presentation, and reflection" (p. 40). This has changed over time as the term cooperative learning has been developed, separating out key aspects between collaborative and cooperative learning practices. A recent definition of collaborative learning is that it is an educational approach to teaching and learning that involves groups of learners working together who are "challenged both socially and emotionally as they listen to different perspectives and are required to articulate and defend their ideas" [20] (p. 491) to solve a problem, complete a task, or create a product.

The main differences between collaborative and cooperative are (1) collaborative learning has a "focus on learners promoting shared responsibility for the goals, work, and other aspects of the assignments" [34] (n.p.), and (2) cooperative learning is focused more on teacher-led activities where "students work in groups to accomplish a common yet, pre-defined goal within specific planning by the instructor or teacher. Compared to the collaborative approach, the teacher has a greater role in affecting task distribution, differentiation of goals, and student input in collaborative learning" [34] (n.p.). Barkley, Cross, & Major [35] described the difference between these two SCTs as opposite ends of a continuum, sharing "Collaborative and cooperative learning [are] positioned on a continuum from most structured (cooperative) to least structured (collaborative)" (pp. 5–6).

3.2.2. Key Characteristics

The main characteristics of collaborative learning are that it is used to (a) promote positive interdependence, (b) employ a high level of student investment, (c) involve student presentations, (d) use collaborative group work, and (e) use activities and lessons that are either teacher-focused (cooperative learning) or student-focused (collaborative learning) [20,25,33,36]. The main component of this method is learning with peer collaboration. Many SCTs can incorporate the element of collaboration to enhance or guide student learning, but in this method, collaboration is the crux of the learning. Collaboration among students working on open-ended activities or lessons is the foundation of collaborative learning, while students working together on teacher-led, more structured activities or lessons is the foundation of cooperative learning. Here, we see the nuance of SCTs' definitions coming into play. In collaborative learning, students should be grouped together in a way that promotes individual strengths within the group. The lessons and activities do not have a set length but do require some form of presentation from the groups at the end. This could be as formal as a slide show or speech or as simple as discussing ideas from their seats.

3.2.3. Example: Collaborative Learning

An example for this SCT is Case Study [26] for recommended grades 6–12, where the instructor creates four to five case studies or problems of similar difficulty. These studies can vary depending on the subject. For example, different poems in a literature class or personal interviews in a sociology class. Students work in groups, typically from three to five, to work through and analyze their tasks. The roles in these groups are decided by the students, along with solutions and outcomes of the case study or problem. Teachers may answer questions and prompt/posit questions as necessary but not take away from the students' investigations. Groups present their analyses to the class, allowing time for other students to ask questions and learn from each other. Teachers can visit http://teaching.cornell.edu/resource (accessed on 11 May 2024) for more examples of collaborative learning and other lessons.

3.2.4. Example: Cooperative Learning

One example of cooperative learning is using Think-Pair-Share [27] for recommended grades 2–12. In a math lesson that requires a nonspecific answer, such as estimation or logic, students are presented with a task or problem. First, students think individually about an answer to the problem, knowing they will have to share it with a group. This inspires in-depth thinking and motivation. Next, they share their ideas with a partner or small group, practicing listening for understanding and communication skills. Lastly, they share their group solution with the whole class or larger group. Teachers can visit http://www.teachervision.com (accessed on 11 May 2024) for more examples of cooperative learning and other lessons.

3.2.5. Relevance to Teaching

By using case studies and think-pair-share as examples, it is easier to see the difference between these two SCTs. Case studies allow the teacher to utilize a more open-ended approach to learning, whereas this version of think-pair-share promotes more structured and rigid work on the part of the student. Both examples require students to use their personal strengths in a group setting by allowing them to share their ideas and perspectives while also listening and responding to others. Each example can require students to share perspectives and prior knowledge, enabling them to co-construct new knowledge alongside their peers. Whether sharing as a pair or a group, both versions require a form of presentation [26,27].

3.3. *Inquiry-Based Learning*

3.3.1. Definition

Lee et al. [21] defined inquiry-based learning as an "array of classroom practices that promote student learning through guided and, increasingly, independent investigation of complex questions and problems, often for which there is no single answer" (p. 9). Inquiry-based learning uses the scientific method to allow students to form, test, and retest hypotheses for solutions to the question. This can be performed individually or in groups, and there is significant emphasis on student exploration and engagement [37].

3.3.2. Key Characteristics

The main characteristics of inquiry-based learning are that it (a) begins with a driving question, (b) follows the scientific method of inquiry, (c) typically has preset steps, (d) requires students to practice hypothesis testing and retesting, (e) requires student exploration, (f) requires student reflection, and (g) may be performed individually or as a group [21,37]. Although many SCTs incorporate the idea of inquiry and exploration in the learning process, inquiry-based learning is specifically organized to follow the steps of the scientific method. Driving questions are used to build student engagement and motivation throughout the lesson. The lessons and activities do not have a set length but typically follow preset steps set up by the instructor. For example, in a traditional high school chemistry lab, the steps are laid out on a sheet of paper, and the students follow the instructions to find out what happens. This is where the hypothesis testing and retesting come in. Students should hypothesize about what will happen during the lesson. The hypothesis could be as simple as a given math problem simplifying to one or as complex as a guess towards what the net forces will be on a moving object. Student reflection is also a crucial piece, as it allows students to process their work, learning, and thoughts more deeply.

3.3.3. Example

An example of inquiry-based learning is The Boat Float [28] for recommended grades 4–12. The creators of this task describe it as:

> In this task, the teacher provides learners with basic information regarding the physics of floatation and buoyancy. They ask students to explore how boats the size of luxury cruise liners and container ships can stay afloat even with the extra weight and then have them use their knowledge to create a boat that can remain afloat in a plastic tub of water. They [students] should experiment with different types of materials and designs while following the scientific concepts they have learned. Once learners have found a way to keep their boat afloat, have them add items such as paperclips or thumbtacks to see if the weight causes their boat to sink. They can also simulate storms and ocean waves by causing disruptions to the water in the tank. Have them observe how the boats that successfully remain afloat also follow the requirements for buoyancy and how this allows shipbuilders to create boats of all sizes that will stay afloat in many different conditions (n.p.).

Teachers can visit https://futurefocusedlearning.net/blog/learner-agency/5-terrific-inquiry-based-learning-examples (accessed on 11 May 2024) for more examples of inquiry-based learning and other lessons.

3.3.4. Relevance to Teaching

This activity represents inquiry-based learning by providing a typical science experiment that allows students and teachers to follow all the characteristics described above. The driving question helps support engagement through the lesson. Hypothesis testing takes the form of asking and examining how boats float with added weight. Retesting occurs after adding weight and the boat sinks. Reflection can occur throughout or at the end from instructor prompting, reflection worksheets, or group discussions. What makes this an inquiry-based task rather than activity-based is the necessity for preset steps, using the scientific method, and the use of hypothesis testing and retesting [21,28,37].

3.4. Problem-Based Learning

3.4.1. Definition

Problem-based learning was originally developed in the medical field as a means of hands-on learning. Barrows and Tamblyn [38] described it as "a method of learning in which the learners first encounter a problem, followed by a systematic, student-centered inquiry process" (p. 1). Over time, it has been adapted to classroom use for student learning centering on solving a complex problem that can be approached through multiple methods and may have multiple ways of being answered. Students engage in the material and use newly constructed knowledge to aid in solving the problem. Students are encouraged to reflect on their solutions and processes. The teacher should act as a facilitator of activities, not a disseminator of knowledge [8].

3.4.2. Key Characteristics

The main characteristics of problem-based learning are (a) it begins with a driving question, (b) uses larger, open-ended problems to enhance or replace a lesson, (c) often employs the use of case studies or fictitious scenarios, (d) allows students to practice hypothesis testing, (e) requires student exploration, (f) requires student reflection, and (g) incorporates community partners for authenticity and application [8,9,39]. The focus of this SCT is on the method of solving a problem. Many SCTs can use problems in their lessons; the difference here is that the problem is the driving force behind the learning. Students construct knowledge through the exploration of solving the problem using hypothesis testing and preset steps; however, students should not be taught how and why the solutions work ahead of time. Rather, solutions are used for discussion and reflection to promote further growth in understanding.

3.4.3. Example

An example of a problem-based learning task is the Design a Food Truck problem for recommended grades 4–9 (adapted from [29]). For this problem, students are tasked with designing their own food truck for their community. Students research popular food truck options and operational costs. The problem of designing their own food truck has the potential of addressing many learning objectives, such as arithmetic, economics, entrepreneurship, vocabulary, reading, and more. Posing an open-ended problem such as this allows students to engage in the material and be invested as a result of students' voice and choice. Students can work individually or in groups to design their own menu and truck layout. Their solutions are presented by students in the form of crafts, pictures, graphics, models, etc. Grade-level appropriate adjustments can be made concerning budgeting and geographical considerations. Teachers can visit http://www.bctf.ca/classroom-resources (accessed on 11 May 2024) for more examples of problem-based learning and other lessons.

3.4.4. Relevance to Teaching

Some of the main deciding factors of problem-based learning are open-endedness, lesson replacement or enhancement, and authentic situations. Designing a food truck meets all three of these, as well as the characteristics described above. This example allows students to voice their ideas and choices in multiple aspects, including the type of food, menu, price, design, and more. With a hands-on approach, students can explore finance, math, art, and design. The fictitious scenario of creating a food truck is grounded in an authentic situation. Students can present their designs and plans at the end to the class, to another group at the school, or community partners. These partners can be local restaurateurs, other teachers, or simply volunteer parents to replicate the idea of a client meeting. Teacher-led learning sessions where new information is developed, challenged, and applied are still valuable, but the lesson should not dominate the class time [8,29].

3.5. Project-Based Learning

3.5.1. Definition

Project-based learning can be defined as a student-centered approach to teaching and learning that involves students working collaboratively on solutions to authentic problems [6,7]. These problems are grounded in real-world situations, and the solutions are presented via an artifact at the end of the project. These projects are typically larger in scope, replacing or enhancing entire units or curricula. Community partners are brought in to facilitate further investigation and realism of the projects. There are a few differences between project-based learning and problem-based learning, the biggest of which is size and scope. On the one hand, problem-based learning is typically completed in one to two classes and usually only involves one or two subjects. On the other hand, project-based learning takes weeks or months to complete and involves multiple subjects. Teachers and students working collaboratively on projects in this manner provide opportunities for cooperative engagement, real-world integration, and encourage intrinsic motivation [6,7,23].

3.5.2. Key Characteristics

The main characteristics of project-based learning are (a) it begins with a driving question, (b) uses larger, open-ended problems to enhance or replace a curriculum or unit, (c) requires students to use tools and technology, (d) requires student work and solutions to be presented at the end of the project to the class or community partners, and (e) incorporates community partners for authenticity and application [6,7,9,23]. Project-based learning often encompasses not only several problems and activities but may also include other SCTs. For example, in a project on building a scale model wooden bridge, inquiry-based learning may be used to investigate the strongest bridge designs, or activity-based learning could be used to investigate materials that will be used during construction. Project-based learning replacing or enhancing entire units or curricula allows the project to become a theme for other assignments and goals, creating unity across disciplines or areas of study [23]. For example, a project on tiny home construction could incorporate learning about vocabulary, reading, measurement, and arithmetic.

3.5.3. Example

An example of a project-based learning task recommended for grades 3–6 is a Design a Garden project, where students are tasked with designing a school garden for herbs and vegetables. This project starts with a driving question: How do we, as consumers and students, create a vegetable garden at school to help diversify food intake in an urban food desert? Students then need to research what it takes to build a garden, how much room the school has available, what costs are involved, and more. Community partners are brought in for demonstrations and examples. These partners could be local farmers or gardeners who can discuss growing and soil with the students or the principal of the school to discuss areas and planning. Teachers can visit http://my.pblworks.org (accessed on 11 May 2024) for more examples of problem-based learning and other lessons.

3.5.4. Relevance to Teaching

For this example, the task of designing a community garden can serve as the theme of an entire unit of learning. To use this in an elementary school, teachers could work with their administration ahead of time to put the final project into place and have students build the garden on school grounds. Students should be prepared to present their ideas formally to the administration directly. Tasks in this unit can be separated into several categories and include individual, group, and full-class activities. Reading and spelling time could focus on literature and vocabulary about growable foods and garden maintenance. Math time could be spent measuring possible areas, calculating area and volume, and creating a budget. Science and social studies could focus on researching local food systems, growers, and challenges to sustaining a garden in their area. Designing a garden meets all the characteristics of project-based learning. It provides ample room for student engagement, self-efficacy, teacher-led and student-led sections, and ownership of a real-world problem that students can solve in a hands-on manner and see their solution come to life in real time [6,7,9,23].

4. Looking across Five SCT Methods

For quick access to the practices each SCT is inherent to, and ease of understanding where the overlap occurs, Table 1 below contains all five SCTS and all of the key characteristics from Section 3. Each collum is labeled with the corresponding SCT, and each row lists out the prominent practices. An "X" has been placed in the corresponding square if the practice was found in the literature reviewed. From this table, teachers can readily seek out a practice they are interested in and see what corresponding SCT contains them or vice versa.

Table 1. Prominent practices that appear in 5 chosen SCTs.

	Project-Based	Problem-Based	Inquiry-Based	Activity-Based	Collaborative
Projects enhance or replace curriculum or units	X				
Uses tools and technology	X				
Open-ended tasks	X	X			
Authentic applications	X	X			
Community partners	X	X			
Collaboration	X	X			X
Student presentation	X				X
Embrace individual strengths in group settings					X
High level of student engagement	X			X	X
More teacher-focused activities				X	X
Uses activities to construct new knowledge				X	
Exploration			X	X	
May be performed individually			X	X	
Generally follows the scientific method			X		
Follows preset steps		X	X		
Hypothesis testing		X	X		
Reflection		X	X		
Begins with a driving question	X	X	X		
Problems enhance or replace lessons		X			
Uses case studies or fictitious scenarios		X			

It is worth noting that, while the focus of this article is on the comparison of SCTs, I recognize that no single approach is universally superior. All five of the methods presented can be utilized in k–12 classrooms of any subject or topic. The suitability of a specific method will depend on various contextual factors, such as the subject matter, student population, available resources, learning goals, and teacher personality. Therefore, this article provides an overview of these five different methods, allowing teachers to further their research and make more informed decisions based on their unique educational contexts.

5. Summary

Understanding the diverse range of SCTs is crucial for educators seeking to create engaging and effective learning environments. Teacher-centered lessons have a place and should not be omitted entirely, especially when helping students learn vocabulary, academic language, and other content-specific conventions. This article contributes to the ongoing discourse on SCT education and provides educators with valuable insights to enhance their instructional practices. The SCTs reviewed here, and many others that have not been discussed, have similarities, but each has their own unique characteristics that are not present in the others. There is not a single practice that all five of these SCTs share in common, and yet, the flexibility of each method allows teachers to include any practice into any other SCT. By examining the principles, characteristics, examples, and relevance of various approaches, educators can better equip their classrooms with multiple effective learning methods and opportunities for students to be active participants in learning.

Funding: This research received no external funding.

Acknowledgments: The author would like to thank Lane Bloome and Jean Lee for their guidance and unwavering support. Thank you.

Conflicts of Interest: The author declares no conflicts of interest.

References

1. Barr, R.B.; Tagg, J. From teaching to learning—A new paradigm for undergraduate education. *Change* **1995**, *27*, 12–25. [CrossRef]
2. Dole, S.; Bloom, L.; Kowalske, K. Transforming Pedagogy: Changing Perspectives from Teacher-Centered to Learner-Centered. *Interdiscip. J. Probl-Based Learn.* **2016**, *10*, 1. [CrossRef]
3. O'Neill, G.; McMahon, T. Student-centred learning: What does it mean for students and lecturers. In *Emerging Issues in the Practice of University Learning and Teaching I*; AISHE: Dublin, Ireland, 2005.
4. Peyton, J.K.; More, S.K.; Young, S. *Evidence-Based, Student Choice Instructional Practices*; Center for Applied Linguistic: Washington, DC, USA, 2010; pp. 20–25. Available online: http://cal.org/caelanetwork (accessed on 10 January 2024).
5. Collins, J.W.; O'Brien, N.P. (Eds.) *Greenwood Dictionary of Education*; Greenwood: Westport, CT, USA, 2003.
6. Bell, S. Project-based learning for the 21st century: Skills for the future. *Clear. House* **2010**, *83*, 39–43. [CrossRef]
7. Blumenfeld, P.C.; Soloway, E.; Marx, R.W.; Krajcik, J.S.; Guzdial, M.; Palincsar, A. Motivating project-based learning: Sustaining the doing, supporting the learning. *Educ. Psychol.* **1991**, *26*, 369–398. [CrossRef]
8. Hmelo-Silver, C.E. Problem-based learning: What and how do students learn? *Educ. Psychol. Rev.* **2004**, *16*, 235–266. [CrossRef]
9. Larmer, J. Project-Based Learning vs. Problem-Based Learning vs. X-BL. 13 July 2015. Available online: https://www.edutopia.org/blog/pbl-vs-pbl-vs-xbl-john-larmer (accessed on 12 December 2023).
10. Vygotsky, L. *Mind in Society*; Harvard University Press: London, UK, 1978.
11. Piaget, J. *Genetic Epistemology*; Columbia University Press: New York, NY, USA, 1970.
12. Bruner, J.S. *Toward a Theory of Instruction*; Belkapp Press: Cambridge, MA, USA, 1966.
13. Bruner, J.S. The Role of Dialogue in Language Acquisition. In *The Child's Concept of Language*; Sinclair, A., Jarvelle, R.J., Levelt, W.J.M., Eds.; Springer: New York, NY, USA, 1978.
14. Lave, J.; Wenger, E. *Situated Learning: Legitimate Peripheral Participation*; Cambridge University Press: Cambridge, UK, 1991.
15. Wenger, E. Communities of practice: Learning as a social system. *Syst. Think.* **1998**, *9*, 2–3. [CrossRef]
16. Von Glasersfeld, E. Cognition, construction of knowledge, and teaching. *Synthese* **1989**, *80*, 121–140. [CrossRef]
17. Leask, M.; Younie, S. Communal constructivist theory: Information and communications technology pedagogy and internationalisation of the curriculum. *J. Inf. Techology Teach. Educ.* **2001**, *10*, 117–134. [CrossRef]
18. Tall, D. *How Humans Learn to Think Mathematically: Exploring the Three Worlds of Mathematics*; Cambridge University Press: Cambridge, UK, 2013.
19. MacGregor, J. Collaborative learning: Shared inquiry as a process of reform. *New Dir. Teach. Learn.* **1990**, *42*, 19–30. [CrossRef]
20. Drew, C. Collaborative Learning: Pros & Cons. 10 May 2023. Available online: https://helpfulprofessor.com/collaborative-learning/ (accessed on 10 January 2024).
21. Lee, V.S.; Greene, D.B.; Odom, J.; Schechter, E.; Slatta, R.W. What is inquiry guided learning. In *Teaching and Learning through Inquiry: A Guidebook for Institutions and Instructors*; Lee, V.S., Ed.; Stylus Publishing: Sterling, VA, USA, 2004; pp. 3–15.
22. Papert, S.; Harel, I. Situating constructionism. *constructionism* **1991**, *36*, 1–11. Available online: https://pirun.ku.ac.th/~btun/papert/sitcons.pdf (accessed on 10 January 2024).
23. Kokotsaki, D.; Menzies, V.; Wiggins, A. Project-based learning: A review of the literature. *Improv. Sch.* **2016**, *19*, 267–277. [CrossRef]
24. Ertmer, P.A.; Newby, T.J. Behaviorism, cognitivism, constructivism: Comparing critical features from an instructional design perspective. *Perform. Improv. Q.* **1993**, *6*, 50–72. [CrossRef]
25. MathSeeds. 7 Classroom Math Activities That Will Make Math Engaging and Fun. Available online: https://mathseeds.com/articles/2018/02/26/classroom-math-activities/ (accessed on 11 May 2024).
26. Center for Teaching Innovation. Examples of Collaborative Learning or Group Work Activities. Available online: https://teaching.cornell.edu/resource/examples-collaborative-learning-or-group-work-activities (accessed on 11 May 2024).
27. Kaddoura, M. Think pair share: A teaching learning strategy to enhance students' critical thinking. *Educ. Res. Q.* **2013**, *36*, 3–24.
28. Future Focused Learning. 5 Terrific Inquiry-Based Learning Examples. Available online: https://futurefocusedlearning.net/blog/learner-agency/5-terrific-inquiry-based-learning-examples (accessed on 11 May 2024).
29. Aquino, P. Design a Food Truck. 2016. Available online: http://bctf.ca/classroom-resources/details/design-a-food-truck (accessed on 12 December 2023).
30. PBL Works. What Is PBL? Buck Institute for Education. 2019. Available online: http://my.pblworks.org (accessed on 10 January 2024).
31. Felder, R.M.; Brent, R. Active learning: An introduction. *ASQ High. Educ. Brief* **2009**, *2*, 1–5.
32. Geneva Global. Introduction to Activity-Based Learning. July 2021. Available online: https://www.genevaglobal.com/wp-content/uploads/2021/10/Activity-Based-Learning.GenevaGlobal.2021-07.pdf (accessed on 10 January 2024).
33. Reid, J.; Forrestal, P.; Cook, J. *Small Group Learning in the Classroom*; Heinemann: Portsmouth, NH, USA, 1989.

34. Gryshuk, R. Collaborative vs Cooperative Learning: Which Will Suit Your Course Best? *Collaborative Learning*, 14 June 2023. Available online: https://www.educate-me.co/blog/collaborative-vs-cooperative-learning (accessed on 10 January 2024).
35. Barkley, E.F.; Major, C.H.; Cross, K.P. *Collaborative Learning Techniques: A Handbook for College Faculty*; John Wiley & Sons: Hoboken, NJ, USA, 2014.
36. Laal, M.; Laal, M. Collaborative learning: What is it? *Procedia-Soc. Behav. Sci.* **2012**, *31*, 491–495. [CrossRef]
37. Pedaste, M.; Mäeots, M.; Siiman, L.A.; De Jong, T.; Van Riesen, S.A.; Kamp, E.T.; Manoli, C.C.; Zacharia, Z.C.; Tsourlidaki, E. Phases of inquiry-based learning: Definitions and the inquiry cycle. *Educ. Res. Rev.* **2015**, *14*, 47–61. [CrossRef]
38. Barrows, H.S.; Tamblyn, R.M. *Problem-Based Learning: An Approach to Medical Education*; Springer Publishing Company: Berlin/Heidelberg, Germany, 1980; Volume 1.
39. Schwartz, P. *Problem-Based Learning*; Routledge: London, UK, 2013.

education sciences

Article

Multidisciplinary Capstone Senior Design Projects: A Comparative Analysis of Industry_Sponsored and Faculty_Sponsored Projects Using Comprehensive Performance Metrics

Mohamed M. Morsy *, Md. Nizam Uddin and Faycal Znidi

Engineering and Physics Department, Texas A&M University Texarkana, Texarkana, TX 75503, USA; muddin@tamut.edu (M.N.U.); fznidi@tamut.edu (F.Z.)
* Correspondence: mmorsy@tamut.edu

Abstract: Engineering education has continually evolved to embrace Project_Based Learning (PBL), a dynamic classroom approach emphasizing learning through engagement in real_world projects. The study conducts a comparative analysis of multidisciplinary Capstone Senior Design Projects across Electrical Engineering, Mechanical Engineering, and Computer Science at Texas A&M University at Texarkana. The research emphasizes understanding the dynamics of student collaboration within these disciplines and scrutinizes the impact of industry and faculty sponsorship on these projects. The methodology involves a comprehensive comparative analysis, employing diverse performance metrics to evaluate the effectiveness of different sponsorship models. This approach aims to uncover the influence of these models on project outcomes and students' educational experiences. The results reveal notable differences between industry_sponsored and faculty_sponsored projects. Industry sponsorship leads to higher performance in overall project execution and professional skills development. In contrast, faculty_sponsored projects are more effective in nurturing teamwork and communication abilities among students. The findings suggest that each sponsorship type presents unique benefits and challenges. Industry_sponsored projects provide valuable hands_on problem_solving experience, though they may suffer from inconsistencies in mentorship and varying expectations. Faculty_sponsored projects offer a more stable and consistent educational environment but might lag slightly in performance metrics. Integrating elements from both sponsorship models could provide students with a more balanced and enriching learning experience.

Keywords: assessment; self_and_peer review; capstone; senior design; multidisciplinary project_based learning; industry sponsorship; faculty sponsorship

1. Introduction

This study examines the application of PBL in multidisciplinary Capstone Senior Design Projects (CSDP) at Texas A&M University at Texarkana (TAMUT), where collaborative efforts extend beyond traditional project work to embody the core principles of PBL—interdisciplinary learning, collaboration, and reflection. By comparing industry_sponsored and faculty_sponsored projects, this research identifies how each sponsorship model aligns with and supports PBL outcomes, such as problem_solving, self_directed learning, and integrating theory with practice, crucial for preparing students for the complexities of modern engineering challenges.

Engineering harnesses mathematical and scientific knowledge gained through academic learning, experience, and real_world application. Professionals creatively develop techniques to utilize nature's materials and forces for human benefit in this discipline. They innovate and build effective devices, systems, and infrastructures. The Accreditation Board of Engineering and Technology (ABET) defines engineering design as a systematic process to create systems, components, or processes that meet specific needs within constraints. It is a repetitive, imaginative process where fundamental sciences and engineering principles are applied to transform resources into practical solutions [1–4]. The capstone design project is a crucial element in design education involving real-world engineering challenges. Successfully conducting capstone courses in electrical engineering (E.E.), mechanical engineering (M.E.), and computer science (C.S.) is vital yet complex. These projects often differ from actual design office scenarios, potentially turning them into analytical rather than design experiences [5–8]. The influence of site-specific conditions and local regulations on E.E., M.E., and C.S. projects highlights the need for faculty with industry experience for more impactful education. To bridge this gap, numerous educational institutions collaborate with industrial clients to sponsor these capstone projects [9,10].

The evolution of multidisciplinary CSDP has significantly enhanced student collaboration across various disciplines and altered the dynamics of industry and faculty sponsorships [11]. Despite this progress, there is a notable deficiency in comprehensive research exploring these aspects in depth. Most existing studies tend to focus on either student collaboration, industry sponsorship, or faculty sponsorship, treating them as isolated variables. Rarely do they examine the interplay and combined impact of these factors on project outcomes and student development. This gap highlights the need for more integrative research to fully understand the synergies and challenges of these elements in engineering education.

In a recent study referenced in [1], the authors investigate the impact of industry involvement on student learning in civil and environmental engineering courses at Florida Gulf Coast University (FGCU). By utilizing surveys from both students and practitioners, the research assesses the benefits of industry participation, focusing on the roles of practitioners as mentors and judges. The paper also examines two capstone projects to illustrate effective industry engagement. In [12], the authors aim to understand the motivation and value of industry sponsors of senior mechanical engineering capstone design projects. The study in [13] discusses the evolution of engineering curricula to meet industry needs, focusing on interdisciplinary teams, team building, and project management.

Further, the research in [14] discusses Seattle University's senior design program in Civil and Environmental Engineering. This year-long, industry-sponsored program meets ABET 2000 requirements, combining technical problem-solving with soft skills development such as leadership and communication. It outlines assessment methods and includes feedback from sponsors, alumni, and faculty. In [15], a capstone course, students developed software for an industry sponsor, comparing test-driven development (TDD) with test-last methods. Surprisingly, the test-last group was more productive and wrote more tests. The study suggests other factors such as ambition and motivation may influence outcomes more than the chosen development approach.

While this research offers valuable insights into the impact of industrial sponsorship on CSDP, it lacks a comparative analysis that would illuminate the perceived values of these projects from both industrial and faculty sponsorship viewpoints. Additionally, involving students from various disciplines in such a comparison study could provide a more comprehensive understanding of how different sponsorship models influence project outcomes and student learning experiences in a multidisciplinary context.

Other research on CSDP tends to focus on specific elements such as student assessments, skill improvement, team formation, and the use of internships, but often lacks a comprehensive comparison of these elements' overall impact on student learning outcomes. For instance, the study in [16] targets enhancing self- and peer-review accuracy by implementing various interventions over four years. Article [17] investigates an engineering capstone project aimed at boosting building information modeling (BIM) skills, employing team-based Learning (TBL) and 360-degree feedback. Study [7] reviews engineering project assessment rubrics to align with international engineering alliance standards, highlighting gaps in complex problem-solving. Research [18] delves into team formation in software engineering, proposing criteria for better cohesion. Lastly, [10] examines the influence of internships on capstone projects in computer science, noting improvements in student skills and project complexity.

This study emphasizes the role of CSDP in fostering collaboration and practical skills in academic settings, particularly at TAMUT. It delves into a detailed comparison between industry_sponsored and faculty_sponsored projects using a variety of performance metrics. This comparative analysis is crucial as it highlights how different types of sponsorships influence student learning and the overall effectiveness of projects. By providing a comprehensive evaluation of these sponsorship models, the study aims to offer valuable insights into optimizing project_based learning in engineering education, enhancing the practical application of theoretical knowledge, and preparing students for real_world challenges.

2. Structure of CSDP

The CSDP at TAMUT is a multidisciplinary venture involving E.E., M.E., and C.S. students. The course's structure facilitates the formation of multidisciplinary teams, matching them with projects based on their interests. Of the 11 projects undertaken, 7 received industry funding, mainly from local manufacturing firms, with two C.S. projects sponsored by TAMUT's local I.T. department and a sheriff's office. This study demonstrates that incorporating real_world, project_based learning with industry engagement in capstone courses is advantageous for students, faculty, and industry partners. Undergraduate teams in the capstone course worked alongside fellow students, faculty members, and potential clients to adhere to project deadlines. Projects involved developing software, hardware, interfaces, system integration, and testing, requiring teamwork with professionals outside the capstone team. This experience brought forth challenges in teamwork, communication, documentation, scheduling, and various project management aspects, mirroring larger_scale industry projects. The CSDP thus serves as a practical platform for students to engage in teams and solve real_world problems through a two_semester, 6_credit_hour design process, either by developing new products/services or contributing to existing industry projects.

The CSDP is typically sponsored by industry partners and faculty members, with academic and industry mentors guiding students through the entire design process. This includes project initiation, scope definition, planning, various design stages, testing, performance analysis, simulation, and final presentations. The industry_sponsored projects provide students with hands_on experience in real_world scenarios, enabling collaboration with engineers and customers. Such projects have been significantly beneficial for the E.E., ME, and C.S. programs at TAMUT. Led by two faculty members from the E.E. and M.E. departments, the course is structured to create multidisciplinary teams matched with projects that align with their interests. Each project was supervised by academic and industry mentors. A total of 11 projects were undertaken in the course, involving teams of 3–4 students, with 7 projects receiving industry funding. These projects mainly involved collaboration with local manufacturing companies, alongside two C.S. projects sponsored by TAMUT's I.T. department and a sheriff's office. The course enrollment for the spring 2023 semester was 39 students. It was held once a week for 2 h and 45 min, where students formed their teams, a strategy aimed at minimizing potential conflicts during the semester.

In the CSDP, students begin the fall term by submitting and presenting their initial proposals. Once these are approved by their academic mentors, they commence work on their projects. Regular weekly meetings with the course instructor are required, where students provide oral updates in class. At the end of the second term, they are expected to submit a final report, deliverables, and an electronic team notebook and participate in a public poster and project presentation. Industry mentors play a crucial role in this process, judging the students' presentations and offering valuable feedback to both faculty and students, thereby enriching the learning experience in the capstone course. This feedback is instrumental in enhancing student performance on their projects and providing them with skills for their future engineering careers. Student performance is evaluated based on individual effort (28%) and teamwork (72%).

Individual contributions include reviews by industry and faculty mentors and peer reviews, while teamwork encompasses various components: 8% for the proposal report and presentation, 7% for oral updates in class, 7% for the electronic team notebook, 15% for the midterm report and presentations, and 35% for the final written reports and design and poster presentations. Industry mentors use a faculty_provided rubric to assess the final design of poster presentations, evaluating the student teams' verbal presentation skills, including organization, delivery, and professionalism, as well as written presentation skills such as content and poster quality.

3. Materials and Methods

This study's research methodology is crafted to meticulously compare industry_sponsored and faculty_sponsored projects, utilizing a set of strategic metrics that offer an all_encompassing evaluation of each project's effectiveness. The metrics applied include:

- *Overall Performance*: This metric assesses the overall success and outcomes of the projects, focusing on how well the objectives were met and the quality of the final deliverables.
- *Mentors' Evaluation*: The input from mentors who oversaw the projects is crucial. Their insights shed light on the teams' methodologies, problem_solving skills, and compliance with project guidelines.
- *Peer_Reviews by Team Members*: This involves the team members assessing each other and highlighting the team dynamics, individual contributions, and the overall cohesion within the group.
- *Self_Review by Team Members*: Important as well, this metric looks at each member's self_review, focusing on their personal development, the challenges they encountered, and their individual input to the project's success.

The assessment of individual contributions and team dynamics in team projects uses specific evaluation criteria for self_review and peer review. These criteria (EC1 to EC6) include:

EC1 Attendance and Punctuality: Regular attendance and timely arrival at team meetings are crucial, reflecting commitment to the team's schedule.
EC2 Responsibility: Team members should responsibly contribute to collaborative tasks and assignments.
EC3 Timeliness: Completing assignments on time, especially for industry projects where deadlines might be strictly defined.
EC4 Quality of Work: High_quality work preparation ensures tasks are completed and performed to a high standard.
EC5 Cooperation and Support: A cooperative and supportive demeanor is essential for maintaining team harmony and effectiveness.
EC6 Listening Skills: Effective listening to fellow team members is crucial, underscoring the importance of communication within the team.

A numerical scoring system is used in the study to enable a clear and measurable comparison. Each project and its components are rated on a scale of 1 to 4, with 4 being the highest. This scale provides an efficient means to assess and compare performance levels across different projects. Moreover, the study calculates the standard deviation for these scores to determine the variability or dispersion in the data. Understanding the consistency of results across various projects and metrics offers a deeper insight into the performance differences between industry_sponsored and faculty_sponsored projects. This methodological approach highlights each sponsorship model's strengths and areas for improvement, providing a comprehensive evaluation of their effectiveness.

4. Results

4.1. Overall Performance

The overall performance assessment encompasses a comprehensive evaluation of all tasks undertaken within the CSDP. This evaluation integrates a variety of components: midterm and final presentations, interim and final reports, assessments from mentors and peers, and the caliber of the electronic notebooks maintained by the participants. The data is categorized according to the nature of the project sponsorship: industry or faculty. This research analyzed the collective efforts of 11 teams spanning three distinct academic disciplines—electrical engineering, mechanical engineering, and computer science—which are detailed in Tables 1 and 2. Of these teams, four were under faculty sponsorship, and the remaining seven were supported by industry partnerships.

Table 1. Industry_sponsored projects in AY 2022/2023 at TAMUT.

Team No.	Students Majors	Project Title	Objectives
2	M.E. and E.E.	Hydraulic Power Unit Design and Overview	The project goal is to design and build a hydraulic power unit for Ledwell & Sons, Texarkana, TX, which will be used to test feed trailers before they are sold to the customer. The unit is mobile and transported by a forklift.
3	CS	Data Management in an Archival System	The project's goal is to reorganize archived data via software. The software will include a Python implementation of Optical Character Recognition (OCR), a database implementation of Microsoft Access, and an offline HTML program for keyword searching and other preferred features.
4	M.E. and E.E.	Transverse Tetris Table	This project aims to design and construct an effective and efficient transverse plasma table for JCM Industries, Texarkana, TX. The current plasma table is slow, inefficient, and unsafe during operation. By redesigning the plasma table, safety in the workplace and the overall production rate at JCM are significantly increased.
7	C.S.	Engineering a Secure Intranet Network	This project aims to engineer and deploy a secure Intranet network for Texas A&M University–Texarkana. The network was engineered to support a secure website and its client systems.
9	M.E. and E.E.	Automated Channel Stacker	The project's goal is to design and construct an automated channel stacker for New Millennium Building Systems, Hope, AR. The problem concerns the automation of the collection of cut channels from a channel cutter.
10	EE	Small Maintenance Rovers	This project aims to design and construct small maintenance tethered rovers to perform inspections inside the pipelines. This project will provide an opportunity for companies to perform inspections efficiently to result in less downtime and prevent any unexpected failures in the surrounding environments.
11	E.E. and C.S.	Control Cabinet Temperature Monitoring System	The project aims to develop a temperature monitoring system for Cooper Tires Texarkana AR control cabinets. The system will provide real_time monitoring and forecasting of the temperature in the control cabinets. The project improves the functionality and productivity of Cooper Tire's manufacturing processes and reduces the costs associated with damaged control panels and inactive processes.

Table 2. Faculty–sponsored projects in AY 2022/2023 at TAMUT.

Team No.	Students Majors	Project Title	Scope
1	M.E. and E.E.	Design and Manufacturing of an Archimedes Screw	The objective of this project is to design and manufacture a prototype Archimedes screw turbine to generate electricity. The design parameters for the Archimedes screw turbine were determined based on the current literature from various researchers. However, this study also highlights opportunities for improving the design and manufacturing processes.
5	CS	Hunter Sunder	This project is an Interactive Media game for Android devices. Its purpose post_creation is simply an interactive experience for users to enjoy in their off time, offering light entertainment to them as they go about their day_to_day.
6	C.S. and M.E.	Fiber Optic Motor Control	The project's goal is to design and construct a fiber optic cabling system that can control equipment in an industrial environment using a central access point and monitor its status. This design demonstrates how using fiber optics creates a flexible industrial environment due to its inherent properties, allowing easy use in harsh environments.
8	CS	ElectricEdge	This project aims to develop a platform that aims to provide a convenient and cost_effective solution to the growing demand for accessible and affordable charging infrastructure for electric vehicles.

Figure 1 compares students' overall performance between faculty_sponsored and industry_sponsored projects, with performance measured on a scale from 1 to 4. The performance for faculty_sponsored projects stands at 3.75 out of 4, with a standard deviation of 0.15, indicating a relatively uniform performance among the participants. In contrast, industry_sponsored projects have a marginally higher overall performance, scoring 3.76 out of 4, with a standard deviation of 0.18, suggesting a slightly broader range of outcomes. The difference in overall performance between the two types of projects is minimal, at just 0.01 points, or a mere 0.27% higher for industry_sponsored projects. The standard deviation is also quite close, with industry_sponsored projects showing only 0.03 points.

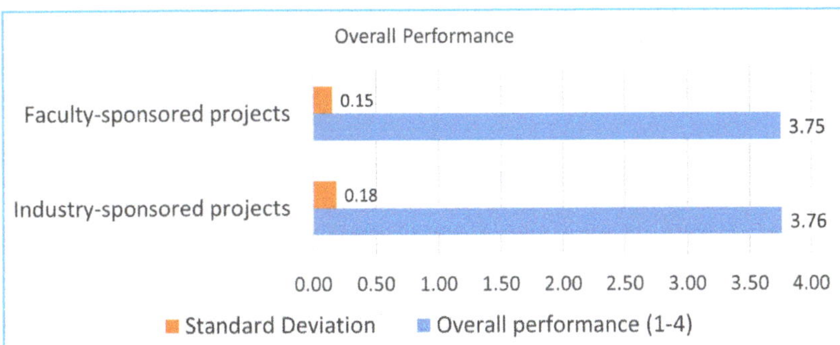

Figure 1. Overall performance in CSDP on a scale of 1–4.

4.2. Mentor Evaluation

The groups of students involved were matched with faculty and industry mentors according to the thematic focus of their projects. This strategic pairing was designed to harness the specific expertise of each mentor type, aiming to provide the most relevant and beneficial guidance possible. A comparative analysis of the evaluations provided by the industry and faculty mentors is presented, reflecting the distinct assessment approaches and expectations derived from their respective professional and academic backgrounds. The juxtaposition of these evaluations yields a nuanced view of the mentorship's effectiveness and the differential impact it may have on the students' project results.

Figure 2 depicts mentor evaluations of student performance in faculty_sponsored and industry_sponsored projects, scored on a scale from 1 to 4. Faculty_sponsored projects received a higher evaluation, with an average score of 3.71, compared to industry_sponsored projects, with an average score of 3.45. This indicates that mentors rated faculty_sponsored projects more favorably by a margin of 0.26 points, translating to a 7.53% higher score compared to industry_sponsored projects. The variability in scores, as indicated by the standard deviation, is higher in industry_sponsored projects, at 0.49, compared to 0.38 for faculty_sponsored projects. In percentage terms, the standard deviation for industry_sponsored projects is 28.95% higher than that for faculty_sponsored projects. This suggests that mentors gave a broader range of evaluations to industry_sponsored projects, pointing to a less consistent performance within this group. Overall, these numbers reflect a trend where faculty_sponsored projects not only scored higher on average but also had more consistent evaluations.

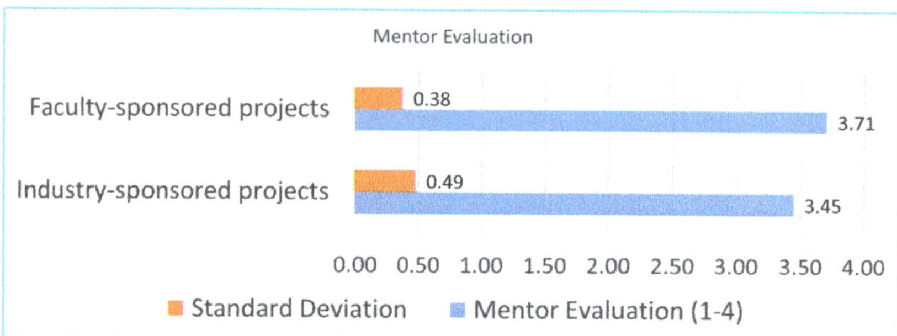

Figure 2. Industry and faculty mentor evaluations on a scale of 1–4.

Figure 3 illustrates a self_ and peer_evaluation form, an essential tool for systematically assessing CSDP. It is thoughtfully crafted to evaluate a range of performance indicators. Common criteria include attendance and punctuality, assessing each member's regular participation and timeliness. Another key aspect is responsibility, reflecting on the degree to which team members fulfill their roles and highlighting accountability in teamwork. The form is likely to include an assessment of how promptly tasks are completed, a vital element in project management, especially stressed in areas such as E.E. and M.E. Work quality is another key criterion, with evaluators examining the completeness and accuracy of the deliverables in relation to the project's aims. Additionally, the form assesses the ability to nurture a cooperative and supportive team atmosphere, evaluating this ability as a measure of teamwork and mutual support.

Furthermore, in collaborative environments, effective communication, including listening skills, is crucial and expected to be included in the evaluation. These aspects are usually rated on a scale ranging from 1 to 4, where 1 indicates the least favorable outcome and 4 is the most favorable. This scoring system allows for a detailed and measurable assessment of each participant's input. The form, serving a dual purpose, facilitates both self_review and peer review, guaranteeing that each team member's performance is thoroughly evaluated from various angles, thereby enriching the learning experience of the capstone project.

Peer Evaluation Form for Team Projects				
Project Title :			**Team no.**	
Write the name of each of your team members (including you) in a separate column. For each person, indicate the extent to which you agree with the statement on the left, using a scale of 1-4 (1=strongly disagree; 2=disagree; 3=agree; 4=strongly agree). Total the numbers in each column.				
	Student #1 (Self-evaluation)	Student #2	Student #3	Student #4
Attends team meetings regularly and arrives on time.				
Take responsibility in team efforts to complete the assigned tasks				
Completes team assignments on time.				
Prepares work in a quality manner.				
Demonstrates a cooperative and supportive attitude.				
Demonstrates effective listening skills to other team members.				
TOTALS				

Figure 3. Self_ and peer_review evaluation forms on a 1–4 scale.

Figure 4′s peer_review chart evaluates team performance for industry_sponsored and faculty_sponsored projects on a 1_to_4 scale. Industry_sponsored projects excelled with a perfect 4.0 in attendance and punctuality, while faculty_sponsored projects scored a slightly lower 3.5, indicating a 12.5% difference. Both types of projects rated equally well at 3.75 for responsibility and timely completion of assignments. Remarkably, both achieved perfect scores in preparing quality work and in exhibiting cooperative, supportive attitudes, reflecting exemplary standards and teamwork. However, industry_sponsored projects maintained perfect scores for effective listening skills, whereas faculty_sponsored projects lagged slightly at 3.5, a 12.5% lower rating.

The standard deviations for industry_sponsored projects were consistently zero, showing uniformity in peer evaluations, but faculty_sponsored projects showed more variability, with a standard deviation of 0.7 in meeting attendance, assignment completion, and listening skills. This suggests a broader range of peer perceptions of faculty_sponsored projects. Despite this, faculty_sponsored projects still received high marks, illustrating a generally positive assessment from peers across all categories, while industry_sponsored projects consistently garnered perfect peer evaluations.

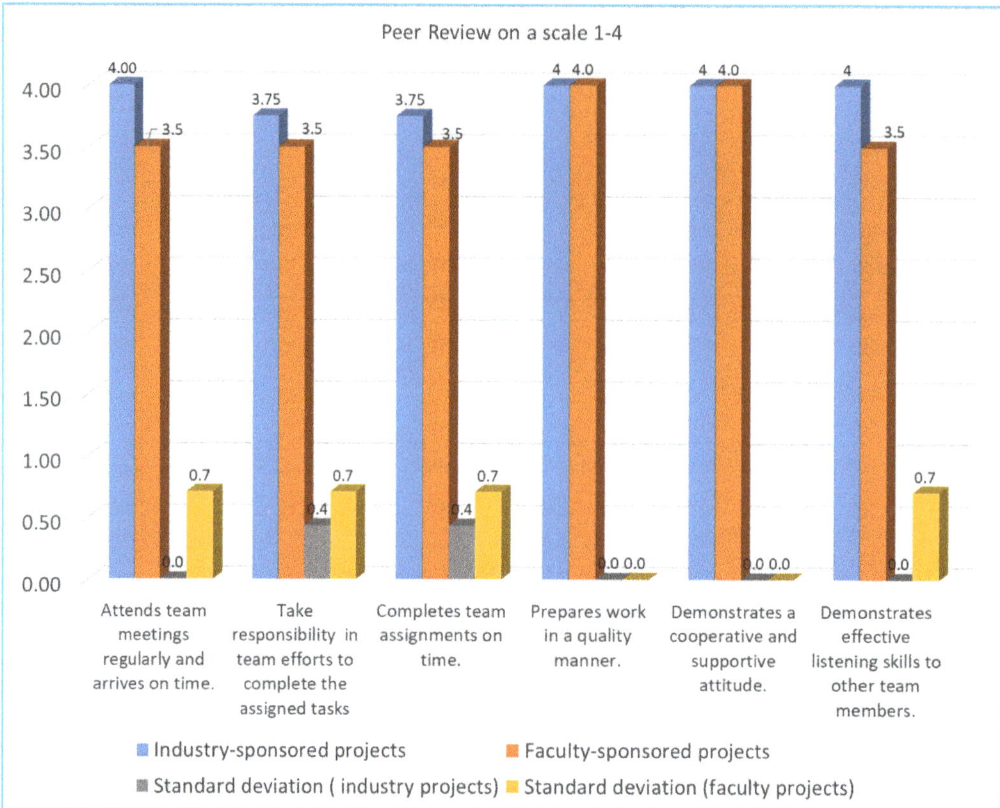

Figure 4. Peer_review results.

Figure 5′s analysis of self_evaluation data in CSDP highlights distinct contrasts between industry and faculty_sponsored projects. Industry_sponsored projects scored a perfect 100% in attendance and punctuality, surpassing faculty_sponsored projects, which achieved 95.75%. In contrast, faculty_led projects showcased superior performance in responsibility, attaining 95.75% compared to the industry's 84%, hinting at a greater sense of commitment. Timeliness in completing assignments was nearly equivalent for both, with industry_sponsored projects slightly leading at 97.73%, against faculty's 95.83%. In terms of work quality, both types of projects maintained high standards, with industry scoring 95.45% and faculty at 95.83%.

However, faculty_sponsored projects outshone in fostering cooperative attitudes and demonstrating effective listening skills, scoring an impeccable 100% in both, exceeding the industry's 95.45% and 97.73%. The standard deviation analysis indicated greater variability in industry_sponsored projects, particularly in "Responsibility in Team Efforts", with a standard deviation of about 0.505. This variation suggests a wider range of individual experiences in industry projects, in contrast to faculty projects, where scores were more tightly clustered, especially in categories where they attained perfect scores. Overall, while industry_sponsored projects have a slight edge in areas such as punctuality and timeliness, faculty_sponsored projects are notable for their strengths in teamwork and communication skills.

Figure 5. Self_review results.

5. Discussion

The comparative analysis of industry_sponsored and faculty_sponsored projects in CSDP, utilizing numerical data and percentages, reveals key differences between these two models. Industry_sponsored projects slightly outperformed in overall performance, scoring an average of 3.76 out of 4 compared to faculty_sponsored projects' 3.75. This minimal difference, just 0.01 points or 0.27% higher for industry projects, suggests a marginally more effective approach to meeting project objectives. The similar standard deviations (0.18 for industry and 0.15 for faculty) indicate consistent project outcomes across both models. The independent samples t_test (Welch's t_test) [19], conducted with the actual data points, resulted in a t_statistic of approximately 0.151 and a p_value of roughly 0.882. Therefore, based on this statistical test, the difference in performance scores between industry_sponsored and faculty_sponsored projects is not statistically significant.

In mentor evaluations, faculty_sponsored projects achieved an average score of 3.71, surpassing industry_sponsored projects' average of 3.45. This difference of 0.26 points, or a 7.53% higher score, suggests faculty mentors may favor projects more aligned with academic standards. Industry_sponsored projects showed a higher standard deviation of 0.49, compared to 0.38 for faculty_sponsored projects, indicating 28.95% greater variability due to diverse industry expectations and standards.

The independent samples t_test (Welch's t_test) for mentor evaluations resulted in a t_statistic of approximately −1.366 and a p_value of approximately 0.192. The negative t-statistic indicates that the average mentor evaluation score for the industry-sponsored projects is lower than for the faculty-sponsored projects. However, the *p*-value is higher than the conventional alpha level of 0.05, meaning that the difference in mentor evaluation scores between the two groups is not statistically significant at the 5% significance level.

Peer and self-reviews in these projects offer a window into team dynamics and the individual roles played. Industry-sponsored projects excelled with perfect punctuality and listening skills scores, whereas faculty-sponsored projects scored a lower 3.5 in these areas, marking a 12.5% difference. However, in areas such as responsibility and cooperative attitudes, faculty-sponsored projects performed better, scoring 0.26 points or 7.53% higher in mentor evaluations. This points to different skill set priorities: industry-sponsored projects tend to enhance professional conduct and communication skills, while faculty-sponsored ones focus more on teamwork and collaboration.

The standard deviations in peer reviews show a notable contrast. Faculty-sponsored projects exhibited more variability (0.7) in areas such as meeting attendance, assignment completion, and listening skills, unlike industry-sponsored projects, which generally showed little to no variability. This suggests a broader spectrum of experiences within faculty-sponsored teams, allowing for greater individual differences. However, the independent samples *t*-test (Welch's *t*-test) was conducted for each of the six peer-review evaluation criteria, comparing scores from industry-sponsored projects with faculty-sponsored projects. For EC1, EC2, EC3, and EC6, despite having positive t-statistics indicating that the average scores for industry-sponsored projects might be higher than those for faculty-sponsored projects, the *p*-values are high (0.500 and above for EC1 and EC6, and 0.710 for EC2 and EC3). This means that for these criteria, there is no statistically significant difference in peer review scores between the two groups.

For EC4 and EC5, the standard deviation of zero indicates no variation in the scores within at least one group, rendering a *t*-test inappropriate for these criteria. In such cases where there is no variance, the mean scores are effectively the same across all observations within the groups, and thus a *t*-test is not needed to infer that there is no difference.

Supporting these observations, self-reviews for faculty-sponsored projects displayed significant consistency, especially in "Cooperative and Supportive Attitude" and "Effective Listening Skills", where they achieved perfect scores of 100%. In contrast, industry projects scored slightly lower at 95.45% and 97.73% in these categories. This consistent scoring in faculty-sponsored projects suggests a more uniform focus on teamwork and communication skills. Yet, all *p*-values of Welch's *t*-test are much greater than 0.05, indicating no statistically significant difference between the scores of peer reviews of industry-sponsored and faculty-sponsored projects for any of the six evaluation criteria.

In summary, Welch's *t*-test, a form of statistical significance testing, indicates no statistically significant difference between the evaluation criteria used for industry-sponsored and faculty-sponsored projects. However, descriptive statistics can still offer valuable insights into the nature of the data and potential areas of interest for future research or practical application.

6. Recommendations

Integrating faculty and industry-sponsored projects represents a forward-looking strategy that leverages the strengths of academic and practical perspectives in educational programs. The next steps could involve:

Developing a Hybrid Model: Creating a framework that combines the structured, theory-based approach of faculty-sponsored projects with the dynamic, real-world challenges of industry-sponsored projects. This model would encourage a balanced curriculum that prepares students for both academic and practical challenges.

Collaboration and Partnership Building: Strengthening partnerships with industries and incorporating their feedback into the curriculum design. This ensures that the projects remain relevant to current industry standards and needs.

Curriculum Integration: Incorporating projects as a core component of the curriculum rather than as extracurricular activities. This integration would ensure that all students gain valuable experience in both types of projects.

Assessment and Continuous Improvement: Establishing robust assessment mechanisms to evaluate the effectiveness of the hybrid model. Feedback from students, faculty, and industry partners should be used to refine project objectives and outcomes continuously.

Scaling and Diversification: Expanding the range of projects to cover more disciplines and industries. This diversification would provide students with a broader exposure to various fields and challenges.

By integrating both faculty and industry_sponsored projects, educational programs can offer a more comprehensive and practical learning experience, better_preparing students for the challenges of the modern workforce.

7. Conclusions

The experiences and outcomes of students in industry_sponsored versus faculty_sponsored projects in CSDP differ significantly, each with its own unique advantages and challenges. Students participating in industry_sponsored projects, scoring an average of 3.76 out of 4 in overall performance, gain invaluable exposure to real_world problems and practical applications of their theoretical knowledge. However, they may face challenges adapting to the industry environment, which could be reflected in the slightly higher standard deviation (0.18) in these projects compared to faculty_sponsored ones (0.15). This variability might stem from industry mentors' fluctuating availability and diverse expectations. Despite these challenges, the value of industry_sponsored projects is considerable. Engaging in real_life problem_solving enhances critical thinking and problem_solving skills and potentially increases job placement prospects. The experience of dealing with tangible, industry_relevant challenges provides a significant advantage in the job market, as students are better prepared for the dynamics of a professional setting.

On the other hand, faculty_sponsored projects scored slightly lower in overall performance (3.75 out of 4) but offered a more consistent and structured learning environment, thanks in part to the more regular availability of mentors. Faculty mentors, typically scoring an average of 3.71 in mentor evaluations compared to 3.45 for industry mentors, provide guidance that is closely aligned with the academic objectives of the projects. These projects may not offer the same level of industry engagement, but they excel in developing foundational skills such as teamwork, communication, and academic rigor—skills that are also critical in professional settings.

Regarding peer evaluations, industry_sponsored projects received higher scores in professional skills such as punctuality and listening, with perfect scores of 4.0, indicating their effectiveness in preparing students for professional environments. While scoring slightly lower in these areas (3.5, a 12.5% lower score), faculty_sponsored projects still foster important collaborative skills and a structured approach to problem_solving.

In summary, the comparative analysis of industry and faculty_sponsored CSDPs provides insights with implications extending into the realms of PBL. Despite the lack of statistically significant differences in performance metrics, the nuanced variations offer a deeper understanding of how PBL principles manifest in a real_world setting. The engagement with actual industrial problems and the academic rigor of faculty_guided projects together reflect the multidimensional benefits of PBL—preparing students academically and for the unpredictable nature of engineering professions. This study advocates for an educational paradigm that integrates the PBL elements found in CSDPs, promoting a balanced approach to engineering education that is theoretically sound and practically oriented.

Author Contributions: Conceptualization, M.M.M. methodology, M.M.M. and M.N.U.; formal analysis, M.M.M. and M.N.U.; investigation, F.Z.; resources, F.Z.; data curation, M.M.M.; writing—original draft preparation, M.M.M., M.N.U. and F.Z.; writing—review and editing, M.M.M. and F.Z.; visualization, M.M.M. and M.N.U.; supervision, M.M.M.; project administration, M.M.M. All authors have read and agreed to the published version of the manuscript.

Funding: This research received no external funding.

Institutional Review Board Statement: Not applicable. The study uses anonymous and aggregated data values.

Informed Consent Statement: Not applicable.

Data Availability Statement: All data used for the article are included.

Conflicts of Interest: The authors declare no conflicts of interest.

References

1. Badir, A.; O'Neill, R.; Kinzli, K.-D.; Komisar, S.; Kim, J.–Y. Fostering Project–Based Learning through Industry Engagement in Capstone Design Projects. *Educ. Sci.* **2023**, *13*, 361. [CrossRef]
2. Steingrimsson, B.; Jones, R.; Estesami, F.; Yi, S. Ecosystem for Engineering Design Learning_A Comparative Analysis. *IJEE Int. J. Eng. Educ.* **2017**, *33*, 1499–1512.
3. Deepamala, N.; Shobha, G. Effective Approach in Making Capstone Project a Holistic Learning Experience to Students of Undergraduate Computer Science Engineering Program. *J. Technol. Sci. Educ.* **2018**, *8*, 420. [CrossRef]
4. Bragós Bardia, R.; Aoun, L.; Charosky Larrieu-Let, G.; Bermejo Broto, S.; Rey Micolau, F.; Pegueroles Vallés, J.R. Correlation Study between the Access Mark and the Performance in Project_Based and Standard Courses. In Proceedings of the Towards a New Future in Engineering Education, New Scenarios That European Alliances of Tech Universities Open up, Universitat Politècnica de Catalunya, Barcelona, Spain, 19–22 September 2022; pp. 151–159.
5. Beyerlein, S.; Davis, D.; Huang, Y.M.; McKenzie, L.; Trevisan, M. Capstone Design Courses and Assessment: A National Study. In Proceedings of the 2004 Annual Conference Proceedings, ASEE Conferences, Salt Lake City, UT, USA, 20–23 June 2004; pp. 9.286.1–9.286.18.
6. Morkos, B.; Joshi, S.; Summers, J.D. Investigating the Impact of Requirements Elicitation and Evolution on Course Performance in a Pre_Capstone Design Course. *J. Eng. Des.* **2019**, *30*, 155–179. [CrossRef]
7. Liew, C.P.; Puteh, M.; Hamzah, S.H. Comparative Study of Engineering Design Project Assessment Rubrics to Address the Washington Accord's Complexity Attributes. *Asean J. Eng. Educ.* **2021**, *4*, 71–94. [CrossRef]
8. Yousafzai, J.; Damaj, I.; El Abd, M. A Unified Approach for Assessing Capstone Design Projects and Student Outcomes in Computer Engineering Programs. In Proceedings of the 2015 IEEE Global Engineering Education Conference (EDUCON), Tallinn, Estonia, 18–20 March 2015; IEEE: Piscataway, NJ, USA, 2015; pp. 333–339.
9. Meah, K.; Hake, D.; Wilkerson, S.D. A Multidisciplinary Capstone Design Project to Satisfy ABET Student Outcomes. *Educ. Res. Int.* **2020**, *2020*, 9563782. [CrossRef]
10. Jaime, A.; Olarte, J.J.; Garcia–Izquierdo, F.J.; Dominguez, C. The Effect of Internships on Computer Science Engineering Capstone Projects. *IEEE Trans. Educ.* **2020**, *63*, 24–31. [CrossRef]
11. Al–Olimat, K. An Industry Sponsored Capstone Project: A Story Of Success. In Proceedings of the 2010 Annual Conference & Exposition Proceedings, ASEE Conferences, Louisville, KY, USA, 20–23 June 2010; pp. 15.155.1–15.155.18.
12. Rawal, V.; O'Shields, S.T.; Summers, J.D. Comparison of Motivations and Perceptions of Capstone Benefits for Industry Sponsors: An Interview_Based Study of Faculty and Industry. *Int. J. Mech. Eng. Educ.* **2022**, *50*, 269–290. [CrossRef]
13. Ray, J.L. Industry_Academic Partnerships for Successful Capstone Projects. In Proceedings of the 33rd Annual Frontiers in Education, 2003, FIE 2003, Westminster, CO, USA, 5–8 November 2003; IEEE: Piscataway, NJ, USA, 2003; pp. S2B_24–S2B_29.
14. Gnanapragasam, N. Industrially Sponsored Senior Capstone Experience: Program Implementation and Assessment. *J. Prof. Issues Eng. Educ. Pract.* **2008**, *134*, 257–262. [CrossRef]
15. Vu, J.H.; Frojd, N.; Shenkel–Therolf, C.; Janzen, D.S. Evaluating Test_Driven Development in an Industry_Sponsored Capstone Project. In Proceedings of the 2009 Sixth International Conference on Information Technology: New Generations, Las Vegas, NV, USA, 27–29 April 2009; IEEE: Piscataway, NJ, USA, 2009; pp. 229–234.
16. Berry, F.C.; Huang, W.; Exter, M. Improving Accuracy of Self_and_Peer Assessment in Engineering Technology Capstone. *IEEE Trans. Educ.* **2023**, *66*, 174–187. [CrossRef]
17. Zhang, J.; Zhang, Z.; Philbin, S.P.; Huijser, H.; Wang, Q.; Jin, R. Toward Next_generation Engineering Education: A Case Study of an Engineering Capstone Project Based on BIM Technology in MEP Systems. *Comput. Appl. Eng. Educ.* **2021**, *30*, 146–162. [CrossRef]
18. Shaikh, M.K. How to Form a Software Engineering Capstone Team? *Heliyon* **2021**, *7*, e06629. [CrossRef] [PubMed]
19. West, R.M. Best Practice in Statistics: Use the Welch t_Test When Testing the Difference between Two Groups. *Ann. Clin. Biochem. Int. J. Lab. Med.* **2021**, *58*, 267–269. [CrossRef] [PubMed]

education sciences

MDPI

Article

Establishing a PBL STEM Framework for Pre-Service Teachers

Lisa N. Pitot *, Maggie Lee McHugh and Jennifer Kosiak

Educational Studies, University of Wisconsin-La Crosse, La Crosse, WI 54601, USA;
mmchugh@uwlax.edu (M.L.M.); jkosiak@uwlax.edu (J.K.)
* Correspondence: lpitot@uwlax.edu

Abstract: Research into pre-service teachers' (PSTs) ability to develop meaningful interdisciplinary, project-based curricula is lacking; at the same time, many young adolescents fail to see the connections between their schoolwork and the real world. As such, there is a need for new methods to prepare elementary and middle school teachers' abilities to integrate mathematics and science through authentic content. This article will examine how elementary and middle PSTs collaborated across their mathematics and science methods courses to design project-based learning (PBL) unit plans that integrate social justice and global awareness in a STEM context. The content analysis of 25 distinct PBL unit plans documented the levels at which PSTs could incorporate practical PBL design elements into their projects, integrate robust mathematical content, and identify connections to social justice and global awareness. Through this analysis, we will share the successes and challenges faced in guiding PSTs to create PBL STEM units and present a series of next steps that could be taken to further this cross-curricular endeavor.

Keywords: project-based learning; STEM; social justice; global awareness; mathematics conceptual understanding

1. Introduction

Initiatives that aim to increase awareness of and develop competencies in science, technology, engineering, and mathematics, or STEM, have deepened as a response to the challenges of the 21st century [1]. *YOU Belong in STEM* is a current focus within the United States Department of Education, as expressed in the launching of a new initiative by which to enhance STEM education for all students. The initiative aims to raise the bar, investing in PK-higher education students so that they may reach higher levels of STEM learning through authentic and challenging experiences [2]. As researchers and educators, we define STEM education as a teaching and learning approach focused on the interdisciplinary integration of science, technology, engineering, and mathematics as a cohesive and interwoven unit. We believe that STEM disciplines "cannot and should not be taught in isolation, just as they do not exist in isolation in the real world or the workforce" [3].

This approach integrates rigorous STEM content standards with authentic and engaging contexts to further student development of workplace competencies such as teamwork, communication, problem-solving, critical thinking, and self-management [3–6]. An integrated STEM education can also develop students' global awareness competencies by promoting scientific and mathematical inquiry from global perspectives [5,7]. These workforce and global awareness competencies are also distinctive attributes of project-based learning (PBL), a pedagogical approach where students engage in authentic inquiry guided by driving questions as they work together to solve real-world problems by creating public products to answer the driving question [8–11].

1.1. PBL STEM Framework

A PBL STEM framework integrating global awareness requires a foundational understanding of two critical components—PBL design elements and integrated STEM instructional elements [12]. While PK-12 education practices may identify and focus on these foundations separately, the realization of an integrated approach encourages each content area to be equally emphasized in the teaching and learning of STEM, where content elements are interwoven throughout the project.

1.1.1. PBL Design Elements

According to McHugh [10], PBL is "a teaching and learning practice where students sustain exploration into an authentic question, challenge, or problem while engaging in academic content and developing critical success skills, such as communication, collaboration, and critical thinking" (p. 24). As a pedagogical approach, the benefits of PBL in improving student learning outcomes have been extensively researched; these benefits include the construction of cognitively demanding content knowledge [13–15], enhanced critical thinking and problem-solving skills [14,15] and the development of success skills such as time management and effective communication [10,14,16].

Designing a high-quality PBL unit involves attention to critical design elements, as outlined by PBLWorks [16], a leading organization in PBL professional development, research, and curricular materials. The learning goals are at the core of the design elements, which include grade-level standards and success skills. A **challenging problem or question** centers on a relevant problem or question that guides student learning and exploration [13]. **Sustained inquiry** refers to the cyclical nature of questioning, exploring, and applying new knowledge. **Authenticity** includes not only a real-world context or topic of interest directly connected to the lives of students but also the use of research methods and tools that align with those used by experts in that field of study [10,16]. **Student voice and choice** highlight students' pivotal role in a project, including providing students with opportunities to determine how they engage in the project and express their knowledge and creativity through the final product [13]. **Critique and revision** outline how students play a role as givers and receivers of feedback to improve project products and project management. **Reflection** centers on teachers and students reflecting upon growth in content understanding and success skills during and at the project's culmination. Lastly, **Public product** focuses on students as creators of a physical or digital product and presentation that is shared with people outside the classroom walls [10,16].

1.1.2. Integrated STEM Instructional Elements

Rather than teaching content in isolated classrooms, an integrated STEM education calls for combining the subject areas through relevant contexts to engage students and increase their understanding of and connection across each subject area [5,12,17,18]. Integrated STEM instruction can enhance student engagement [5], increase interest in STEM [12], and make learning more meaningful [18].

Designing integrated STEM curricular material can be conceptualized through six design elements [4]. The first element focuses on situating STEM integration in motivating and engaging contexts. These contexts, such as global, social, and environmental contexts, should allow students to use their prior knowledge to make sense of the context and provide a purpose for learning [17]. The second and third elements require students to engage in engineering design challenges with opportunities to learn from failure through redesign. The fourth element requires students to conceptually understand and apply scientific and mathematical concepts that align with grade-level standards. Student-centered pedagogies, which form the fifth element, allow students to participate actively in their learning [17]. The final element emphasizes teamwork and communication in which students collaboratively discuss scientific and mathematical concepts through multiple representations [17].

The PBL design elements lead directly to the goals of an integrated STEM curriculum. Jolly [19] tells educators that STEM is an interwoven, integrated practice that focuses "students on local, national, and global situations or problems, [that will] bring the classroom alive for students and deepen their learning" (p. 8). In STEM experiences, students apply knowledge to real-world situations by using tools or manipulating objects found in STEM careers while building social skills such as decision-making and collaborative problem-solving. As such, these integrated STEM elements align with several PBL design elements, as shown in Table 1 below.

Table 1. Alignment between an integrated STEM curriculum and PBL design elements.

Integrated STEM Instructional Elements	PBL Design Elements
Motivating and engaging contexts	Challenging problem or question authenticity
Science and mathematics concept	Learning goals sustained inquiry reflection
Student-centered pedagogies	Sustained inquiry critique and revision reflection
Teamwork and communication	Critique and revision public product

1.1.3. Focusing on the M (Mathematics) in STEM

Research has noted that mathematics often plays a secondary role in the integrated STEM classroom, which researchers call a "service role" or an "auxiliary discipline" to science, engineering, and technology concepts [20]. For example, Roehrig et al. [18] analyzed STEM curricula and found that mathematics concepts represented less than 10% of new learning, often being used as a tool for data analysis in service of science and engineering concepts. Roehrig et al. [18] further state that engaging in science and engineering practices inherently includes mathematical practices; however, in the curricular review, these practices are not made transparent but are implied, again leading to mathematics playing a service role in STEM curricula.

Therefore, national mathematics organizations have insisted that STEM educators make the M "transparent and explicit," recognizing that not all of our (K-12) students "will 'see' the mathematics that is involved in a particular problem" [21]. Furthermore, the mathematics used should move beyond procedural computations that a computer or calculator could quickly compute towards using and applying conceptual mathematical knowledge as an integral, intentional component of the STEM unit [18].

To assist with making mathematics visible in integrated STEM instruction, Guzey et al. [17] developed the STEM Integration Curriculum Assessment Tool (STEM-ICA). This tool consists of various rubric components related to high-quality integrated STEM curricular material, including several PBL design elements such as motivating and engaging questions, student-centered instructional strategies, implicit opportunities for teamwork and communication, and integrating science and mathematics content. Concerning the integration of mathematics content, the STEM-ICA tool operationally defines this integration as the alignment of the curricular material to appropriate grade-level mathematics standards and the incorporation of mathematical concepts so that students can "learn, understand, and use fundamental mathematics concepts" to "promote coherent understanding of mathematical thinking" [17] (p. 17).

These elements of mathematics integration in STEM are consistent with calls from national mathematics organizations highlighting the need for conceptual understanding and procedural fluency in the mathematics classroom. Conceptual understanding is operationally defined as "an integrated and functional grasp of mathematical ideas" so that students "know more than isolated facts and methods" [22] (p. 118). Conceptual understanding lays the foundation for procedural fluency, providing pathways for students to become flexible and efficient users of mathematics in real-world and mathematical problems [23].

1.1.4. Global Awareness in STEM Education

One way to realize the PBL design element of authenticity within an integrated STEM education is through a global awareness foundation. Global awareness has been defined as a "set of knowledge and skills to understand the world, comprehend current global problems and affairs, and devise solutions considering human dimensions as well as a positive attitude towards interacting peacefully, respectfully, and productively with people from diverse cultures" [24] (p. 1). Schools can and do play a critical role in developing globally aware students, providing classroom opportunities to examine local to global issues, engage in dialogue with people from diverse cultures, and analyze current issues impacting our global society [25].

For the most part, global awareness in STEM education naturally leads to the constructs of social justice, equity, and diversity across geographic levels, locally to globally [25,26]. According to Freire [27], educators should teach for social justice by fostering critical consciousness and empowering students to challenge and change oppressive structures in society. Social justice pedagogy includes facets of a caring classroom, where teachers and students learn together through dialogue about real-world issues and culturally relevant content, intending to develop students' critical consciousness [28]. Student empowerment, respect for diversity, and an emphasis on inclusion are central tenets of teaching and learning for social justice [27].

Specifically in STEM, social justice ensures that all students, regardless of their background, have equal access to and are represented within the curriculum. STEM educators must be responsive and welcoming to students' diverse backgrounds, including their culture, religion, sexual orientation, gender, and socio-economic backgrounds [29]. According to Mackenzie [30], social justice in STEM promotes academically rigorous content grounded in students' lives, democratic classrooms, safe havens, and promotion of activism. Mackenzie [30] suggests a range of topics that educators can use to infuse social justice in the science classroom. These topics in the literature are referred to as socioscientific issues or SSIs. SSIs are controversial, socially relevant, real-world problems informed by science that often include an ethical component [31]. Therefore, social justice in STEM from an SSI lens aligns with the PBL design elements of a challenging problem or question and student voice and choice.

Proponents of teaching science using SSIs have found that SSI-based instruction can promote the development of students' global awareness [32,33]. Therefore, global awareness and social justice aim to align directly with the PBL design elements of authenticity and public products. Both design elements center on students as agents of change when the public product aligns with awareness, advocacy, or action goals. Students can bring awareness to a critical topic, such as access to clean water, through a social media campaign. Students can then move towards advocacy by proposing a bill for the legislature to aid in access to clean water. Students can even move towards actionable change, such as assisting in water cleanup efforts or fundraising for clean water filters to give to families. These change agency products can also occur from a local to a global scale. For example, in a PBL STEM middle school classroom, students embodied the role of environmental engineers, where they designed "awareness campaigns to address environmentally destructive habits" at a local level, then translated individual human activities and lifestyle choices to realize the "global costs of these same activities at national or global levels" [34] (p. 73). Students then created "language-neutral posters that emphasize images over words [to] contextualize findings for a global audience" [34] (p. 73). This integrated PBL STEM unit exemplified students as local and global change agents, bringing awareness through campaigns. As students engage in awareness, advocacy, or action, they may move from sharing their ideas locally, such as the whole school, district, or community, to a national and global level through social media or fundraising efforts [10].

1.2. PST's Abilities to Produce PBL STEM Curricular Units

Much of the current research has highlighted the ability of in-service educators to integrate PBL and STEM [12,17]; however, research into pre-service teachers' (PSTs') ability to develop meaningful interdisciplinary, project-based STEM curricula is lacking. Research also suggests that teacher education programs fail to train PSTs for diverse classrooms or prepare them to integrate global awareness through social justice issues [25,35]. A gap exists between theory and classroom approaches related to integrating social justice theory with STEM practices [36]. As such, there is a need for new methods to prepare elementary and middle school teachers' abilities to integrate mathematics and science through authentic content. This content engagement should connect quality standards to real-world projects about students' interests.

Our study aimed to answer the overarching question: How does using an integrated PBL unit plan across undergraduate science and math methods courses support PSTs' abilities to produce meaningful PBL STEM units that increase students' global awareness and incorporate a social justice lens? To answer this question, we sought to answer the following questions:

- How do PSTs incorporate effective PBL design elements in a socioscientific PBL STEM unit?
- How do resulting PBL STEM units integrate concepts of global awareness and social justice?
- How do PSTs emphasize mathematics in PBL STEM units?

2. Methodology

2.1. Participants

A qualitative case study design was employed to provide an in-depth understanding of PST's use of a PBL STEM social justice framework. Specifically, the research methodology is a collective case study that includes the analysis of multiple unit plans developed by PSTs of senior status enrolled in a university Bachelor of Science Education degree program [37]. Over four semesters, 76 PSTs worked in groups of 2–4 developing the units. A convenience sampling technique was employed as the PSTs were required to enroll in the semester-long courses taught by two of the authors; additionally, informed consent was obtained from each student. The classes were designed to prepare the participants in the mathematics and science methodologies specific to the teaching of students in elementary and middle schools (grades 1–8).

Positionality Statement from Researchers

Two of the three authors for the current study were instructors of the methods course that supported PSTs in developing their PBL STEM units. Both authors contributed to the data analysis and interpretation. To avoid bias in the scoring and interpreting the findings, the authors brought in an external third author who independently scored the projects to determine consistency across all rubric categories. Additional parties independently read the article to ensure consistency and lack of bias.

2.2. Data Sources

Methods course instructors collaborated on implementing the PBL STEM unit plan assignment. The completed written unit plan proposals, developed over the semester, served as the data source for this research study. Before introducing the unit plan assignment, the first science methods unit focused on the nature of science (NOS). PSTs examined science as a noun, a verb, and a way of knowing. Identifying an SSI and how it related to the NOS discussion board helped them identify topics they thought would be relevant to their future students' lives. In math methods, PSTs discussed the importance of using mathematics to catalyze change and as an introduction to the standards for mathematical practice.

By the fourth week of the semester, instructors focused on introducing the PBL STEM unit plan as part of learning the intricacies of teaching K-9 students science and mathematics. Instructors connected the unit plan final assignment to the globally responsive teaching attributes explicitly called for within the university's conceptual framework. While valuing human diversity and the various talents of their future students, PSTs at this university were expected to infuse a rigorous integrated curriculum linked to global events to make the world a healthy, sustainable, and just environment. While promoting global responsiveness and a socially just curriculum, instructors used a modified PBLWorks template and rubric to guide the assignment. PSTs self-selected into groups based on similar SSI topic interests. Beginning with a concept mapping activity, PSTs brainstormed sub-topics they could include in their projects. Using a flow chart or storyboard helped the PSTs to illustrate how their unit topics would flow, connecting the essential question with a series of activities to the culminating project; each series of activities is grouped into a milestone (Appendix A, project template).

Additional topics discussed during each science methods course included formative diagnostic pre-assessments, the learning cycle model, literacy integration, environmental science standards, and pedagogical content knowledge. Math methods classes focused on the five strands of mathematical proficiency: conceptual understanding, procedural fluency, adaptive reasoning, strategic competence, and productive disposition (National Research Council, 2001). In addition, PSTs discussed and practiced engineering design during science methods, followed by creating a STEM experience, which they implemented for a group of middle schoolers in the community. Feedback from the instructors on each group's project progress was given approximately bi-weekly for the remaining weeks of the semester. This required both instructors to stay on pace with PSTs' project completion by the end of the semester. Before their final submission, peer feedback was given anonymously based on the PBLWorks rubric supplied to the PSTs at the project's onset. Expectations on the project template included requiring PSTs to reflect and act upon both instructor and peer feedback.

2.3. Data Analysis

Rubric Development

The PBL Design Elements rubric was adapted from the Project Design Rubric from PBLWorks [16]. The development of the rubrics for (1) application of social justice and global awareness (Table 2) and (2) mathematical emphasis (Table 3) began with a review of the literature within each area, followed by initial development by the authors. Because the established PBLWorks rubric contained three performance levels for each criterion, the two additional rubrics developed for this study included three. Drafts of each rubric were sent to university colleagues for expert review. Rubric edits were completed, and, when applicable, the rubric was revisited by content experts until a consensus was reached that the rubric was sufficient for this study.

Table 2. Rubric for Application of Social Justice and Global Awareness.

Criteria	3 Demonstrating	2 Developing	1 Beginning
Application of Social Justice Issue	Teacher candidates integrate social justice issues * that deepen and extend students' understanding of the world.	Teacher candidates integrate social justice issues that develop students' understanding of the world.	Teacher candidates integrate social justice issues that pay little attention to students' understanding of the world.
Global Awareness	The project examines local issues and their connection to the global community or vice versa.	The project thoroughly examines a local OR global issue.	The project has a limited examination of a local OR global issue.

* Social justice incorporates environmental, racial, gender, disability, and economic injustices/inequities.

Table 3. Rubric for Mathematics Emphasis.

Criteria	3 Demonstrating	2 Developing	1 Beginning
Mathe- matics Standard	Targets a grade-level mathematics standard(s) to the full depth of the standard.	Targets a grade-level mathematics standard(s) but does not address the entire standard(s).	Targets a below-grade level mathematics standard(s) or unrelated mathematics standard(s).
Procedural and Conceptual	The project focuses on a balance of mathematical procedures and deeper conceptual understanding.	The project focuses on mathematical procedures with some connection to conceptual understanding.	The project focuses on mathematical procedures with no connection to conceptual understanding.
Application	Provides opportunities for students to apply mathematical concepts in authentic problem-solving situations.	Provides limited opportunities for students to apply mathematical concepts in authentic problem-solving situations.	Provides no opportunities for students to apply mathematical concepts in authentic, problem-solving situations.

Thematic analysis was employed as the PBL STEM unit plans were scored according to the three rubrics, in most cases by each of the three authors. Projects were individually scored according to the rubric criteria. Cross-case analysis was utilized to identify commonalities, differences, and overarching themes.

Trustworthiness and rigor: If scores were more than one half-point apart, the reviewers engaged in member checking by examining the unit plans together to find evidence to support their initial score. When necessary, the individual scores from each reviewer were averaged for each criterion. For example, initial scores for the *Water Waste* project for challenging problem or question were scored 2, 2, and 2.75 by each of the researchers. The higher scorer noted the driving question, "*How is water wasted in our community, and what can you do to reduce water waste?*" This was aligned closely with a three on the rubric, scoring 2.75 as the level of challenge was lacking. The other two scorers initially scored this a 2 for similar reasons, thinking the question lacked rigor for the grade level. Discussion ensued on appropriate levels of rigor, which led to an average score of 2.25 for this criterion.

3. Findings

Over four semesters, PSTs working in groups created 25 PBL unit plans. Teacher candidates had selected a variety of topics related to meaningful SSIs. The broad issues ranged from genetically modified organisms, climate change, vaccines, and endangered species to water quality and access. Table 4 highlights six projects that stood out across the three rubrics. These projects support key findings after scoring (see Appendix B for a complete list of 25 projects and final scores for all three rubrics).

Table 4. PBL design element results for exemplar projects.

		PBL Design Elements					
	Unit Driving Question	**Problem or Question**	**Sustained Inquiry**	**Authenticity**	**Student Voice and Choice**	**Reflection**	**Public Product**
Our Changing World	What is climate change, and how do you interact with it on a personal, communal, and global level?	2	2	2.5	2.5	1	2
Water Waste	How is water wasted in our community, and what can you do to reduce water waste?	2.25	2	2.5	3	2	2.5
Sustainable Farming	How can sustainable farming practices benefit our school?	2	1.5	2	1	2	1.5
Climate Change Social Media	Who will be affected the most by a changing climate, and what can we as middle schoolers do to make an impact and help people facing the most struggles with a changing climate?	2.75	3	3	3	2.5	3
Recycling in Wisconsin	How can we, as earth citizens, contribute to recycling efforts in our schools and homes?	3	2	2.5	2	2.5	2.5
Viruses	How do we protect our immune system from viruses, and how does it differ globally?	2	2	2	2	1.5	2

3.1. PBL Design Elements

The PBL STEM units were first examined for alignment to six PBL design elements: challenging problem or question, sustained inquiry, authenticity, student voice and choice, reflection, and public product. The PBL design element of learning goals was examined in the mathematics emphasis section of the rubric with the criterion of standard. The researchers did not discuss the design element of critique and revision as the time allotted for developing PBL STEM units was limited. Given the limited time, the PSTs were never explicitly taught how to build critique and revision within a student project; hence, the researchers did not feel justified in assessing PSTs on a concept they had yet to learn. The reviewers scored each of the six design elements. Table 5 highlights a rubric with modified criteria and identifies the results as a mean score and standard deviation, rounded to the hundredth place (see full rubric Appendix C).

Table 5. PBL design elements rubric and overall results (n = 25).

Criteria	3 Demonstrating	2 Developing	1 Beginning	Results
Challenging Problem or Question	The project is focused on a central problem at the appropriate level of challenge.	The project is focused on a central problem, but the level of challenge might be a mismatch for the intended students.	The project is not yet focused on a central problem, or the problem or driving question is too quickly answered to justify a project.	M: 2.21 SD: 0.52
Sustained Inquiry	Inquiry is sustained over time and academically rigorous.	The project includes limited opportunities for inquiry.	The project is more like an activity than an extended inquiry process.	M: 1.78 SD: 0.57

Table 5. *Cont.*

Criteria	3 Demonstrating	2 Developing	1 Beginning	Results
Authenticity	The project has an authentic context, impacts the world, and speaks to students' personal concerns, interests, or identities.	The project has some authentic features, but opportunities exist to deepen connections to the real world and students' interests.	The project resembles traditional "schoolwork;" no evidence of a real-world context or connection to students' interests exists.	M: 2.20 SD: 0.52
Student Voice and Choice	Students have opportunities to express their voices, make choices on important matters, and have opportunities to work independently from the teacher.	Students are given some low-stakes opportunities to express their voice and make choices. Students work independently from the teacher to some extent.	The project is primarily teacher-directed and does not include opportunities for students to express their voice and make choices that affect the content or process of the project.	M: 1.81 SD: 0.66
Reflection	Students and teachers reflect both during the project and after its culmination.	Students and teachers engage in brief or intermittent opportunities for reflection during the project and after its culmination.	The project does not include explicit opportunities for reflection.	M: 1.54 SD: 0.56
Public Product	Student work is made public by presenting, displaying, or offering it to people beyond the classroom.	Student work is made public to classmates and the teacher.	The teacher is the primary audience for student work.	M: 1.91 SD: 0.59

3.2. Challenging Problem or Question

After examining the PBL STEM unit plans, the average score on the challenging problem or question component was 2.21, with a standard deviation of 0.52. Of the 25 PBL STEM units, 19 scored a two or better, indicating that PSTs were on their way toward demonstrating a solid grasp of creating a question that challenged students appropriately. Within this rubric component, three criteria were established to analyze a challenging problem or question, namely that the question is (1) open-ended, (2) aligned to learning goals, and (3) understandable and inspiring to students. One strong example from the PBL STEM unit *Recycling in Wisconsin* was this challenging question posed to 3rd-grade students, "How can we, as earth citizens, contribute to recycling efforts in our school and home?" This question was rated as a three as it met all three criteria of being open-ended, aligned with learning goals, and inspiring to students. Contributing to recycling efforts for their school and personal household has the potential to excite 3rd-grade students who are eager to be helpful to the community.

In the *Viruses* project, the question posed to 7th-grade students is, "How do we protect our immune system from viruses, and how does it differ globally?" This question received a score of 2 for "Developing." Although the question was open-ended and aligned with learning goals, the question does not seem readily understandable and inspiring to potential 7th-grade students.

3.3. Sustained Inquiry

The average score on the sustained inquiry component across all 25 PBL STEM units was 1.78, with a standard deviation of 0.57. One of the main focuses of this component is student-driven inquiry. The only project to receive a score of 3 for "Demonstrating," *Climate Change Social Media* exemplified the practice of middle school students driving the inquiry. In milestone 2 of that project, students take notes on diverse informational materials regarding where or when the effects of climate change are happening; they then add their findings to a graffiti wall over a massive world map drawing. This research milestone then connects to milestone 3, where students use the graffiti wall map to identify which global communities are most affected by climate change to begin creating a climate change social media campaign. The PSTs authoring that project also included an opportunity for their future middle school students to investigate any topics they have further questions or concerns about, aligning sustained inquiry with student-driven questions.

Very little sustained inquiry existed in the *Sustainable Farming* project, leading to a 1.5 score. Each milestone read like a short one- or two-day lesson plan connected to the next milestone based on the theme of sustainable farming. For example, in milestone 2, students spend one day addressing misconceptions about percentages, decimals, and fractions. Then, in milestone 3, students spend one day examining the critical characteristics of a farming practice. In milestone 4, students spend two days creating mathematical story problems related to sustainable farming. Students are not generating questions, nor are the milestones showing the cyclical nature of students posing questions, gathering data, developing and evaluating solutions, and then asking further questions.

In the project Our Changing World, sustained inquiry scored a 2. Unlike Sustainable Farming, the thread from one milestone to the next was evident as students posed questions and interpreted data. However, each investigation lacks the depth and rigor to challenge students. The activities created by the PSTs led their students to merely graze over concepts without looking deeply at each topic, preventing this project from scoring higher.

3.4. Authenticity

The average score on the authenticity component was 2.20, with a standard deviation of 0.52. In this component, only four projects received a score of less than a 2, indicating a solid attainment of this standard by many PSTs. The project *Climate Change Social Media* exemplified a highly authentic project, scoring a 3. This project directly speaks to students' personal concerns, interests, and identities through the study topic and the final product. Students build empathy for environmental/climate refugees, coastal developing nations, and people struggling to access clean water, among others, through their research, humanizing climate change for middle-school students. Students examine various sources, from articles to TikTok videos to Instagram posts. Students then use real-world tools to create social media campaigns to impact the world. This leads to a very authentic experience for students throughout the project.

The *Viruses* project scored a 2 for authenticity. The topic of examining viruses may interest students, especially after COVID-19. However, the academic investigations did not deepen students' connection at a personal level. For example, students looked at prevention methods from a general standpoint. At no point were those prevention methods examined for the home, school, or local community. In the final product, students propose prevention methods for a country they researched, again keeping this topic from becoming personal to students' immediate lives and interests.

3.5. Student Voice and Choice

After examining the unit plans, the average student voice and choice score was 1.81, with a standard deviation of 0.66. A PBL STEM unit scoring a 1, *Sustainable Farming*, led with the question, *"How can sustainable farming practices benefit our school?"* This project centered on teacher-directed lessons rather than student-centered inquiry. For example, in one milestone, the teacher leads students through a lab, creating a 'wormery', a clear container of sand and soil to watch worms decompose organic matter to make richer soil. All students follow the exact directions throughout the lab and are posed the same questions. Students then use this lab and the results to persuade their school to install a compost pile. Although these activities are hands-on and engaging, there were several missed opportunities to provide students with voice and choice. For example, the driving question asked generally about sustainable farming practices. Still, the project led students only to consider a compost pile, failing to provide students voice and choice regarding other potential sustainable farming practices they may see as beneficial. After students were led to accept the solution of a compost pile, they focused on persuading their school to install one. To provide more voice and choice, PSTs could have engaged students in scientific engineering practices to design a better wormery, including mathematical skills and continued student-led research.

Contrastingly, a project that scored a 3, *Water Waste*, highlights multiple opportunities for students to express their voices and work as independent learners. For example, in the project, students act as engineers to create their filtration system, investigate their water usage, and develop action plans to share with others, often working in small groups independently from the teacher. For the final product, students create a persuasive argument to the government to advocate for people who do not have access to clean water, choosing the format most suitable for their argument with options of an infographic, presentation, poster, or podcast. In this project, students have multiple opportunities to express their voice, from the design of filtration systems to the research and creation of an argument with choice in the format of the final product.

3.6. *Reflection*

Of the PBL design elements examined, Reflection had the lowest mean score, with a 1.54 and a standard division of 0.56. Only one project scored a 3 for reflection. The project *Recycling in Wisconsin* proved to be a commendable example of reflection with a 2.5 score. In the project, 3rd-grade students are given two opportunities to reflect on the content they are learning. This content reflection occurs during the entry event in milestone one and as the kick-off to the final milestone. Before completing the final milestone, students are asked to consider how they can organize the ideas they have been learning to educate their peers. The reflection points range from considering content to reflecting on the successful skills of the organization and effective communication, which are critical indicators in the rubric. What would have moved this project from a 2.5 to a three on the rubric would have been more consistent reflection opportunities and the opportunity to reflect on academic and success skill growth after the project.

Contrastingly, the project *Our Changing World* lacked intentional reflection moments, scoring a 1. The closest opportunity for reflection described in the project is during an exit ticket where students were asked to share what they liked about the lesson's activity. However, this question does not prompt students to think deeply or carefully about content knowledge or success skills, which is the hallmark of an exemplary reflection question. The project itself has multiple missed opportunities for reflection. For example, in milestone 3, students take a carbon footprint quiz individually before compiling a classroom set of data. Students then analyze and interpret carbon footprint data. However, neither individually nor as a whole class do students examine the data and reflect upon their carbon footprint related to the world or how their carbon footprint could be decreased. Additionally, students never reflect upon their success or project management skills.

3.7. *Public Product*

The average score on the public product component across all 25 PBL STEM units was 1.91, with a standard deviation of 0.59. In a project that scored a 1.5, *Sustainable Farming*, 6th-grade students work towards creating a compost pile for their school. After the project, students tend to a school garden by continuously making compost. However, students have yet to present their ideas for compost piles to anyone in the school. Students appear to follow the steps provided by the teacher. The public product resembles a service-learning opportunity, where students enrich a pre-existing school garden with their compost. At no point do students create and deliver presentations or display public products. The teacher is the sole point of contact in this project.

Conversely, a project that scored a 2.5 for public product is the 6th-grade *Water Waste* unit. After examining local to global issues in water waste, students create a persuasive argument for the government to advocate for people who do not have access to clean water. Students share these persuasive campaigns virtually with the community and their school by uploading presentations to the school website. These project opportunities highlight how student products can be made public to people outside of the classroom. What kept this project from scoring a 3 was the need for more description of student reasoning and choice behind their public product.

3.8. Social Justice and Global Awareness

The PBL STEM units were examined based on the PST's abilities to integrate global awareness and social justice concepts. As defined above and outlined in the rubric (Table 2), PST's abilities within the criterion of global awareness were viewed as the ability of the teacher candidates to integrate a social justice issue that would also support the deepening of their students' global awareness by making connections between a students' local understanding and a larger global community. PST's abilities to integrate social justice, including a connection to environmental, racial, gender, disability, and economic injustices/inequities, was measured on a 3-point scale.

3.9. Social Justice Issue

The analysis of 25 PBL STEM projects for their application of social justice resulted in an average rubric score of 2.06 with a standard deviation of 0.60 (Table 6). Most of the PBL STEM projects (n = 20) integrated a social justice issue, but this integration was limited to developing (n = 16) rather than deepening students' global awareness. For example, the *Our Changing World* project investigated the driving question, "What is climate change, and how do you interact with it on a personal, communal, and global level?" and scored a 2 for its application to a social justice issue as the final product was an infographic with no connection to students applying mitigation strategies that made a true impact to the social or economic wellbeing of their community. On the other hand, in the *Water Waste* project, which scored a 3 in this category, students developed action plans to lessen their impact on water waste. Their project further directed students to conduct research and create a persuasive argument for the local government to advocate for people who do not have access to clean water. The *Climate Change: Social media* project scored a 3 for this criterion. PSTs included numerous opportunities for their students to use their voices via discussion, including within a social justice circle, which allows students to process and express their frustrations, concerns, and emotions. Their final project outlined various social media platforms that allowed young adolescents to act on their learning in a manner they felt was most effective based on their strengths as adolescents.

Table 6. Social justice, global awareness, and mathematics emphasis overall results (n = 25).

Criteria	Results
Application of Social Justice Issue	M: 2.06 SD: 0.60
Global Awareness	M: 1.92 SD: 0.65
Mathematics Standard	M: 1.98 SD: 0.93
Procedural and Conceptual	M: 1.68 SD: 0.60
Application	M: 1.87 SD: 0.63

3.10. Global Awareness

Upon analysis of the project's ability to connect local issues to the global community (or vice versa), the result was an average rubric score of 1.92 with a standard deviation of

0.65 (Table 6). This analysis revealed that most projects (n = 22) focused on a local or global issue with few connections. For example, within the *Sustainable Farming* project, PSTs did include a visit from a local organic farmer and the development of a community school garden. However, there was no extension of the benefits these practices would have on a larger national or global scale.

A few projects made explicit connections between a local issue and connected it to the global community. In the *Water Waste* project, students investigated their personal water usage and water issues where groundwater is drained internationally. Furthermore, they investigated water quality issues in their local environment related to PFAS contamination and extended this issue to national water contamination issues such as that in Flint, Michigan. Students then selected different countries to explore statistics related to water. In the *Viruses* project, which led with the driving question, "How do we protect our immune system from viruses, and how does it differ globally?" students learned about how to keep themselves safe from contracting illnesses by investigating a country of their choice on the policies and procedures enacted because of the Coronavirus pandemic.

3.11. Emphasizing Mathematics

The examination of the ability of PSTs to integrate mathematics in PBL STEM units focused on how PSTs addressed the full extent of a grade level standard within the mathematics portion of their project, how they build procedural fluency from conceptual understanding, and their ability to apply mathematics in accurate and relevant contexts within the project. Additionally, units were examined to determine whether mathematics was an integral component of the PBL STEM unit or whether the mathematics was isolated within a particular lesson or milestone.

3.12. Grade Level Standard

In analyzing 25 PBL STEM unit plans, most received either a 3 (n = 10) or a 1 (n = 10), indicating that PSTs could either address the standard or not. Projects that scored a one typically indicated that PSTs chose a standard one or more grade levels above the target grade. For example, in the *Climate Change Social Media* project, PSTs selected Grade 7 statistics standards in which students need to understand the meaning of sampling. Instead, the lesson focused on graphing data on either line plots or bar graphs using categorical or numerical data, content that is applied in grades 5 and 6. Though the data were collected from classmates during the lesson, there was no discussion about sampling techniques or the difference between a sample and a population, which would have moved this unit toward grade level.

On the other hand, projects that scored a three could connect the standard to mathematical activities found within their project. For example, in the *Sustainable Farming* project, PSTs selected a 6th-grade ratio standard focused on finding the percent of a quantity as a rate per 100. In the lesson, middle-school students were asked to create percentage tasks from their research on sustainable farming, thus aligning the standard and appropriate grade-level mathematics.

3.13. Conceptual Understanding

After examining the PBL STEM unit plans, the average procedural and conceptual components score was 1.68, with a standard deviation of 0.59 (Table 6). This indicated that teacher candidates developed PBL STEM units in which the project focused on mathematical procedures with limited (n = 9) to no (n =14) connections to conceptual understanding. A few projects emphasized conceptual understanding as the primary focus of the project. For example, in the *Recycling in Wisconsin* project, PSTs focused on a 3rd-grade standard centered on making scaled bar graphs. In this project, 3rd-grade students are tasked with collaboratively drawing scaled bar graphs with different scales. Then, students discuss questions such as "What is similar and what is different between these scaled bar graphs? What fraction of the class recycles? How did this fraction show up in each of the different graphs?" These questions lead to a rich discussion and a conceptual focus on the represented data.

On the other hand, in projects where similar standards were addressed, the lesson focused on mimicking how the teacher created a graph, scoring a two or below. For example, in the *Viruses* project, students were asked, "How do we choose data to create a mathematical representation?" After posing that question, the students engage in an *I Do, We Do, You Do* lesson where they mimic how the teacher creates a bar graph with the data they researched. A lack of critical questioning and analysis leads to a procedural lesson with little connection to a conceptual understanding of the mathematics standard.

3.14. *Application*

Over half of the projects scored at or above a 2 (n = 14), which allowed elementary and middle-school students to apply mathematical concepts through authentic problem-solving. A total of four projects provided multiple opportunities to engage students in doing mathematics through accurate and relevant contexts. For example, in the *Recycling in Wisconsin* project, the students applied their knowledge of scaled bar graphs from the data collected on their class recycling habits to create infographics related to the school's recycling program. This information was part of the public product, enhancing mathematics' critical role in the PBL unit.

On the other hand, the remaining unit plans (n = 11) needed to provide students with opportunities to apply mathematical concepts and procedures throughout. These projects focused on building mathematical content knowledge within a single lesson that did not extend across the PBL STEM unit plans. For example, students were asked to take a carbon footprint survey in the Our Changing World project. They used class data from this survey to create graphical displays. This mathematical milestone was limited to a single lesson, and neither the data nor the statistical learning was applied beyond the single milestone.

4. Discussion

4.1. *Summary and Contextualizing the Findings*

This study sought to answer three research questions related to PST's ability to incorporate PBL design elements, social justice and global awareness issues, and mathematics in PBL STEM unit plans. As such, our study begins to address the gap in the literature related to how PSTs incorporate effective PBL design elements into PBL STEM units. Through a content analysis of 25 PBL STEM units, this study also outlines the strengths and challenges of developing these units.

4.1.1. How Do PSTs Incorporate Effective PBL Design Elements in a Socioscientific PBL STEM Unit?

Based on our analysis of the PBL unit plan proposals, the PSTs were most successful with the PBL design element related to positioning the project within an authentic context, which is a significant criterion within both PBL design and STEM integration. This finding is consistent with prior research [12,17] that practicing teachers often infuse authenticity to motivate and engage students in learning through real-world contexts into their teacher-developed STEM PBL curricular material. By situating their PBL STEM units in an SSI, the PSTs inherently created an authentic situation that would motivate future K-12 students.

In our study, PSTs were also relatively successful in creating a challenging problem or question that was operationalized in part by the statement of a driving question. For example, the *Recycling in Wisconsin* project utilized the driving question "How can we, as earth citizens, contribute to recycling efforts in our school and home?" to guide the development of their STEM PBL unit. This driving question is aligned with the PBL design element of challenging problem or question as it centered the project on a relevant issue to guide student learning [13]. Studies focused on teacher-developed STEM PBL curricular material have found that teachers struggled with creating and implementing well-defined driving questions [9,12]. The differences in our results from these findings may be attributed to the substantial feedback loop we utilized with PST project teams. PSTs wrote several versions of their driving question in the science methods course. Students then engaged in a critique and revision process, providing targeted feedback on that specific aspect of PBL.

After peer feedback, PSTs submitted their revised driving question to their science and mathematics methods instructors, who provided feedback on the driving question before a final version was integrated into the STEM PBL unit. This significant feedback loop, therefore, led to powerfully written driving questions by the PSTs in this research study compared to cited research studies. Although future opportunities for critique and revision occurred, those opportunities focused on the overall project, which included multiple design elements. Therefore, using critique and revision to focus on one design element seemed to elevate PST's ability to succeed in the PBL design of challenging questions or problems.

The PSTs could have been more successful in integrating the PBL design elements of sustained inquiry, student voice and choice, reflection, and public product. Other studies focusing on teacher-developed PBL STEM units have also noted difficulty in the design elements of student voice and choice and public product [9,12]. For example, in the sustainable farming unit, the PSTs asked, "How can sustainable farming practices benefit our school?" In developing the public product, however, the unit funneled students into creating and tending to a school garden. This focused public product narrowly answers the driving question and limited student voice and choice throughout the project. This narrow application of the public product aligns with some of the findings by Markula and Askela [9], who studied teacher-developed PBL STEM units. These researchers examined PBL STEM public products, which they termed artifacts, and determined that public products took several forms—from one singular public product that may or may not have fully answered the driving question to several smaller public products that addressed various themes of the project topic, sometimes aligning clearly to the driving question and other times tangentially addressing the driving question. Markula and Askela [9] have noted that most teacher developed PBL STEM units showed inconsistent application of a public product, which aligns with our findings in this study of PSTs and their capability with the public product.

The instructors needed to link theory and practice more purposefully to strengthen the PST's abilities to incorporate the PBL design element of critique and revision. Instructors engaged PSTs in critique and revision processes, such as the feedback loop regarding the driving question. However, the instructors needed to connect the ways PSTs were more explicitly engaging in feedback throughout the development of their PBL unit plan proposal with ways to invite their future K-12 students to engage in critique and revision. More explicitly connecting theory and practice would have led to more robust PBL unit plan proposals.

In this study, the peer feedback cycle using the Gold Star PBL rubric, which was required by the instructors towards the end of the semester, resulted in project improvement. For example, PSTs in the *Recycling in Wisconsin* project realized their projects improved by engaging in their critique and revision process, and their PBL design skills deepened. They added a reflection activity to address prior learning during the entry event so students could connect their previous knowledge to the new content, and they included more independent work, which increased student autonomy, known as "student voice and choice".

4.1.2. How Do Resulting PBL STEM Units Integrate Social Justice Concepts and Global Awareness?

PSTs were also generally successful in incorporating elements of social justice within their PBL STEM units. This finding aligns with research that advocates for science teaching with SSIs [31]. Most projects are centered on the environment as a social justice issue, which is a topic that is readily accessible. Few PSTs incorporated what might be considered controversial subject matter, such as race, gender, disabilities, and economic injustices, into their final project proposal. While studies such as that of Cahill and Bostick [38] indicate that PSTs have the desire to discuss social justice issues in their future classroom openly, the OECD [25] report reasoned that teachers often find it challenging to engage in more controversial topics and focus on only "safe" topics, like the topics of the PBL STEM units within our study. A key idea for educators to take away is echoed in Cochran-Smith's theory of social justice teaching [28], wherein teachers must acknowledge their tensions and challenges with social justice-centered teaching, knowing they can be managed in concrete ways.

Despite prompting through multiple feedback loops to PSTs, the PBL STEM units they created tended to focus on either a local or a global issue. OECD [25] calls for teacher-learning communities to focus on dimensions of global competence (examining local to global problems, understanding and appreciating diversity, and acting for sustainable development) and the knowledge, skills, values, and attitudes of global competence. Global competence, like excellent teaching, is a process that develops over time. While teachers are often asked to include "one more thing" into their curriculum, this construct must not be considered an "add-on." Tichnor-Wagner et al. [39] (p. 156) assert that infusing global learning into a standard course is "akin to drizzling gravy over the turkey, stuffy, and potatoes," globally responsive teaching provides a richer, more enticing learning experience and is an essential part of all 21st-century curricula. Given the mission statement of the university education department, our PSTs are charged to become globally responsive educators, embodying the mindset and actions of a worldly educator preparing the future stewards of the planet.

4.1.3. How Do PSTs Emphasize Mathematics in PBL STEM Units?

Similar to other research findings centered on teacher developed PBL STEM curricular material [12,17,18], PSTs in our study demonstrated varied abilities to integrate mathematics content into their units. For example, the unit *Recycling in Wisconsin* scored 3's (demonstrating) in all categories of the mathematics rubric, indicating that they could align mathematical learning to the appropriate grade-level standards, integrate a balance of procedural and conceptual knowledge of mathematics, and provide multiple opportunities for students to connect to meaningful mathematics throughout the project. The project Vaccines scored 1's (developing) in all three categories. This lower score indicates difficulty aligning math content to grade-level standards and a view of mathematics as a procedural tool that can be applied in a limited capacity, such as a single lesson, during the PBL STEM unit.

In this research study, slightly over half of the 25 PBL STEM units scored 1.5 or below (developing) on the procedural and conceptual rubric. These scores indicate that many PBL STEM projects focused on procedural skills with little to no understanding of the significant concepts in mathematics. Guzey et al. [17] also found that scores on math integration in teacher-developed PBL STEM curricula did not significantly contribute to the overall score. Two factors might have contributed to these scores when aligned with this research. First, the PSTs may have focused more on the integration of science through an SSI lens [17]. Second, the mathematics content often served in an auxiliary capacity as a tool for data analysis rather than applying conceptual mathematical knowledge [18].

Additionally, PSTs in this study tended not to apply mathematics in authentic problem-solving situations throughout the project; instead, mathematics was often isolated to a single lesson or project milestone. Many of the PBL STEM units did include authentic contexts related to their overall projects. The units did not meaningfully contribute to the public products, even with the connection between math and authenticity. This result is also consistent with Wieselmann et al. [12], who found that much of the teacher-developed mathematics integration tended to align with a standard instead of advancing a deep understanding of both the mathematics and science content. A feedback loop later in the PBL STEM unit development phase (like the feedback loop for the driving question) may enhance the quality of mathematics integration. Additional support of PSTs is also needed to connect the mathematics to the authentic context and overall learning goals of the project to enhance a deep understanding of mathematical concepts [12].

4.2. Limitations

One fundamental limitation of the PBL STEM project was time. Even with both instructors dedicating time to PBL STEM unit development, PSTs were also heavily involved in completing essential pre-student teaching requirements within their degree programs. When instructors provided instruction and work time during class, the focus on those PBL design elements that were unique (e.g., challenging problem or question, authenticity, and public product) tended to be the focus. The challenging problem or question criterion was a central focus of the project launch and revisited often throughout the student's work time; this could have led to the overall highest average score for the 25 projects. On the other hand, the PBL design element related to reflection was noted as a part of the rubric; however, this element was not emphasized within the project template. Thus, PSTs were less successful using this pedagogical strategy within their projects.

In addition, within the final project template, PSTs were tasked with conceptualizing their whole project rather than focusing intensely on each PBL design element. For example, after identifying their topic and ideas, they began their project design with a concept map and storyboard, an outline of mathematics and science standards, and critical content knowledge for teachers. The key project milestones contained depth as required for a single math lesson and two science lessons in their respective courses. Though PSTs academically discussed STEM and applied their knowledge of STEM to an experience within the community, the PBL STEM unit plan template did not specifically address how engineering and technology could have been incorporated, nor were these components part of our analysis.

5. Implications for STEM Education and Future Research

Using an integrated PBL unit plan across undergraduate science and math methods courses did seem to support PSTs' abilities to produce meaningful PBL STEM units that incorporated a social justice lens and increased global awareness. Utilizing meaningful socioscientific topics to launch the project allowed PSTs to develop authentic student projects with challenging projects or problems. In the end, some PSTs were more aware of the need to push for public products and empower their students as agents of change.

Challenges related to STEM integration need to be noted. While PSTs integrated mathematics and science standards, the STEM component of our framework did not fully materialize within the PST's final projects. While STEM research pays attention to integrating science, technology, engineering, and mathematics as a cohesive curriculum [19], the shortcomings of numerous projects that embrace STEM entirely will need to be addressed in future iterations of this project.

Nevertheless, collaboration across university education courses allowed the authors to model how professionals plan and collaborate on a common curriculum. Our PSTs came away with the knowledge and ability to plan integrated curricular units focused on learning content and improving success skills such as communication and collaboration. PBL is both research-based and successful at engaging PK-12 students in authentic inquiry. When coupled with a focus on social justice issues and global awareness, our PSTs, as future educators, have the tools to make a difference in the lives of their students.

Author Contributions: Conceptualization, L.N.P.; Methodology, L.N.P., M.L.M. and J.K.; Validation, M.L.M. and J.K.; Formal analysis, L.N.P., M.L.M. and J.K.; Resources, M.L.M. and J.K.; Writing – original draft, L.N.P., M.L.M. and J.K.; Writing – review & editing, L.N.P., M.L.M. and J.K.; Visualization, M.L.M. and J.K. All authors have read and agreed to the published version of the manuscript.

Funding: This research received no external funding.

Institutional Review Board Statement: Ethical review and approval were waived for this study due to the research, conducted in established or commonly accepted educational settings, that specifically involves normal educational practices that are not likely to adversely impact students' opportunity to learn required educational content or the assessment of educators who provide instruction. This includes most research on regular and special education instructional strategies, and research on the effectiveness of or the comparison among instructional techniques, curricula, or classroom management methods.

Informed Consent Statement: Informed consent was obtained from all subjects involved in the study.

Data Availability Statement: Data are available from the authors and can be provided upon request.

Conflicts of Interest: The authors declare no conflict of interest.

Appendix A

Unit plan template used across science and mathematics courses.

Integrated Project-Based Unit Plan Template	
I. Overview of the Unit Plan and Project	
Project Title	
1. **Driving question**	
Grade level/ subjects	
Timeframe	Estimate the number of class days for the project.
2. **Culminating project summary**	Describe the central focus of your culminating project and how it reflects the elements of project-based learning design (see rubric below).*Be sure to include service-learning components.
Student product(s) (individual/team)	Note which products are individual or team and the product/performance's intended audience.

II. Project Pre-planning tools

3. **Use this space to complete a** concept map **(or feel free to import your map from another source). The concept map should outline/list all of the big ideas within your project AND include linking words/phrases explaining how ideas connect.**
4. **Storyboard:** Use the frames below to show the critical unit plan milestones representing significant moments or stages and indicate how the inquiry extends throughout the unit plan.

Authentic context:	
Entry event	
	6. Culminating Project

III. Learning Goals, Standards, and Objectives

5. Standards: A list of the standards being covered in your sequence of lessons. (Based on your methods courses, please ensure that you at least include the respective professional standards aligned to your current enrollment, e.g., NGSS, NCSS, CCSSM, etc.)

6. Learning objectives: Write a list of learning objectives for the unit (make sure they are aligned with the standards).
7. **Vocabulary list: A list of the key vocabulary students will need to comprehend and apply their understanding of towards the final project**
8. **Literacy skills:** A description of the key literacy skills students will be practicing within the unit (should correspond with the listed literacy standards).
9. Success/SEL skills: A description of success/social-emotional skills students will be practicing within the unit.
10. A T chart with a bulleted list of **math and science** concepts: What students should know from previous lessons or grade levels and what they are expected to learn versus what they do not know (the common misconceptions held by learners).

Mathematics		Science	
Should know/ previous grade level	May not know	Should know/ previous grade level	May not know/research-based misconceptions

11. This is a detailed description of the teacher's math and science content knowledge needed to teach the unit, **sufficient for a novice teacher to have a strong grasp of the content.**
12. Interventions/accommodations: From what you know thus far about student learning needs, what specific skill/information would you target for intervention or accommodations? Why? Describe an intervention or accommodation you might use to provide instruction in the particular skill/information targeted.

IV. Unit Plan Milestones and Lesson Plans

13. **Milestones and focus questions table:** This section creates a high-level overview of your unit plan and project. Think of this as the broad outline of the story of your project, with the milestones representing the significant 'moments' or 'stages' within the story. As you develop these, consider how the inquiry process unfolds and what learning will occur.

Milestone #1	**Milestone #2**	**Milestone #3**	**Milestone #4**	**Milestone #5**	**Milestone #6**
Consider indicating if this is tied to team or individual learning/products					
Description of big idea and what students will be doing.					
Key Inquiry Question	**Key Inquiry Question**	**Key Inquiry Question**	**Key Inquiry Question**	**Key Inquiry Question**	**Key Inquiry Question**
This is the anticipated need-to-know question that guides the learning for the milestone. Be sure the questions are student friendly.					
Connections	Connections	Connections	Connections	Connections	
Identify the number of instructional day(s) and how you will make a connection to the next milestone. That is, how does each milestone connect to the next milestone?					

14. **Unit plan lessons:** Include the following:

- Lesson Objectives
- Brief description of what will occur in each phase of the lesson
- Each phase of the lesson connects to the next phase
- Lesson formative assessments present
- For science lessons (at minimum), strive to use the 5Es to guide each phase (this is your 5E lesson plan assignment; it is not an additional requirement).
- Use the launch, explore, and summarize lesson plan framework for the math lesson as a guide.

V. Field II Unit Plan Reflective Narrative

Use this section to create a narrative describing how your unit plan and culminating project address critical components of impactful teaching as defined in ALL of your Field II courses. This narrative should reflect your conceptual understanding of key course outcomes.

15. A description of how the project connects to the social and cultural assets of the young adolescent learner and learner's community (ages 10–15). (EDS 445/452)
16. A description of how your unit plan and culminating project addresses conceptual understanding, procedural fluency, mathematical reasoning, and problem-solving skills (EDS 422).
17. An explanation of how your unit plan and cumulative project provide students with opportunities to use **mathematics** as a lens to understand, critique, and create solutions for the world (EDS 422).
18. An explanation of how your unit plan and the cumulative project allow students to engage in science disciplinary core ideas and scientific practices (EDS 421).
19. An explanation of how your unit plan provides students with opportunities better to understand the nature of science (NOS).

VI. Convention, Style, and Feedback

20. Creative and critical thinking will be evaluated—review your unit plan and ensure novel thinking and logical sequencing throughout.
21. Conventions: Review your document for spelling, grammar, and writing style, and include APA citations where appropriate.
22. Feedback: Your project will be peer-reviewed using the PBL design rubric (see Assignment document). You will be scored on your reflective use of feedback from peers and instructors. Please include a link to your peer review rubric in the final submission.

Appendix B

Complete List of Projects and Scores (n = 25).

		PBL Design Elements						Globally Responsive		Mathematics Emphasis		
Title ***Grade Level***	**Driving Question**	**Problem or Question**	**Sustain Inquiry**	**Authenticity**	**Student Voice & Choice**	**Reflect**	**Public Product**	**Social Justice**	**Local to Global**	**Standard**	**Proceedural & Conceptual**	**Application**
Our Changing World *6th*	What is climate change and how do you interact with it on a personal, communal and global level?	2	2	2.5	2.5	1	2	2	2.75	2	1	1
Water Waste *6th*	How is water wasted in our community, and what can you do to reduce water waste?	2.25	2	2.5	3	2	2.5	3	2.75	2	2	2.25
Sustainable Farming *6th*	How can sustainable farming practices benefit our school?	2	1.5	2	1	2	1.5	1.5	1.5	3	2	2
Climate Change Social Media *6th–8th*	Who will be affected the most by a changing climate and what can we as middle schoolers do to make an impact and help people who are facing the most struggles with a changing climate?	2.75	3	3	3	2.5	3	3	2	1	2	2
Recycling in WI *3rd*	How can we, as earth citizens, contribute to recycling efforts in our school and home?	3	2	2.5	2	2.5	2.5	2	2	3	3	3
Viruses *7th*	How do we protect our immune system from viruses, and how does it differ globally?	2	2	2	2	1.5	2	2	3	1	1	1.5
Climate Change States *5th*	How does your life here in Wisconsin compare to lives of other 5th grade students around the country when looking at life through the lens of climate change?	1.75	2.5	2	2	2	1.25	2	1.5	1	1.5	2

		PBL Design Elements						Globally Responsive		Mathematics Emphasis		
Title Grade Level	**Driving Question**	**Problem or Question**	**Sustain Inquiry**	**Authenticity**	**Student Voice & Choice**	**Reflect**	**Public Product**	**Social Justice**	**Local to Global**	**Standard**	**Proceedural & Conceptual**	**Application**
Vaccines 7th	What role do vaccines play in our society?	1.5	2	2.25	2.5	1.5	1.5	2	1.75	1	1	1
Human impact on Earth Systems 7th	As humans, how does our lifestyle impact Earth Systems?	1.5	1.5	2.75	2	2	2	2.5	2	3	2	2
Endangered Species 6th	How can we protect endangered species in our state?	2.25	1.5	2.25	2	1	2	2	2	1	1	1
Get Outside 7th	How can nature benefit our well-being?	2.75	2.5	2.25	3	2.5	2.75	3	1.75	1	2.5	3
Water Access 6th	Is safe water accessible to all? Why or why not?	1.75	1	2	1	1	2	1	2	3	1.5	1.5
Plastic Waste 6th	How does plastic waste affect our environmental systems?	2.25	1	3	1	1.5	2.25	2	3	3	2	2
Climate Change Impact 8th	What small changes can you make in your life that if done at a larger scale would reduce the negative effects of climate change?	2.25	2	3	2	1.5	2.25	2.5	3	1	1.5	1.5
What's your impact? 8th	What is your impact on the environment?	1.5	1	2	1.5	2	1.25	2	1.5	3	2	2
Human Impact on Water 4th	How do our actions impact local and global waterways?	2.5	1.5	2	1	1	2	2	2.5	1	2	2
Single Plastic use 6th–8th	In what ways can we, as environmentalists, limit single use plastic at the school, community, or global level?	2.75	2.5	2	2	1	2.75	2	2.5	3	1.5	3
Oil Consumption 8th	How does oil production and consumption affect our world?	2	1	1.5	1	1	1	2	1.5	2.5	1.5	1.5

		PBL Design Elements						Globally Responsive		Mathematics Emphasis		
Title* *Grade Level	**Driving Question**	**Problem or Question**	**SUSTAIN INQUIRY**	**Authenticity**	**Student Voice & Choice**	**Reflect**	**Public Product**	**Social Justice**	**Local to Global**	**Standard**	**Proceedural & Conceptual**	**Application**
Organic vs. *Non-organic* *6th*	Should we provide organic food options for students in school?	3	2.5	3	1.5	1	2	2.5	2	1.5	1.5	2
Sustainable practices *6th–8th*	Who should be responsible for sustainable practices and choices?	1	2.25	2	2.25	2	2	2.25	1.5	3	1.5	1.5
Ag Run-off *7th*	How can we positively impact Wisconsin waterways?	2.5	1.25	2	1.75	1	1	1	1	1	1	1.5
Save the Bees *6th-7th*	How can we as middle school students positively impact biodiversity through supporting the bee population?	2.75	2	1.5	1.5	1	1	1.25	1	3	3	1.5
The green-house effect *6th-8th*	How can we, as environmentalists, limit our impact on climate change by reducing our carbon footprint?	2.5	1.5	1.5	1.75	1	2	2	1.5	1.5	1	2
Radiation *6th*	How does radiation affect you and your community?	2	1	1	1	1	1	1	1	1	1	1
GMO's 7th	How can I make an informed decision on what type of food we consume?	2.75	1.5	2.5	1	2	2.25	3	1	3	2	3
Average		2.21	1.78	2.2	1.81	1.54	1.91	2.06	1.92	1.98	1.68	1.87
SD		0.52	0.57	0.52	0.66	0.56	0.59	0.60	0.65	0.93	0.59	0.63

Appendix C. Project Design Rubric—PBLWorks.org

PROJECT DESIGN RUBRIC

	Beginning This element is not yet strongly evident in this project. There are opportunities to brighten this Element in future revisions of the project.	**Developing** The project includes some evidence of this Essential Project Design Element, as well as opportunities to further brighten the Element in future iterations.	**Demonstrating** The project shows clear and strong evidence of this Essential Project Design Element.
Student Learning Goals: Key Knowledge, Understanding & Success Skills	• Clear and specific student learning goals aligned to standards are not yet evident in the project. • The project does not yet explicitly target, assess, or scaffold the development of success skills.	• The project is focused on standards-derived knowledge and understanding, but it may target too few, too many, or less important goals. • Success skills are targeted, but there may be too many to be adequately taught and assessed.	• The project is focused on teaching students specific and important knowledge, understanding, and skills derived from standards and central to academic subject areas. • Success skills are explicitly targeted to be taught and assessed, such as critical thinking, collaboration, creativity, and project management.
Essential Project Design Elements			
Challenging Problem or Question	• The project is not yet focused on a central problem or question (it may be more like a unit with several tasks); or the problem or question is too easily solved or answered to justify a project. • The central problem or question is not framed by a driving question for the project, or the question: • has a single or simple answer. • may be difficult for students to understand or connect with.	• The project is focused on a central problem or question, but the level of challenge might be a mismatch for the intended students. • The driving question relates to the project but does not capture its central problem or question (it may be more like a theme). • The driving question meets some of the criteria (in the Includes Features column) for an effective driving question, but lacks others.	• The project is focused on a central problem or question, at the appropriate level of challenge. • The project is framed by a driving question, which is: • open-ended; there is more than one possible answer. • understandable and inspiring to students. • aligned with learning goals; to answer it, students will need to gain the intended knowledge, understanding, and skills.
Sustained Inquiry	• The overall project is more like an activity or "hands-on" task, rather than an extended process of inquiry. • There is no process yet for students to generate questions to guide inquiry.	• The project includes brief or intermittent opportunities for inquiry, primarily focused on information-gathering. • Students generate questions, but while some might be addressed, they are not yet used to guide inquiry and do not affect the path of the project.	• Inquiry is sustained over time and academically rigorous (students pose questions, gather & interpret data, develop and evaluate solutions or build evidence for answers, and ask further questions). • Inquiry is driven by student-generated questions throughout the project.

 www.pblworks.org Page 1

Authenticity	• The project resembles traditional "schoolwork;" there is not yet evidence of a clear connection to a real-world context, tasks and tools, impact on the world or connection to students' personal interests.	• The project has some authentic features, but there are opportunities to deepen connections to the real world and to students' personal interests.	• The project has an authentic context, involves real-world tasks, tools, and quality standards, makes an impact on the world, and/or speaks to students' personal concerns, interests, or identities.
Student Voice & Choice	• The project is primarily teacher-directed, and does not yet include opportunities for students to express their voice and make choices affecting the content or process of the project. • (Or) Students have opportunities to work on their own, but could benefit from clearer structures and guidance.	• Students are given some low-stakes opportunities to express their voice and make choices (deciding how to divide tasks within a team or which website to use for research). • Students work independently from the teacher to some extent, but they could do more on their own.	• Students have opportunities to express their voice and make choices on important matters (topics to investigate, questions asked, texts and resources used, people to work with, products to be created, use of time, organization of tasks). • Students have opportunities to take significant responsibility and work as independently from the teacher as is appropriate, with guidance.
Reflection	• The project does not yet include explicit opportunities for reflection about what and how students learn or about the project's design and management.	• Students and teachers engage in brief or intermittent opportunities for reflection during the project and after its culmination.	• Students and teachers engage in thoughtful, comprehensive reflection both during the project and after its culmination, about what and how students learn and the project's design and management.
Critique & Revision	• Students get some feedback about their products and work-in-progress from teachers. • Students do not yet know how or are not required to use feedback to revise and improve their work.	• Students are provided with opportunities to give and receive feedback about the quality of products and work-in-progress, but they may be unstructured or only occur once. • Students look at or listen to feedback about the quality of their work, but do not have opportunities to substantially revise and improve it.	• Students are provided with regular, structured opportunities to give and receive feedback about the quality of their products and work-in-progress from peers, teachers, and if appropriate from others beyond the classroom. • Students use feedback about their work to revise and improve it.
Public Product	• The teacher is the primary audience for student work.	• Student work is made public to classmates and the teacher. • Students present products, but are not asked to explain how they worked and what they learned.	• Student work is made public by presenting, displaying, or offering it to people beyond the classroom. • Students are asked to explain the reasoning behind choices they made, their inquiry process, how they worked, what they learned, etc.

References

1. Widya, R.R.; Rahmi, Y.L. STEM education to fulfill the 21st century demand: A literature review. *J. Phys. Conf. Ser.* **2019**, *1317*, 012208. [CrossRef]
2. U.S. Department of Education. *U.S. Department of Education Launches New Initiative to Enhance STEM Education for All Students*; U.S. Department of Education: Washington, DC, USA, 2022. Available online: https://www.ed.gov/news/press-releases/us-department-education-launches-new-initiative-enhance-stem-education-all-students#page-header (accessed on 22 January 2024).
3. California Department of Education: STEM Task Force Report (2014). Innovate: A Blueprint for Science, Technology, Engineering, and Mathematics in California Public Schools. Available online: https://www.cde.ca.gov/pd/ca/sc/documents/innovate.pdf (accessed on 7 December 2023).
4. Moore, T.J.; Stohlmann, M.S.; Wang, H.-H.; Tank, K.M.; Glancy, A.W.; Roehrig, G.H. Implementation and integration of engineering in K–12 STEM education. In *Engineering in Pre-College Settings: Research into Practice*; Purzer, S., Strobel, J., Cardella, M., Eds.; Purdue University Press: West Lafayette, IN, USA, 2014; pp. 35–60.
5. Kelley, T.R.; Knowles, J.G. A conceptual framework for integrated STEM education. *Int. J. STEM Educ.* **2016**, *3*, 11. [CrossRef]
6. Wan, Z.H.; So, W.M.W.; Zhan, Y. Developing and validating a scale of STEM project-based learning experience. *Res. Sci. Educ.* **2022**, *52*, 599–615. [CrossRef]
7. Kennedy, T.; Odell, M.R. Engaging students in STEM education. *Sci. Educ. Int.* **2022**, *25*, 246–258.
8. Hall, A.; Miro, D. A study of student engagement in project-based learning across multiple approaches to STEM education programs. *Sch. Sci. Math.* **2016**, *116*, 310–319. [CrossRef]
9. Markula, A.; Aksela, M. The key characteristics of project-based learning: How teachers implement projects in K-12 science education. *Discip. Interdiscip. Sci. Educ. Res.* **2022**, *4*, 2. [CrossRef]
10. McHugh, M.L. *Bringing Project-Based Learning to Life in Mathematics, K-12*; Corwin: Thousand Oaks, CA, USA, 2023; ISBN 978-107-188-072-2.
11. Thomas, J.W. *A Review of Research on Project-Based Learning*; The Autodesk Foundation: San Rafael, CA, USA, 2000.

12. Wieselmann, J.R.; Sager, M.T.; Price, B.C. STEM project-based instruction: An analysis of teacher-developed integrated STEM PBI curriculum units. *Educ. Sci.* **2022**, *12*, 626. [CrossRef]
13. Blumenfeld, P.C.; Soloway, E.; Marx, R.W.; Krajcik, J.S.; Guzdial, M.; Palincsar, A. Motivating project-based learning: Sustaining the doing, supporting the learning. *Educ. Psychol.* **1991**, *26*, 369–398. [CrossRef]
14. Dag, F.; Durdu, L. Pre-service teachers' experiences and views on project-based learning processes. *Int. Educ. Stud.* **2017**, *10*, 18–39. [CrossRef]
15. Park, J. Pre-service teachers' project-based instruction with mathematics problem-solving. *Educ. Sci.* **2022**, *12*, 526. [CrossRef]
16. PBLWorks. Project Design Rubric. Available online: https://my.pblworks.org/resource/document/project_design_rubric (accessed on 20 February 2024).
17. Guzey, S.S.; Moore, T.J.; Harwell, M. Building up STEM: An analysis of teacher-developed engineering design-based STEM integration curricular materials. *J. Pre-Coll. Eng. Educ. Res* **2016**, *6*, 11–29. [CrossRef]
18. Roehrig, G.H.; Dare, E.A.; Ring-Whalen, E.; Wieselmann, J.R. Understanding coherence and integration in integrated STEM curriculum. *Int. J. STEM Educ.* **2021**, *8*, 2. [CrossRef]
19. Jolly, A. *STEM by Design: Strategies and Activities for Grades 4-8*; Routledge: New York, NY, USA, 2017; ISBN 978-113-893-106-3.
20. Just, J.; Siller, H.-S. The role of mathematics in STEM secondary classrooms: A systematic literature review. *Educ. Sci.* **2022**, *12*, 629. [CrossRef]
21. Shaughnessy, J.M. Mathematics in a STEM context. *Math. Teach. Middle Sch.* **2013**, *18*, 324. [CrossRef]
22. National Research Council. *Adding It up: Helping Children Learn Mathematics*; The National Academies Press: Washington, DC, USA, 2001; ISBN 978-030-921-895-0. [CrossRef]
23. National Council of Teachers of Mathematics. *Principles to Actions*; NCTM: Reston, VA, USA, 2014; ISBN 978-087-353-774-2.
24. Kulturel-Konak, S. Person-centered analysis of factors related to STEM students' global awareness. *Int. J. STEM Educ.* **2020**, *7*, 40. [CrossRef]
25. OECD. *Preparing our Youth for an Inclusive and Sustainable World: The OECD PISA Global Competence Framework*; OECD Publishing: Paris, France, 2018; Available online: https://www.oecd.org/pisa/Handbook-PISA-2018-Global-Competence.pdf (accessed on 16 January 2024).
26. Adams, J.; Avraamidou, L.; Jacobs, D.B.; Boujaoude, S.B.; Bryan, L.; Christodoulou, A.; Couso, D.; Danielsson, A.T.; Dillon, J.; Evagorou, M.; et al. *The Role of Science Education in a Changing World*; NIAS Lorentz Center: Leiden, The Netherlands, 2018.
27. Freire, P. *Pedagogy of the Oppressed*; Penguin Classics: London, UK, 2017; ISBN 978-024-130-111-1.
28. Cochran-Smith, M. Toward a theory of teacher education for social justice. In *Second International Handbook of Educational Change*; Hargreaves, A., Lieberman, A., Fullan, M., Hopkins, D., Eds.; Springer: Dordrecht, The Netherlands, 2009; pp. 445–467; ISBN 978-90-481-2659-0.
29. Madden, P.E.; Wong, C.; Vera Cruz, A.C.; Olle, C.; Barnett, M. Social Justice-Driven STEM Learning (STEMJ): A curricular framework for teaching STEM in a social justice-driven, urban, college access program. *Catal. A Soc. Justice Forum* **2017**, *7*, 24–37.
30. Mackenzie, A.H. Social justice in the science classroom. *Sci. Teach.* **2020**, *87*, 7.
31. Sadler, T.; Barab, S.; Scott, B. What do students gain by engaging in socioscientific inquiry? *Res. Sci. Educ.* **2007**, *37*, 371–391. [CrossRef]
32. Johnson, J.; Macalalag, A.Z.; Dunphy, J. Incorporating socioscientific issues into a STEM education course: Exploring teacher use of argumentation in SSI and plans for classroom implementation. *Discip. Interdiscip. Sci. Educ. Res.* **2020**, *2*, 9. [CrossRef]
33. Lee, H.; Chang, H.; Choi, K.; Kim, S.; Zeidler, D.L. Developing character and values for global citizens: Analysis of pre-service science teachers' moral reasoning on socioscientific issues. *Int. J. Sci. Educ.* **2012**, *34*, 925–953. [CrossRef]
34. Fester, J.; Valenzuela, J. *Environmental Science for Grades 6-12: A Project-Based Approach to Solving the Earth's Most Urgent Problems*; International Society for Technology in Education: Washington, DC, USA, 2021; ISBN 978-156-484-925-0.
35. Anabousy, A.; Daber, W. Pre-service teachers design of STEAM learning units: STEAM capabilities' analysis. *J. Technol. Sci. Educ.* **2022**, *12*, 529–546. [CrossRef]
36. Mattheis, A.; Nava, L.; Beltran, M.; West, E.B. Theory-practice divides and the persistent challenges of embedding tools for social justice in a STEM urban teacher residency program. *Urban Educ.* **2023**, *58*, 2407–2436. [CrossRef]
37. Creswell, J.W. *Qualitative Inquiry & Research Design: Choosing among the Five Approaches*; Sage Publications: Thousand Oaks, CA, USA, 2013; ISBN 978-150-633-021-1.
38. Cahill, J.; Bostic, J.D. Preparing pre-service mathematics teachers to teach for social justice. *Sch. Sci. Math.* **2024**, *124*, 48–59. [CrossRef]
39. Tichnor-Wagner, A.; Parkhouse, H.; Glazier, J.; Cain, J.M. *Becoming a Globally Competent Teacher*; ASCD: Alexandria, VA, USA, 2019; ISBN 978-141-662-751-7.

education sciences

Article

From Seeds to Harvest in Seven Weeks: Project-Based Learning with Latina Girls and Their Parents

Peter Rillero [1,*], Margarita Jiménez-Silva [2], Katherine Short-Meyerson [3] and Kim Marie Rillero [4]

[1] Mary Lou Fulton College for Teaching and Learning Innovation, Arizona State University, Phoenix, AZ 85306, USA
[2] School of Education, University of California, Davis, CA 95616, USA; mjimenezsilva@ucdavis.edu
[3] Department of Social Work, University of Wisconsin Oshkosh, Oshkosh, WI 54901, USA; shortmey@uwosh.edu
[4] Urban Farming Education, Phoenix, AZ 85009, USA; kr@weareufe.org
* Correspondence: rillero@asu.edu

Abstract: This study examines the impact of a culturally responsive, garden-based STEM program designed for Latina girls (grades 5–6) and their parents. The "Our Plot of Sunshine" project integrates Family Project-Based Learning with garden education to create meaningful STEM engagement opportunities. Drawing on the science capital, science identity, and community cultural wealth frameworks, the program leverages families' cultural and linguistic resources while developing science knowledge and identity. Nineteen families from low socioeconomic schools participated in three pilot implementations across two Western U.S. cities. Using a mixed-methods approach with repeated measures over 19 weeks, the study tracked changes in participants' science identity, interest, and career aspirations. Results showed significant increases in science identity and career aspirations, with effects maintained at three-month follow-up. While interest/enjoyment showed positive trends, changes were not statistically significant. Parent ratings of program elements were consistently higher than daughter ratings, though both groups reported strong engagement. The successful integration of bilingual instruction emerged as a particularly valued program component. These findings suggest that family-centered, culturally responsive garden education can effectively support Latina girls' STEM identity development and future orientation, while highlighting the potential of leveraging family and cultural resources in STEM education.

Keywords: science education; project-based learning; STEM education; garden-based education; Latina girls; science identity

1. Introduction

The persistent underrepresentation of women and Latiné communities in STEM fields represents a critical challenge in American education and workforce development. Despite making up a growing percentage of the U.S. population, Latina women remain significantly underrepresented across most STEM disciplines, from university enrollment to professional careers (Crisp & Nora, 2012; National Center for Science and Engineering Statistics, 2023; National Science Foundation, National Center for Science and Engineering Statistics, 2021). This disparity not only limits individual opportunities but also deprives the STEM workforce of diverse perspectives and talent essential for innovation and problem solving. To this point, Strategic Goal 1 in the National Science Foundation's (2022) strategic plan for 2022–2026 is to "Empower STEM talent to fully participate in science and engineering"

(p. 30) and includes objectives to increase the involvement of communities underrepresented in STEM and to "grow a more diverse STEM workforce to advance the progress of science and technology" (p. 32).

Multiple factors contribute to this underrepresentation of Latinas in STEM. In the K-12 educational system, there is limited access to science education (Blank, 2013) in general and, more specifically, science education through bilingual education (Suárez, 2020). As Latinas proceed from K-12 education into higher education, there is a significant lack of representation and role models within STEM careers, which can lead to a sense of isolation and lack of mentorship opportunities (Mendieta, 2023). Cultural stereotypes and biases can also play a significant role, as Latina women may face discrimination or have their abilities underestimated due to gender and ethnic stereotypes (Verdugo-Castro et al., 2021). Additionally, there might be a lack of resources and support systems, such as scholarships, networking opportunities, and institutional support, which are crucial for success in STEM fields (Bravo & Stephens, 2023).

Research indicates that early intervention is crucial, particularly during the middle school years when many students, especially girls and minoritized communities, begin to form lasting attitudes toward science and mathematics that influence their future academic and career choices (Archer et al., 2012). Despite increasing opportunities for engagement with STEM and recognition of the value of a diverse workforce, there remains persistent underrepresentation of minorities in STEM fields, leading to an "urgent need for concerted efforts to promote inclusivity" (Dormer, 2023, p. 1).

Traditional approaches to addressing these disparities have often focused solely on students, overlooking the crucial role that families, particularly parents, play in shaping educational outcomes. This oversight is especially significant in Latiné communities, where family involvement and cultural values are deeply intertwined with educational aspirations and achievement (Moll et al., 1992). Furthermore, many existing STEM programs fail to recognize and leverage the rich cultural capital, language, and knowledge that Latiné families bring to educational settings (Habig et al., 2021; Rincón & Rodriguez, 2021; Yosso, 2005). Rincón and Rodriguez (2021) highlight the role that engaging families in STEM learning has, and how leveraging cultural and linguistic resources enhances Latina students' science identities.

The Our Plot of Sunshine project addresses these challenges through an innovative approach that integrates project-based learning, garden-based learning, family engagement, and cultural responsiveness. By engaging fifth- and sixth-grade Latina girls alongside their parents in hands-on gardening activities, the program creates an environment where scientific learning becomes a family endeavor, building upon existing community strengths while developing new skills and understanding. This approach aligns with recent research highlighting the effectiveness of culturally responsive, family-centered interventions in promoting STEM engagement among underrepresented groups. This is an area of research that is underexplored with diverse and bilingual populations, as most studies have focused on predominantly White or higher-income participants (D. Williams, 2018).

2. Theoretical Framework

Our study integrates science capital, science identity, and Community Cultural Wealth (CCW) as complementary theoretical lenses for examining STEM engagement among Latina girls and their families.

2.1. Science Capital and Science Identity

Science capital encompasses an individual's accumulated science-related resources, including knowledge, experiences, attitudes, and social connections (Archer et al., 2014). Rather than viewing scientific literacy in isolation, this framework recognizes how science engagement is embedded within broader social and cultural contexts. It includes not only scientific knowledge, but also science-related social networks, everyday engagement with science, and an understanding of science's value (Archer et al., 2012).

Science identity refers to how individuals see themselves, and believe others see them, as someone who engages with and belongs in science (Carlone & Johnson, 2007). It develops through both personal experiences with science and social interactions that validate one's role as a science learner or practitioner (Kim et al., 2018). According to Gee (2000), science identity emerges from the recognition of oneself and by others as a "certain kind of person" in science-related contexts. This process of identity formation is especially important during early adolescence, as students start to explore their academic interests and consider potential career paths (Archer et al., 2010). Research suggests that developing a strong science identity is especially important for students from underrepresented groups, as it can help them persist in STEM fields despite potential challenges or stereotypes they may encounter (Hazari et al., 2013).

The relationship between science identity and science capital is bidirectional. Science identity emerges from self-categorization and identification with particular groups or roles (Stets & Burke, 2000). A strong science identity can drive the accumulation of science capital through increased participation in scientific activities and pursuit of science-related opportunities (Vincent-Ruz & Schunn, 2018). Similarly, access to science capital—through resources, experiences, and supportive networks—can nurture the development of science identity.

Research shows that science capital is not fixed but flexible, with the potential to grow through intentional interventions, particularly during pre- and early adolescence (DeWitt & Archer, 2015). This highlights the significant role of targeted educational experiences and family involvement in enhancing science capital (Archer et al., 2015).

2.2. Community Cultural Wealth

Yosso's (2005) Community Cultural Wealth (CCW) framework identifies six distinct forms of capital that communities of color possess and utilize. Aspirational capital represents the ability to maintain hopes and dreams for the future, even in the face of obstacles. Linguistic capital encompasses the intellectual and social skills attained through communication experiences in more than one language. Familial capital comprises the cultural knowledge cultivated among family that carries a sense of community history, memory, and cultural intuition. Social capital consists of networks of people and community resources. Navigational capital includes the skills of maneuvering through social institutions. Finally, resistance capital represents the knowledge and skills fostered through oppositional behavior that challenges inequality. Together, these intersecting forms of capital contribute to identity formation, shaping how individuals understand themselves and their roles within their communities and broader society. More recently, Yosso and Burciaga (2016) have expanded the CCW framework, calling on us to reclaim our histories and to be intentional about recovering community cultural wealth. Habig et al. (2021) drew from Yosso's CCW theory and discuss the need to disrupt deficit narratives in informal science education by applying CCW theory to youth learning and engagement. In recent years, an increasing number of studies have used CCW as a framework. Denton et al. (2020) conducted a systematic literature review of 33 studies using CCW in science, technology, engineering, and mathematics education. They found that most of the studies focused on higher education and used qualitative research methods and provided valuable insight into how asset-based frameworks are being interpreted in the field.

2.3. Integration of Frameworks and Application to Latina Families in STEM

The integration of science capital, science identity, and CCW provides a comprehensive lens for understanding and supporting Latina girls and their families in STEM education. This three-part framework recognizes that Latina families bring valuable resources to STEM learning environments, while acknowledging how identity formation and capital accumulation mutually reinforce each other (Yap et al., 2024). The intersection of these frameworks reveals multiple pathways through which families can support their daughters' STEM engagement.

When families' aspirational capital aligns with science capital and identity formation, their hopes for their daughters' futures intersect with STEM opportunities, helping girls envision themselves as future scientists and engineers. Linguistic capital serves as an asset in scientific discourse and identity development, particularly when bilingual students can engage with scientific concepts in multiple languages, potentially developing unique perspectives that strengthen their identification with science. Research by Civil (2016) demonstrated that leveraging bilingual students' language skills in mathematics instruction improved their problem-solving abilities and confidence. Through familial capital, science learning is supported by intergenerational knowledge transfer and provides role models that contribute to science identity formation, particularly in areas such as gardening, cooking, and sustainability. Through qualitative research in Mexican–American communities in Arizona, Moll et al. (1992) introduced the concept of "funds of knowledge," emphasizing that students' household knowledge can be a valuable resource in education.

The findings from Galindo et al. (2018) reinforce the importance of culturally responsive educational interventions that build upon existing family strengths. Fernández et al. (2023) discuss how that familial capital is re-created in higher education settings in ways that support Latino/a students pursuing STEM majors. Linguistic capital is further developed when STEM programs are provided in Spanish. Leman et al. (2023) studied the impact on kindergarten through fifth-grade students, their parents, and mentors when participating in a STEM outreach program that centered the use of Spanish. Social capital plays a crucial role by expanding science learning opportunities through community connections and shared resources, while also providing access to STEM mentors and role models who can reinforce positive science identities (Morales-Chicas et al., 2022; Saw, 2020).

Navigational capital enables families to support their daughters in accessing STEM education resources and opportunities, while also helping them persist in developing their science identities within potentially challenging institutional contexts (Bueno, 2024). A study by Chemers et al. (2011) and another by Morales-Chicas et al. (2022) highlighted that mentorship positively impacts the persistence of minority students in STEM fields. Through resistance capital, girls and their families are empowered to persist in STEM despite systemic barriers, contributing to the development of resilient science identities that can withstand and challenge stereotypes and obstacles (Yosso, 2000). Jimenez (2024) refers to this resistance capital as a cultural asset that supports Latina leadership.

This integrated theoretical framework guides our approach to family engagement in STEM education in several ways:

1. We recognize and build upon existing family strengths and knowledge while acknowledging how these assets contribute to both capital accumulation and identity formation.

2. We celebrate diverse forms of expertise and ways of knowing, understanding that science identity can develop through multiple cultural pathways.
3. We create opportunities for families to leverage their various forms of capital in support of their daughters' STEM engagement while nurturing positive science identities.
4. We foster environments where science capital, science identity, and community cultural wealth can grow simultaneously, recognizing their interconnected nature.
5. We acknowledge the dynamic interplay between identity development and capital accumulation, understanding that strengthening one often reinforces the other.

This integrated approach recognizes that successful STEM engagement for Latina girls involves not only building knowledge and resources (science capital) and leveraging community strengths (CCW), but also developing robust science identities that allow them to see themselves as legitimate participants in STEM fields. The majority of previous work on shaping science identity and career aspirations has focused on high school and college students. The present study expands on the literature by examining these topics at a younger developmental period, specifically elementary and middle school. The middle school period may be especially impactful because it is when children begin exploring their own interests and selecting some of their own coursework and extracurricular activities. This may shape their science identity and aspiration for future science careers. Furthermore, Denton et al. (2020), in their systematic literature review of research in STEM which used the CCW framework, found few studies that used quantitative methods, with most using qualitative methods and others using mixed-methods approaches. This present study used a robust quantitative approach, addressing a current gap in the research.

3. Literature Review

3.1. Project-Based Learning in STEM Education

Project-based learning (PBL) is a student-centered pedagogical approach where learners actively engage with real-world, authentic problems and meaningful projects over an extended period (Bell, 2010; Hmelo-Silver, 2004; Larmer & Mergendoller, 2015). Essential elements of effective PBL include a challenging problem or question, sustained inquiry, authenticity, student voice and choice, reflection, and a culminating celebration (Blumenfeld et al., 1991; Krajcik & Shin, 2014; Thomas, 2000). This approach transforms learning by making the project the primary driver of learning rather than using projects simply to demonstrate previously learned content (Ertmer & Newby, 1993).

Within STEM education, PBL shows particular promise when it creates opportunities for students to develop deep conceptual understanding through hands-on experiences while engaging in authentic practices of the discipline (Freeman et al., 2014; Beier et al., 2019). According to Krajcik and Blumenfeld (2006), PBL is characterized by student engagement in real-world investigations where they pursue solutions to nontrivial problems by asking and refining questions, debating ideas, making predictions, designing plans and/or experiments, collecting and analyzing data, drawing conclusions, and communicating their findings. Research indicates that compared to traditional instruction, PBL can enhance student achievement, motivation, critical thinking, collaboration skills, and ability to apply knowledge in new situations (Johnson & Johnson, 2018).

The effectiveness of PBL in STEM education has been well documented for traditionally underrepresented students. A comprehensive review by Thomas (2000) found that PBL can lead to increased student engagement, improved content understanding, and enhanced critical thinking skills when implemented with appropriate scaffolding and support. Capraro et al. (2016) demonstrated in their study of a diverse urban district that sustained STEM PBL implementation led to significant improvements in student achievement, with particularly positive impacts for historically underserved students. Their research suggests that PBL can be especially effective when it connects to students' lived experiences and community contexts.

3.2. Garden-Based Learning

Garden-based learning (GBL) represents a powerful approach for engaging students and families in authentic STEM experiences. GBL extends beyond teaching about food sources, integrating lessons across multiple disciplines including environmental studies, mathematics, science, and language arts (Klemmer et al., 2005). This educational approach leverages gardening activities to enhance student learning across multiple domains, transforming outdoor spaces into dynamic classrooms where students interact directly with nature (Desmond et al., 2004).

Research demonstrates both direct and indirect positive outcomes from GBL (D. R. Williams & Dixon, 2013). School-based gardening activities provide students with opportunities for inquiry-based learning grounded in real-world experiences (Papadopoulou et al., 2020; Corson, 2003), while fostering deeper understanding of academic concepts and promoting personal growth. Studies have documented numerous benefits including improvements in physical, mental, and socio-emotional health among participants (Blair, 2009; Mastropieri & Scruggs, 2018).

Academic benefits of GBL are particularly noteworthy. Graham and Zidenberg-Cherr (2005) identified multiple content areas that showed improvement through garden-based curriculum integration, with nutritional health, environmental studies, and STEM concepts showing most growth. Klemmer et al. (2005) found that school gardens provided valuable opportunities to practice language arts, mathematics, and science in authentic contexts that engage students in multiple ways of learning.

Beyond academic achievement, GBL shows significant impact on student engagement and social development. Skelly and Bradley (2007) demonstrated positive social and behavioral outcomes, with teachers observing improvements in student motivation, enthusiasm, and sense of community. Riggs and Lee (2022) also found that experienced teachers who use GBL reported more engaged students in science and having higher science self-perceptions than no-GBL students. Students reported an increased sense of responsibility and more positive environmental attitudes after participating in garden programs (Conte, 2022). In a YMCA summer camp experience for fourth to six grade children, Heim et al. (2009) found that 95.6% of the children enjoyed learning in the garden setting, with high percentages reporting enthusiasm for growing and preparing their own food (97.8% and 93.4%, respectively).

Multiple qualitative studies have documented increased student enthusiasm for learning through GBL. Elementary and middle-grade students showed particular excitement about hands-on garden exploration (Faddegon, 2005), and studies reported improved interpersonal relations among participants (Dirks & Orvis, 2005; Murphy & Schweers, 2003). This enhanced sociability through gardening activities provides additional motivation for learning while building community connections.

While evidence suggests benefits of GBL, our understanding is limited as most studies have been carried out with predominantly White participants (Lohr et al., 2022). While the number of gardens in US schools rose from 2006 to 2014, unfortunately, gardens are significantly less common in schools with higher percentages of students eligible for free and reduced lunches (a measure of SES) (L. Turner et al., 2016). Greater opportunities for and more research on GBL with diverse children could have promising results. For example, in an analysis of their data for gardening projects at 22 schools, Lohr et al. (2022) concluded the following:

Regardless of past school garden exposure, however, fifth-grade students, females, and those who identify as Latino/a (Hispanic) reported that school garden programming improves their learning. Latino/a (Hispanic) students who participate in school garden programming also indicated feeling a greater sense of connection to their teachers and peers at school.

3.3. Cultural Relevance in STEM Education

Cultural relevance in STEM education extends beyond mere inclusion of diverse examples to encompass a deeper understanding and validation of students' cultural identities, experiences, and ways of knowing. Ladson-Billings (1995) established three critical components of culturally relevant pedagogy: academic success, cultural competence, and critical consciousness. For Latina students, culturally relevant STEM education acknowledges and builds upon their cultural and linguistic resources while challenging inequitable educational practices.

Research has demonstrated several key outcomes of culturally relevant approaches in STEM education. Studies have shown increased student engagement and participation, with Tan and Calabrese Barton (2009) documenting how culturally responsive approaches transformed science learning participation among minority students. Academic achievement gains have been documented by Lee and Buxton (2013), particularly among English language learners in science classrooms. Their research demonstrated that culturally relevant pedagogical approaches, when combined with appropriate linguistic support, led to improved science and literacy achievement.

The integration of cultural relevance in STEM education requires thoughtful consideration of curriculum design, instructional strategies, and assessment practices. Effective culturally relevant STEM education acknowledges the fundamental role of students' cultural backgrounds while maintaining high academic expectations and developing critical perspectives about the scientific enterprise.

4. Program Description

The "Our Plot of Sunshine" program we created fostered an integrated learning community through garden-based activities that engage Latina girls and their parents in collaborative STEM experiences at local schools. The core structure features Family Project-Based Learning (FPBL) sessions, where parent–daughter dyads (one parent with one daughter) spend 90 min engaged in hands-on science activities. This was followed by 30 min Conversation Groups for parents and daughters in separate rooms. Each group was facilitated by a member of the research team. This approach leverages both science capital (Archer et al., 2012) and community cultural wealth (Yosso, 2005) through targeted discussions and activities.

The overall challenge in the FBPL was to produce a small garden where seeds are sown in order to harvest food for a culminating celebration in seven-weeks. This challenge involved choices of seeds (from plants such as bok choy, radish, arugula, and lettuce), specific plans for where the seeds would be planted, caring for and measuring the growing plants, and the harvest. In addition, there were experiences to deepen understanding about soils and structures and functions of plants. For example, parents and daughters were given small plants and magnifying glasses to examine plant roots, and through discussion, surface area was introduced. Then, on a thin plastic cutting board, families were challenged to use Play-Doh to create a root system that had the most surface area. While "doing" is important for the development of science capital, thinking, talking, and developing concepts are equally important. The project-based learning framework in design and implementation stressed (a) discussion before action and then (b) exploration before explanation. After challenges were presented, materials were withheld until families had sufficient time to discuss the challenge and how to meet it. Instructions were given in both English and Spanish and families could converse in a language of their choice. This opportunity to use language is critical for both linguistic and concept development. After the explorations—the first-hand experiences, which created shared understandings—the activity was discussed, and in this explanation phase, concepts and terminology were introduced. Parents and daughters both engaged equally in the activities; it was not a situation where daughters did the activity and parents watched. The curriculum was designed by the research team and included culturally responsive topics and pedagogies. For example, the choice of seeds to plant expanded as families shared information about plants that had cultural significance.

Informed by the CCW framework, Conversation Groups provide dedicated spaces for exploring cultural connections to science, discussing bilingual advantages in STEM careers, and building science identity. Parent groups focus particularly on developing strategies to support their daughters' STEM interests and aspirations, while student groups explore science careers and concepts through culturally relevant contexts. These conversations were always grounded in at least one specific area of CCW, for example, focusing on aspirational or navigational wealth and both the parents and the girls became familiar with the language of CCW.

4.1. *Family Project-Based Learning*

The theoretical foundation of the program integrates multiple frameworks, building from PBL approaches (Bell, 2010; Blumenfeld et al., 1991) to incorporate both language learning theory and cultural wealth perspectives. This integration reflects a deliberate evolution from traditional PBL to address the specific needs and strengths of bilingual learners (Lucas & Grinberg, 2008) and their families through the development of Family Project-Based Learning (FPBL).

A critical theoretical intersection occurs between Halliday's (1993) Language-Based Theory of Learning and Yosso's (2005) Community Cultural Wealth framework. This synthesis recognizes language as both a cognitive tool and a cultural asset, acknowledging how linguistic practices serve dual roles in learning and identity development. Within this integrated framework, bilingualism and cultural linguistic practices are viewed as valuable resources that enhance both scientific understanding and community connections (Schleppegrell, 2004).

The FPBL approach (Figure 1), derived from our previous work with Problem-Based Enhanced Language Learning (PBELL) (Rillero et al., 2018), leverages these theoretical foundations to create learning experiences that validate and build upon families' linguistic capital while supporting science learning (Maxwell-Jolly & Gandara, 2006). This perspective recognizes that language acquisition and use occur within specific sociocultural contexts, where heritage languages and cultural communication patterns contribute significantly to learning and identity formation (Wellington & Osborne, 2001).

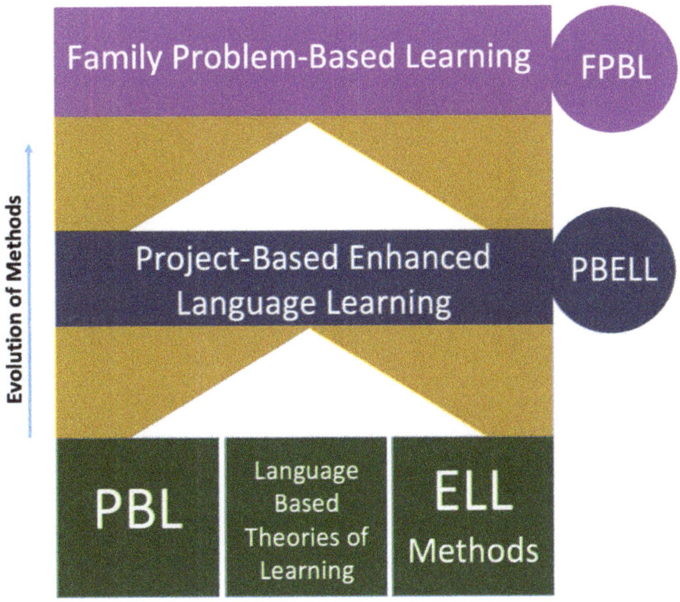

Figure 1. The evolution of the FPBL.

4.2. Learning Sequence for FPBL

The "Our Plot of Sunshine" project centers on a driving challenge that engages Latina girls and their parents: planning, growing, and harvesting food from seeds within a seven-week timeframe for a culminating tostada party. Each parent–daughter dyad is assigned one square foot of growing space, creating an authentic context for applying scientific practices while working toward a meaningful goal. This project structure aligns with key elements of effective Project-Based Learning (PBL), including a challenging problem, sustained inquiry, authenticity, and a culminating celebration (Bell, 2010; Blumenfeld et al., 1991).

The learning sequence integrates scientific tools and practices through a carefully structured progression. Beginning with science notebooks/garden journals (Gilbert & Kotelman, 2005; Klentschy, 2005), each dyad documents their journey from seed selection and garden planning through harvest. This documentation process supports both scientific thinking and family collaboration as participants explore fundamental questions: What can we grow from seeds in seven weeks? How do we maximize our small space? What foods would be best for our tostada party? The sequence moves through observation and measurement of plant growth, investigation of plant structures and functions, and analysis of environmental factors, all within the authentic context of growing food for a shared celebration.

The project culminates in the harvest and tostada party celebration, with families sharing their growing journey through graphs and stories. This structure exemplifies key PBL principles while leveraging the unique potential of garden-based learning. As documented by Heim et al. (2009), such garden programs can achieve high levels of engagement, with over 95% of students reporting enjoyment in learning and working in the garden. The combination of a clear challenge, family collaboration, hands-on investigation, and a meaningful culminating event creates a powerful context for both scientific learning and cultural connection.

5. Research Methods

5.1. Study Context and Participants

This study reports on the pilot implementations of three gardening programs examined across two Western U.S. cities. Nineteen families completed one of the three pilot programs, with participants recruited from eight Title 1 schools. Parents completed the demographic survey, with the following results. All parents considered their daughters as Latina and themselves as Latiné/o/a. Of the girls, 61.1% had Spanish and 38.9% had English as a first language. About 33.3% of participants reported speaking Spanish at home, 38.9% English, with the remainder (27.8%) speaking both English and Spanish at home. The average age of the participating parent was 39.8 years old, and 83.3% were female. For parents' first language, 76.5% indicated it was Spanish and 23.5% English. About 22.2% of the parents had not finished high school and 33.3% reported high school as their highest degree. About 92.8% said their daughter was receiving free or reduced lunches. About 27.7% reported a family income of less than $15,000, 5.5% up to $29,999, 38.9% up to $44,999, 11.1% up to $59,999, 0% up to $74,999, 0% up to $89,999, 5.6% up to 104,999, and 11.1% above $105,000, reflecting a range of socioeconomic circumstances.

5.2. Data Collection Procedures

We incorporated diverse assessment methods to comprehensively measure program impact. Participants began by providing demographic information, followed by a series of assessments using 5-point Likert-scale surveys (ranging from 1 = strongly disagree to 5 = strongly agree). Our survey measures were extrapolated and adjusted from previous researchers, such as the Child and Adolescent Social Support Scale (CASS) (Malecki et al., 2000; S. L. Turner et al., 2004), as well as measures used by Martin and Mullis (2012) and Silander et al. (2018). They were then piloted (in English and Spanish) and revised prior to use in our study. We conducted measurements at four key points: program initiation, mid-program (week 4), program completion (week 7), and a delayed posttest three months after program completion. This extended longitudinal approach enabled us to track both immediate program effects and the sustainability of changes over time. Questions about the program were included in the mid- and post-surveys. These items were designed to evaluate the sustainability of participant engagement, enabling us to determine whether initial enthusiasm was maintained or diminished during the program's latter half.

To maintain data integrity, participants completed their assessments independently, a practice that research has shown enhances the reliability of program evaluations involving multiple stakeholders (Holtrop et al., 2008). The inclusion of a three-month follow-up assessment provided valuable insights into the durability of program effects beyond immediate completion. This comprehensive assessment approach provided detailed insights into both immediate program impacts and longer-term effectiveness.

6. Results

This section presents findings from our quantitative analysis of program impact, examining changes in participants' science-related attitudes over time and perspectives from both daughters and parents about program elements. We first present results from three key measures—science identity, interest/enjoyment, and career aspirations—tracked across four time points. We then examine participant feedback about specific program components, comparing daughter and parent perspectives at mid-program and post-program points.

Three scales were constructed to measure girl participants' science identity, interest/enjoyment, and career aspirations. All scales showed good internal consistency ($\alpha = 0.82$–0.89). A series of repeated-measure ANOVAs were conducted to examine changes over time. Repeated-measure analysis helped address the limitations of the small sample size by allowing each participant to serve as their own control, reducing variability and increasing statistical power. This approach enhances the ability to detect meaningful changes over time by accounting for within-subject differences rather than relying solely on between-group comparisons. Additionally, repeated measures maximize the use of available data, improving the validity and reliability of the findings despite the limited number of participants.

The Science Identity scale showed significant increases over the study period: $F(3,54) = 4.82$, $p = 0.004$, $\eta^2 = 0.21$. Post hoc comparisons revealed significant increases from baseline to week 7 ($p = 0.008$) and to the three-month follow-up ($p = 0.002$), as well as from week 4 to the follow-up ($p = 0.015$).

The Career/Future scale also showed significant improvement over time: $F(3,54) = 2.76$, $p = 0.046$, $\eta^2 = 0.13$, with significant increases observed between baseline and the three-month follow-up ($p = 0.032$) and between week 4 and follow-up ($p = 0.028$). While the Interest/Enjoyment scale showed slight increases through week 7, the overall changes were not statistically significant: $F(3,54) = 1.94$, $p = 0.128$, $\eta^2 = 0.09$. Figure 2 displays the trajectories of these three measures over the 19-week study period.

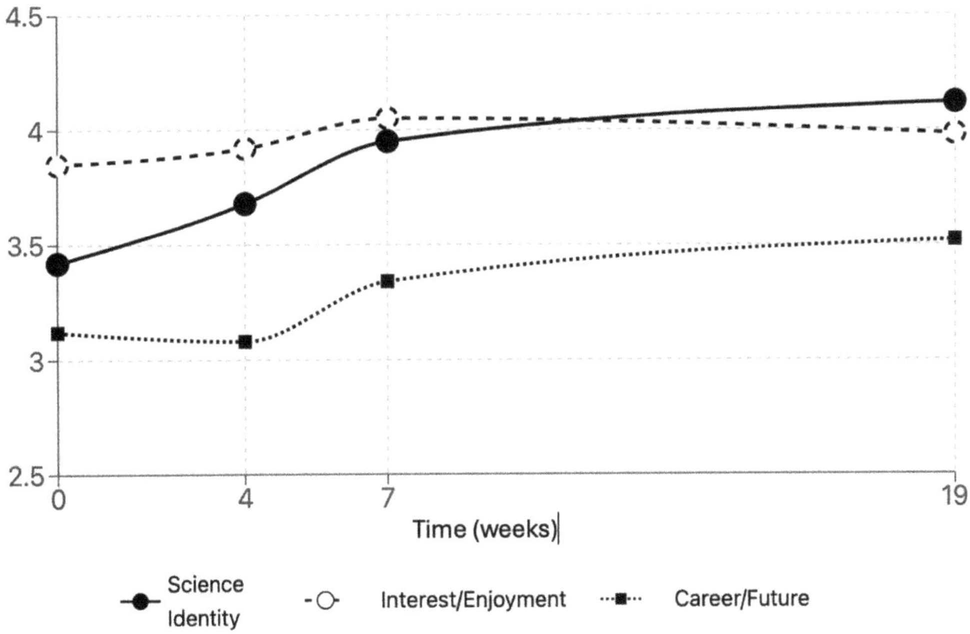

Figure 2. Changes in science identity, interest, and career aspirations over time.

Parent and daughter perspectives on the program were captured through mid-program and post-program surveys (Tables 1 and 2). Results indicate consistently positive views, with daughter means ranging from 3.65 to 4.44 and parent means ranging from 4.38 to 4.94. For daughters, the highest-rated aspect was the program's use of both Spanish and English ($M = 4.44$), while parents most strongly endorsed recommending the program to a friend ($M = 4.94$). Comparing daughters' mid-survey to post-survey responses, two items showed modest increases and one remained constant, with the remaining items showing slight decreases, though none of these changes reached statistical significance.

Table 1. Daughter means and standard deviations for mid- and post-survey perspectives.

Item	Daughter Mid-Mean	*SD*	Daughter Post-Mean	*SD*
1. I benefited from participating in this program.	4.06	1.30	3.76	1.31
2. Participating with my parent/s in this program strengthened our family.	4.13	0.99	4.06	1.06
3. It was a good experience to be able to observe other families doing the same science activities as us.	4.25	0.75	4.06	0.80
4. I would recommend this program to a friend.	4.19	1.07	4.12	0.96
5. The use of both Spanish and English in the program was a good thing.	4.44	0.93	4.44	0.77
6. The program created a supportive environment where I felt comfortable participating.	4.06	0.90	4.00	1.03
7. I enjoyed the program's science activities.	4.38	0.99	4.18	1.00
8. I learned a lot from the program's science activities.	4.38	0.74	4.12	0.83
9. I like the topic for our 7-week program.	4.31	0.92	4.16	1.00
10. The science activities promoted interaction between me and my parent.	4.25	1.03	3.94	0.83
11. I learned a lot during the Girl Conversation Groups.	3.94	1.09	4.19	0.88
Because of the program, I feel greater support from my parents for my science learning.	3.88	0.93	3.65	0.97
The program helped me develop a greater interest in science.	3.88	0.78	4.18	0.94

Table 2. Parent means and standard deviations for mid- and post-survey perspectives.

Item	Parent Mid Mean	*SD*	Parent Post Mean	*SD*
1. I benefited from participating in this program.	4.69	0.58	4.63	0.79
2. Participating with my daughter in this program strengthened our family.	4.44	1.00	4.50	0.71
3. It was a good experience to be able to observe other families doing the same science activities as us.	4.38	1.05	4.69	0.68
4. I would recommend this program to a friend.	4.88	0.33	4.94	0.24
5. The use of both Spanish and English in the program was a good thing.	4.75	0.66	4.63	0.79
6. The program created a supportive environment where I felt comfortable participating.	4.63	0.78	4.63	0.79
7. I enjoyed the project's science activities with my daughter.	4.63	0.60	4.81	0.53
8. I learned a lot from the project's science activities.	4.63	0.60	4.69	0.58
9. I like the topic for our 7-week project	4.75	0.43	4.88	0.33
10. The science activities promoted interaction between me and my/daughter.	4.63	0.70	4.69	0.58
11. I learned a lot during the Parent Conversation Groups.	4.31	0.98	4.50	0.71
I enjoyed the discussion with other parents.	4.25	1.03	4.38	0.93
I think my daughter benefited from participating in this program.	4.69	0.58	4.69	0.68
My participation in the program gives me ideas about how to work on science with my daughter.	4.63	0.78	4.56	0.86
The program helps me develop knowledge of resources that support my daughter's interest in science.	4.56	0.70	4.50	0.87

Table 2. *Cont.*

Item	Parent Mid Mean	*SD*	Parent Post Mean	*SD*
The program helps me learn about my daughter's abilities in science.	4.50	0.71	4.56	0.79
The program helps me learn about my daughter's interests in science.	4.44	0.70	4.63	0.79
The program increases my ability to support my daughter's interest in science.	4.44	0.86	4.38	0.99

Analysis of parallel items between parent and daughter post-surveys revealed consistently higher parent ratings, with statistically significant differences on most items. Only three items showed no significant parent–daughter differences: program strengthening family bonds, bilingual program delivery, and learning from Conversation Groups. These patterns suggest strong overall program engagement while highlighting some differences in how parents and daughters experienced program elements.

Parent and Daughter Views

Table 1 displays the daughter mid-survey and post-survey items and Table 2 displays parent mid-survey and post-survey items. The results suggest overall positive perspectives, with the lowest mean for girls at 3.65 and the lowest parent mean at 4.41. For parents, the item with the highest mean (4.94) was about recommending the program to a friend, while for daughters it was the use of both Spanish and English in the program (4.44). While comparing daughters' mid-survey to post-survey responses, two items showed modest increases and one remained constant, with the remaining items showing slight decreases; however, none of these changes were statistically significant. Parallel items between the parent and daughter post-survey are numbered from one to eleven in the table. On the post-survey, parent means were always higher, and these were statistically significant for all items except for 2, 5, and 11.

Parent responses (Table 2) were notably more positive overall, with means consistently above 4.25 and many exceeding 4.50. Parallel items between the parent and daughter post-survey are numbered from one to eleven in the table. On the post-survey, parent means were always higher, and these were statistically significant for all items except for 2, 5, and 11. The highest-rated item was recommending the program to a friend, which scored 4.88 at mid-program and 4.94 at post-program. Parents particularly valued the program's bilingual nature (4.75 mid, 4.63 post), their daughter's participation benefits (4.69 both mid and post), and the program topic (4.75 mid, 4.88 post). Similar to the daughter results, parent ratings showed slight decreases from mid- to post-survey for most items, though they maintained strongly positive responses throughout. Parents' lowest-rated item was still notably high at 4.38 (enjoying discussions with other parents).

7. Discussion

The results of this study demonstrate the potential of family-centered, culturally responsive garden-based learning to support Latina girls' STEM engagement and identity development. The significant increase in science identity over time, maintained through the three-month follow-up, suggests the program's effectiveness in helping participants see themselves as capable science learners. This finding aligns with previous research on the importance of early identity development in STEM (Vincent-Ruz & Schunn, 2018) and demonstrates how garden-based learning can provide an accessible entry point for developing a scientific concept of self (Lohr et al., 2022).

The growth in career/future orientation scores is particularly noteworthy, as it indicates the program's potential to influence longer-term STEM engagement. This increase, significant at the three-month follow-up, suggests that participants began to see STEM careers as viable options for their futures. The garden context may have helped make abstract STEM concepts more concrete and relatable, allowing participants to envision themselves in STEM roles. Research further supports the role of school garden programs in fostering connections to STEM learning, particularly for Latina students, who reported greater connections to teachers and peers through gardening activities (Lohr et al., 2022). This aligns with research demonstrating that family engagement can positively influence students' STEM career trajectories (Bueno, 2024; Fernández et al., 2023).

While interest/enjoyment showed positive trends without reaching statistical significance, the consistently high ratings across time periods suggest sustained engagement throughout the program. This maintained interest aligns with previous research showing high engagement levels in garden-based learning (Heim et al., 2009; Papadopoulou et al., 2020). Further, integrating culturally responsive approaches within garden-based STEM programs has been shown to increase student engagement and identity formation in science (Riggs & Lee, 2022; Gülhan, 2023). These findings highlight the garden as a setting that supports active, hands-on learning, which is often more engaging than traditional classroom approaches (Graham & Zidenberg-Cherr, 2005).

The role of gender and ethnicity combined warrants attention, as the participants in this study—Latina girls—consistently showed strong engagement and positive perceptions of the program. This is particularly encouraging given the well-documented disparities in STEM participation and interest among Latina students (Bravo & Stephens, 2023). By providing culturally responsive, family-centered experiences, the program appears to have created an inclusive and supportive environment that empowered participants to see themselves as capable STEM learners. This aligns with broader efforts to address equity in STEM education by fostering early confidence and interest among underrepresented groups (Jimenez, 2024).

The disparity between daughter and parent ratings, with parents consistently rating program elements higher, merits consideration. This pattern might reflect different expectations and experiences between generations, or perhaps indicates areas where the program could better bridge intergenerational perspectives. However, the high ratings from both groups suggest strong overall program engagement. Similar trends have been observed in family-centered STEM programs, where parental support plays a crucial role in reinforcing science identity and aspirations (Morales-Chicas et al., 2022; Saw, 2020).

The successful integration of bilingual instruction and cultural relevance appears to have resonated strongly with participants, as evidenced by the highest daughter ratings for the program's use of both Spanish and English. This finding supports the value of leveraging linguistic capital, as described in the community cultural wealth framework (Yosso, 2005). Recent studies highlight the importance of bilingual education in STEM settings, emphasizing that linguistic capital can enhance comprehension, engagement, and identity development (Leman et al., 2023; Suárez, 2020). These results highlight several implications for practice. The study demonstrates the importance of sustained family engagement in STEM learning and underscores the value of culturally and linguistically responsive approaches. The findings reveal the potential of garden-based contexts for developing science identity and illustrate the effectiveness of combining hands-on activities with cultural connection. Research indicates that culturally relevant pedagogy, when integrated with science learning, improves both academic performance and long-term interest in STEM (Rincón & Rodriguez, 2021; Yap et al., 2024).

Future research would benefit from examination of the long-term impact of such programs on academic and career trajectories and how specific program elements contribute to observed outcomes. Additionally, exploring how this model might be adapted for other cultural contexts and age groups could expand its potential impact. Finally, research is needed to better understand the mechanisms through which garden-based learning supports science identity development and how these can be optimized for diverse learners.

8. Conclusions

This study demonstrates the effectiveness of integrating family engagement, cultural responsiveness, and garden-based learning to support Latina girls' STEM development. Through the "Our Plot of Sunshine" project, we found that a carefully structured program incorporating these elements could significantly enhance participants' science identity and future career aspirations, with effects persisting three months after program completion.

The program's success in engaging both daughters and parents highlights the value of leveraging family and community resources in STEM education. The consistently high ratings of the program's bilingual approach underscore the importance of incorporating linguistic capital as a resource rather than treating it as a barrier. The garden-based context proved effective in making STEM concepts accessible and meaningful within participants' cultural frameworks.

These findings have important implications for addressing the persistent underrepresentation of Latina women in STEM fields. By integrating project-based learning with cultural wealth perspectives, programs can create environments where diverse students not only learn science but come to see themselves as legitimate participants in scientific endeavors. This understanding points toward educational approaches that recognize and build upon the rich resources that students and families bring to STEM learning, potentially opening new pathways for broadening participation in STEM fields.

Author Contributions: Conceptualization, P.R., M.J.-S. and K.S.-M.; Methodology, K.S.-M.; Investigation, P.R.; Resources, K.M.R.; Data curation, K.S.-M.; Writing—original draft, P.R. and M.J.-S.; Writing—review & editing, K.S.-M. and K.M.R.; Project administration, M.J.-S., K.S.-M. and K.M.R.; Funding acquisition, K.S.-M. All authors have read and agreed to the published version of the manuscript.

Funding: This research was funded by National Science Foundation (NSF) grant number DRL-2005319.

Institutional Review Board Statement: The study was conducted in accordance with the Declaration of Helsinki, and approved by the University of Wisconsin Oshkosh Institutional Review Board (IRB) (NE20-56, 22 December 2020).

Informed Consent Statement: Informed consent was obtained from all subjects involved in the study.

Data Availability Statement: The raw data supporting the conclusions of this article will be made available by the authors on request.

Conflicts of Interest: The authors declare no conflict of interest.

References

Archer, L., Dawson, E., DeWitt, J., Seakins, A., & Wong, B. (2015). "Science capital": A conceptual, methodological, and empirical argument for extending bourdieusian notions of capital beyond the arts. *Journal of Research in Science Teaching, 52*(7), 922–948. [CrossRef]

Archer, L., DeWitt, J., & Willis, B. (2014). Adolescent boys' science aspirations: Masculinity, capital, and power. *Journal of Research in Science Teaching, 51*(1), 1–30. [CrossRef]

Archer, L., DeWitt, J., Osborne, J., Dillon, J., Willis, B., & Wong, B. (2010). "Doing" science versus "being" a scientist: Examining 10/11-year-old schoolchildren's constructions of science through the lens of identity. *Science Education, 94*(4), 617–639. [CrossRef]

Archer, L., DeWitt, J., Osborne, J., Dillon, J., Willis, B., & Wong, B. (2012). Science aspirations, capital, and family habitus: How families shape children's engagement and identification with science. *American Educational Research Journal, 49*(5), 881–908. [CrossRef]

Beier, M. E., Kim, M. H., Saterbak, A., Leautaud, V., Bishnoi, S., & Gilberto, J. M. (2019). The effect of authentic project-based learning on attitudes and career aspirations in STEM. *Journal of Research in Science Teaching, 55*(3), 271–291. [CrossRef]

Bell, S. (2010). Project-based learning for the 21st century: Skills for the future. *The Clearing House, 83*, 39–43. [CrossRef]

Blair, D. (2009). The child in the garden: An evaluative review of the benefits of school gardening. *Journal of Environmental Education, 40*(2), 15–38. [CrossRef]

Blank, R. K. (2013). Science instructional time is declining in elementary schools: What are the implications for student achievement and closing the gap? *Science Education, 97*(6), 830–847. [CrossRef]

Blumenfeld, P. C., Soloway, E., Marx, R. W., Krajcik, J. S., Guzdial, M., & Palincsar, A. (1991). Motivating project-based learning: Sustaining the doing, supporting the learning. *Educational Psychologist, 26*(3–4), 369–398. [CrossRef]

Bravo, E. I., & Stephens, D. P. (2023). RESISTIR: Hispanic undergraduate STEM majors' perceptions of barriers and supports toward degree persistence. *Journal of Latinx Psychology, 11*(2), 104. [CrossRef]

Bueno, E. H. (2024). *The role of familial engagement on Latina adolescents' identity, self-efficacy, and persistence in STEM* [Doctoral dissertation, The University of Arizona].

Capraro, R. M., Capraro, M. M., Scheurich, J. J., Jones, M., Morgan, J., Huggins, K. S., & Han, S. (2016). Impact of sustained professional development in STEM on outcome measures in a diverse urban district. *The Journal of Educational Research, 109*(2), 181–196. [CrossRef]

Carlone, H. B., & Johnson, A. (2007). Understanding the science experiences of successful women of color: Science identity as an analytic lens. *Journal of Research in Science Teaching, 44*(8), 1187–1218. [CrossRef]

Chemers, M. M., Zurbriggen, E. L., Syed, M., Goza, B. K., & Bearman, S. (2011). The role of efficacy and identity in science career commitment among underrepresented minority students. *Journal of Social Issues, 67*(3), 469–491. [CrossRef]

Civil, M. (2016). STEM Learning Research through a Funds of Knowledge Lens. *Cultural Studies of Science Education, 11*(1), 41–59. [CrossRef]

Conte, A. (2022). *Benefits of school gardening programs in education: Opportunities and challenges towards sustainability.* [Capstone project, California State University, Monterey Bay]. Digital Commons@CSUMB. Available online: https://digitalcommons.csumb.edu/caps_thes_all (accessed on 16 December 2024).

Corson, C. (2003). *Grounds for learning: Hope for America's derelict schoolyards.* Available online: https://www.cherylcorson.com/publications.html (accessed on 12 August 2008).

Crisp, G., & Nora, A. (2012). *Overview of Hispanics in science, mathematics, engineering and technology (STEM): K-16 representation, preparation and participation.* Hispanic Association of Colleges and Universities.

Denton, M., Borrego, M., & Boklage, A. (2020). Community cultural wealth in science, technology, engineering, and mathematics education: A systematic review. *Journal of Engineering Education, 109*(3), 556–580. [CrossRef]

Desmond, D., Grieshop, J., & Subramanian, A. (2004). *Revisiting garden-based learning in basic education. International institute for educational planning.* Food and Agriculture Organization International Institute of the United Nations.

DeWitt, J., & Archer, L. (2015). Who aspires to a science career? A comparison of survey responses from primary and secondary school students. *International Journal of Science Education, 37*(13), 2170–2192. [CrossRef]

Dirks, A. E., & Orvis, K. (2005). An evaluation of the junior master gardener program in third grade classrooms. *HortTechnology, 15*(3), 443–447. [CrossRef]

Dormer, A. (2023, June 19). *The lack of minorities in STEM: An urgent call for diversity and inclusion. LinkedIn.* Available online: https://www.linkedin.com/pulse/title-lack-minorities-stem-urgent-call-diversity-inclusion/ (accessed on 27 January 2024).

Ertmer, P. A., & Newby, T. J. (1993). Behaviorism, cognitivism, constructivism: Comparing critical features from an instructional design perspective. *Performance Improvement Quarterly, 6*(4), 50–72. [CrossRef]

Faddegon, P. A. (2005). *The kids growing food school gardening program: Agricultural literacy and other educational outcomes* [Doctoral dissertation, Cornell University].

Fernández, É., Rincón, B. E., & Hinojosa, J. K. (2023). (Re) creating family and reinforcing pedagogies of the home: How familial capital manifests for students of color pursuing STEM majors. *Race Ethnicity and Education, 26*(2), 147–163. [CrossRef]

Freeman, S., Eddy, S. L., McDonough, M., Smith, M. K., Okoroafor, N., Jordt, H., & Wenderoth, M. P. (2014). Active learning increases student performance in science, engineering, and mathematics. *Proceedings of the National Academy of Sciences, 111*(23), 8410–8415. [CrossRef] [PubMed]

Galindo, C., Sonnenschein, S., & Montoya-Ávila, A. (2018). Latina mothers' engagement in children's math learning in the early school years: Conceptions of math and socialization practices. *Early Childhood Research Quarterly, 45*, 34–48. [CrossRef]

Gee, J. P. (2000). Identity as an analytic lens for research in education. *Review of Research in Education, 25*(1), 99–125. [CrossRef]

Gilbert, A., & Kotelman, M. (2005). Five good reasons to use science notebooks. *Science and Children, 43*(3), 28–32.

Graham, H., & Zidenberg-Cherr, S. (2005). California teachers perceive school gardens as an effective nutritional tool to promote healthful eating habits. *Journal of the American Dietetic Association, 105*, 1797–1800. [CrossRef] [PubMed]

Gülhan, F. (2023). The order of garden-based learning from science education to STEM education. *Eurasian Journal of Science and Environmental Education, 3*(1), 17–23. [CrossRef] [PubMed]

Habig, B., Gupta, P., & Adams, J. D. (2021). Disrupting deficit narratives in informal science education: Applying community cultural wealth theory to youth learning and engagement. *Cultural Studies of Science Education, 16*, 509–548. [CrossRef]

Halliday, M. A. K. (1993). Towards a Language-based Theory of Learning. *Linguistics and Education, 5*(2), 93–116. [CrossRef]

Hazari, Z., Sadler, P. M., & Sonnert, G. (2013). The science identity of college students: Exploring the intersection of gender, race, and ethnicity. *Journal of College Science Teaching, 42*(5), 82–91.

Heim, S., Stang, J., & Ireland, M. (2009). A garden pilot project enhances fruit and vegetable consumption among children. *Journal of the American Dietetic Association, 109*, 1220–1226. [CrossRef]

Hmelo-Silver, C. E. (2004). Problem-based learning: What and how do students learn? *Educational Psychology Review, 16*(3), 235–266. [CrossRef]

Holtrop, K., Smith, A. C., & Scott, J. L. (2008). Family-based interventions to enhance child and adolescent mental health. *American Journal of Family Therapy, 36*(4), 305–319.

Jimenez, M. (2024). Resistance capital as a cultural asset that supports Latina leadership development & address environmental leadership challenges in K-12 schools. *Journal of Latinos and Education*, 1–19. [CrossRef]

Johnson, D. W., & Johnson, R. T. (2018). Cooperative learning: The foundation for active learning. In S. M. Brito (Ed.), *Active learning—Beyond the future*. IntechOpen. [CrossRef]

Kim, A. Y., Sinatra, G. M., & Seyranian, V. (2018). Developing a STEM identity among young women: A social identity perspective. *Review of Educational Research, 88*(4), 589–625. [CrossRef]

Klemmer, C. D., Waliczek, T. M., & Zajicek, J. M. (2005). Growing minds: The effect of a school gardening program on the science achievement of elementary students. *HortTechnology, 15*(3), 448–452. [CrossRef]

Klentschy, M. P. (2005). Science notebooks: Writing about inquiry. *Science and Children, 43*(3), 20–24.

Krajcik, J. S., & Blumenfeld, P. C. (2006). Project-based learning. In R. K. Sawyer (Ed.), *The Cambridge handbook of the learning sciences* (pp. 317–334). Cambridge University Press. [CrossRef]

Krajcik, J. S., & Shin, N. (2014). Project-based learning. In R. K. Sawyer (Ed.), *The Cambridge handbook of the learning sciences* (2nd ed., pp. 275–297). Cambridge University Press. [CrossRef]

Ladson-Billings, G. (1995). Toward a theory of culturally relevant pedagogy. *American Educational Research Journal, 32*(3), 465–491. [CrossRef]

Larmer, J., & Mergendoller, J. R. (2015). *Gold standard PBL: Essential project design elements* (pp. 1–4). Buck Institute for Education.

Lee, O., & Buxton, C. A. (2013). Integrating Science And English Proficiency For English Language Learners. *Theory Into Practice, 52*(1), 36–42. [CrossRef]

Leman, A. M., Hernandez, A. L., & Gutierrez, P. B. (2023). Exploring the impact of a Spanish Language STEM outreach program on participants, families, and mentors. *Journal of STEM Outreach, 6*(2), 1–15. [CrossRef]

Lohr, A. M., Bell, M. L., Coulter, K., Marston, S., Thompson, M., Carvajal, S. C., Wilkinson-Lee, A. M., Gerald, L. B., & Korchmaros, J. (2022). The association between duration of school garden exposure and self-reported learning and school connectedness. *Health Education & Behavior, 50*(5), 637–646. [CrossRef]

Lucas, T., & Grinberg, J. (2008). Responding to the linguistic reality of mainstream classrooms: Preparing all teachers to teach English language learners. In M. Cochran-Smith, S. Feiman-Nemser, & J. McIntyre (Eds.), *Handbook of research on teacher education: Enduring issues in changing contexts* (3rd ed., pp. 606–636). Lawrence Erlbaum.

Malecki, C. K., Demaray, M. K., & Elliott, S. N. (2000). *The child and adolescent social support scale*. Northern Illinois University.

Martin, M. O., & Mullis, I. V. S. (Eds.). (2012). *Methods and procedures in TIMSS and PIRLS 2011*. TIMSS & PIRLS International Study Center, Boston College.

Mastropieri, M. A., & Scruggs, T. E. (2018). *The inclusive classroom strategies for effective differentiated instruction*. Pearson.

Maxwell-Jolly, J., & Gandara, P. (2006). Critical issues in preparing teachers of English learners. In *Crucial issues in California education 2006: Rekindling reform*. Policy Analysis for California Education.

Mendieta, A. B. (2023). *Navigating the STEM landscape: Exploring the challenges and opportunities for Latinas in pursuit of representation and inclusion* [Doctoral dissertation, St. John Fisher College]. Available online: https://fisherpub.sjf.edu/education_etd/579 (accessed on 7 February 2024).

Moll, L. C., Amanti, C., Neff, D., & Gonzalez, N. (1992). Funds of knowledge for teaching: Using a qualitative approach to connect homes and classrooms. *Theory into Practice, 31*(2), 132–141. [CrossRef]

Morales-Chicas, J., Gomez, M., Gussman, M., & Kouyoumdjian, C. (2022). A cultural wealth approach to understanding Latin@s' STEM mentee and mentor experiences. *Equity & Excellence in Education, 55*(4), 371–385. [CrossRef]

Murphy, M., & Schweers, E. (2003). *Evaluation of a food systems-approach to fostering ecological literacy.* Final Report to Center for Ecoliteracy. Available online: www.ecoliteracy.org (accessed on 11 November 2024).

National Center for Science and Engineering Statistics (NCSES). (2023). *Diversity and STEM: Women, minorities, and persons with disabilities 2023* (Special Report NSF 23-315); National Science Foundation. Available online: https://ncses.nsf.gov/wmpd (accessed on 11 January 2024).

National Science Foundation. (2022). *Leading the world in discovery and innovation, STEM talent development, and the delivery of benefits from research: NSF Strategic Plan for Fiscal Years (FY) 2022–26.* Available online: https://www.nsf.gov/about/performance/strategic-plan (accessed on 4 March 2023).

National Science Foundation, National Center for Science and Engineering Statistics. (2021). *Women, minorities, and persons with disabilities in science and engineering: 2021*; Special Report NSF 21-321. Available online: https://ncses.nsf.gov/pubs/nsf21321 (accessed on 29 June 2024).

Papadopoulou, A., Kazana, A., & Armakolas, S. (2020). Education for sustainability development via school garden. *European Journal of Education Studies, 7*(9), 194–206. [CrossRef]

Riggs, C., & Lee, D. N. (2022). Assessing educator perceptions of garden-based learning in K–12 science education. *The American Biology Teacher, 84*(4), 213–218. [CrossRef]

Rillero, P., Thibault, M., Merritt, J., & Jimenez-Silva, M. (2018). Bears in a Boat: Science Content and Language Development through a Problem-Based Learning Experience. *Science Activities, 55*(1), 28–33. [CrossRef]

Rincón, B. E., & Rodriguez, S. (2021). Latinx students charting their own STEM pathways: How community cultural wealth informs their STEM identities. *Journal of Hispanic Higher Education, 20*(2), 149–163. [CrossRef]

Saw, G. K. (2020). Leveraging social capital to broaden participation in STEM. *Policy Insights from the Behavioral and Brain Sciences, 7*(1), 35–43. [CrossRef]

Schleppegrell, M. J. (2004). *The language of schooling: A functional linguistics perspective.* Lawrence Erlbaum Associates.

Silander, M., Grindal, T., Hupert, N., Garcia, E., Anderson, K., Vahey, P., & Pasnik, S. (2018). *What parents talk about when they talk about learning: A national survey about young children and science.* Education Development Center, Inc.; SRI International.

Skelly, S. M., & Bradley, J. C. (2007). The growing phenomenon of school gardens: Measuring their variation and their effect on students' sense of responsibility and attitudes toward science and the environment. *Applied Environmental Education and Communication, 6*(1), 97–104. [CrossRef]

Stets, J. E., & Burke, P. J. (2000). Identity theory and social identity theory. *Social Psychology Quarterly, 63*(3), 224–237. [CrossRef]

Suárez, E. (2020). "Estoy Explorando Science": Emergent bilingual students problematizing electrical phenomena through translanguaging. *Science Education, 104*(5), 791–826. [CrossRef]

Tan, E., & Calabrese Barton, A. (2009). Transforming science learning and student participation in sixth-grade science: A case study of a low-income, urban, racial minority classroom. *Equity & Excellence in Education, 43*(1), 38–55.

Thomas, J. W. (2000). *A review of research on project-based learning.* The Autodesk Foundation.

Turner, L., Eliason, M., Sandoval, A., & Chaloupka, F. J. (2016). Increasing prevalence of US elementary school gardens, but disparities reduce opportunities for disadvantaged students. *Journal of School Health, 86*(12), 906–912. [CrossRef] [PubMed]

Turner, S. L., Steward, J. C., & Lapan, R. T. (2004). Family factors associated with sixth-grade adolescents' math and science career interests. *The Career Development Quarterly, 53*(1), 41–52. [CrossRef]

Verdugo-Castro, S., García-Holgado, A., Sánchez-Gómez, M. C., & García-Peñalvo, F. J. (2021). Multimedia analysis of Spanish female role models in science, technology, engineering and mathematics. *Sustainability, 13*(22), 12612. [CrossRef]

Vincent-Ruz, P., & Schunn, C. D. (2018). The nature of science identity and its role as the driver of student choices. *International Journal of STEM Education, 5*(1), 48. [CrossRef] [PubMed]

Wellington, J., & Osborne, J. (2001). *Language and literacy in science education.* Open University.

Williams, D. (2018). *Garden-based education.* Oxford Research Encyclopedia of Education. Available online: https://oxfordre.com/education/view/10.1093/acrefore/9780190264093.001.0001/acrefore-9780190264093-e-188 (accessed on 17 December 2024).

Williams, D. R., & Dixon, P. S. (2013). Impact of garden-based learning on academic outcomes in schools: Synthesis of research between 1990 and 2010. *Review of Educational Research, 83*(2), 211–235. [CrossRef]

Yap, M. J., Foriest, J., Walker, K., Sanford, S., & Rice, A. (2024). Family helps transform the STEM pathways of community college women of color STEM majors. *CBE Life Sciences Education, 23*(1), ar10. [CrossRef] [PubMed]

Yosso, T. J. (2000). *A critical race and LatCrit approach to media literacy: Chicana/o resis-tance to visual microagressions* [Unpublished doctoral dissertation, University of California].

Yosso, T. J. (2005). Whose culture has capital? A critical race theory discussion of community cultural wealth. *Race Ethnicity and Education*, *8*(1), 69–91. [CrossRef]

Yosso, T. J., & Burciaga, R. (2016). Reclaiming our histories, recovering community cultural wealth. *Center for Critical Race Studies at UCLA Research Brief*, *5*, 1–4.

education sciences

MDPI

Article

Transforming Learning Orientations Through STEM Interdisciplinary Project-Based Learning

Soobin Seo [1,*], Dustin S. J. Van Orman [2], Mark Beattie [1], Lucrezia Cuen Paxson [3] and Jacob Murray [4]

1 School of Hospitality Business Management, Washington State University Everett, Everett, WA 98201, USA; mabeattie@wsu.edu
2 Science, Math, and Technology Education (SMATE), Western Washington University, Bellingham, WA 98225, USA; vanormd2@wwu.edu
3 The Edward R. Murrow College of Communication, Washington State University Everett, Everett, WA 98201, USA
4 Voiland School of Engineering, Washington State University Everett, Everett, WA 98201, USA; jamurray@wsu.edu
* Correspondence: soobin.seo@wsu.edu

Abstract: Science, technology, engineering, and math (STEM) education is challenged by industries to incorporate business, engineering, and communication experiences to prepare students for workplace success. In this study, we outline an approach—the STEM Oriented Alliance for Research (SOAR)—to enhance student experience by offering interdisciplinary project-based learning (IPBL) for undergraduate students majoring in electrical engineering, communications, and marketing. We examined how students' disciplinary and cooperative orientations toward learning shifted in response to their experiences in a semester-long interdisciplinary project-based learning experience with authentic industry outputs. Using a multi-method approach, we explored how interdisciplinary projects influenced student experiences in terms of five collaboration abilities: positive interdependence, accountability, promotive interaction, group processing, and social skills. Further, we observed a shift from fixed- to more growth-oriented mindsets, and from a primarily disciplinary to interdisciplinary focus for their future professional work. The outcomes of the SOAR project make clear that providing structure for professional cooperation on interdisciplinary projects can have profound effects on how students learn to cooperate and position themselves as learners. For most SOAR participants, the experience was deeply formative and contributed to their readiness to cooperate and learn within the interdisciplinary and STEM-oriented workforce.

Keywords: project-based learning; cooperative learning; interdisciplinary learning; mindset; STEM

1. Introduction

In this study, we examine important outcomes of an evidence-based and industry-modeled interdisciplinary project-based learning initiative intended to engage undergraduate students as professionals who can innovate, collaborate, communicate, and work skillfully and diligently across domains [1–5]. The rapid social and economic change occurring as we experience a fourth industrial revolution requires exploration of project-based learning in interdisciplinary settings that can enhance student engagement and understanding, particularly in STEM [6]. Given the high demand of the benefits of project-based learning on student development, including skill enhancement, teamwork, and critical thinking, project-based courses can improve students' collaboration skills and overall learning experience [7,8], and higher education is challenged to create frameworks for project-based learning effective across disciplines [9].

Some industry initiatives such as Google's Oxygen and Aristotle programs provide evidence that interdisciplinary teams composed of professionals from various fields can enhance both work processes and products [10,11]. To encourage interdisciplinary research and collaboration in STEM, business, and liberal arts fields, which are our respective areas of expertise, we have extended evidence-based models. Our goal is to introduce interdisciplinary principles to college classrooms by creating an environment that fosters cohesive interaction centered on real-world problems. This research details the STEM Oriented Alliance for Research (SOAR), a project-based interdisciplinary initiative, and examines its impact on undergraduate students. We designed a transformative educational experience that promotes interdisciplinary understanding, collaboration, and a growth mindset, enhancing students' skills, knowledge, satisfaction, and confidence to engage as modern professionals.

1.1. *Theory of Action for Interdisciplinary Project-Based Learning*

Several overlapping and research-based educational practices underpin the design of the SOAR project and the hypothesized educational and social outcomes of students' participation. A theory of action for interdisciplinary project-based learning guided this work and our examination of outcomes. We drew from decades of research on project-based [12], cooperative learning [13], interdisciplinary learning [14], growth mindset [15], and formative assessment [16,17], to describe processes and outcomes of educator and student actions within interdisciplinary project-based learning.

In the theory of action, educators initiate interdisciplinary project-based learning through planning for diverse teams comprising of multiple disciplines. This planning includes defining interdisciplinary products, identifying goals, information collection opportunities, supports for students' self-directed efforts, opportunities for student ownership, activation of peers as resources for one another, and considering when feedback on student efforts will be appropriate. Altogether, these combined efforts have the potential to increase student learning, cooperation, learning mindset, and interdisciplinary understanding as students work to build quality products together. In the sections below, we highlight research around interdisciplinary, project-based, and cooperative learning, mindset, and a formative assessment process that underpin the theory of action informing our study.

1.1.1. Interdisciplinary Learning

It is often challenging for scientists and engineers to convey or explain their knowledge and concepts to non-experts without any engineering background [18]. On the other hand, business, and communications professionals are often equally challenged to describe or communicate topics and ideas in science and technology. Despite initial challenges to interdisciplinary learning (e.g., shared language, disciplinary techniques), the benefits are wide-ranging, including the potential for generating new knowledge, meaningful collaboration, and new relationships [19,20]. Further, interdisciplinary learning can enhance students' awareness of interconnectivity among disciplines, innovation, and creativity [14,21,22]. Finally, by engaging students in cooperative cross-disciplinary work, peers and educator teams can develop trust and confidence in one another and make work more fulfilling [23].

1.1.2. Project-Based Learning

Project-based learning is experiential education that places value on student-led creative and goal-directed efforts and outputs [24]. When compared to traditionally passive lecture-based courses, active and project-based STEM courses contribute to higher student achievement [25]. If used effectively, project-based learning can also promote students' positive perceptions of their own skillsets, the utility of courses, and students' interest in pursuing STEM-oriented careers [26]. To achieve these benefits, [12] described the essential elements of project-based learning including promoting critical problem-solving, creativity, and the refinement of work and skillsets across time. However, [27] found that individual characteristics (e.g., attitudes, behavior, learning approaches) and group cultures (e.g., finishing culture vs. collaborative learning culture) that groups bring to collaboration impacts the depth of learning in groups. Cooperation among group members can impact the learning process and products made.

1.1.3. Cooperative Learning

Teams without structure can lead to conflicts, disparate contributions, and mismanagement of tasks [13]. Cooperative learning is needed for students to learn from interaction while working as a team and to complete tasks and achieve shared goals that individuals could not complete alone [28]. Structured effectively, cooperative learning can have many positive impacts on students, including on achievement, motivation, and peer relationships [29,30]. Ref. [13] outline five essential components to successful cooperative learning: positive interdependence, promotive interaction, individual accountability, interpersonal social skills, and group processing.

First, groups need to be arranged in such a way as to promote positive interdependence—delineated roles for each person to contribute and take responsibility for an aspect of the work. Another key aspect of successful cooperative learning is promotive interaction. Here, encouragement, helpfulness, the provision of feedback, and constructive work together helps a team be successful [31]. A third component is individual accountability. When students feel responsible for contributing to the group and that their contributions are identifiable in the products of their work, it is more likely each group member will make the effort [13]. Fourth, interpersonal social skills are essential. This includes the abilities to communicate, actively listen, participate in democratic decision-making, and manage potential disagreements. Each of these are vital to ensure students respect one another and make progress toward goals together [13]. Finally, group processing involves the inclusion of all in discussions, decision-making, and the establishment of group norms. This final component is essential for the group members to identify as a collective whole [32].

1.1.4. Mindset

There are barriers to learning including preconceptions, predispositions, and mindsets students bring with them, which prevent students from fully realizing the full potential of learning experiences [27]. Reference [15] described the mindsets learners bring to educational experiences as a continuum from a fixed to a growth mindset. A fixed mindset is characterized by rigidity in approaches to learning—potentially equating intelligence to talent and avoiding risks or challenges. Individuals with a fixed mindset may believe that they possess (or do not) the skills necessary to do a task and may be less receptive to growth-oriented feedback and redoubling of efforts to achieve a goal. These individuals are more likely to quit when faced with challenges and achieve less than their growth-oriented peers [33]. A growth mindset is exemplified by positioning effort and engagement as the key to achieving success and may consider intelligence to be malleable. Individuals adopting a growth mindset may approach challenging tasks iteratively—trying out strategies, seeking feedback and further opportunities to challenge themselves, and learning from mistakes [33].

2. The SOAR Project

We incorporated evidence and guidance for effective practices into the design of the SOAR project—an interdisciplinary project-based learning initiative that engages a team in bringing a product to market. These projects centered around a prototype developed by electrical engineering students (e.g., an airfoil glider electricity generating system, a current calibration coil). The SOAR project emulated an industry setting with a series of assignments, multiple checkpoints, and feedback. This project also allows students to develop team-building abilities and collaboration skills. Throughout the semester, students are asked to reflect on their group's interdisciplinary collaboration and project overall (see Figure 1 for project timeline, deliverables, and surveys). Students had to complete four modules; each module required specific group tasks along with rubrics. Groups needed to:

1. Identify stakeholders, broader impacts, team roles, a timeline for completion, and a joint statement synthesizing the project.
2. Provide a research-based description of their product's significance and rationale, a product, and a market description.
3. Present a business pitch to communicate their product to an audience of clients, investors, and other stakeholders.
4. Create a press release, a written and performed product pitch in a shark tank-style format, and a video.

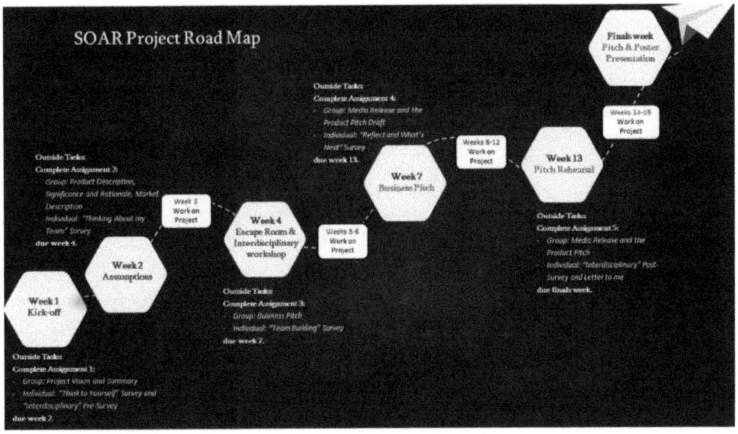

Figure 1. SOAR project road map.

After each module, groups submitted their work to the interdisciplinary teaching team where they received feedback based on the criteria for exemplary work and were given an opportunity to implement feedback into their progressive portfolios. At the end of the course, each group submitted final portfolios that displayed their best work (see BLINDED for a full description of the SOAR program including development and piloting).

3. Present Study

Study Objectives

To explore the interdisciplinary and cooperative learning orientations of groups of engineering, communications, and business/marketing students, we collected artifacts and analyzed students' reflections on their cooperative interdisciplinary project-based learning experience. The following questions frame our study:

1. How does the SOAR program impact cooperative learning orientations of students over the semester?
2. What dispositions and mindsets toward interdisciplinary learning are exemplified in student reflections?

4. Methods

This descriptive study drew on survey reflections to understand the impact of the SOAR program on interdisciplinary understanding, cooperative learning, and student dispositions and mindsets over time. We elicited authentic and anonymous reflections on groups and projects. We analyzed outcomes over time to better understand how students perceived their experiences throughout the project.

4.1. Participants

In Spring 2020 at a university located in the United States, we had a total of 51 students comprising 22 business-majored, 14 communications-majored, and 20 engineering-majored students who were tasked to work on seven industry-sponsored projects over 15 weeks (8 weeks for business students). Examples of industry sponsors include Boeing, Fluke, and OceanGate, and each group consisted of a range of 8 to 13 students. This study was reviewed and approved by our institution's Institutional Review Board to collect data without identifying information. All participants gave consent to participate.

4.2. Data Sources

We used a questionnaire and five open-ended surveys to elicit student reflections on their interdisciplinary team collaboration over time.

4.2.1. Disciplinary, Interdisciplinary, and Collaboration Questionnaire

During the first SOAR session, we used a synchronous polling site to elicit anonymous responses to six questions. Students (n_{Range} = 34–40) rated their knowledge of their own major, perceptions of what people from other majors know about their area of study, and their collaboration abilities (1 = poor, 4 = excellent). Students also reported their motivation to collaborate and do well in the project (1 = not motivated, 4 = very motivated). Finally, students chose their greatest concern for interdisciplinary collaboration (i.e., group dynamics, unequal work, time constraints, conflict, or other) and what they value most in collaboration (i.e., gaining new perspectives, improving collaboration skills, improving communication skills, gaining career skills, or other). These questions were developed following open-ended feedback from an earlier iteration of the SOAR project.

4.2.2. Reflections

Students provided their own reflections on group roles, aspects of interdisciplinary learning and collaboration, goal setting and achievement, and reflective thinking on experiences throughout the project (Table 1). The questions were created and reviewed by a panel of experts to ensure the validity of the measurement.

Table 1. SOAR reflections.

Reflection	Prompts/Description
1	• What does an {Electrical Engineering, Communications, Business} major do? • What are their strengths for your project?
2	• Explain in a few sentences the role you perceive your team members to have. What do you expect each person will need to do to ensure your team's success? Complete this for all team members including yourself.
3	• How has your understanding about other disciplines changed? • How is your team interdependent? • Does each member contribute toward your goals? Why or why not? • How have your individual roles contributed to your success and/or failures as a team? • How has your group functioned overall? Explain please. • How have your social skills contributed to communication, clarification, and encouragement of team members? • What is the interaction between members of your group like? • Overall, what can you and the team do together to ensure you meet your goals?
4	• How did your team members do on their pitches? • What information did your team consider in making decisions for the final pitch? • Reflect how your team will do on the rubric, as of this moment. • How confident are you about your team's success? Why or why not?
5	Write a "Letter to Me." In it, write to yourself on the first day of the semester. Give advice to yourself. Consider assumptions you had about others, things you have learned, and things you would have done differently. Encourage yourself to take on challenges and explain ways to approach them. The letter should be between 1-2 single spaced pages.

Reflection 1. Within the first two weeks of the project and after the first interdisciplinary session, we elicited students' (n = 42) initial understandings of what people in electrical engineering, communications, and business majors do. After each major, prompts ask students to write what they see as disciplinary strengths for their group project.

Reflection 2. Between the second and fourth weeks of the project, we elicited student (n = 37) reflections on their team's organization and expectations. Specifically, we asked students to explain each person's role within their team, and their expectations for contributions from that person that would make the team successful. For example, roles include meeting arrangement, facilitating communication, making PowerPoint presentations, creating videos, or conducting market research.

Reflection 3. Between weeks four and seven, after completing their business pitch, students (n = 36) were asked to comment on how their understanding of other disciplines had changed, and to reflect on aspects of collaboration within their team. Finally, we asked students to comment on what the group needs to do to reach their goals.

Reflection 4. During the period of preparation for the final pitch (weeks 7–13), students (n = 37) responded to five questions eliciting their perception of their team's performance, how effective they were, and future team achievement.

Reflection 5. In the final reflection in weeks 13–15 and just before the product pitch and poster presentation, students (n = 38) wrote a 'letter to me'. This was a letter to the students themselves—the person they were on the first day of the semester. Students were prompted to offer advice, reflect on the assumptions we held about others, share the valuable lessons that they have learned, contemplate on the things they would have done differently, and provide encouraging words to embrace challenges while suggesting effective approaches to overcome them. A writing prompt and rubric were provided to guide their writing.

4.3. Analysis

With a focused attention on our research questions, an in-depth analysis of the questionnaire responses and thoughtful reflections, we have been able to draw meaningful inferences regarding how students perceive disciplines and their orientations toward learning and interdisciplinary groups. Responses to the questionnaire were summarized by the proportions of responses to questions and summarized in relation to other items (e.g., knowledge of one's own major and perceptions of others' knowledge of their major). To make sense of the information from reflections, we iteratively and recursively read responses and assigned codes to the data—assigning (or using participants' own words in vivo) words and phrases to describe qualitative information [34]. We drew from current information in data but also imposed codes to capture theoretical variables of interest (e.g., disciplinary, and cooperative orientations [34]. Through discussion and collaborative coding, we established a coding and scoring scheme to characterize emergent themes quantitatively. Using the coding scheme, two members of our research team coded all responses and made notes about feasible alternative codes and borderline cases. Both coders met and discussed discrepancies, resulting in full agreement. The coding scheme was presented and discussed with the full research team. Following discussion and critique, all responses were reexamined with the final coding scheme to ensure criteria and codes were consistently applied.

In all reflections, we coded for disciplinary/interdisciplinary orientations and facets of cooperative learning (i.e., positive interdependence, individual accountability, group processing, social skills, and promotive interaction (Table 2)). For cooperative learning orientations, we looked across each participant's responses to prompts within a reflection occasion and determined the degree of collaboration present in the responses (0 = N/A, 1 = some evidence, 2 = abundant evidence). For instance, if we found a single reference to either positive relationships with group members or acknowledging the contributions of group members, this response would receive a score of 1 for positive interdependence. If we found multiple references to establishing and enacting group goals and interaction among the group to meet goals, a response received a score of 2 for group processing. In the final reflection, which took the form of a 'letter to me', we conducted coding to examine various aspects. First, we analyzed whether students mentioned their initial confusion or difficulty in understanding the SOAR project. Additionally, we looked at how students described their initial and final dispositions toward working in groups, categorizing them as positive, negative, neutral, mixed, or characterized by nervousness. Furthermore, we explored the mindsets toward learning apparent in the letters, such as differentiating between a growth mindset and a fixed mindset.

Table 2. Descriptions of cooperative learning.

Element	Description
Positive interdependence	Positive relationships and contributions of group members
Individual accountability	Dependence of each group members' contributions
Promotive interaction	Mutual encouraging and facilitated communications
Group processing	Group functioning through the establishment and enactment of goals, and interaction
Social skills	Interpersonal communication skills (e.g., clarification, gratitude)

Note: Adapted from [35].

5. Results

We examined SOAR students' orientations toward disciplines, group cooperation, the project, and learning over a fifteen-week semester (eight weeks for business students). We report on our first information collection occasion, and themes identified in reflections over the semester. We provide descriptions of themes and exemplify them in students' own words.

5.1. Disciplinary, Interdisciplinary, and Collaboration Questionnaire

At the onset of the SOAR project, we observed patterns in students' perceptions of their own disciplinary knowledge, positioning of their peers' knowledge of their major, as well as project motivations and concerns (Table 3). Unsurprisingly, most students rated their knowledge of their own discipline highly, however, they rated their peers' knowledge of their major lower. On average, students rated their interdisciplinary knowledge as fair or good, but in rating their abilities to collaborate, most students rated themselves highly—good or excellent. All participants were motivated or very motivated to do well in the project. Considering their upcoming interdisciplinary project collaborations, we found students were concerned with potential time constraints ($n = 14$, 41%), group dynamics ($n = 11$, 32%), and conflict ($n = 3$, 9%)—six (18%) listed that they had other concerns. Finally, students responded to a question about what they valued most in collaboration. Students reported they hoped to gain new perspectives ($n = 15$, 38%), gain career skills ($n = 10$, 25%), improve collaboration skills ($n = 5$, 13%), and improve their communication ($n = 5$, 13%) skills. Five (13%) said they retained other values for collaboration.

Table 3. Disciplinary, interdisciplinary, and collaborative questionnaire.

	Poor	Fair	Good	Excellent	n	M	SD
Own major understanding	2 (5%)	4 (10%)	20 (51%)	13 (33%)	39	3.13	0.80
Others' understanding of your major	15 (38%)	16 (40%)	8 (20%)	1 (3%)	40	1.88	0.82
Interdisciplinary knowledge	6 (15%)	18 (45%)	12 (30%)	4 (10%)	40	2.35	0.86
Collaboration abilities	1 (3%)	3 (8%)	27 (68%)	9 (23%)	40	3.10	0.63
	Not motivated	Somewhat motivated	Motivated	Very motivated			
Motivation to collaborate	6 (16%)	3 (8%)	21 (55%)	8 (21%)	38	2.82	0.95
Motivation to do well	1 (3%)	1 (3%)	12 (30%)	26 (65%)	40	3.58	0.68

5.2. Disciplinary and Professional Conceptions

In the initial reflection, we identified misconceptions regarding the nature of each major based on the responses provided. Specifically, we found that 17% of engineering responses, 33% of communications responses, and 2% of business responses demonstrated misconceptions about their respective fields. In the case of engineering, the misconceptions primarily revolved around oversimplifying the role of engineers, with responses such as, "They engineer products with electrical components" or "Math, building things." On the other hand, misconceptions related to communications often involved confusion regarding professional roles, as seen in responses like "...create and deliver creative advertising and marketing strategy" or "They will market better and be able to reach out and talk to more people about our project."

As the reflections progressed and students engaged further in the project, we observed notable changes in how they perceived other majors. In fact, by the third reflection, a significant 58% of students reported a shift in their conceptualization of other majors. This transformation was evident through recurring statements such as, "It has made me have a newfound respect for the skills that each member of my team possesses" and "Before, I was a little confused about the difference between communication and marketing. I think I have a better understanding now". In addition to changing conceptions, we also found students evolved in their understanding of the professional roles one another might take in the future. At the beginning, we found that students tended to view disciplines and their groupmates from other majors as instrumental for the course project, rather than a focus on what they will be doing in their careers. For instance, one student commented on the question about what engineering majors do, "I would guess the electrical engineer designs the hardware side of the kites, and the software engineer designs the computer side." By the end of the project, we saw a clear increase in statements from students that extended work on the project to the professional world. One student's comment on their 'letter to me' captures this transformation:

> "Get ready to be challenged as a professional with your SOAR project. You are going to have to step out of your role as a student and become a professional communicator. You are not alone in wanting your project to be successful."

5.3. Interdisciplinary Orientations

Initiating the SOAR project was a challenge for many students, and each came with a diverse set of disciplinary understandings and preconceptions about what the project would entail. At the beginning of the project and extending through the mid-point, most students delineated disciplinary roles for one another—using phrases to describe group roles like, ". . .in charge of. . .", ". . .responsible for. . ..", ". . .expected to. . .." While this may be a natural product of the nature of work (i.e., an engineering project brought to market), we found that on each successive reflection, fewer students kept a primarily disciplinary focus, with more students adapting interdisciplinary orientations to the project over time (Table 4). The focus slowly shifted from specific responsibilities of individuals to group responsibilities and processes.

Table 4. Group proportions for interdisciplinary learning orientations.

	Reflection 1 (n = 42)	Reflection 2 (n = 37)	Reflection 3 (n = 36)	Reflection 4 (n = 37)	Reflection 5 (n = 38)
Disciplinary orientation	36 (86%)	30 (81%)	28 (78%)	26 (68%)	14 (39%)
Interdisciplinary orientation	5 (14%)	7 (19%)	8 (22%)	11 (32%)	24 (63%)

Progressive reflections co-occurred with team experiences and challenges. We observed that challenges, particularly for groups that were well-prepared, boosted team morale and perceived authenticity of the work. By the final reflection, 'letter to me', we observed extensive gratitude and fondness for one another's contributions. For example:

> "There will be some challenges you have no control over, but it is vital to maintain discipline among yourself and help your team members if they are falling behind. The keyword in this project is teamwork."

> "One thing I really loved about SOAR was the ability to work with students from other majors. Not only was I able to meet new people, but I learned a lot about engineering and business that I otherwise would not learn."

However, for many students, this cohesive interdisciplinary collaboration remained lacking. We observed that some students maintained a focus on their own disciplinary skillset for collaboration, had a disposition of self-reliance, and/or deficit perspectives of their peers. For some of these students, they may perceive their collaborators as less able than themselves. For example, the following student comment to themselves in the 'letter to me' occurring at the end of the project:

> "I know you will let the business and communication students edit your work because you think they can write better, but you will see that is not the case. You and the other engineering students can do much better job than they are, because you care about this project much more and you understand it better..."

This comment, and others, represent more than just a disciplinary orientation—extending to personal characteristics and a more general dynamic that may have been occurring within groups with diverse individuals (e.g., lacking contributions from all, conflict, predispositions).

5.4. Cooperative Learning Orientations

Upon analyzing the data, we identified notable increases in all five cooperative learning orientations over time, although the change was not consistently linear when examined collectively. During the initial survey, we observed some evidence of positive interdependence, individual accountability, and limited indications of promotive interaction among the participants. Following a team-building activity conducted during the third reflection, we detected significant improvements in positive interdependence, promotive interaction, group processing, and social skills. By the time of the final reflection, coinciding with the submission of the final group work, we witnessed substantial and demonstrable increases in all cooperative learning orientations. These trends indicate a clear pattern of enhanced cooperation resulting from continuous engagement in interdisciplinary group projects (for descriptive statistics, refer to Table 5, and for a visual representation of the cooperative learning orientations over time, consult Figure 2).

Table 5. Descriptive statistics for cooperative orientations.

	Reflection 1 (n = 42)		Reflection 2 (n = 37)		Reflection 3 (n = 36)		Reflection 4 (n = 37)		Reflection 5 (n = 38)	
	M	*SD*	*M*	*SD*	*M*	*SD*	*M*	*SD*	*M*	*SD*
Positive interdependence	1.00	0.00	0.95	0.74	1.11	0.71	0.95	0.81	1.50	0.76
Individual accountability	1.02	0.47	1.35	0.72	1.13	0.91	0.97	0.87	1.53	0.73
Promotive interaction	0.52	0.67	0.51	0.77	0.97	0.83	0.97	0.87	1.50	0.76
Group Processing	N/A	N/A	0.73	0.73	0.88	0.77	0.86	0.89	1.45	0.76
Social skills	N/A	N/A	0.46	0.77	0.91	0.75	0.70	0.81	1.42	0.83

Note: Scale is 0 = NA; 1 = Some Evidence, 2 Extensive Evidence.

> "Open yourself up earlier so you can understand everything you can about this amazing product you have the honor of working on with some awesome engineers and don't be afraid to ask questions."

> "Everything will work out great when you address assumptions and have the chance to talk about things in person."

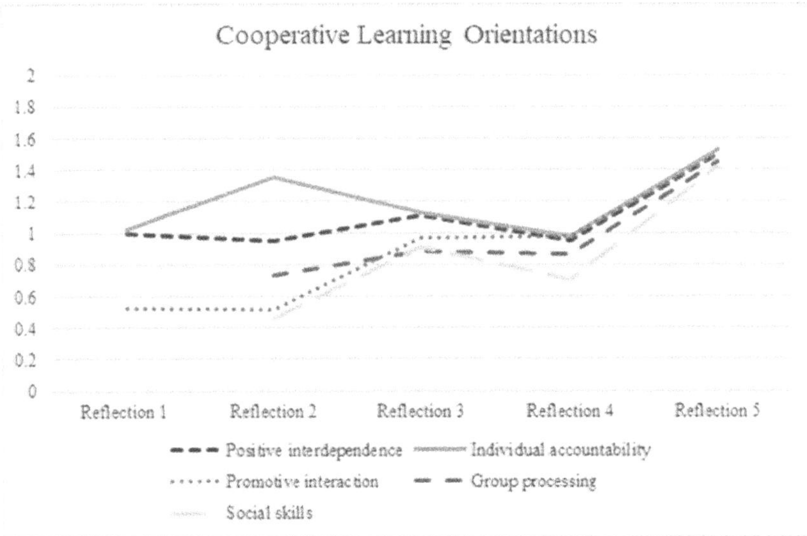

Figure 2. Cooperative learning orientations. Note: DV is the mean value of cooperative learning orientation: Scale is 0 = N/A, 1 = some evidence, 2 = extensive evidence.

During the final reflection, we assessed the orientations of students towards their groups and the project (Table 6). At the beginning of the semester, when asked about their initial experiences working in groups, about a half of students (48%) expressed negative predispositions. However, by the end of the semester, only one student reported negative feelings about their group. This significant shift in disposition toward group work is evident in the following comment provided by a student:

Table 6. Proportions of emotions characterizing the pre- and post-dispositions.

	Predispositions	Post-Dispositions
Positive	4 (11%)	28 (74%)
Negative	18 (47%)	1 (3%)
Neutral	10 (26%)	1 (3%)
Mixed	2 (5%)	8 (21%)
Nervous	4 (11%)	0 (0%)

Note: *n* = 38.

> "In my previous group projects, most... barely contributed to the final product. I used to be one of these students... I really decided to crack down and contribute to the group."

At the end of the project, more than a half of students (about 74%) reported enthusiastically positive feelings about their groups. We found that as most students reflected on the experience holistically, they were able to see the many actions taken and not taken that affected the process and recognize that they could not have succeeded alone. For example, one student commented:

> "You will find this experience extremely rewarding and you should make the effort to experience all aspects of the process. The multi-discipline aspects of this project amplify this even more..."

> "Your passive behavior in the group will lead to an unsuccessful project. Only finishing your own portion is not enough to succeed."

5.5. Mindset

On the final reflection, from the 'letter to me', we were able to gain a more rounded window into student thinking and to establish, with confidence, whether they had adopted a primarily fixed vs. growth orientation toward learning about other disciplines and skills for their future endeavors. The letters provided evidence that 84% of students exhibited a growth mindset, evidencing students overcoming their aversion to risk or discomfort and encouraging themselves to take on new challenges. Comments from students often are hedged with a desire to have embraced a more growth- and open-minded perspective earlier, for example:

> "Congratulations!! You just won the ticket to be a part of a group that is filled by some extraordinary, talented, and kind people. So, you! Pretentious, judgmental, despicably self-involved wanker better fight with every fiber of your being to put yourself out there and truly be a part of this amazing group of young people right at the beginning."

However, we identified a subset of students who exhibited a fixed mindset (16%) and a grade-focused orientation toward the course (13%), rather than prioritizing the project goals. One student's final comment exemplified this perspective: "You don't really need me to tell you what to do to be successful in this class because you already know." We recognize that these comments may also reflect preexisting biases that were reinforced by the behaviors of group members and individual experiences.

5.6. Educational Progression

In the 'letter to me', each student provided insights into their approach to the project at the beginning. Students (58%) openly expressed their confusion or difficulties during the initial stages of the project. The students overwhelmingly recommended embracing an open-minded growth mindset and shared instances during the project that altered their perspectives. For example, regarding the initial challenge at the project's onset, one student remarked: "During this semester, you'll be faced with a project proposal for this course that seems very difficult and damn near impossible at first, but it won't be."

Other students commented about past behaviors and encouraged themselves to make a transformation sooner. For instance:

> "Throughout this semester, I found multiple solutions for my time management problems. Most of the time if you communicate with your superiors whether at work or at school, they will help you come up with a solution. Don't be afraid to tell others about your problems: Most of the time people will help you."

Finally, students commented on how crucial communication was to engage in the project and build group cohesion. One student wrote this to their past self:

> "I think the biggest thing I could tell you, is that you will need to communicate with your groupmates and teacher a lot more. When things get confusing, and you don't know where to go or where to look, that is the perfect time to ask for some help."

6. Significance and Implications

Across the United States, teacher-centered instruction in undergraduate classrooms remains common and assessments remain one-off high-stakes tests used for accountability and marking purposes. This is despite longstanding research that demonstrates students learn better through active, student-centered, and collaborative learning environments [13,25]. Guided by a theory of action for interdisciplinary project-based learning, most students were engaged in the SOAR project and experienced enhanced outcomes in learning, cooperation, mindset, and interdisciplinary understanding.

Our study revealed that implementing an interdisciplinary group project for students from various majors posed challenges, yet it proved to be a rewarding experience for both students and instructors. Although students initially faced confusion and difficulties, along with some misconceptions about their peers' majors, there was ample evidence of improved interdisciplinary understanding, group dynamics, satisfaction, and mutual appreciation as the project progressed. In line with research on project-based cooperative learning and formative assessment, the structure of the project and groups was essential to realizing these outcomes. Notably, by embedding a formative assessment process within the project, we enabled students to iteratively apply clear criteria for success to both group and individual work. It also provided opportunities for frequent low-stakes critique via the provision of peer and instructor feedback on checkpoints, and structured opportunities for self-reflection [17,36].

By offering students a template for the project that was broken down by deliverables, we enabled students to set their own goals, roles, and timelines for the project. This scaffolded a shared understanding of the work of each discipline and the purposes of the SOAR project. We believe this all contributed to students' positive interdependence, promotive interaction, individual accountability, interpersonal social skills, and group processing as shown in Table 5 and Figure 2—in line with the work of [13,29]. The observed trend across student reflections implies that students tended to focus more on individual accountability before later adopting other facets of cooperative learning such as promotive interaction and social skills. Further, we found evidence that cooperative work among students of different disciplines led to many developing a sense of trust and confidence [23].

The results of our analysis of students' 'letter to me' also indicate the project cultivated a growth mindset in students by breaking down disciplinary silos and misconceptions among students of different majors. The structured collaborative opportunities afforded by the SOAR project appears to have enabled students to see their work improving with each iteration and embrace the diverse contributions of their groupmates, which is consistent with the findings of [33]. We also found corroborative evidence for the beliefs about intelligence and learning were associated with students' academic experiences, observations of peers, social cues, and formal learning opportunities. Further, we found SOAR projects influenced students' interests in STEM, perceptions of their own skillsets, and the utility of the course [26]. We believe this is particularly due to the authenticity of the project to the professional world and real-world outputs that students generated [37]. Upon completion of the more summative aspects of the project (i.e., the product pitch to stakeholders), it is clear most students took considerable pride in their work, had gratitude for their peers' contributions, and experienced significant learning that could be continued into their careers.

Limitations

This study has several limitations that bound our interpretation and opened avenues for further research. Our study is a description of one semester implementing and examining the outcomes of the SOAR project at one university campus and is not representative of other contexts. Further, we were only able to collect information anonymously and we were not able to link data to the same students over time—limiting inferences that can be made at the individual level. We acknowledge also that there were students who did not participate in all reflections. The scope of our study is, therefore, bound by these factors and should be interpreted as such. Another limitation is the lack of statistical analyses due to the small sample size. Hence, a more robust study with statistical analyses, or longitudinal and larger-scale research, is needed to confirm our findings across contexts.

7. Conclusions

The present study underscores the power and potential of interdisciplinary project-based approaches, so-called SOAR, in fostering deeper collaboration and cultivating essential academic and workplace skills among future professionals. It highlights the significant role of such approaches in promoting interdisciplinary learning, teamwork, and the development of valuable competencies sought after in professional settings. Bringing together electrical engineering, communications, and marketing educators and students to work on industry-sponsored projects with real-world implications led to increased authenticity, collaboration, and achievement in the work and products of groups. This approach also led to a transformation in the learning orientations of students who shifted from the view of themselves as students to professionals capable of more than they originally envisioned. Further research is needed to explore how facets of interdisciplinary projects and teams affect motivation, mindset, collaboration, and the ultimate quality of products.

Author Contributions: Conceptualization, all authors; methodology, S.S. and D.S.J.V.O.; software and formal analysis, S.S. and D.S.J.V.O.; data curation, D.S.J.V.O.; writing—original draft preparation, S.S. and D.S.J.V.O.; writing—review and editing, L.C.P., J.M. and M.B.; funding acquisition, all authors. All authors have read and agreed to the published version of the manuscript.

Funding: Washington State University, Smith Teaching and Learning Grant (Internal Grant).

Institutional Review Board Statement: The study was approved by the Institutional Review Board of Washington State University (IRB: 18034-002, 02/28/2020).

Informed Consent Statement: Informed consent was obtained from all subjects involved in the study.

Data Availability Statement: Data is not publicly available, but can be offered by request.

Conflicts of Interest: The authors declare no conflict of interest.

References

1. Andrade, H.L.; Hefferen, J.; Palma, M.E. Formative assessment in the arts. In *Handbook of Formative Assessment in the Disciplines*; Andrade, H.L., Bennett, R.E., Cizek, G.L., Eds.; Routledge: Oxfordshire, UK, 2019; pp. 126–145.
2. Johnson, D.W.; Johnson, R.T. *Active Learning: Cooperation in the Classroom*; Interaction Book Company: West Reno, NV, USA, 1998.
3. Manyika, J.; Lund, S.; Chui, M.; Bughin, J.; Woetzel, J.; Batra, P.; Ko, R.; Sanghvi, S. *Jobs Lost, Jobs Gained: Workforce Transitions in a Time of Automation*; McKinsey Global Institute: New York, NY, USA, 2017; Available online: http://hdl.voced.edu.au/10707/444873 (accessed on 1 September 2024).
4. Schwab, K. *The Fourth Industrial Revolution*; Penguin Random House: Manhattan, NY, USA, 2017.
5. Zaloom. STEM is Overrated: College Is Not just Job Prep, and the Job Market Changes Constantly. The Atlantic, 10 September 2019. Available online: https://www.theatlantic.com/ideas/archive/2019/09/college-not-job-prep/597487/ (accessed on 1 September 2024).
6. Bolick, M.A.; Thomassen, M.; Apland, J.; Spencer, O.; Nicole, F.; Tran, S.K.N.; Voigt, M.; Lazar, K.B. Project-Based Learning in Interdisciplinary Spaces: A Case Study in Norway and the United States. *Educ. Sci.* **2024**, *14*, 866. [CrossRef]
7. Balleisen, E.J.; Howes, L.; Wibbels, E. The impact of applied project-based learning on undergraduate student development. *High. Educ.* **2023**, *87*, 1141–1156. [CrossRef]
8. Johnsen, M.M.W.; Sjølie, E.; Johansen, V. Learning to Collaborate in a Project-based Graduate Course: A Multilevel Study of Student Outcomes. *Res. High. Educ.* **2023**, *65*, 439–462. [CrossRef]
9. Lavado-Anguera, S.; Velasco-Quintana, P.-J.; Terrón-López, M.-J. Project-Based Learning (PBL) as an Experiential Pedagogical Methodology in Engineering Education: A Review of the Literature. *Educ. Sci.* **2024**, *14*, 617. [CrossRef]
10. Duhigg, C. What google learned from its quest to build the perfect team. *The New York Times Magazine*. 25 February 2016. Available online: https://www.nytimes.com/2016/02/28/magazine/what-google-learned-from-its-quest-to-build-the-perfect-team.html (accessed on 1 September 2024).
11. Garvin, D.A.; Wagonfeld, A.B.; Kind, L. Google's project oxygen: Do managers matter? *Harv. Bus. Sch. Case* **2013**, 313-110. Available online: https://www.hbs.edu/faculty/Pages/item.aspx?num=44657 (accessed on 1 September 2024).
12. Larmer, J.; Mergendoller, J.; Boss, S. *Setting the Standard for Project-Based Learning: A Proven Approach to Rigorous Classroom Instruction*; Association for Supervision and Curriculum Development: Alexandria, VA, USA, 2015.
13. Johnson, D.; Johnson, R. Cooperative learning and achievement. In *Cooperative Learning: Theory and Research*; Sharan, S., Ed.; Praeger: Westport, CT, USA, 1990; pp. 23–37.
14. Jacobs, H.H. The growing need for interdisciplinary curriculum content. In *Interdisciplinary Curriculum: Design and Implementation*; Jacobs, H.H., Ed.; Association for Supervision and Curriculum Development: Alexandria, VA, USA, 1989; pp. 1–11.
15. Dweck, C.S. *Mindset: The New Psychology of Success*; Random House Digital, Inc: New York, NY, USA, 2008.
16. Black, P.; Wiliam, D. Assessment and Classroom Learning. *Assess. Educ. Princ. Policy Pract.* **1998**, *5*, 7–74. [CrossRef]
17. ETS (Educational Testing Service). Research Rationale for the Keeping Learning on Track® Program. 2009. Available online: https://files.eric.ed.gov/fulltext/ED567844.pdf (accessed on 1 September 2024).
18. Brownell, S.E.; Price, J.V.; Steinman, L. Science communication to the general public: Why we need to teach undergraduate and graduate students this skill as part of their formal scientific training. *J. Undergrad. Neurosci. Educ.* **2012**, *12*, E6–E10. Available online: https://www.ncbi.nlm.nih.gov/pmc/articles/PMC3852879/ (accessed on 1 September 2024).

19. Jacobs, J.A.; Frickel, S. Interdisciplinarity: A critical assessment. *Annu. Rev. Sociol.* **2009**, *35*, 43–65. [CrossRef]
20. National Academy of Sciences. *Facilitating Interdisciplinary Research*; National Academies Press: Washington, DC, USA, 2004.
21. Frodeman, R.; Mitcham, C. New directions in interdisciplinarity: Broad, deep, and critical. *Bull. Sci. Technol. Soc.* **2007**, *27*, 506–514. [CrossRef]
22. Levinson, B.; Thornton, K.W. Managing interdisciplinary research: Lessons learned from the EPA-STAR/NSF/USDA Water and Watersheds Research Program. In Proceedings of the First Interagency Conference on Research in the Watersheds, US Department of Agriculture, Agricultural Research Service, Washington, DC, USA, 5–8 June 2023; Available online: http://www.tucson.ars.ag.gov/icrw/Proceedings/Levinson.pdf (accessed on 1 September 2024).
23. Dailey, R.; Hauschild-Mork, M. Making it all count: A cross-disciplinary collaboration model incorporating scholarship, creative activity, and student engagement. *InSight J. Sch. Teach.* **2013**, *12*, 64–78. [CrossRef]
24. Capraro, R.M.; Capraro, M.M.; Morgan, J.R. (Eds.) *STEM Project-Based Learning: An Integrated Science, Technology, Engineering, and Mathematics (STEM) Approach*; Sense Publishers: Rotterdam, The Netherlands, 2013. [CrossRef]
25. Freeman, S.; Eddy, S.L.; McDonough, M.; Smith, M.K.; Okoroafor, N.; Jordt, H.; Wenderoth, M.P. Active learning increases student performance in science, engineering, and mathematics. *Proc. Natl. Acad. Sci. USA* **2014**, *111*, 8410–8415. [CrossRef] [PubMed]
26. Beier, M.E.; Kim, M.H.; Saterbak, A.; Leautaud, V.; Bishnoi, S.; Gilberto, J.M. The effect of authentic project-based learning on attitudes and career aspirations in STEM. *J. Res. Sci. Teach.* **2018**, *56*, 3–23. [CrossRef]
27. Krishnan, S.; Gabb, R.; Vale, C. Learning cultures of problem-based learning teams. *Australas. J. Eng. Educ.* **2011**, *17*, 67–78. [CrossRef]
28. Johnson, D.W.; Johnson, R.T. Cooperative learning: The foundation for active learning. In *Active Learning—Beyond the Future*; Intechopen: London, UK, 2018.
29. Johnson, D.W.; Johnson, R.T.; Roseth, C.; Shin, T.S. The relationship between motivation and achievement in interdependent situations. *J. Appl. Soc. Psychol.* **2014**, *44*, 622–633. [CrossRef]
30. Kyndt, E.; Raes, E.; Lismont, B.; Timmers, F.; Cascallar, E.; Dochy, F. A meta-analysis of the effects of face-to-face cooperative learning. Do recent studies falsify or verify earlier findings? *Educ. Res. Rev.* **2013**, *10*, 133–149. [CrossRef]
31. Johnson, D.; Johnson, R. Learning together and alone: Overview and meta-analysis. *Asia Pac. J. Educ.* **2002**, *22*, 95–105. [CrossRef]
32. Johnson, D.; Johnson, R. An educational psychology success story: Social interdependence theory and cooperative learning. *Educ. Res.* **2009**, *38*, 365–379. [CrossRef]
33. Smiley, P.A.; Buttitta, K.V.; Chung, S.Y.; Dubon, V.X.; Chang, L.K. Mediation models of implicit theories and achievement goals predict planning and withdrawal after failure. *Motiv. Emot.* **2016**, *40*, 878–894. [CrossRef]
34. Saldaña, J. *The Coding Manual for Qualitative Researchers*, 4th ed.; Sage: Washington, DC, USA, 2021.
35. Kern, A.L.; Moore, T.J.; Akillioglu, F.C. Cooperative learning: Developing an observation instrument for student interactions. In Proceedings of the 2007 37th ASEE/IEEE Frontiers in Education Conference—Global Engineering: Knowledge Without Borders, Opportunities Without Passports, Milwaukee, WI, USA, 10–13 October 2007; pp. T1D-1–T1D-6. [CrossRef]
36. National Research Council [NRC]. *Knowing What Students Know: The Science and Design of Educational Assessment*; National Academies Press: Washington, DC, USA, 2001.
37. Kidron, A.; Kali, Y. Boundary breaking for interdisciplinary learning. *Res. Learn. Technol.* **2015**, *23*, 26496. [CrossRef]

education sciences

MDPI

Article

Conceptualizing an Initial Framework to Support Discipline-Rich Project-Based Learning in STEM

Monica Sircar [1,*], Sheila Orr [2,*], Carlee Madis [3] and Sarah DiMaria [4]

1 Graduate School of Education, Stanford University, Stanford, CA 94305, USA
2 Department of Teacher Education, Michigan State University, East Lansing, MI 48824, USA
3 Desmos Mathematics, Amplify Education, Brooklyn, NY 11201, USA; carlee.madis@knowlesteachers.org
4 Cedars Next Generation High School, Austin, TX 78748, USA; sarah.dimaria@knowlesteachers.org
* Correspondence: msircar@stanford.edu (M.S.); smorr11@msu.edu (S.O.)

Abstract: Project-Based Learning (PBL) is positioned as a pedagogical approach to support authentic, discipline-rich STEM curricula. However, much of the research has focused on the effectiveness of researcher-created curricula rather than teacher-created curricula. In this manuscript, we seek to illuminate the ways in which teachers create discipline-rich STEM projects. Drawing on the theory of the curriculum enactment process, we analyzed curricular artifacts from our teaching practices that we created as secondary STEM teachers who designed and enacted project-based learning. From the analysis, we propose a framework grounded in disciplinary standards to support teachers in creating discipline-rich STEM projects by attending to (1) the Elements of PBL; (2) Content Storyline; (3) Practice Pathway.

Keywords: project-based learning; curriculum development; PK-12 teachers; teacher learning; STEM education; standards

1. Introduction and Presentation of the Problem

To prepare students for a dynamic future, STEM education demands a bold and ambitious vision for math and science education, where all students build deep conceptual understandings and skills in scientific and mathematical thinking through their engagement in rich performance tasks [1,2]. Enacting this vision requires shifts in both curriculum materials and instructional practice, both "what students learn" and "how students learn". Moreover, deep alignment to these standards involves not only "covering" all the individual components, but also designing learning experiences and tasks that weave components together for coherent and deep learning.

Project-Based Learning (PBL) is a pedagogical approach "in which students learn by actively engaging in real-world and personally meaningful projects" [3] that shows promise for powerfully engaging students in complex work [4]. This approach is seen as a leading instructional model for enacting the vision of NGSS and has been shown to narrow the gap in achievement for children from backgrounds underrepresented in the STEM fields [5,6]. Moreover, research on PBL in math and science suggests that this approach can support students' content knowledge acquisition, process skill development, ability to apply skills and knowledge in new situations, and ability to draw connections between concepts—all goals underlying the design of new math and science standards [7].

Despite great interest in PBL, science and math educators struggle to utilize PBL in their classrooms, particularly for driving the learning of core disciplinary standards [8,9]. Additionally, previous research has called for increased support for STEM teachers who use a PBL approach to design projects towards disciplinary learning goals [9,10]. As four current and former secondary-school STEM teachers with extensive PBL experience across various contexts in the United States, we have grappled with how projects can be designed to support robust disciplinary learning goals. Across our experiences as classroom teachers, we each have found PBL to be an instructional method that allowed us to engage students in complex tasks and foster profound conceptual understanding and skills in scientific and mathematical thinking among all students. Individually, we each have taught from 5 to 10 years in PBL environments and experienced significant professional learning related to the pedagogical approach. However, each of us found the professional support to engage in PBL in math and science not meeting our needs in relation to unique demands facing STEM teachers. We came together through our shared participation in the Removed for Peer Review Fellowship program. In the spring of 2018, we began our collaborative work around our shared experiences of PBL as a potent pedagogical strategy that provides students with the access to the power of math and science. Our goal was to find a way to support teachers in developing discipline-rich projects for their STEM courses.

Drawing on various bodies of literature related to PBL and the STEM curriculum, in this article, we put forth a conceptual framework for discipline-rich PBL projects in STEM education. We then draw on the theory of the curriculum enactment process [11] to reflect on and refine our framework by analyzing the curriculum we created as PK-12 STEM teachers who employed project-based learning. Taken together, we seek to answer the question: what are the key features of teacher-created, discipline-rich STEM projects?

2. Review of the Literature Related to Discipline-Rich Projects

As we conceptualized the ways in which teachers plan discipline-rich STEM PBL projects, we drew on three different bodies of literature: teaching content standards through content storylines, student learning of disciplinary practices, and PBL in STEM classrooms.

2.1. Teaching Content Standards through Content Storylines

The design of content storylines is an approach to designing learning sequences where the disciplinary content ideas in a lesson or unit are "sequenced and linked to one another and to lesson activities to help students construct a coherent "story" that makes sense to them" [12]. In contemporary science education, storylines represent "coherent units in which engagement in science practices is driven by questions arising from phenomena, and teachers and students work as partners in constructing and managing the trajectory of the resulting investigations and sensemaking" [13]. For example, at the start of a unit, students might encounter a compelling phenomenon or problem that they iteratively work to make sense of and/or solve. Across the sequence of lessons in the unit, teachers elicit and leverage students' questions about what they need to know next to motivate students' thinking across the unit and to promote conceptual coherence from the students' perspective.

While content storylines are not a new concept in curriculum development [11,14–18], this approach has garnered renewed interest as part of current reform efforts in science education, such as the shift towards the Next Generation Science Standards (NGSS), which emphasizes student sensemaking about phenomena and problems to drive deeper understandings of science ideas [2,18]. In particular, scholars have argued that designing storylines is supportive to these science education reform efforts when combined with project-based learning [19,20].

Although the inclusion of content storylines is most prominent in science education, Dietiker has been conceptualizing how mathematical concepts build to create a mathematical storyline [15,21]. As in science, the selection and sequencing of the progression of mathematical ideas that students develop across a unit should similarly promote coherence, a characteristic that previous research suggests is especially critical for learning in mathematics [22–24]. In project-based STEM learning, the content storyline describes the logical, coherent sequence of mathematical and/or scientific ideas that students are intended to build and use across the project, articulated as a narrative within the project context. Students' progress on this sequence of ideas is driven by students' questions and decisions across the project.

In our framework, we conceptualize the *Content Storyline* as a tool that teachers develop during the project design process to help themselves design for conceptual coherence within their projects. The Content Storyline anchors teachers' decisions about the selection and sequencing of project activities to ensure that their project builds towards the intended disciplinary content understandings in a way that is driven by students' engagement with the project context.

2.2. Disciplinary Practice Standards

Current reform efforts in both science and math education emphasize the importance of students developing skills and knowledge that are important to the practice of the discipline [1,2]. Such practice-oriented standards are intended to emphasize ways that students can participate in scientific, engineering, and mathematical activities and mirror the ways that scientific, engineering, and mathematical knowledge is constructed and used in the broader world [2,25,26] (see Table 1).

Table 1. Disciplinary practices for science and mathematics.

Disciplinary Practices in the Next Generation Science Standards	Disciplinary Practices in the Common Core—Math Standards
1. Asking questions and defining problems	1. Make sense of problems and persevere in solving them
2. Developing and using models	2. Reason abstractly and quantitatively
3. Planning and carrying out investigations	3. Construct viable arguments and critique the reasoning of others
4. Analyzing and interpreting data	4. Model with mathematics
5. Using mathematics and computational thinking	5. Use appropriate tools strategically
6. Constructing explanations and designing solutions	6. Attend to precision
7. Engaging in argument from evidence	7. Look for and make use of structure
8. Obtaining, evaluating, and communicating information	8. Look for and express regularity in repeated reasoning

The term "practices" is used instead of "skills" to emphasize that the development of these competencies requires the simultaneous coordination of both disciplinary knowledge and skill [2,25]. As with disciplinary content knowledge, students need scaffolded opportunities to develop the disciplinary knowledge and skills targeted by these practices as they build their competency with these practices over time [26,27]. Moreover, these practices are not intended to be rote process skills to be taught in isolation, but rather, students' engagement in these disciplinary practices should be embedded into meaningful contexts, such as making sense of a phenomenon or designing solutions to problems [27]. Thus, the context-situated nature of project-based learning can provide robust opportunities for students to engage in disciplinary practices in STEM.

In our framework, we conceptualize *disciplinary practices* as the ways that people think and act in scientific and mathematical manner when making or doing things in the broader world—both within and beyond formal science and mathematical contexts. When teachers identify the scientific and mathematical ways that people think and act that are authentically elicited by students' work towards the End Product, the overall project can be designed to intentionally develop students' capacity with a key disciplinary practice. In order to highlight the need for students to develop their use of a disciplinary practice over time, we introduce the concept of a *Practice Pathway*—a component of the curriculum design where teachers select a disciplinary practice or practices that align with authentic task demands of the end product and then sequence opportunities for students to build their capacity with the practice across the project. The Practice Pathway is a conceptual tool to support teachers to sequence and design multiple opportunities for students to iteratively build their use of key disciplinary practice(s) across the flow of project activities.

2.3. Project-Based Learning in STEM Classrooms

PBL is typically characterized as an instructional approach in which the teacher provides a well-defined outcome, within an authentic, real-world context, and guides students as they draw on various disciplines to achieve the desired end goal or product [28]. Other necessary components of PBL include students' engagement in design work, opportunities for formative assessment and revision, student inquiry of problems they define, and collaboration with peers [29].

Research on PBL in math and science suggests that this approach can support students' content knowledge acquisition, process skill development, ability to apply skills and knowledge in new situations, and ability to draw connections between concepts —all goals underlying the design of current math and science standards [7]. A meta-analysis of effective strategies for integrated STEM education suggests that using PBL positively impacts student learning and interest in STEM [30]. Recently, studies of PBL curricula used randomized control trials to test the efficacy of a rigorous PBL curriculum and found that students in PBL classrooms outperformed students in control classrooms on a variety of measures [4]. Additionally, Pupik Dean and colleagues examined teachers' practices in enacting PBL and found that teachers had four goals in their enactment: (1) subject area learning; (2) project authenticity; (3) feedback, reflection, and revision; (4) agency in learning communities [31].

As Pupik Dean and colleagues discussed, there is some ambiguity around the criteria for what makes a high-quality PBL environment [31]. This ambiguity makes for a wide variety in what are considered essential elements of PBL projects. For this paper, we draw on DiMaria and colleagues to describe the essential elements as follows: Entry Events, Knows and Need to Knows, a Focus Statement, Sustained Inquiry, Checkpoints, Scaffolding and Assessment, Student Voice and Choice, Rubrics, and End Product and Presentation [32].

In PBL classrooms, projects often begin with a Project Launch, which incorporates the Entry Event, Knows and Need to Knows, and the Focus Statement [33]. Entry events are designed to engage students in the project from the beginning [34]. These can be real-world scenarios, provocative questions, multimedia presentations, or guest speakers that pique students' interest and motivate them to explore the project's topic. Often, during the Entry Event, the project's rubric is shared with the students. Providing the rubric during the Project Launch not only provides clear expectations and guidelines for the students [33,35], but also is a way to encourage the students to ask about the content standards during the Knows and Need to Knows routine. Knows and Need to Knows are a routine used to organize students' existing knowledge (Knows) and identify what they need to learn (Need to Knows) in order to complete the project successfully. This helps guide the students' learning throughout the project. Finally, during the Project Launch, a Focus Statement is shared with the students. The Focus Statement succinctly connects to the purpose, the Content Storyline, and the Practice Pathway of the project. It provides clarity and direction for both students and teachers, guiding them throughout the project's duration [36].

Across the middle of projects, students engage in a variety of activities which support students to engage in sustained inquiry over the period of the project. Sustained Inquiry includes students "asking questions, finding and using resources and other learning experiences to help develop answers to those questions, then ask deeper questions—and the process repeats" [37]. To support students in this process, teachers create a series of scaffolding activities to support students throughout the project. Some of these scaffolding activities mirror what may have already been done in traditional classrooms (e.g., a favorite lab or math exploration). However, other activities may be classified as Checkpoints. Checkpoints are predetermined moments throughout the project that are necessary to complete the End Product [38]. Checkpoints are critical opportunities for students to reflect on their progress, receive feedback, and make necessary adjustments.

PBL projects end with a cumulative End Product and public Presentation. Krajcik and Shin discuss how meaningful End Products and Presentations provide students with opportunities to demonstrate their learning and communicate their ideas effectively while increasing their motivation for engaging with the disciplinary content [39]. The End Product is an artifact that is the culmination of the students' work in the project, showcasing their learning and understanding of the topic. These artifacts could be a research paper, a presentation, a multimedia project, a performance, or any other form of output that demonstrates mastery of the project's objectives. Presentations provide students with the opportunity to share their knowledge with others, receive feedback, and reflect on their learning journey.

In our framework, we conceptualize *Elements of PBL* as the key aspects of a PBL project that differentiate a project from a more traditional classroom "dessert project" such that engagement in the project drives student learning rather than merely following a learning sequence as a retrospective application [40]. As described above, these elements are spiraled throughout different phases of the project to ensure that students are having authentic touchpoints back to the context.

2.4. Towards an Understanding of Discipline-Rich PBL

A common misconception is that the Elements of PBL are removed from the standards being taught in the classroom; however, that is not the case. Each of the elements are driven by and selected from the standards. For instance, the End Product is selected based on what is authentic for that specific set of standards. If the standards are about human impacts on earth systems, global climate change, and weather and climate, it may not make sense to have students create scale models. However, it would make sense to develop a project that has students researching climate change impacts and using that understanding to create an awareness campaign for the impact on local communities. Additionally, these ideas are not separate from the disciplinary practice standards. For instance, given the early example, it would make sense to select "constructing explanations and designing solutions" as the practice standard, given the project context of an awareness campaign around the impacts of climate change [2].

In this paper, we argue teachers need to balance all three aspects (disciplinary practice standards, content standards, and elements of PBL) evenly to create a PBL project that is discipline-rich. To do this, we propose the following PBL *Project Planning Pyramid* (Figure 1) that explicitly attends to (1) Elements of PBL; (2) Content Storyline; (3) Practice Pathway.

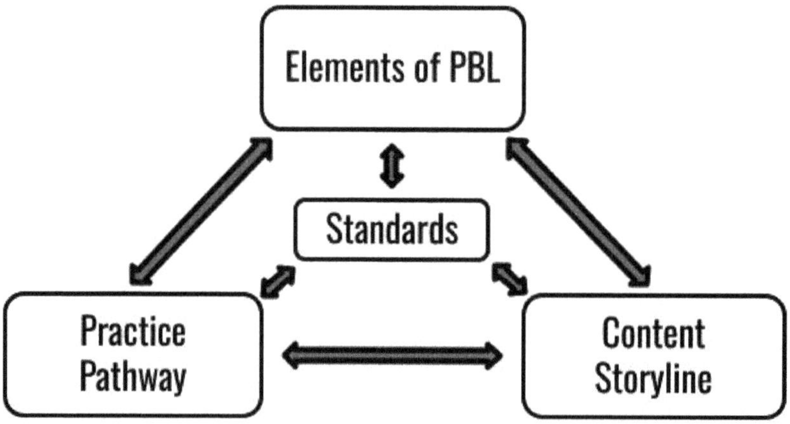

Figure 1. The *Project Planning Pyramid: A Framework to Ensure Discipline-Rich STEM Projects.*

Grounded in disciplinary standards, this framework draws attention to the balance and coherence of the disciplinary content and practices threaded throughout the elements of the project. Together, the integration of disciplinary content and practices offers a discipline-rich learning experience. PBL elements give motivation and meaning to this discipline-rich experience. Together, these domains create a discipline-rich PBL project.

3. Context of Framework Refinement

In order to refine our understanding of discipline-rich STEM projects, we drew on the theory of the curriculum enactment process [11] to analyze the curriculum we created as PK-12 STEM teachers who employed project-based learning to answer the question: what are the features of teacher-created discipline-rich STEM projects?

3.1. Theory of the Curriculum Enactment Process

We drew upon the theory of the curriculum enactment process [11] to inform the approach we took to investigate the features of teacher-created discipline-rich STEM projects. The curriculum enactment process is informed by inputs that are within, and outside of, a teacher's control. Our study is situated within the operational curriculum portion of the curriculum enactment process. Remillard and Heck described the operational curriculum as "the teacher-intended curriculum, the curriculum that is actually enacted with students, and student outcomes" [11]. An enacted curriculum is the ways students and teachers interact with content and tasks in the classroom. Remillard and Heck argued that an enacted curriculum cannot be scripted, because teachers must respond in the moment to student needs. Additionally, a teacher-intended curriculum is created as teachers transform elements of the official curriculum and guidelines from instructional materials into the curriculum that is experienced by students. In this paper, we conceptualize this transformation as happening when teachers engage in curriculum design to develop PBL projects for their classrooms.

Similar to Orr and Bieda [41], we assert that while the teacher-intended curriculum (e.g., teacher-created projects) evolves during the curriculum enactment process, teachers make intentional moves in response to students in order to support the continued development of their understanding. In this paper, we focus on the curricular materials created by teachers to understand what makes discipline-rich projects and to analyze the teacher-intended curriculum. Remillard and Heck remind the reader that the study of the teacher-intended curriculum is often difficult to access, as "it exists in its most detailed state in the teacher's mind" [11]. Thus, in this paper, we rely on the physical artifacts of our created projects to analyze the teacher-intended curriculum.

3.2. Project Selection

As we sought to determine what makes a strong STEM PBL project, we took a deep dive into our own teacher-created projects from our secondary STEM classrooms. We each brought projects that we found fell short of being a discipline-rich learning experience for our students. We also brought projects that we believed were discipline-rich experiences for our students. In total, there were 20 projects spanning a course content (Algebra I, Geometry, Integrated Physics/Algebra I, Calculus, Biology, and Environmental Science).

3.3. Examination of the Projects

Since our goal was to refine our understanding of discipline-rich STEM projects, we drew on our conceptualization that discipline-rich STEM projects attend to the Content Storyline, Practice Pathway, and the Elements of PBL. To do this, we drew on Lather's concept of praxis-oriented research [42]. This approach allows for "the interactive, reciprocal shaping of theory and practice", which "requires a reciprocal relationship between data and theory" [42] (p. 258). According to Lather, this relationship is where the data are viewed through the lens of the literature, but "keeps a particular framework from becoming the container into which the data must be poured" [42] (p. 267). To do this, we iteratively viewed the data and the framework through the lens of the other to build our understanding of both [43]. Given the conceptual nature of this article, the goal was not to provide a detailed analysis of how each project did or did not meet the ideas of discipline-rich projects. Instead, the goal was to highlight the ways some projects fell short, and others provided discipline-rich opportunities for students. In the following sections, we will elaborate and provide illustrative examples.

4. Types of Projects

As we analyzed the selected projects, we identified several ways that these projects, the intended curriculum, diverted from or achieved the goal of reflecting discipline-rich project experiences. In this section, we share the three ways projects fell short and close with an example of a project that engaged all the aspects of discipline-rich projects. We use "broken" images of the Project Planning Pyramid to illustrate several ways that projects can fail when the components of this framework are not attended to in a balanced way across the design of the project.

4.1. Superficial Project Due to Weak Elements of PBL

The Farm Project was an AP Environmental Science project that asked students to justify the best farming practices to use to grow crops for a selected client. Students were assigned the role of deciding which farming practices to use on a fictional farm. Initially, students learned about various agricultural practices. Then, students applied what they learned to design a farming plan that best met the needs and values of one of six predetermined potential clients for their farm (e.g., a large chain grocery store, a local farmer's market). At the end of the project, students presented and justified their choices to the class.

As represented in Figure 2, this project primarily connected content standards and the Content Storyline, as common in more traditional, didactic teaching methods. To some extent, the project moved beyond a singular focus on content by also engaging students in disciplinary practices. However, this largely traditional unit lacked key elements of project-based learning, such as an authentic project context that could support Sustained Inquiry, meaningful Student Voice and Choice, or an authentic End Product. The dotted lines and position of the Elements of PBL in this figure represent the superficial integration of this aspect of the *Project Planning Pyramid*.

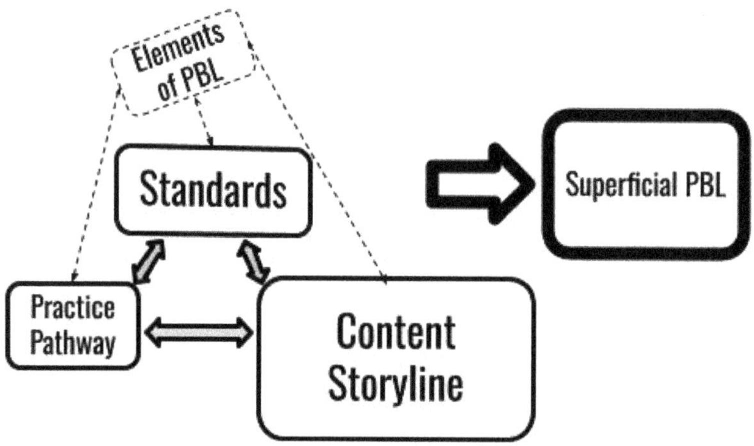

Figure 2. Superficial project due to weak Elements of PBL. This "broken" Project Planning Pyramid illustrates a project with an imbalanced emphasis on the Content Storyline and content-related standards and limited attention to the Elements of PBL.

The context of this project required students to apply both disciplinary content knowledge and practices to meet the task demands. However, while The Farm Project contained some surface elements of project-based learning, overall, this project failed to embody discipline-rich PBL due to its weak integration of the Elements of PBL. Students demonstrated limited engagement and motivation during the project due to its inauthentic tasks and lack of open-endedness. During the first two weeks of the unit, students wondered aloud about when the project was going to start, as the unit was sequenced to frontload content learning about agricultural methods prior to engaging with the farm design task. After students selected their clients from the pre-set client options, they described feeling as though there was a single "right answer" that they could reasonably justify for each client. Thus, the project context was not designed to drive students' need to know about the intended content learning, nor did the project offer students opportunities to make meaningful choices as they navigated open-ended challenges. Instead, students seemed to experience the unit as a drawn-out short-answer question with predetermined correct answers. This superficial engagement with the Elements of PBL in the project could have been rectified through adjusting the role that students took on to be more authentic to real-world contexts where the intended content knowledge would be used to inform open-ended decisions. For instance, students could take on the role of advising the director of a farmers' market tasked with considering the impacts of various farming practices on social and ecological systems to recommend vendor requirements that reflect the needs and goals of their community.

4.2. Gaps in Project Content through a Weak Content Storyline

Greeting Card Design is a project from a Geometry course. This project was launched right before Mother's Day and challenged students to design greeting cards with two-dimensional composite figures. The focus statement was 'How can we as thoughtful humans, design and create geometric inspired greeting cards so that we can bring joy to others?' Students started the project by exploring the history of Mother's Day and greeting cards. They looked at geometric designs and how two-dimensional shapes came together to create larger designs. The project also had constraints in the rubric to ensure that students included the correct shapes from this geometry unit in their End Product. Through the Project Launch, students asked many Need to Know questions about what materials they could use to make the cards, whom they were allowed to send them to, the history of Mother's Day, and occasionally, the shapes they needed to use. Students were grouped with feedback partners, but each student designed their own card. Although this project engaged many Elements of PBL and supported students in receiving feedback on their work, it still fell short due to a weak Content Storyline. As demonstrated in Figure 3, when the *Project Planning Pyramid* is missing a strong Content Storyline, the project results in content gaps in the project.

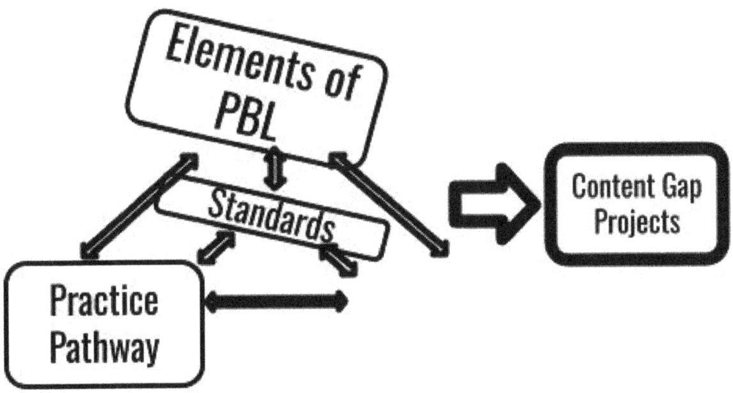

Figure 3. Content gaps in the project from a weak Content Storyline. This "broken" Project Planning Pyramid represents a project with a missing or underdeveloped Content Storyline.

For this specific project, the gaps showed up as the project progressed. Some of the more artistically driven students had full card designs even before we conducted workshops on composite figures and proportions. Although the instructor designed project activities where students had to discuss the proportions of the card, the area of their design, or the specifics of the shapes, students did not see the connection to the project, asking "How does this connect again?" Although the End Products were beautiful, and students were proud of their work, the videos where students were supposed to describe the mathematics included descriptions of the art but no specifics of the mathematical constructions. The content had been lost along the way, and this became an art project with a separately taught unit of math. This gap in content in the project could have been rectified by spiraling learning activities, so that students created part of their card each day after they learned a new content idea.

4.3. Loss of Coherence from Missing Disciplinary Practices

Can You Hear Me Now? was a project from an integrated Algebra 1 and Physics course. The purpose of the project was for students to create the most cost-efficient amplifier for a cell phone, drawing on their knowledge of sound waves and systems of linear equations. Students took on the role of entrepreneurs to design and build an amplifier that was cost-efficient while also producing the loudest sound in decibels. The End Product was a prototype of the amplifier as well as a production report. This report included the materials used to build the amplifier, the cost of the materials, an equation to represent the cost of the amplifier (including the USD 5.50 overhead assigned to every group). Additionally, the report included the amount they would charge for the speaker, with a justification why they believed people would pay for it. Finally, they had to find the breakeven point for the number of amplifiers they needed to sell to break even. Over the course of the three weeks this project spanned, students learned about the relationship between frequency, wavelength, and the speed of waves, as well as how to construct and solve systems of equations with varying constraints. The last few days of the project period involved students engaging in an iterative design process and constructing mathematical models for the cost of their amplifier and potential revenue from sales of their amplifier. Although this project included a strong focus on the content standards, with many workshops to support new learning, and engaged with many of the Elements of PBL, it still ended up falling short because it did not intentionally support a coherent Practice Pathway. As demonstrated in Figure 4, when the *Project Planning Pyramid* is missing a Practice Pathway, the project results in a loss of coherence.

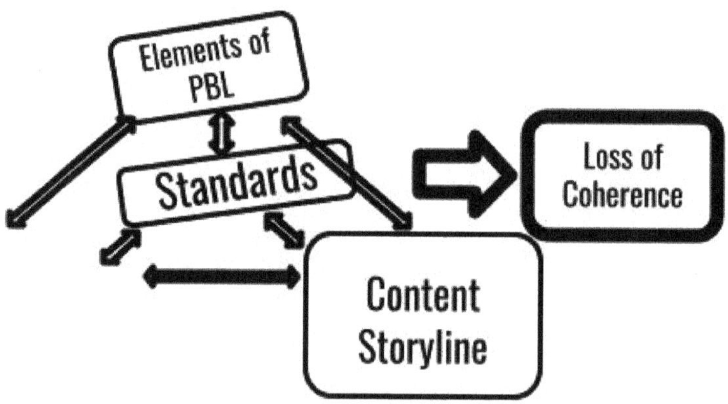

Figure 4. Loss of Coherence without a Practice Pathway. This "broken" Project Planning Pyramid represents a project that does not integrate a Practice Pathway.

This project was identified as a "dessert project" because much of the learning happened prior to the construction of the End Product and there were no meaningful Checkpoints along the way, leading to a loss of coherence. Additionally, this project did not have a focus on disciplinary practice standards, even though much of the project required constructing and refining models. This lack of identifying a disciplinary practice standard created loss of coherence from the student perspective because the practice of modeling was not intentionally developed along a Practice Pathway. This lack of coherence could have been rectified with an intentional focusing on modeling throughout the project and having students journal about how this knowledge of modeling would be taken up in their End Product.

4.4. Discipline-Rich Project

An example in our work of a discipline-rich project is The Community Garden Project [44]. In this project, we see an intentional development of the Elements of PBL, the Content Storyline, and the Practice Pathway. This project built on previous work carried out during the academic year, focused on food insecurity in the community where the school was located. This project asked students to take on the role of activists and urban farmers to design a proposal for a community garden on the school campus. The End Product was an oral presentation to the school administration where students presented a scale model of the proposed garden, a budget proposal for how much the garden would cost, and an explanation of how the proposed garden would address food insecurity in their community.

In addition to a community-centered End Product, this project also engaged with several other Elements of PBL. The project was launched through the principal giving the students a charge to propose a way for the students to find a way to address food insecurity in the neighborhood. To focus the learning over the course of the project, the following focus statement was developed:

> "We need to understand surface area and volume of three-dimensional shapes and be able to strategically select tools given various limitations in order to create a model to persuade the school administration to approve our community garden proposal" .
>
> (Project Materials)

Throughout the Project Launch, students asked many questions (Need to Knows) that both applied in general to how we would create a community garden and were specific to Geometry. These were publicly recorded by the teacher, as shown in Figure 5.

Figure 5. Sheila Orr recording Knows and Need to Knows during the Project Launch.

Over the course of the project, Checkpoints were used to ensure students were making progress. Some examples of Checkpoints included having a blueprint diagram of the space and calculating the area, a rough draft sketch of a potential garden design, a spreadsheet showing the calculations to support determining the budget for the garden, and a final draft sketch of the garden. These Checkpoints ensured that students were making progress towards designing the scale model and calculating the cost of the garden.

This project was situated in a Geometry classroom, and the Content Storyline was developed to support the standards related to three-dimensional shapes (see Table 2).

Table 2. Common Core Standards covered in *The Community Garden Project*.

Descriptor of Content Standards
Give an informal argument for the formulas for the circumference of a circle, area of a circle, volume of a cylinder, pyramid, and cone.
Use volume formulas for cylinders, pyramids, cones, and spheres to solve problems.
Identify the shapes of two-dimensional cross sections of three-dimensional objects and identify three-dimensional objects generated by rotations of two-dimensional objects.
Use geometric shapes, their measures, and their properties to describe objects (e.g., modeling a tree trunk or a human torso as a cylinder)
Apply geometric methods to solve design problems (e.g., designing an object or structure to satisfy physical constraints or minimize cost; working with typographic grid systems based on ratios)

Note. These descriptors of standards are from the Common Core State Standards, Geometric Measurement and Dimension, and Modeling with Geometry Sections [1].

To develop students' understanding of three-dimensional figures, the standards were used to develop the following Content Storyline for this project (Figure 6).

What should students be able to figure out/explain once they have mastered the standards in this project?
Geometric shapes can be used individually and combined to model various aspects of the physical world. In order to do this, first geometric shapes need to be identified as potential models for the aspect of the physical world. Then the shapes need to be decomposed into smaller shapes to which we know how to find surface area and volume. In particular, knowing the surface area and volume of various geometric figures can be useful to solve design problems and determine the amount of materials needed.

Figure 6. Content Storyline for The Community Garden Project.

Through the Content Storyline of this project, students needed to approximate shapes based on objects in the physical world, then use their knowledge of surface area and volume to solve design problems, such as building a community garden. However, instead of just listing the content standards, the Content Storyline was written in a manner that connected to and considered the learning progression for students. It gave purpose to the content and would help with answering questions like "Why do we need to learn this?" and "What are you working on"?

The implementation of a Content Storyline through The Community Garden Project planning can be seen through varied components of the learning process. The snapshot of classroom activities (Figure 7) shows a portion of the progression from the beginning to the end of a project and how the Content Storyline would weave alongside. Through these learning activities, there is an arc of the story of learning in the context that students experienced.

Independently, using a Content Storyline in classroom planning will lead to deeper content understanding; however, weaving together a consistent Content Storyline with the Elements of PBL and a Practice Pathway could generate discipline-rich contextualized learning for all. For The Community Garden Project, the practice "uses appropriate tools strategically" was selected as the practice to intentionally scaffold throughout the project [1]. Specifically, the aspect of the practice that was focused on throughout the project was "students consider the available tools when solving a mathematical problem" and "make sound decisions about when each of these tools might be helpful, recognizing both the insight to be gained and their limitations" [1]. To scaffold this practice, the following Practice Pathway was constructed (Figure 8).

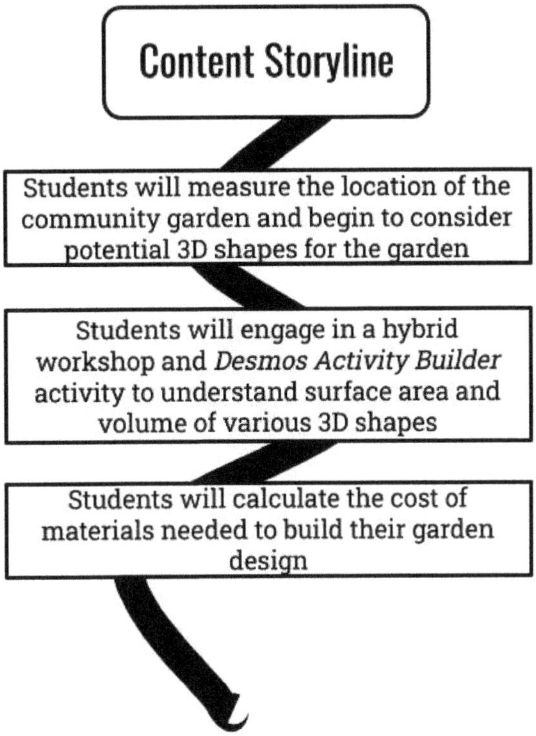

Figure 7. Opportunities for students to showcase and improve their knowledge of the Content Storyline.

How is the Disciplinary Practice elicited by the End Product(s)?

Disciplinary Practice: Uses appropriate tools strategically
End Product:
An oral presentation to the school administration where students
- presented a scale model of the proposed garden
- a budget proposal for how much the garden would cost
- an explanation of how the proposed garden would address food insecurity in their community.

How the practice is elicited by making/doing the End Product:
Students will use various tools across the project. They will need to find tools that will best support them measuring and recording a large area. Additionally, they will need to decide on a tool that will best support creating a scale model for the proposed garden. As part of selecting the tool, students will receive feedback on the tool selected and asked to consider limitations of a specific tool.

Figure 8. Practice Pathway for The Community Garden project.

Similar to the Content Storyline, the Practice Pathway builds in natural connection spaces throughout the learning process of a project. The snapshot of classroom activities (Figure 9) shows students' experiences of engaging in a focal practice from the beginning to the end of a project. This regular surfacing of the focal practice foregrounds to learners their iterative and growing facilities with the practice situated within the real-world context of the project.

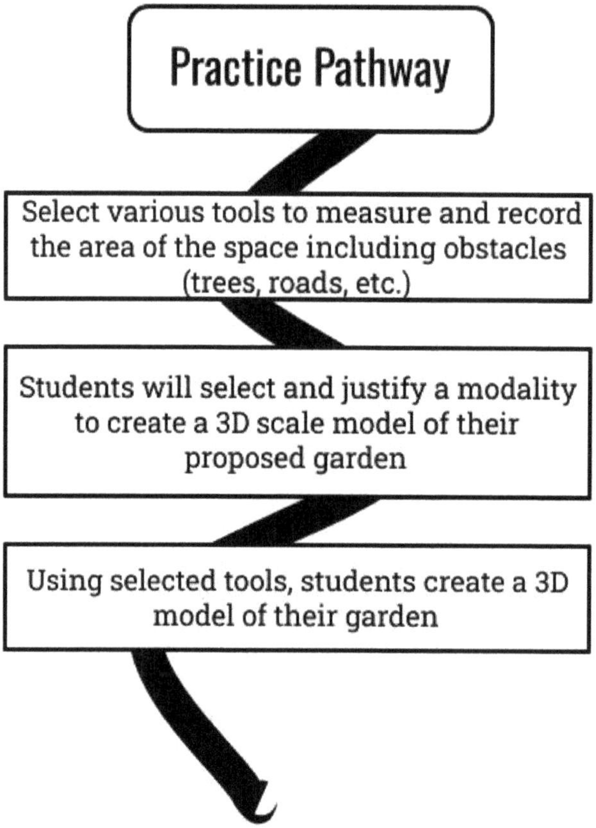

Figure 9. Opportunities for intentional exposure and feedback on the Practice Pathway in The Community Garden Project.

5. Discussion: Revisiting the Framework

As described by the theory of the curriculum enactment process, teachers act upon instructional materials in order to coordinate their multiple goals for the intended curriculum. By putting forth a framework for discipline-rich PBL in STEM, we aim to support teachers in this coordination work. As teachers create project-based STEM learning experiences, they grapple with how their curriculum can advance students' understandings of disciplinary content and capacity with disciplinary practices in ways that are authentically driven by the project context and reflect strong elements of PBL. We argue that these components of strong STEM PBL design—elements of PBL, disciplinary practices, disciplinary content, and attention to standards—should be interwoven across a STEM project such that they support and strengthen each other in service of student learning. Thus, integrating these multiple components across the design of a project requires iterative and complex decision-making during curriculum development. As our project examples illustrate, failing to attend to any one of these components can result in STEM projects that fail to realize the potential of project-based STEM to generate motivating, authentic project experiences for students that also rigorously advance discipline-specific learning outcomes.

Drawing from the literature and our deep experiences as STEM PBL practitioners, we developed and refined a framework, the *Project Planning Pyramid*, to capture key components embedded across the design of discipline-rich project-based STEM learning. Building on existing literature on the effective teaching of disciplinary content and practices in STEM education [27,45], we offer the constructs of a Practice Pathway and a Content Storyline as components of a strong STEM PBL design that support teachers to integrate and scaffold rigorous STEM learning outcomes within project-based curriculum materials. We argue that the *Project Planning Pyramid* has potential as a conceptual tool that aids teachers in substantively attending to and integrating these components as they work to design STEM PBL projects. Moreover, the use of the *Project Planning Pyramid* as a framework for thinking about project design has the potential to support teachers in analyzing how projects can succeed or fail at balancing these multiple components, aiding teachers in building their capacity to develop what we term "discipline-rich STEM projects". This use of our framework has potential to support teachers to reflect on and iteratively refine their STEM projects after they have enacted them.

Developing discipline-rich STEM projects requires teachers to develop and coordinate multiple forms of skill and knowledge: disciplinary content knowledge, pedagogical content knowledge for both content ideas and disciplinary practices, knowledge of the elements of PBL, as well as pedagogical design capacity for PBL instructional approaches, to name a few [46–48]. We argue that our framework can function as a tool for teachers and teacher educators to think with as they build and use these capacities during project design. However, teachers need opportunities to build their capacities with this framework. We argue that the potential of this framework may be greatest when integrated into sustained professional learning experiences for teachers. Prior research demonstrated that curriculum design frameworks coupled with professional learning can support teachers to design experiences that support students' learning in STEM disciplines [46]. In this vein, we developed and enacted a sustained professional learning experience for secondary STEM teachers, built around the *Project Planning Pyramid*, to help scaffold and develop teachers' capacities to design discipline-rich STEM projects. Although this study was a retroactive analysis of the projects, we see potential in using it to examine the ways in which it supports teachers to create discipline-rich projects from scratch. Additionally, future work with this tool can include examining how teachers take the projects from the intended curriculum to the enacted curriculum [11]. This framework is currently in use as a tool for in-service secondary school teacher learning as part of a sustained professional learning experience. Future teacher education research could examine the extent to which this framework supports the development of teachers' pedagogical design capacity for STEM projects and how the application of this model might vary across different STEM learning contexts. Furthermore, teacher educators might extend and adapt this work to support in-service and preservice teachers across K-12 education, for example by exploring the *Project Planning Pyramid*'s potential application in elementary school settings.

Our framework is designed to support teachers' pedagogical design capacity for discipline-rich STEM PBL by focusing on the alignment between disciplinary content, practices, PBL, and standards during the design of project-based STEM curricula [48]. Nonetheless, we recognize that our framework does not encompass all the components needed for strong PBL or strong STEM teaching. Developing and enacting powerful project-based learning experiences in classrooms requires teachers to utilize additional lenses beyond this framework. For example, teachers will need to consider how to scaffold language and literacy demands within the project and how they will develop aligned assessments. Moreover, our framework does not highlight how decisions about the project might reflect commitments to center culturally sustaining pedagogies or justice-oriented societal issues [49–51]. However, the use of this framework may be coupled with additional lenses in order to integrate such commitments into the act of project design. We believe that our framework provides a valuable foundation for thinking about the core components of discipline-rich STEM projects which can be productively extended to reflect additional needs and goals.

6. Conclusions

In this paper, we argue that teachers can coordinate complex goals for project-based STEM learning in order to create discipline-rich projects and we present and illustrate the use of a framework to support such curriculum development efforts. By drawing on the literature related to content storylines, disciplinary practices, and elements of PBL, we put forth the *Project Planning Pyramid: A Framework to Ensure Discipline-Rich STEM Projects* (see Figure 1). By examining projects from PBL classrooms, we show how this framework can be used as a lens to view PBL projects in order to analyze strengths and growth areas of these curricula, supporting teachers' capacity building for designing STEM projects and the iterative development of discipline-rich STEM PBL. Through examining teacher-created STEM projects, we have contributed a new perspective to the literature on project-based learning, which previously focused on teacher practices [31], effectiveness for student learning [4,6,8], and dilemmas that arise during PBL [52].

Author Contributions: Conceptualization, M.S., S.O., C.M. and S.D.; methodology, M.S. and S.O.; data curation, M.S., S.O., C.M. and S.D; writing—original draft preparation, M.S. and S.O.; writing—review and editing, M.S., S.O., C.M. and S.D.; funding acquisition, M.S., S.O., C.M. and S.D. All authors have read and agreed to the published version of the manuscript.

Funding: This material is based upon work supported by the Knowles Teacher Initiative. Additionally, this material is based upon work supported by the National Science Foundation Graduate Research Fellowship Program under Grant No. DGE-1656518. Any opinions, findings, and conclusions or recommendations expressed in this material are those of the author(s) and do not necessarily reflect the views of the National Science Foundation.

Institutional Review Board Statement: Not applicable.

Informed Consent Statement: Not applicable.

Data Availability Statement: No new data were created or analyzed in this study. Data sharing is not applicable to this article.

Conflicts of Interest: The authors declare no conflict of interest.

References

1. National Governors Association. Common Core State Standards. 2010. Available online: https://preview.fadss.org/resources/webinars/webinar2/FSBAPresentationforCommunities_transcribed.pdf (accessed on 28 January 2024).
2. National Research Council. *A Framework for K-12 Science Education: Practices, Crosscutting Concepts, and Core Ideas*; National Academies Press: Washington, DC, USA, 2013. [CrossRef]
3. What is PBL? PBLWorks. Available online: https://www.pblworks.org/what-is-pbl (accessed on 28 January 2024).
4. Krajcik, J.; Schneider, B.; Miller, E.A.; Chen, I.-C.; Bradford, L.; Baker, Q.; Bartz, K.; Miller, C.; Li, T.; Codere, S.; et al. Assessing the Effect of Project-Based Learning on Science Learning in Elementary Schools. *Am. Educ. Res. J.* **2023**, *60*, 70–102. [CrossRef]
5. Krajcik, J. Projected-Based Science. *Sci. Teach.* **2015**, *82*, 25–27.
6. Harris, C.J.; Penuel, W.R.; D'Angelo, C.M.; DeBarger, A.H.; Gallagher, L.P.; Kennedy, C.A.; Cheng, B.H.; Krajcik, J.S. Impact of Project-Based Curriculum Materials on Student Learning in Science: Results of a Randomized Controlled Trial. *J. Res. Sci. Teach.* **2015**, *52*, 1362–1385. [CrossRef]
7. Kingston, S. *Project Based Learning & Student Achievement: What Does the Research Tell Us? Pbl Evidence Matters*; Buck Institute for Education: Novato, CA, USA, 2018; Volume 1, No. 1. Available online: https://eric.ed.gov/?id=ED590832 (accessed on 28 January 2024).
8. Diego-Mantecon, J.-M.; Prodromou, T.; Lavicza, Z.; Blanco, T.F.; Ortiz-Laso, Z. An Attempt to Evaluate Steam Project-Based Instruction from a School Mathematics Perspective. *ZDM-Math. Educ.* **2021**, *53*, 1137–1148. [CrossRef]
9. Markula, A.; Aksela, M. The Key Characteristics of Project-Based Learning: How Teachers Implement Projects in K-12 Science Education. *Discip. Interdiscip. Sci. Educ. Res.* **2022**, *4*, 2. [CrossRef]
10. Kokotsaki, D.; Menzies, V.; Wiggins, A. Project-Based Learning: A Review of the Literature. *Improv. Sch.* **2016**, *19*, 267–277. [CrossRef]

11. Remillard, J.T.; Heck, D.J. Conceptualizing the Curriculum Enactment Process in Mathematics Education. *ZDM* **2014**, *46*, 705–718. [CrossRef]
12. Roth, K.J.; Garnier, H.E.; Chen, C.; Lemmens, M.; Schwille, K.; Wickler, N.I.Z. Videobased Lesson Analysis: Effective Science Pd for Teacher and Student Learning. *J. Res. Sci. Teach.* **2011**, *48*, 117–148. [CrossRef]
13. Reiser, B.J.; Novak, M.; Fumagalli, M. Using Storylines to Design or Adapt Curriculum and Instruction to Make It Three-Dimensional. 2016. Available online: https://www.academia.edu/24083676/Using_Storylines_to_Design_or_Adapt_Curriculum_and_Instruction_to_Make_It_Three_Dimensional (accessed on 22 April 2024).
14. Arons, A. What Science Should We Teach. In *Curriculum Development for the Year 2000*; BSCS: Colorado Springs, CO, USA, 1989.
15. Dietiker, L. Mathematical Texts as Narrative: Rethinking Curriculum. *Learn. Math.* **2013**, *33*, 14–19.
16. Hanuscin, D.; Lipsitz, K.; Cisterna-Alburquerque, D.; Arnone, K.A.; van Garderen, D.; de Araujo, Z.; Lee, E.J. Developing Coherent Conceptual Storylines: Two Elementary Challenges. *J. Sci. Teach. Educ.* **2016**, *27*, 393–414. [CrossRef]
17. Ramsey, J. Developing Conceptual Storylines with the Learning Cycle. *J. Elem. Sci. Educ.* **1993**, *5*, 1–20. [CrossRef]
18. Reiser, B.J.; Novak, M.; McGill, T.A.W.; Penuel, W.R. Storyline Units: An Instructional Model to Support Coherence from the Students' Perspective. *J. Sci. Teach. Educ.* **2021**, *32*, 805–829. [CrossRef]
19. Nordine, J.; Krajcik, J.; Fortus, D.; Neumann, K. Using Storylines to Support Three-Dimensional Learning in Project-Based Science. *Sci. Scope* **2019**, *42*, 86–93. [CrossRef]
20. Penuel, W.R.; Reiser, B.J.; McGill, T.A.W.; Novak, M.; Van Horne, K.; Orwig, A. Connecting Student Interests and Questions with Science Learning Goals through Project-Based Storylines. *Discip. Interdiscip. Sci. Educ. Res.* **2022**, *4*, 1. [CrossRef]
21. Dietiker, L. Mathematical Story: A Metaphor for Mathematics Curriculum. *Educ. Stud. Math.* **2015**, *90*, 285–302. [CrossRef]
22. Dietiker, L.; Richman, A.S. How Textbooks Can Promote Inquiry: Using a Narrative Framework to Investigate the Design of Mathematical Content in a Lesson. *J. Res. Math. Educ.* **2021**, *52*, 301–331. [CrossRef]
23. Schmidt, W.H.; Houang, R.T. Curricular Coherence and the Common Core State Standards for Mathematics. *Educ. Res.* **2012**, *41*, 294–308. [CrossRef]
24. Tyburski, B. The Meta-Narratives about Function Conveyed by a Commonly Used Multivariable Calculus Textbook. In Proceedings of the 26th Annual Conference on Research in Undergraduate Mathematics Education, Omaha, NE, USA, 22–24 February 2024.
25. Koestler, C.; Felton, M.; Bieda, K.; Otten, S. *Connecting the Nctm Process Standards and the Ccssm Practices*, 1st ed.; National Council of Teachers of Mathematics: Reston, VA, USA, 2013.
26. Osborne, J. Teaching Scientific Practices: Meeting the Challenge of Change. *J. Sci. Teach. Educ.* **2014**, *25*, 177–196. [CrossRef]
27. Schwarz, C.V.; Passmore, C.; Reiser, B.J. *Helping Students Make Sense of the World Using Next Generation Science and Engineering Practices*; NSTA Press: Arlington, VA, USA, 2017.
28. Savery, J. Overview of Problem-Based Learning: Definitions and Distinctions. *Interdiscip. J. Probl.-Based Learn.* **2006**, *1*, 5–15. [CrossRef]
29. Barron, B.J.S.; Schwartz, D.L.; Vye, N.J.; Moore, A.; Petrosino, A.; Zech, L.; Bransford, J.D. Doing with Understanding: Lessons from Research on Problem- and Project-Based Learning. *J. Learn. Sci.* **1998**, *7*, 271–311. [CrossRef]
30. Mustafa, N.; Ismail, Z.; Tasir, Z.; Mohamad Said, M.N.H. A Meta-Analysis on Effective Strategies for Integrated STEM Education. *Adv. Sci. Lett.* **2016**, *22*, 4225–4228. [CrossRef]
31. Pupik Dean, C.G.; Grossman, P.; Enumah, L.; Herrmann, Z.; Kavanagh, S.S. Core Practices for Project-Based Learning: Learning from Experienced Practitioners in the United States. *Teach. Teach. Educ.* **2023**, *133*, 104275. [CrossRef]
32. DiMaria, S.; Madis, C.; Orr, S.; Sircar, M. STEM Project-Based Learning: Finding Balance of Content Standards, Disciplinary Practices, and Elements of Project-Based Learning. *Kaleidosc. Educ. Voices Perspect.* 2024.
33. Adams, J.; Grand, D.D. *New Tech Network: Driving Systems Change and Equity through Project-Based Learning*; Learning Policy Institute: Palo Alto, CA, USA, 2019.
34. Larmer, J.; Mergendoller, J.R. Eight Essentials for Project-Based Learning. *Educ. Leadersh.* **2010**, *68*, 34–37.
35. Arter, J.; McTighe, J. *Scoring Rubrics in the Classroom: Using Performance Criteria for Assessing and Improving Student Performance*; Corwin Press: Thousand Oaks, CA, USA, 2001.
36. Miller, A. How to Write Effective Driving Questions for Project-Based Learning. Edutopia. Available online: https://www.edutopia.org/blog/pbl-how-to-write-driving-questions-andrew-miller (accessed on 1 March 2024).
37. Gold Standard PBL: Essential Project Design Elements. PBLWorks. Available online: https://www.pblworks.org/blog/gold-standard-pbl-essential-project-design-elements (accessed on 7 September 2023).
38. Dennis, M. Benchmarks: What Are They and Why Do They Matter? Magnify Learning. Available online: https://www.magnifylearningin.org/project-based-learning-blog/2019/10/20/benchmarks-what-are-they-and-why-do-they-matter (accessed on 13 March 2024).
39. Krajcik, J.S.; Shin, N. Project-Based Learning. In *The Cambridge Handbook of the Learning Sciences*; Sawyer, R.K., Ed.; Cambridge Handbooks in Psychology; Cambridge University Press: Cambridge, UK, 2014; pp. 275–297. [CrossRef]
40. "Doing a Project" vs. Project Based Learning. PBLWorks. Available online: https://www.pblworks.org/doing-project-vs-project-based-learning (accessed on 28 January 2024).
41. Orr, S.; Bieda, K. Learning to Elicit Student Thinking: The Role of Planning to Support Academically Rigorous Questioning Sequences during Instruction. *J. Math. Teach. Educ.* **2023**. [CrossRef]

42. Lather, P. Research as Praxis. *Harv. Educ. Rev.* **1986**, *56*, 257–278. [CrossRef]
43. Augustine, S.M. Living in a Post-Coding World: Analysis as Assemblage. *Qual. Inq.* **2014**, *20*, 747–753. [CrossRef]
44. Harper, F.K.; Kudaisi, Q.J. Geometry, Groceries, and Gardens: Learning Mathematics and Social Justice through a Nested, Equity-Directed Instructional Approach. *J. Math. Behav.* **2023**, *71*, 101069. [CrossRef]
45. Penuel, W.R.; Allen, A.-R.; Henson, K.; Campanella, M.; Patton, R.; Rademaker, K.; Reed, W.; Watkins, D.; Wingert, K.; Reiser, B.; et al. Learning Practical Design Knowledge through Co-Designing Storyline Science Curriculum Units. *Cogn. Instr.* **2022**, *40*, 148–170. [CrossRef]
46. Carlson, J.; Daehler, K.R.; Alonzo, A.C.; Barendsen, E.; Berry, A.; Borowski, A.; Carpendale, J.; Kam Ho Chan, K.; Cooper, R.; Friedrichsen, P.; et al. The Refined Consensus Model of Pedagogical Content Knowledge in Science Education. In *Repositioning Pedagogical Content Knowledge in Teachers' Knowledge for Teaching Science*; Hume, A., Cooper, R., Borowski, A., Eds.; Springer Nature: Singapore, 2019; pp. 77–94. [CrossRef]
47. Davis, E.A.; Krajcik, J.S. Designing Educative Curriculum Materials to Promote Teacher Learning. *Educ. Res.* **2005**, *34*, 3–14. [CrossRef]
48. Brown, M.W. The Teacher–Tool Relationship: Theorizing the Design and Use of Curriculum Materials. In *Mathematics Teachers at Work*; Routledge: New York, NY, USA, 2009.
49. Paris, D.; Alim, H.S. What Are We Seeking to Sustain through Culturally Sustaining Pedagogy? A Loving Critique Forward. *Harv. Educ. Rev.* **2014**, *84*, 85–100. [CrossRef]
50. Krajcik, J.S.; Miller, E.C.; Chen, I.-C. Using Project-Based Learning to Leverage Culturally Relevant Pedagogy for Science Sensemaking in Urban Elementary Classrooms. In *International Handbook of Research on Multicultural Science Education*; Atwater, M.M., Ed.; Springer International Handbooks of Education; Springer International Publishing: Cham, Switzerland, 2022; pp. 913–932. [CrossRef]
51. Lee, O.; Grapin, S. The Role of Phenomena and Problems in Science and STEM Education: Traditional, Contemporary, and Future Approaches. *J. Res. Sci. Teach.* **2022**, *59*, 1301–1309. [CrossRef]
52. Clark, N. Why Do We Have Such Dilemmas?—An Reflection on Shadowing a PBL Mentor Teacher. *J. Educ.* **2022**, *202*, 543–548. [CrossRef]

MDPI AG
Grosspeteranlage 5
4052 Basel
Switzerland
Tel.: +41 61 683 77 34

Education Sciences Editorial Office
E-mail: education@mdpi.com
www.mdpi.com/journal/education

www.ingramcontent.com/pod-product-compliance
Lightning Source LLC
Chambersburg PA
CBHW061512210926
51850CB00008B/1894
* 9 7 8 3 7 2 5 8 4 6 7 3 3 *